THE CAMBRIDGE COMPANION TO
BOXING

While humans have used their hands to engage in combat since the dawn of man, boxing originated in ancient Greece as an Olympic event. It is one of the most popular, controversial, and misunderstood sports in the world. For its advocates, it is a heroic expression of unfettered individualism. For its critics, it is a depraved and ruthless physical and commercial exploitation of mostly poor young men. This *Companion* offers engaging and informative chapters about the social impact and historical importance of the sport of boxing. It includes a comprehensive chronology of the sport, listing all the important events and personalities. Chapters examine topics such as women in boxing, boxing and the rise of television, boxing in Africa, boxing and literature, and boxing and Hollywood films. A unique book for scholars and fans alike, this *Companion* explores the sport from its inception in ancient Greece to the death of its most celebrated figure, Muhammad Ali.

Gerald Early is Professor of English and African American Studies at Washington University in St. Louis. He has written about boxing since the early 1980s. His book, *The Culture of Bruising*, won the 1994 National Book Critics Circle Award for criticism. He also edited *The Muhammad Ali Reader* and *Body Language: Writers on Sports*. His essays have appeared several times in the Best American Essays series.

THE CAMBRIDGE COMPANION TO
BOXING

EDITED BY
GERALD EARLY
Washington University, St. Louis

CAMBRIDGE
UNIVERSITY PRESS

CAMBRIDGE
UNIVERSITY PRESS

University Printing House, Cambridge CB2 8BS, United Kingdom

One Liberty Plaza, 20th Floor, New York, NY 10006, USA

477 Williamstown Road, Port Melbourne, VIC 3207, Australia

314–321, 3rd Floor, Plot 3, Splendor Forum, Jasola District Centre,
New Delhi – 110025, India

79 Anson Road, #06-04/06, Singapore 079906

Cambridge University Press is part of the University of Cambridge.

It furthers the University's mission by disseminating knowledge in the pursuit of
education, learning, and research at the highest international levels of excellence.

www.cambridge.org
Information on this title: www.cambridge.org/9781107058019
DOI: 10.1017/9781107415355

First published 2019

Printed in the United Kingdom by TJ International Ltd, Padstow Cornwall

A catalogue record for this publication is available from the British Library.

Library of Congress Cataloging-in-Publication Data
Names: Early, Gerald Lyn, editor.
Title: The Cambridge companion to boxing / edited by Gerald Early,
University of Washington, St Louis.
Other titles: Companion to boxing
Description: Cambridge, United Kingdom; New York, N.Y.:
Cambridge University Press, 2018. |
Includes bibliographical references and index.
Identifiers: LCCN 2018039104 | ISBN 9781107058019 (Hardback) |
ISBN 9781107631205 (Paperback)
Subjects: LCSH: Boxing – History. | Boxers (Sports) – History.
Classification: LCC GV1121.C34 2018 | DDC 796.83–dc23
LC record available at https://lccn.loc.gov/2018039104

ISBN 978-1-107-05801-9 Hardback
ISBN 978-1-107-63120-5 Paperback

CONTENTS

CONTENTS

NOTES ON CONTRIBUTORS

COLLEEN AYCOCK, PhD, lives in Albuquerque, New Mexico. She is the co-editor for the International Boxing Research Organization and member of the New Mexico Boxing Hall of Fame. She has authored and co-edited five books on boxing and numerous articles in sports magazines and journals.

KASIA BODDY is Reader in American Literature at the University of Cambridge. Her books include *Boxing: A Cultural History* (2008), *The American Short Story Since 1950* (2010), *The New Penguin Book of American Short Stories* (2011), and *Geranium* (2013).

BENJAMIN CAWTHRA is Professor of History and Associate Director of the Center for Oral and Public History at California State University, Fullerton. He is the author of *Blue Notes in Black and White: Photography and Jazz* (2011).

ADAM CHILL is Associate Professor of European and World History and Global Studies at Castleton University in Vermont. He is the author of *Bare-Knuckle Britons and Fighting Irish: Boxing, Race, Religion and Nationality in the 18th and 19th Centuries* (2017).

GERALD EARLY is the Merle Kling Professor of Modern Letters in the Departments of English and African and African American Studies at Washington University in St. Louis. He also serves as the executive editor of the *Common Reader*, the online interdisciplinary journal of Washington University. He is the editor of the *Muhammad Ali Reader*.

ROSALIND EARLY is the associate editor of periodicals at Washington University and freelance writer in St. Louis. Her work has appeared in *American Theater* magazine, *Humanities*, the magazine for the national endowment for the humanities, as well as *St. Louis Magazine*.

SCOTT D. EMMERT is Professor of English at the University of Wisconsin, Oshkosh. With Steven Trout he is the co-editor of *World War I in American Fiction: An*

Anthology of Short Stories (2014), and with Michael Cocchiarale he co-edited *Critical Insights: American Short Story* (2015), *Critical Insights: American Sports Fiction* (2013), and *Upon Further Review: Sports in American Literature* (2004). He is the author of *Loaded Fictions: Social Critique in the Twentieth-Century Western* (1996) and of articles on Midwestern literature and American literary naturalism.

LEWIS A. ERENBERG is Professor of History Emeritus at Loyola University, Chicago. An authority on the Second World War and American culture, he has been on NPR, the Milt Rosenberg Show, and the Studs Terkel program and has been interviewed for articles in *The New York Times, Chicago Tribune, Vanity Fair,* and *The Nation*. He is the author of *The Greatest Fight of Our Generation: Louis vs. Schmeling* (2005, paperback 2007) and *Steppin' Out: New York Nightlife and the Transformation of American Culture, 1890–1930* (1981, paperback 1984). He is also the author of the forthcoming *The Rumble in the Jungle: Muhammad Ali and George Foreman in Africa*.

MICHAEL EZRA is Professor of American Multicultural Studies at Sonoma State University. He is the author of the book *Muhammad Ali: The Making of an Icon* and the editor of the *Journal of Civil and Human Rights*. His book *The Bittersweet Science: Fifteen Writers in the Gym, in the Corner, and at Ringside*, co-edited with Carlo Rotella, was published in 2017.

SHELLEY FISHER FISHKIN is the Joseph S. Atha Professor in the Humanities, Professor of English, and Director of American Studies at Stanford. She is the author, editor, or co-editor of over forty books, and has published over 100 articles, essays, and reviews, many of which have focused on issues of race and racism in America, and on recovering previously silenced voices from the past. Her award-winning books include *Was Huck Black? Mark Twain and African American Voices* (1993), *Feminist Engagements: Forays into American Literature and Culture* (2009), and *Writing America: Literary Landmarks from Walden Pond to Wounded Knee* (2015). Her research on race and American literature has been featured twice on the front page of the *New York Times*.

TONY GEE is a former kickboxer, and a Xen-Do black belt, and is now considered one of the leading authorities on eighteenth- and nineteenth-century bare-knuckle fighting. He is a contributor on the subject to the *Oxford Dictionary of National Biography* and author of the acclaimed publication on the London Prize Ring, *Up to Scratch: Bareknuckle Fighting and Heroes of the Prize-ring* (1998). He has recently been inducted into the Bare Knuckle Boxing Hall of Fame for his work as a historian.

ELLIOTT J. GORN is Joseph Gagliano Professor of History at Loyola University Chicago. He is the author of several books, including *The Manly Art: Bare-Knuckle Prize Fighting in America; Mother Jones: The Most Dangerous Woman in America;*

Dillinger's Wild Ride, the year that Made America's Public Enemy Number One; and co-author with Warren Goldstein of *A Brief History of American Sports*. His most recent book is about the 1955 murder of Emmett Till, *Let the People See: The Story of Emmett Till* (2018).

LEGER GRINDON is the Walter Cerf Professor of Film and Media Culture at Middlebury College in Vermont. He is the author of *Knockout: Boxing and the Boxer in American Cinema; Hollywood Romantic Comedy: Conventions, Histories, Controversies*, and *Shadows on the Past: Studies in the Historical Fiction Film*. He is currently writing a book on contemporary documentary film.

WIL HAYGOOD, author of *Sweet Thunder: The Life and Times of Sugar Ray Robinson* (2009), has written eight nonfiction books. His latest is *Tigerland: 1968– 1969: A City Divided, a Nation Torn Apart, and a Magical Season of Healing*. A Guggenheim and National Endowment for the Humanities Fellow, Haygood serves as Distinguished Scholar-in-Residence at Miami University, in Ohio.

BENITA HEISKANEN is Director of the John Morton Center for North American Studies at the University of Turku, Finland. She is the author of *The Urban Geography of Boxing: Race, Class, and Gender in the Ring* (2012, paperback 2014). She has published a number of book chapters and journal articles on sport in English, including the *European Journal of American Studies, European Journal of Cultural Studies, Diálogos Latinoamericanos, Auto/Biography*, and *Journal of Sport History*, as well as two edited volumes in Finnish.

ADEYINKA MAKINDE is a Visiting Lecturer in Law at the University of Westminster in the United Kingdom. He is the author of two books on pugilists, *Dick Tiger: The Life and Times of a Boxing Immortal* and *Jersey Boy: The Life and Mob Slaying of Frankie DePaula*.

LOUIS MOORE is Associate Professor of History at Grand Valley State University.

BYRON J. NAKAMURA is Associate Professor of History at Southern Connecticut State University.

STEVEN A. RIESS is a Bernard Brommel Research Professor Emeritus in the Department of History at Northeastern Illinois University, Chicago.

RANDY ROBERTS, one of the leading sports scholars in the United States, is Distinguished Professor of History at Purdue University. He is the author of several biographies of professional boxers, including *Jack Dempsey: The Manassa Mauler* (1979), *Papa Jack: Jack Johnson and the Era of White Hopes* (1983), *Joe Louis: Hard Times Man* (2010). His latest book, with co-author Johnny Smith, is *Blood Brothers: The Fatal Friendship Between Muhammad Ali and Malcolm X* (2016).

TROY RONDINONE is Professor of History at Southern Connecticut State University. He additionally serves on the Executive Board of the Greater New Haven Labor History Association. Troy received his PhD in history at UCLA, and his areas of scholarly interest include working-class history, economic history, and radical studies. He has published articles in *American Quarterly*, *Journal of the Gilded Age and Progressive Era*, *Connecticut History*, and *Labor Studies* as well as writing two books, *The Great Industrial War: Framing Class Conflict in the Media, 1865–1950* (2010) and *Friday Night Fighter: Gaspar "Indio" Ortega and the Golden Age of Television Boxing* (2013). He is also the recipient of the Norton Nezvinsky Trustees Research Award for 2010. He is currently working on an analysis of working-class language with Graham Cassano of Oakland University.

CARLO ROTELLA is Professor of American Studies, Journalism, and English at Boston College and a regular contributor to the *New York Times Magazine*. His books include *Cut Time: An Education at the Fights*, *Good With Their Hands: Boxers, Bluesmen, and Other Characters from the Rust Belt*, *Playing in Time: Essays, Profiles, and Other True Stories*, and, with co-editor Michael Ezra, *The Bittersweet Science: Fifteen Writers in the Gym, in the Corner, and at Ringside*.

MARK SCOTT is a writer and former Golden Glove boxer who lives in Austin, Texas. He has written four books with Colleen Aycock: *Joe Gans: A Biography of the First African American World Boxing Champion* (2008), *The First Black Boxing Champions: Essays on Fighters of the 1800s to the 1920s* (2011), *Tex Rickard: Boxing's Greatest Promoter* (2012), and *Boxing Short Stories* (2014).

CATHY VAN INGEN is an Associate Professor at Brock University (Department of Kinesiology). Dr. van Ingen's research is on the cultural study of sport, focusing on issues of inequality, violence, and social change. She is the founder of Shape Your Life, a free, non-contact boxing program for female identified survivors of violence in Toronto, Canada.

REBECCA WANZO is Associate Professor of Women, Gender, and Sexuality Studies at Washington University in St. Louis.

CHRONOLOGY

The Ancient World

2400 BC   Earliest depictions of boxing in Ancient Mesopotamia.

1500 BC   Boxing Boys Fresco on the island of Thera.

1350 BC   Boxing emerges in Egypt.

776 BC   First Olympic Games are held.

700 BC
(circa)   Homer's account of boxing in the *Iliad* and *Odyssey*. Virgil's boxing match between Dares and Entellus in the *Aeneid* is similar to boxing matches found in the *Iliad* and *Odyssey*.

688 BC   Pygmachia, ancient Greek boxing, is added to the Olympic Games. This combat sport is fought with leather wrappings around the hands, knuckles, and wrist. As the sport developed, more sharp-edged gloves were used that could lacerate the skin. Fighters fought to the finish, until one was unable or unwilling to continue. Blows were only permitted with the fists. Kicks were not allowed nor were blows to the genitals. Fights were refereed and confined to a space called the skamma. There were no rounds, no time limit, or rest periods.

648 BC   Pankration, a no-holds barred, unrestrained combat sport that combines boxing and wrestling is introduced at the Olympics. Despite its violence or perhaps because of it, it maintains its popularity for centuries, well into the days of the Roman Empire. The sport was meant to resemble the combat of war and was so brutal that some contestants were actually killed during the contest. Biting and gouging were not permitted but nearly everything else was, including breaking fingers and choking.

5th century BC   Diagoras of Rhodes and his family dominate Pan Hellenic boxing.

480 BC   Theagenes of Thasos wins his first of multiple Olympic titles. A novel about the great athlete called *The Olympian: A Tale of Ancient Hellas* by E. S. Kraay is published in 2008.

2nd century AD   Melankomas of Caria retires undefeated. He is known to us from the 28th and 29th Discourses of Dio Chrysostom. It is not entirely clear whether Melankomas was a real person or a fictive creation.

393 AD   Christian emperor Theodosius I abolishes boxing, indeed the Olympics as well, in the Roman Empire due to excessive brutality. Pugilatus, as it was called in Rome, usually employed gloves with embedded sharpened metal studs, reminiscent of the gloves used in Pan Hellenic boxing but even more deadly.

The Modern World

1681   First known reported bare-knuckle boxing match. The combatants were an unnamed butcher and the Duke of Albemarle's footman.

1719   James Figg becomes first British heavyweight champion and opens his Amphitheatre. This date is much in dispute in both regards. At least one scholar explains that there is no contemporary evidence that Figg's Amphitheatre existed this early. Figg was known predominantly as England's premiere swordsman and his actual fistic participation was minor. Figg is regarded today as England's first pugilistic champion but the date here is considered by some scholars to be arbitrary.

1725   First known international pugilistic contest. This was between John Whitacre, English, and the Venetian Gondolier, Italian.

1740   Jack Broughton beats George Taylor and becomes champion.

1743   Jack Broughton's Rules are published and become the governing rules of the sport and will remain so until the London Prize Ring Rules replace them nearly a century later. Broughton's Rules required that fighters must come to a "scratch" mark in the center of the area that has been marked off for the bout and each man must be "set," that is, in a fighting position, before fighting can commence or resume. A fight was over when one of the combatants could not make it back to the scratch mark within the time allotted after a knockdown. The Rules outlawed blows below the waist and limited who could enter the ring and when. A fighter was considered down if he fell to his knees. An umpire was established to settle disputes about knockdowns, fouls, and the like. The Rules greatly reduced the chaos that surrounded bouts in the early days of prizefighting. But the Rules were designed largely to provide clarification for betting rather than to safeguard boxers. Betting was the major impetus for boxing. Also, opening of Broughton's Amphitheatre, the first establishment dedicated to pugilism. James Figg's Amphitheatre, although showcasing the first regular pugilistic contests, nevertheless concentrated on "trials of skill" involving weapons, rather than "trials of manhood" involving fists. (Contrary to popular belief, weapons and fists were not used in the same contest.) Broughton's Amphitheatre did, on occasions, include other entertainments but boxing predominated.

1777   Former American slave Bill Richmond goes to England where he achieves considerable fame as a boxer, the first black man to do so. He was defeated by Tom Cribb in 1805 and seconded Tom Molineaux, when the latter fought Cribb for the title.

1787–1795   This is the era of Daniel Mendoza, the first prominent Jewish boxer, the most scientific and intelligent fighter of his time, and the 16th champion of England. The latter point is disputed by at least one scholar who can find no evidence in contemporary sources that Mendoza was ever referred to as champion. He himself claims to be champion. He is, nonetheless, one of the dominant fighters of this period and the most famous Jewish fighter of the time.

1788–1790   During these years Daniel Mendoza fights Richard Humphries three times, winning the last two. These fights reflect a high point of interest in boxing. There is simply unprecedented interest in these fights with extensive newspaper coverage of the combatants. At this point, it might be said that bare-knuckle fighting has "arrived" as a truly popular sport. Indeed, for their last fight, in a barn at Doncaster in Yorkshire, Mendoza erects a gate and, for the first time in boxing history, spectators have to pay an admission.

1810   Tom Cribb beats Tom Molineaux in thirty-nine rounds. Molineaux, a former American slave, followed Richmond to England and practiced the profession of boxing, which he had learned on plantations in the United States. The fight with Cribb is the first international and interracial bout for the championship. Richmond serves as Molineaux's second. Molineaux actually knocks out Cribb but through seeming chicanery in Cribb's corner and the complicity of the partisan crowd is unable to claim victory. Cribb recovers his senses and defeats a badly fatigued Molineaux. The fight generated massive interest at the time. There is a debate among scholars about whether Molineaux was "robbed." What happened to Molineaux in this fight was not at all unusual for a prizefight at this time, which were typically quite rowdy affairs.

1811   Tom Cribb beats Tom Molineaux in rematch in eleven rounds. Molineaux, under-trained, dissipated from rowdy living, and somewhat demoralized by the results of the first fight, is much easier for Cribb to defeat this time.

1812   Journalist Pierce Egan's first edition of *Boxiana or Sketches of Ancient and Modern Pugilism* is published and becomes the first prominent and well-regarded history of the sport.

1822   William Hazlitt's famed essay, "The Fight," is published, describing the journey to and from the December 1821 fight between Bill Neate and Tom Hickman as well as the fight itself. As boxing is illegal in England at the time, followers of the sport often have to go on pilgrimages to get to fights. Locations are frequently changed at the last minute if it is learned that the constables know about the fight. The essay is considered one of the finest pieces of first-person sports reportage and certainly the best description of the atmosphere surrounding a bare-knuckle fight. Norman Mailer uses the essay as a model for his 1975 book, also entitled *The Fight*, about the 1974 championship fight between Muhammad Ali and George Foreman that took place in Zaire.

1838   The London Prize Ring Rules are established, commonly called the "New Rules" in contemporary sources. They are revised in 1843, 1853, and 1864. The LPRR outlaw biting, butting, gouging, holding and hitting, scratching, hitting an opponent when he is down, and kicking. The LPRR requires the ring to be 24 ft. square and with designated corners for each fighter. The LPRR reiterate the Broughton Rules that each fighter must come up to scratch for each round. A round ends when a man is knocked down. Fighters have thirty seconds to come to scratch and resume the fight. Although very different from modern boxing, under LPRR bare-knuckle boxing comes to resemble somewhat what boxing is like today. The new rules have made the sport a little less gruesome and brutal to watch than under the Broughton Rules. Fights are still to the finish, with one man quitting or so badly beaten as to be unable to continue. The LPRR are designed to safeguard fighters a bit. Nonetheless, bare-knuckle boxing remains a rough, tough, vicious, unseemly sport.

1858   John Morrissey defeats John C. Heenan to win the American heavyweight championship. Morrissey later served two terms in the US Congress.

1860   The first "world" heavyweight championship fight takes place in Farnborough, England, between John C. Heenan (United States) and Tom Sayers (England). After two hours of hard scrapping, the two fighters abandon the ring when spectators begin to scramble to escape the police who never officially stop the fight. The referee declares the fight a draw. Among the spectators are Charles Dickens, William Thackeray, and Lord Palmerston.

1861   Britain passes an anti-prizefight law that, among other things, makes it illegal to transport anyone to a prizefight. The sport diminishes in popularity in Britain.

1867   The Marquess of Queensberry Rules are published and will replace the London Prize Ring Rules. At first these rules apply only to amateur boxers but gradually catch with professional fighters as well. Boxers are required to wear gloves which protect the hands and enable the combatants to throw more blows. Wrestling, with the exception of clinches, has been eliminated. Rounds are now timed at three minutes. Fighters are given a one-minute rest between rounds. Fights are fought for a set number of rounds and if the bout ends with both fighters still standing, designated judges using a point system will designate who, in their judgment, won the fight on the basis of which fighter won the most rounds.

Although bare-knuckle boxing will continue for several years, these rules are the launch of modern boxing. By the end of the nineteenth century, bare-knuckle fighting has been virtually eliminated from the sport.

1873   Richard K. Fox launches *Police Gazette, the Leading, Illustrated Sporting Journal of America* in New York. Lurid and sometimes unreliable, the paper becomes the leading publication about boxing in the United States. It ceases publication in 1932.

1877   Jem Mace, boxing champion in England and the United States, goes to Australia and meets Larry Foley, the undisputed champion of Australia. Using Queensberry Rules, they usher in a golden age of boxing in Australia.

1877   John Knifton defeats Tom Tully for the championship of England in the first heavyweight championship fight under Marquess of Queensberry Rules

1880   Henry Downes Miles's *Pugilistica* is published, intended to succeed Egan's *Boxiana* as the definitive (and more accurate) history of boxing.

1880   Prizefighting is illegal in every state in the United States.

1882   George Bernard Shaw publishes a boxing novel, *Cashel Byron's Profession.*

1886   Peter Jackson, The Black Prince, émigré to Australia from the West Indies, defeats Tom Lees for the Australian heavyweight becoming the first black man to win the professional heavyweight of any country. He challenges American champion John L. Sullivan who draws the color line and refuses to fight him.

1889   John L. Sullivan beats Jake Kilrain in Mississippi and wins the American championship, becoming America's first celebrity boxer.

1889   Jem Smith draws with Frank Slavin in Belgium, the last Prize Ring championship fight in Europe.

1889   The manual *Boxing* is published by R. G. Allanson-Winn (Lord Headley). An Irish peer and accomplished amateur boxer, Headley famously converts to Islam in 1913.

1892   James J. Corbett knocks out John L. Sullivan to become the first heavyweight champion under Marquess of Queensberry Rules. The era of gloved boxing and timed rounds has begun. Distinct weight divisions have been firmly established now. George Dixon becomes the first African American to win a boxing title when he knocks out Jack Skelly to win the world featherweight title. Both fights were at the Carnival of Champions in New Orleans. In 1893, Richard K. Fox, owner of the *Police Gazette*, "officially" recognizes Dixon as the featherweight champion.

1894   Thomas Edison films the first boxing match, a staged match for film between heavyweight champion James J. Corbett and Peter Courtney in Orange, New Jersey.

1896   The Horton Act legalizes professional boxing in New York state from 1896 to 1900 when it expires. It would not be until 1920 that boxing would again be legal in the state of New York.

1897   Nellie Verrill Mighels Davis becomes the first woman reporter to cover a prizefight when she reports the Bob Fitzsimmons–Jim Corbett heavyweight championship fight for the Nevada Appeal. The fight ends with Fitzsimmons knocking out Corbett with his famous "solar plexus" punch. Fitzsimmons will win titles as a middleweight, light heavyweight, and heavyweight, becoming the first fighter to do so.

1897   The state of Nevada legalizes boxing and becomes an important site for championship matches.

1899   Peter Felix, émigré to Australia from St. Croix, defeats Bill Doherty to become the second black man to win the Australian heavyweight title.

1901   Joe Walcott of Barbados becomes the first black man to win the welterweight title by knocking out Jim "Rube" Fern in Fort Erie, Ontario, Canada.

1902   Joe Gans, considered one of the greatest fighters of all time, becomes the first African American to win the lightweight title, knocking out Frank Erne.

1904   Men's boxing is introduced in the Olympics Games held in St. Louis.

1905 Jack London publishes *The Game*, a boxing novel. London will publish several other boxing stories over the course of his career.

1906 Jack Johnson defeats Sam Langford, the Boston Tarbaby, one of the great black fighters of his age, who manages to give Johnson a competitive battle despite the fact Johnson outweighed him by nearly 30 pounds and was six inches taller. Unlike the other black fighters of this era whom Johnson would fight several times, he would never fight Langford again. Seventy-six of Langford's fights were against black opponents as black fighters often were forced to fight one another because of Jim Crow.

1906 Joe Gans wins a 42-round lightweight title defense against Oscar "Battling" Nelson at Goldfield, Nevada. It was the most talked-about and publicized non-heavyweight title fight of the era. For instance, reporters read by bullhorn the round-by-round Gans-Nelson fight results from Western Union Telegraph transmissions at their various newspaper headquarters. Famed promoter Tex Rickard promoted the fight.

1907 Andrew Jeptha of Cape Town, South Africa, becomes the first black fighter to hold a British title (unofficially) when he wins the British welterweight championship.

1908 Jack Johnson defeats Tommy Burns in Sydney, Australia to become the first African American heavyweight boxing champion. The cry goes up from writer Jack London for a "Great White Hope" to defeat Johnson and return the title to the white race. Battling Nelson defeats Joe Gans to win the lightweight title. In a return match a few months later, Nelson retains the title and defeats Gans a second time.

1910 On July 4, "Great White Hope" and former champion Jim Jeffries returns to the ring to face champion Jack Johnson in what is billed at the time as "the Fight of Century," the most publicized sporting event in American history to that point. Johnson easily wins the match, the result causing racial violence throughout the United States. Tex Rickard, the promoter, vowed not to promote another interracial heavyweight championship fight again. The federal government interdicts the film of the fight under the Interstate Commerce Clause in the interest of public safety.

1910   Former lightweight champion Joe Gans dies in Baltimore from complications from tuberculosis.

1911   National Sporting Club imposes a "color bar" in British boxing after Home Secretary Winston Churchill bows to pressure to declare as illegal and ban a fight between heavyweight champion Jack Johnson and "Bombardier" Billy Wells scheduled for October.

1912   Jerry Jerome becomes the first Aboriginal to win an Australian boxing title, defeating Ted Whiting to win the Australian middleweight title.

1912   In Australia, Sam Langford defeats Sam McVey, a noted black American fighter of the period, to win the Australian heavyweight championship. McVey and Langford would fight six bouts against each other while both were in Australia.

1913   Jack Johnson is convicted in federal court of violation of the Mann Act and is sentenced to a year and a day in prison. He flees the country rather than serve the sentence.

1915   Jess Willard knocks out Jack Johnson in Havana, Cuba, ending the controversial reign of the first black heavyweight champion. Johnson claims that he threw the fight in order to have the Justice Department drop his conviction for violation of the Mann (or White Slavery) Act so that he could return to the United States. He left the United States in 1913, immediately after his conviction of transporting a woman across state lines for immoral purposes.

1917   Benny Leonard, "The Ghetto Wizard," considered by many boxing authorities to be the greatest of all Jewish boxers, wins the lightweight title by defeating Freddie Welsh. He holds the title until his retirement in 1925.

1920   Jack Johnson returns to the United States to serve his one-year prison sentence at Leavenworth federal prison.

1920   Walker Law legalizes professional boxing in the state of New York and forms the basis for legalization in other states.

1921   Jack Dempsey defeats Georges Carpentier in the first live radio broadcast of a championship boxing match.

1922 Tex Rickard is jailed and charged with statutory rape of a 15-year old girl. The charges stem from his relationship with the 15-year old and two other girls, 11 and 12. He is acquitted by an all-male jury despite the fact that the prosecution had a strong case. Rickard's attorney successfully attacks the reputation of the girl in question after he is unable to shake her testimony under cross-examination. Despite the acquittal, Rickard's reputation is stained.

1922 Battling Siki becomes the first African to win a world championship when he defeats the popular French fighter Georges Carpentier to win the light heavyweight title.

1922 Nat Fleischer, former sports editor at the *New York Telegram*, launches *The Ring* magazine, the Bible of Boxing, which becomes the most famous boxing publication in the United States.

1923 Shelby, Montana holds a heavyweight championship match between champion Jack Dempsey and challenger Tom Gibbon. The town's desire for the match is the result of an oil boom which convinced the town's leaders that a boxing match would make the town famous and increase tourism. The tourism never materializes; the fight draws a disappointing attendance and the promoter, Tex Rickard, and Dempsey's manager, Jack "Doc" Kearns fleece the town for everything they can in the demands they make for the fight to be held there. Dempsey wins the lackluster fight and Kearns absconds with the gate receipts as Dempsey's share of the fight. The match actually bankrupts the town's four banks that backed the fight and is one of the most disastrous boxing ventures in the history of the sport.

1923 Luis Firpo, an Argentine nicknamed the Wild Bull of the Pampas, becomes the first Latin American fighter to contend for the heavyweight title when he loses to Jack Dempsey in September at the Polo Grounds in New York. It is considered to be one of the most exciting title fights ever with Firpo being knocked down seven times in the first round. But in the same round, Firpo manages to trap Dempsey against the ropes and knock the champion clean out of the ring. Dempsey, who lands on the typewriters of the reporters at ringside, manages, with some support from the reporters, to get back in the ring before being counted out. (A fighter is given twenty seconds to get back in the ring if knocked out of it, rather than the ten seconds to get up if knocked down inside the ring.) Dempsey then knocks out Firpo in the second round. The moment of Firpo knocking Dempsey out of the ring was captured by Ashcan painter George Bellows in 1924 in one of the most famous pieces of art dealing with boxing or indeed any sport.

1925   Promoter Tex Rickard builds the third iteration of Madison Square Garden between 49th and 50th Streets on Eighth Avenue which becomes the most famous site in the world for professional boxing. It would be replaced by a new Garden built above the Pennsylvania Station by Irving Mitchell Felt in 1968.

1926   Tiger Flowers becomes the first African American middleweight champion, defeating Harry Greb.

1926   Black British middleweight Len Johnson goes to Australia as he is unable to fight for the title in England because of his color. He has some success outclassing several Aussie fighters including welterweight and middleweight champion Harry Collins. When his career ends, Johnson becomes a lorry and bus driver and an active member of the Communist Party.

1927   The first Jack Dempsey–Gene Tunney fight in 1926 ends with Tunney defeating Dempsey in ten rounds, thoroughly outboxing the hard-charging champion. The controversial rematch one year later features "the long count." Dempsey once again is being outclassed by Tunney's stylish boxing but knocks Tunney down in the seventh round. Instead of immediately going to a neutral corner as the rules stipulate, Dempsey hovers over Tunney for several seconds. The referee actually has to push Dempsey to a neutral corner. It is only when Dempsey is finally pushed away that the referee actually starts the count over Tunney who rises at nine, although he has been down on the canvas for at least fourteen seconds. By then, Tunney has regained his senses, continues to outbox Dempsey, indeed, knocking Dempsey down in the eighth round. Dempsey loses the rematch as well. Both Dempsey–Tunney fights are among the biggest sports events of the 1920s with multi-million dollar gates, with a glamorous audience of the rich, the beautiful, the celebrity, and smart set crowds. Boxing, especially big-time matches, is attracting these sorts of people during this era all over the Western world, in Europe and the

United States. Tunney is the first true intellectual-gentleman type, modeled after George Bernard Shaw's Cashel Byron, to become heavyweight champion. Tunney in fact is friends with Shaw and lectured on Shakespeare at Trinity College, Dublin. He marries a wealthy socialite. One of his sons, John V. Tunney, becomes a US senator in the early 1970s.

1927   *The Atlantic Monthly* publishes Ernest Hemingway's "Fifty Grand," a story about a fixed fight that does not go as planned. It becomes one of the most famous and well-regarded pieces of boxing fiction in American literary history.

1931   Mahonri Young casts a bronze statue of Joe Gans from a wax cast that was used in a Paul Muni movie called *Seven Faces*. Gans's wax statue in the movie, one among seven of famous men in different fields, represented sport. The other six wax statues were destroyed but Young's bronze casting of Gans wound up in Madison Square Garden sometime during the 1930s. Surprisingly, no one at Madison Square Garden had any idea that it was a bronze of Joe Gans.

1933   Middleweights Archie Sexton and Lauri Raiteri fight the first televised boxing match – an exhibition aired by the BBC.

1933   Adolph Hitler listens to radio transmission of the Max Baer v. Max Schmeling heavyweight fight. Baer wins the fight.

1934   Heavyweight boxer Max Baer stars in *The Prizefighter and the Lady* opposite leading actress Myrna Loy. He wins the heavyweight title in May 1934, knocking out Primo Carnera in the eleventh round. Gillette sponsors the Baer–Carnera match and it is broadcast internationally in three languages. Don Dunphy begins his sports broadcasting career announcing the fight.

1937   Joe Louis knocks out Jim Braddock to become the second African American to win the heavyweight title. Louis owes much to his promoter Mike Jacobs, the most powerful man in boxing during the Depression, for being able to get an opportunity to fight for the title at a time when much of the boxing establishment was reluctant to have a black heavyweight champion or even entertain the thought of one.

1937   Clifford Odets's *Golden Boy* opens on Broadway and runs for 250 performances. The film version with William Holden and

Barbara Stanwyck and directed by Rouben Mamoulian was released in 1939.

1938   Joe Louis knocks out German fighter Max Schmeling to retain the heavyweight title in one of the most publicized fights of the century: the American versus the Nazi. Louis had previously lost to Schmeling by knockout in 1936 and the German fighter was confident of winning the rematch. Louis's victory makes him a genuine hero in the eyes of many white Americans. He has long been the toast of black America.

1938   Nat Fleischer's *Black Dynamite: The Story of the Negro in the Prize Ring from 1782 to 1938*, five-volume series is the first comprehensive history of African Americans and boxing.

1938   Henry Armstrong wins both the welterweight and lightweight championships, adding them to the featherweight crown he already possesses, to become the only fighter in boxing history to hold three titles simultaneously. Armstrong is considered by most boxing experts to be one of the greatest fighters of the twentieth century.

1938   Joe Louis portrays a boxer and the romantic lead in the all-black cast film *Spirit of Youth*.

1939   Lou Nova defeats Max Baer in the first major televised boxing match in the United States.

1939   Henry Armstrong stars in the all-black cast film, *Keep Punching*, portraying an aspiring boxer.

1942   Joe Louis gives a speech at a military charity event, saying "We're going to do our part … and we'll win because we're on God's side." The words became a patriotic slogan for the Second World War and were used on a poster featuring Louis charging with a bayonet. Actually, Louis mangles his speech as he was supposed to say, "God's on our side." What he wound up saying was actually better. The promotion of Louis as an image during the war was meant to encourage patriotism especially among African Americans whose loyalty became an issue in the early days of America's entry into the war. Many blacks remembered their horrendous military experience during the First World War and were conscious that the nation was fighting a war for democracy against a nation, Germany, which looked upon the United States as a model racist society.

1944   While at Camp Siebert in Gadsden, Alabama, Sugar Ray Robinson jumps a racist white military policeman to prevent Joe Louis from hitting him when the MP pokes Louis with his billy club and tells him to move to the black waiting area to wait for the segregated camp bus. Other MPs arrive and recognize Louis so no harm comes to either Louis or Robinson, and no charges are filed. But Louis and Robinson are asked to drive around the camp in an open jeep to show black soldiers that they have not been harmed as rumors have spread and there is fear that there may be reprisals because of the incident.

1944   Gillette sponsors boxing at Madison Square Garden, telecasting *Friday Night Fight* between Willie Pep and Chalky Wright.

1946   Heavyweight champion Joe Louis returns to action after more than three years away for military service, defeating Billy Conn in the first televised heavyweight boxing match, shown on NBC.

1946   *Gillette Cavalcade of Sports* runs on NBC's New York City station WNBT intermittently beginning in 1943 and is picked up by the NBC television network three years later. It becomes one of the most famous, well-remembered of the many boxing programs on television during the 1950s, when boxing is the most televised sport of the era.

1946   Sugar Ray Robinson wins the welterweight title.

1947   John Garfield plays a boxer very loosely based on the career of the great Jewish fighter Barney Ross (who won titles in the lightweight, junior lightweight, and welterweight divisions) in *Body and Soul*, which also features African American character actor Canada Lee. Nominated for several Academy Awards, it is considered by many critics to be the best boxing film ever made.

1947   Sugar Ray Robinson knocks out Jimmy Doyle in a welterweight title fight that results in Doyle's death as the 22-year-old never regains consciousness. It is the first time that a fighter dies in a world title fight.

1947   British Boxing Board of Control abrogates the color bar in British boxing.

1947   Budd Schulberg's boxing novel, *The Harder They Fall,* loosely based on the career of Primo Carnera, is published. Carnera, who held the heavyweight championship from 1933 to 1934, is accused of being controlled by gangsters and unknowingly participating in fixed fights. His size is his calling card and he is considered the biggest heavyweight in history. Actually, at 6 feet 6 inches he is an inch shorter than Jess Willard who won the title from Jack Johnson in 1915 and lost it to Jack Dempsey in 1919. But Carnera weighs more than any other heavyweight champion until Russian Nikolai Valuev who weighs 328 pounds and who stands 7 feet tall wins the title in 2005. Schulberg's novel is made into a 1956 film starring Humphrey Bogart, his last film. Carnera unsuccessfully sues Columbia Pictures for invasion of privacy because of the film.

1948   The passage of the British Nationality Act of 1948 creates circumstances for a migration of African fighters from the British colonies. They would play a major role in keeping the game alive in the face of a boxing recession and the experience would enable the emergence of the likes of Roy Ankrah, Hogan "Kid" Bassey, and Dick Tiger.

1948   Marcel Cerdan, a Pied-Noir born in Algeria and reared in French Morocco, and one of the most successful boxers to learn his craft in Africa, defeats Tony Zale to become world middleweight champion. He becomes perhaps equally famous for having an affair with singer Edith Piaf in the last year of his life. He dies in a plane crash in 1949.

1949   Robert Ryan stars in Robert Wise's film noir boxing classic, *The Set-Up,* based on the 1928 long narrative poem by Joseph Moncure March of the same title. The poem is actually about a black fighter and the film would have had more dramatic power had the race of the protagonist not been changed. Nonetheless, the film is considered among the best film noirs ever made and certainly one of the best boxing noirs.

1949   Joe Louis, considered by many experts to be the greatest fighter of all time and almost unanimously considered the greatest fighter of his era, announces his retirement. It does not last long as Louis is forced back into the ring because of tax problems.

1949 James D. Norris and Arthur M. Wirtz form the International Boxing Club to promote boxing matches at Madison Square Garden, Yankee Stadium, Chicago Stadium, St. Nicholas Arena, and the Detroit Olympia. The IBC, backed by Murder Inc. gangsters Frankie Carbo and Blinky Palermo, develops a stranglehold on boxing for most of the 1950s, controlling nearly all championship fights of the period. They also fix fights while paying the fighters next to nothing. It is nearly impossible for a fighter to get a chance at a championship unless he plays ball with the IBC. Norris splits the corporation, setting up a new corporation in Chicago, with African American lawyer Truman Gibson taking over the New York share of the business. (In effect, Gibson, who is Joe Louis's lawyer, becomes the first significant black promoter in boxing.) This smokescreen does not fool anyone and the IBC is found to be a monopoly and in restraint of trade in federal court and forced to dissolve. In 1960, Gibson, Carbo, and Palermo are charged with extortion and conspiracy. Gibson is given five years' probation and a fine. Carbo and Palermo are sentenced to 25 years in prison.

1949 Jack Hassen, an Australian Aborigine, wins the Australian lightweight championship in a bout with Archie Kemp. But Kemp dies from injuries he sustains in the fight. Kemp's death so upsets Hassen that he loses all effectiveness as a fighter, being afraid to punch hard, and as a result loses most of his fights between 1949 and 1951, when he retires. He becomes politically active in retirement, for instance demonstrating in 1967 in support of Muhammad Ali's opposition to the draft.

1950 The British Empire Championships Committee is formed, later renamed "Commonwealth" instead of "Empire." Empire titles have previously been contested by whites from the British Isles and the old dominion nations such as Australia, Canada, and South Africa. Black African countries (still under colonial rule) could have a representing steward each. One of the first Nigerian fighters to migrate to England was Israel "Battling" Boyle who was instrumental in welcoming other Nigerian fighters to Liverpool such as Hogan "Kid" Bassey and Dick Tiger. There are now fifty-four Commonwealth states.

1951   Joe Louis's comeback is brutally ended when he is knocked out in the eighth round by rising heavyweight Rocky Marciano who was reluctant to fight his aging boyhood hero. Louis retired for good after this fight. Marciano would go on to defeat Jersey Joe Walcott and become champion.

1951   Sugar Ray Robinson defeats middleweight champion Jake LaMotta to win the title. He and LaMotta would fight six times altogether, going back to their first bout in 1943. Robinson would win five of them. Robinson would win and lose the middleweight title five times over his long career. He is commonly considered to be the greatest fighter pound-for-pound who ever fought. He was Muhammad Ali's favorite fighter, icon, and hero. Ali patterned much of his own style after Robinson.

1952   Light-heavyweight Floyd Patterson wins the gold medal at the Helsinki Olympics. He will go on to become heavyweight champion in 1956 when he beats Archie Moore. He loses the title in 1959 to Sweden's Ingemar Johansson. Patterson regains the title in 1960, knocking out Johansson. He knocks Johansson out again in a third match. Patterson loses the title for good when he is knocked out in one round by the indomitable ex-convict Sonny Liston in 1962. Patterson is knocked out again in one round in the rematch against Liston in 1963. He will go on to lose matches against champion Muhammad Ali, whom he at first detests for joining the Nation of Islam and changing his name, but later learns to respect and support in his stance against the draft.

1954   Elia Kazan's *On the Waterfront* is released featuring Marlon Brando playing an ex-boxer working for his brother on a mob-controlled New York waterfront. The film wins eight Oscars including Best Picture but is not a movie about boxing.

1956   Another Robert Wise boxing film, but considerably more upbeat is *Somebody Up There Likes Me*, based on the autobiography of middleweight champion and street tough Rocky Graziano. James Dean was originally cast to play Graziano but was killed in an auto accident. Paul Newman replaced him. The film won Oscars for best cinematography and art direction. It is considered among the best boxing films ever made by Hollywood. The 1955 autobiography on which the film is based is far more harrowing and grittier than the movie and is among the best sports autobiographies ever written.

1956   New Yorker writer A. J. Liebling's *The Sweet Science*, a collection of his boxing essays, is published and gains the reputation as the best writing in English on the sport. *The Sweet Science* has become the classic text on boxing and probably the most famous of all American nonfiction works on the sport.

1957   Andre DeToth's *Monkey on My Back* is released. It is based on the career of Barney Ross, including his heroic service during the Second World War. Ross becomes a drug addict as a result of the injuries he sustains during the war. The film is, as are most films of this type, heavily fictionalized.

1957   Hogan "Kid" Bassey defeats Cherif Hamia to win the world featherweight title becoming the first Nigerian to win a world title.

1960   Senator Estes Kefauver conducts a Congressional investigation of boxing as part of an investigation into organized crime that was launched in 1950. Jake LaMotta, Sonny Liston, Frankie Carbo, and James D. Norris are among those who testify, with Norris admitting that organized crime was in control of the sport. The hearings end in 1964.

1960   Charlie Mohr, a middleweight at the University of Wisconsin, Madison, dies eight days after fighting in the NCAA boxing tournament, the result of a blow he took in the ring. Almost immediately the University of Wisconsin ends its collegiate boxing program. The NCAA soon follows suit by ending its national boxing tournament and, in effect, pulling the plug on collegiate boxing. The NCAA began sponsoring the championship tournament in 1932 and the tournament reached its peak in 1948 with fifty-five colleges participating. By 1960, the number dwindled to twenty, a sign that boxing is losing popularity in the United States.

1961   Jimmy Toppi Sr. opens the Blue Horizon in North Philadelphia which becomes, after Madison Square, the most famous boxing venue in the United States.

1962   Welterweight champion Emile Griffith knocks out Benny "Kid" Paret in this tragic fight. Paret dies ten days later never regaining consciousness. This was the third fight between the two men, each having won previously. At the weigh-in for this fight, Paret angered Griffith by calling him "a faggot." Indeed, Griffith was gay, which he would publicly acknowledge years later. This fight was televised and the brutality of it results in calls from various corners of the public to ban boxing.

1962   Elvis Presley plays a naïve boxer with a big punch in *Kid Galahad*, this musical remake of the 1937 boxing film that starred Edward G. Robinson, Humphrey Bogart, and Bette Davis. It is Presley's only boxing film and it is considered by critics to be among his better performances.

1962   The feature film version of Rod Serling's noir-ish boxing drama, *Requiem for a Heavyweight*, about a washed-up fighter stars Anthony Quinn, Mickey Rooney, and Julie Harris with a brief but memorable appearance by Cassius Clay (Muhammad Ali) at the beginning of the film.

1962   The National Boxing Association, the sole sanctioning body in boxing since 1921, changes its name to the World Boxing Association in recognition of the growing international dimensions of boxing and the need for a sanctioning body to be able to speak for the sport beyond the United States.

1963   Sugar Ramos knocks out Davey Moore in a featherweight championship fight in which Moore loses both the title and his life as a result of injuries he sustained in the ring. At this point, following the highly publicized death of Benny "Kid" Paret a year earlier, boxing is really reeling from bad publicity and the calls for its outlawing are loud and many.

1963   The World Boxing Council, headquartered in Mexico, is established in eleven countries as an international sanctioning body meant to unify all boxing commissions. Currently, 161 countries are members.

1964   Cassius Clay defeats champion Sonny Liston to become heavyweight champion and immediately after the fight announces that he is a member of the Nation of Islam, known in the press as the Black Muslims, a controversial black separatist group whose most famous spokesperson is Malcolm X, who shortly after this fight will leave the group and a year later will be assassinated by members of the NOI. Immediately after this fight, Clay is given the new name of Muhammad Ali by Elijah Muhammad, leader of the NOI and self-styled Messenger of Allah. Ali goes on to become the most famous man in the world during his days as an active fighter. Before Ali's announced conversion, he has, through his poetry recitation, predictions, and humorous bragging, greatly revived interest in boxing in the United States.

1964   Joe Frazier wins the gold medal in the heavyweight division at the Olympic Games, establishing himself as one of the most promising heavyweights in the world.

1964   Musical version of Clifford Odets's *Golden Boy* with an interracial romance and references to the current-day civil rights movement opens on Broadway at the Majestic Theater and runs for 568 performances. Sammy Davis, Jr., the biggest black star of the era, and Paula Wayne play the leads.

1964   First run of post-Second World War regular television boxing ends with final episode of *Gillette Cavalcade of Sports Friday Night Fights*. The fight is between middleweights Dick Tiger and Gene Fullmer.

1965   In one of the most bizarre heavyweight title fights ever, Muhammad Ali retains the title by knocking out Sonny Liston in one round in the small town of Lewiston, Maine. Ali knocks out Liston with a punch no one sees, stands over him telling the fallen ex-champion to get up, and refuses to go to a neutral corner for many seconds. Indeed, so befuddled is referee Jersey Joe Walcott that he actually has both fighters resume fighting before being told that the fight is over and that Liston was down for more than ten seconds. Few people believe that this fight was not fixed, but there is disagreement regarding by whom and why. One belief is that Liston went to the canvas because he was convinced that a follower of Malcolm X was going to shoot Ali in the ring. The fight took place just a few months after Malcolm X had been murdered in Harlem by members of the Nation of Islam just as he was preparing to give a speech. Malcolm split acrimoniously from the NOI a year before his murder and had been warned that he would be killed for badmouthing NOI leader Elijah Muhammad, who had grown to hate his former favorite minister. After Malcolm's death, rumors abounded that Malcolm's followers were going to avenge their leader's death by killing Ali, now the most prominent member of the NOI. Ali had particularly incensed many of Malcolm's followers because he had been good friends with the slain leader but on orders from the NOI cut Malcolm cold and publicly denounced him. Another belief is that Liston had been approached by NOI toughs and told to throw the fight or else. The NOI certainly had the muscle and cold-bloodedness to make such a threat and to make good on it. Another is that Liston was told by the mob to take a dive as they could make more on bets if he lost the fight than if he won it. All of the conspiracy theories make some sense, but only some. On the other hand, Liston may have been hit by a punch that legitimately knocked him down for ten seconds. The fight completely ruined whatever was left of Liston's reputation. The fight did not do Ali's reputation much good either, although no one ever accused him of being a partner to a fix, if there was one.

1966   Rubin "Hurricane" Carter is arrested for robbing a bar and grill in Paterson, New Jersey and murdering three people, the bartender, and two customers. Carter is a middleweight fighter whose career had been in decline since his surprise victory over Emile Griffith in 1963. He had served time in prison and was dismissed from the military after four courts martial. Carter, along with John Artis, is convicted of murder in 1967 and sentenced to life in prison. Carter begins a campaign to clear his name and prove his innocence. He is able to secure a new trial in 1977 but is convicted again. In 1985, Carter was granted a writ of habeas corpus and freed without bail. The prosecution chose not to try him a third time. Carter was the subject of a song by Bob Dylan and a 1999 film entitled *Hurricane* directed by Norman Jewison and starring Denzel Washington. Carter wrote an autobiography, *The Sixteenth Round: From Number One Contender to Number 45472*, which was published in 1974.

1967–1970   In 1967, Muhammad Ali is convicted in federal court for violation of the Selective Service Act for his refusal to be inducted into the Army on the grounds of his religious faith. He is stripped of his WBA title and New York State boxing license.

He is subsequently unable to fight anywhere in the United States for more than three years but he remains a notable public figure during this time, lecturing on college campuses, acting (*Big Time Buck White*, a musical about Black Power based on a play written by a white author), and participating in a computer-simulated fight with retired undefeated champion Rocky Marciano.

1967   Howard Sackler's play *The Great White Hope*, a fictionalized account of part of Jack Johnson's career and his marriage to Etta Duryea, who committed suicide in her husband's Chicago nightclub, premiers at Arena Stage. Muhammad Ali identifies with the character of Johnson, particularly with Johnson's fight against the federal government when he was charged under the Mann Act. Ali feels he is being persecuted because of his race, as Johnson was for his sexual proclivities toward white women. The difference for Ali is that his persecution stems from his religion. The play is made into a highly regarded film in 1970.

1968   George Foreman, after winning the Olympic gold medal in boxing, walks around the ring waving an American flag in a counter-protest to sprinters Tommie Smith and John Carlos who gave a clenched-fist salute to the National Anthem after winning their medals earlier during the Olympics.

1969   Leonard Gardner publishes *Fat City*, regarded as one of the finest boxing novels ever written. John Huston makes it into a film in 1972.

1970   Argentine Carlos Monzon defeats champion Nino Benvenuti to win the middleweight title. Monzon proceeds to dominate the division, successfully defending his title fourteen times before retiring. Monzon's personal life was turbulent, accused of physically abusing both his wives and his many mistresses. In 1989, he is convicted of killing his second wife and sentenced to eleven years in prison. While on a weekend furlough, Monzon is killed in an automobile accident. Monzon is remembered as one of the finest middleweights in boxing history.

1970   Muhammad Ali is granted a boxing license in the state of Georgia and defeats Jerry Quarry in Ali's first fight in over three years. Growing black political power in Georgia made it possible for Ali finally to get a license.

1970   Trumpeter Miles Davis scores the documentary *Jack Johnson*, about the first black heavyweight champion, produced and directed by Bill Cayton and Jim Jacobs.

1970   Sonny Liston is found dead in his home by his wife, Geraldine. He dies from an apparent heroin drug overdose. He had been dead for several days, so despite the fact that his wife discovered him in early January 1971, the official date of death is late December 1970. His wife did not call the police until two or three hours after she found the body and so there is no way of knowing how she may have tampered with the house to disguise or destroy the evidence of his death. Foul play was not considered a cause of death. Indeed, at the time of his death, Liston was scheduled to fight Canadian George Chavulo. He had just beaten Chuck Wepner and seemed to be making a successful comeback. But Liston's ties to the underworld, his rather unsavory personal life, and his fear of hypodermic needles have led many to suspect that he may have been murdered.

1971   Joe Frazier defeats Muhammad Ali in one of the biggest fights of the century. Both fighters are paid $2.5 million, an unheard-of sum at the time (each would have made much more had they taken a percentage of the gate instead of the guarantee). Both fighters are undefeated and each claims to be the champion. Ali has been stripped of his titles as a result of his conviction in 1967 for violating the Selective Service Act. Frazier wins Ali's vacated title in an elimination tourney. Ali is taken to the hospital immediately after the fight. Frazier is hospitalized for a few weeks as a result of the punishment he endures in the fight. Ali suffers a fifteenth-round knockdown and a severely bruised and swollen jaw. Despite losing the fight, Ali remains by far the more popular of the two fighters which annoys Frazier greatly.

1971   The United States Supreme Court unanimously (8-0) overturns Muhammad Ali's lower court conviction of violating the Selective Service Act.

1973   George Foreman wins the heavyweight title by knocking out titleholder Joe Frazier in a surprising turn of events as Frazier was favored to win. Frazier would never regain the title.

1974   Muhammad Ali and Joe Frazier, both men without championships, fight a non-title fight with Ali winning a decision, although he nearly knocked Frazier out in the second round, which ended several seconds early because referee Carlos Padilla thought he heard the bell. The fight sets up Ali's opportunity to fight titleholder George Foreman.

1974   Muhammad Ali regains the heavyweight title by defeating a heavily favored, younger George Foreman in Kinshasa, Zaire, the first heavyweight title to be held on the continent of Africa. Ali described his technique of leaning against the ropes for leverage against Foreman's onslaughts, or "Rope-a-dope," which becomes a slang expression for fooling someone by playing his strength against him. Don King, a controversial figure in boxing, becomes well-known as a result of promoting this fight. King emerges as the most powerful African American in the sport, going on to promote many fights with Ali and other champions in various weight divisions. King killed a man in 1954 for trying to rob one of his gambling houses and served nearly four years in prison for non-negligent manslaughter for stomping one of his employees to death.

1975   The World Boxing Association moves its headquarters to Panama.

1975   Muhammad Ali defeats Joe Frazier in the Philippines, "the Thrilla in Manila," to retain the heavyweight title in the third match between the two men. It is the first live satellite broadcast and the first boxing match to be on pay-per-view. The fight is so brutal that neither man will be the same as a result of the beating each took at the hands of the other.

1975   Random House publishes Muhammad Ali's autobiography *The Greatest: My Own Story*. Edited by Toni Morrison, heavily ghosted and shaped by the Nation of Islam, the book never seems genuine because it does not sound authentically like Ali. Nonetheless it contains useful information about the fighter and more importantly a useful perspective on how the fighter wanted his life to be seen by the public. The book is made into a film the following year with Ali playing himself.

1976   John G. Avildsen's *Rocky*, written by and starring Sylvester Stallone, becomes the first boxing film to win the Best Picture

Oscar. Seven sequels (and counting) will be made to the original film.

1976   The Olympic Games in Montreal produces five American gold medal winners who go on to have significant professional careers: Howard Davis, Jr., Sugar Ray Leonard, Michael and Leon Spinks, and Leo Randolph. Four of the five go on to win championship titles.

1978   Cathy "Cat" Davis becomes the first woman fighter to make the cover of *The Ring* magazine. She becomes the most noted woman fighter of her era, indeed, in post-Second World War America. Several of her fights were televised on major networks. It is discovered that some of her fights are fixed and her reputation suffers as a result.

1978   Olympic champion Leon Spinks, having only eight professional fights, defeats an aging Muhammad Ali to win the heavyweight title in a shocking upset.

1978   Muhammad Ali defeats champion Leon Spinks to become the first fighter to win the heavyweight title three different times. Ali retires after this fight.

1978   DC Comics publishes a special seventy-two-page, oversize edition entitled *Superman versus Muhammad Ali*, with Ali teaming up with Superman to stop an alien invasion. It is a sign of how widely accepted Ali is as a cultural icon and celebrity hero since his defeat of George Foreman four year earlier. He is now as mythical, as larger than life, as Superman.

1980   Martin Scorsese's *Raging Bull*, based on the autobiography of middleweight champion Jake LaMotta, is released and becomes the most celebrated of all boxing movies. The film was nominated for eight Academy Awards including Best Picture but won only two, one of which was for Robert De Niro's performance as LaMotta. The film brought LaMotta back into the public spotlight for a time and also brought attention to his book, which ranks among the best autobiographies of a boxer.

1980   Larry Holmes, former sparring partner of the aging champion, defeats Muhammad Ali easily and brutally, as Ali attempts a comeback from retirement. Ali's slurred speech and slower reflexes are signs of the Parkinson's syndrome, aggravated by punishment in the ring, that will gradually afflict him more severely in his later years.

1980   Boxing Hall of Fame announcer Al Bernstein announces the first boxing match for cable channel ESPN (Entertainment and Sports Network).

1980   Roberto Duran defeats Sugar Ray Leonard in Montreal in June to win the welterweight title in what is one of the most profitable and most publicized non-heavyweight title fights of the twentieth century. Duran becomes the most famous Latino fighter in the United States, despite the fact that he does not speak English and that he lives in Panama. Duran will be the subject of a 2014 biopic entitled *Hands of Stone*.

1981   Heavyweight champion Larry Holmes defeats Jerry Cooney in one of the most highly publicized, interracial boxing matches in decades, as Cooney is one of the first white fighters in some time who is considered to have a good chance to win.

1981   Joe Louis dies at the age of sixty-six in Nevada of cardiac arrest. He is in poor health in the years before he died, suffering from a number of ailments including drug addiction, strokes, heart ailments, and paranoiac delusions. He had been working as a greeter at a Las Vegas casino for several years before his death.

1981   Trevor Berbick defeats Muhammad Ali in the Bahamas, ending Ali's career.

1982   Actor Sylvester Stallone commissions A. Thomas Schomberg to create a bronze Rocky statue for the film *Rocky III*. The statue is currently at the base of the steps of the Philadelphia Museum of Art.

1983   A splinter group from the World Boxing Association forms this third major sanctioning body, the only one headquartered in the United States (Springfield, New Jersey). The increase in sanctioning bodies increases the number of boxing titles as each organization rarely if ever recognizes the champion of its rival.

1986   Mike Tyson, at the age of twenty, becomes the youngest man to win the heavyweight title when he knocks out WBC champion Trevor Berbick in one round. He is the most powerful, destructive, and feared heavyweight champion since Sonny Liston. No heavyweight can survive more than a handful of rounds against him. He is the most dominant young champion of the heavyweight division in the post-Second World War era.

1987   *On Boxing* by novelist Joyce Carol Oates is published and becomes one of the important meditations of the sport and the first such book written by a woman.

1988   Mike Tyson marries television actress Robin Givens. The marriage lasts for eighteen months. Tyson is accused of assaulting her. His behavior generally is erratic. Many think that Tyson is headed for an emotional breakdown. He is still dominating his opponents in the ring. He is one of the most written about and publicized fighters since Muhammad Ali.

1988   A group of disgruntled businessmen from the World Boxing Association form a new sanctioning body, the World Boxing Organization, headquartered in Puerto Rico. It is the fourth major boxing sanctioning organization.

1989   Former light heavyweight champion Jose Torres's biography of Mike Tyson, *Fire & Fear: The Inside Story of Mike Tyson* is published. Torres, of Puerto Rico, who won the light heavyweight championship in 1965 defeating Willie Pastrano, becomes a writer after retiring from the ring, given encouragement and support from Norman Mailer. In 1971, he co-authored *Sting like a Bee*, a biography of Muhammad Ali. Torres becomes one of the most important boxing writers on the scene. He dies in Puerto Rico in 2009.

1989   Sugar Ray Robinson dies in Los Angeles at the age of sixty-seven from complications from Alzheimer's Disease.

1990   James "Buster" Douglas knocks out Mike Tyson in a stunning upset to become heavyweight champion. Tyson was a 42-1 favorite, making this fight one of the biggest upsets of twentieth-century boxing.

1992   Mike Tyson is found guilty of raping Miss Black America contestant Desiree Washington in Indianapolis and sentenced to six years in prison. He serves three before being released on parole. The case generates a great deal of commentary about sex, race, and gender privilege. Some question whether

Tyson would have been convicted had he been white. Others wonder whether Washington had set him up for a big civil settlement. While still others see it as a victory for women, particularly black women, and see Washington as courageous for bringing criminal charges and testifying during the trial. She is a very poised and credible witness and holds up well under cross-examination. There is controversy in the African American community as some noted black leaders support Tyson as a wrongly convicted black man and even celebrate his release which many black feminists find disgusting. Other black women are torn between sympathizing with Tyson and identifying with Washington. Tyson has always vehemently maintained his innocence. He would never be the same dominant fighter he was before he went to prison.

1992   Oscar De La Hoya wins the gold medal in the lightweight division in the Olympic Games.

1994   Oscar De La Hoya wins the World Boxing Organization (WBO) junior lightweight title. He will go on to win titles in the lightweight, junior welterweight, welterweight, junior middleweight, and middleweight divisions. De La Hoya would become third highest grossing pay-for-viewer fighter, behind only Floyd Mayweather Jr. and Manny Pacquiao.

1994   At the age of forty-five George Foreman defeats Michael Moorer to become the oldest man to win the heavyweight title. For Foreman it is redemption for his ignominious loss to Muhammad Ali in Zaire in 1974.

1996   Leon Gast's documentary about the Muhammad Ali–George Foreman fight in Zaire in 1974, *When We Were Kings*, is released. It will win the Academy Award for Best Feature-Length Documentary.

1996   Congress passes the Professional Boxing Safety Act that ensures that no boxer can fight in a state without a boxing commission unless supervised by the boxing commission of another state. The bill also requires medical insurance to cover the fighter during the bout, a doctor or ambulance available at the venue where the match is being held, and that boxers be registered with a state boxing commission and be issued a health certificate clearing them to fight.

1998   Manny Pacquiao wins the world flyweight championship, the first of the championship titles he would win across eight different weight classes including featherweight, lightweight, and welterweight. He is considered one of the finest boxers in the history of the sport and one of the most gifted of all Filipino athletes. In 2016, he is elected to the Philippine Senate.

1998   Floyd Mayweather, Jr., two years after winning a bronze medal in the 1996 Olympics and turning pro, wins super featherweight title. Mayweather, often touted as the best pound-for-pound fighter of his era, will go on to win titles in the lightweight, light welterweight, welterweight, and light middleweight divisions. He will also earn more than any other fighter in the history of the sport.

1999   Jerry Quarry, one of the accomplished white heavyweights of the Ali era, dies from complications resulting from boxing-induced dementia. Quarry fought Ali twice, in 1970 and 1972, losing first by technical knockout and then by knockout.

2000   Congress passes the Muhammad Ali Boxing Reform Act amending the 1996 Professional Boxing Safety Act by adding further safeguards to protect fighters from rigged rankings, fixed fights, and exploitation by promoters and managers.

2001   Will Smith, with many added pounds, portrays Muhammad Ali in Michael Mann's biopic *Ali*. The film also stars Jamie Foxx, Jon Voight, and Mario Van Peebles. The film generally receives favorable reviews but is not a box office success.

2001   Laila Ali, the daughter of Muhammad Ali, defeats Jacqui Frazier-Lyde, daughter of Joe Frazier, by majority decision in the first pay-per-view fight card ever headlined by women. This is her tenth straight win as a super middleweight. She will go to win all twenty-four of her bouts. Her father was not happy about her becoming a boxer when she informed him in 1999 of her decision to enter the profession. She is criticized for avoiding difficult opponents like Ann Wolfe, considered the hardest puncher among women boxers.

2001   Former heavyweight champion and National Golden Gloves amateur champion Greg Page, a native of Louisville who fought in a style reminiscent of Muhammad Ali, is knocked out and badly injured in a fight in Kentucky. The injuries are exacerbated by the fact that no ambulance, no oxygen, indeed, no doctor is present at the time of the knockout. The ringside physician, who is not licensed to practice in the state of Kentucky, left early and had to be brought back. Page, suffering severe head trauma, goes more than twenty minutes without any medical attention, precious time that might have made a real difference in his outcome. During the post-fight surgery, Page suffers a stroke and is paralyzed on his left side. Page suffers many health complications as a result of this fight: seizures, sepsis, pneumonia, hypothermia, and other maladies and is in need of constant medical care. He settles out of court with the state of Kentucky for $1.2 million. In 2009 he dies at his Louisville home from asphyxia, a direct result of his injuries as he smothers himself in bed, unable to extricate his head which had become lodged between the mattress and the bedframe. Page is fifty years old at the time of his death. His pay for his last fight is $1,500.

2002   Light welterweight Micky Ward, trained by his half-brother, Dick Eklund, narrowly defeats Arturo Gatti in one of the roughest, most savagely fought, welterweight fights in modern memory. Both men are hospitalized after the bout. *The Ring* magazine votes it the Fight of the Year. The men would fight twice more, in 2002 and 2003, each fight a slugfest. Gatti defeats Ward in these two fights. The 2003 fight is also voted Fight of the Year by *The Ring*. Ward and his colorful half-brother Eklund were the subjects of a 2010 Hollywood film entitled *The Fighter*, starring Mark Wahlberg as Ward and Christian Bale as Eklund. Bale wins a Best Supporting Actor Oscar for his efforts. Ward retires after the third Gatti fight. Gatti continues to fight, winning the light welterweight title but losing badly to Floyd Mayweather. Eventually, Gatti hires Micky Ward as his trainer. He retires in 2007. He dies in 2009 under unusual circumstances. Initially, his wife is accused of killing him but she is eventually cleared of all charges as Gatti's death is ruled a suicide.

2003   French sociologist Loic Waquant's *Body and Soul: Notebooks of an Apprentice Boxer,* considered by reviewers and scholars to be one of the most in-depth sociological and ethnographic studies of boxing, is published.

2004 Clint Eastwood's film adaptation of F. X. O'Toole's story "Million Dollar Baby" is released and will become the second boxing themed movie to win the Academy Award for Best Picture. *Million Dollar Baby* along with *Girl Fight* (2000) become the two cornerstone movies about women boxers. Jazz trumpeter Wynton Marsalis scores Ken Burns's documentary *Unforgivable Blackness: The Rise and Fall of Jack Johnson*. The book by Geoffrey C. Ward that accompanies the film is one of the best researched biographies of Johnson.

2005 The Muhammad Ali Center, a non-profit museum and cultural center, in Louisville, Kentucky, Ali's hometown, opens. The six-story facility costs $80 million and is the most expensive tribute ever made to a boxer.

2008 Kasia Boddy's *Boxing: A Cultural History* is published, a far-reaching examination into the history and cultural significance of boxing. It becomes one of the leading studies of the sport and the second significant book on boxing by a woman.

2011 Bernard Hopkins at the age of forty-six defeats Jean Pascal to win the light heavyweight title, becoming the oldest man to ever win a boxing title. Hopkins, overcoming a wayward youth and a term in prison, has a long and illustrious career dominating in the middleweight and light heavyweight divisions, fighting some of the most legendary fighters of his era including Roy Jones Jr., Oscar De La Hoya, Winky Wright, Antonio Tarver, and Felix Trinidad.

2012 Women's boxing is introduced at the Olympics.

2013 The opera *Champion*, about the career of boxer Emile Griffith and composed by jazz trumpeter Terrence Blanchard, premieres at Opera Theater in St. Louis, garnering good reviews. Emile Griffith dies in Hempstead, New York from complications of pugilistica dementia.

2014 Amateur boxer Malissa Smith's *A History of Women's Boxing* is published; it is the first full-scale account of women in the sport.

2016 Muhammad Ali dies from septic shock, having suffered for years from Parkinson's syndrome that increasingly disabled him. Ali is seventy-four years old.

2016   Retired champion Robert Duran publishes *I Am Duran: My Autobiography* with Blue Rider Press. He provides his first full explanation about why he quit during the middle of his championship rematch against Sugar Ray Leonard in 1980, an act that disgraced him in his native Panama for several years.

2017   Jake LaMotta dies at ninety-five in a nursing home from complications from pneumonia. Floyd Mayweather, Jr. comes out of retirement to defeat Ultimate Fighting welterweight champion Conor McGregor. It is Mayweather's fiftieth victory without a loss, leaving him with a better record than Rocky Marciano, the only boxing champion to retire undefeated, who was 49-0.

    Andre Ward, who held world titles in the super middleweight and light heavyweight divisions, retires undefeated with thirty-two straight wins in his career.

2018   In September, HBO announces it will no longer broadcast boxing. The premium cable network had broadcast some of the biggest fights of the past forty-five years.

    In October, middleweight champion Canelo Alvarez signs a five-year, eleven-fight deal worth a minimum of $365 million with DAZN, a sports streaming service. The contract makes him the highest paid athlete in the world.

The editor thanks Wil Haygood, Kasia Boddy, Rosalind Early, Michael Ezra, Troy Rondinone, Leger Grindon, Scott Emmert, Randy Roberts, Lewis Erenberg, Steve Riess, and especially Colleen Aycock, Byron Nakamura, Tony and Hazel Gee, and Adeyinka Makinde for their invaluable assistance in constructing this chronology.

GERALD EARLY

Introduction: The Last Sport Standing

The most lasting impression of all, however, was the fight itself. On the evening of June 30, 1927 I grasped for the first time how much concentration, mercilessness, and toughness American boxers brought to their profession. The way Walker hammered down his challenger, the ditchdigger Milligan, remained an unforgettable lesson for me. Here it was demonstrated to me for the first time *how unconditionally the boxer puts his existence on the line.*

– German boxer Max Schmeling (1905–2005), on watching the championship fight between Tommy Milligan and Mickey (the Toy Bulldog) Walker in London[1]

Was it worth all the blood and the sweat and the heartaches?

Absolutely! Besides, what else could I have become? With education and the right breaks, anyone can aspire to become a doctor or a lawyer – but you have to know real poverty to want to earn your living as a fighter. During much of my career, poverty was a constant companion …

To me, boxing has always represented the purest and truest form of athletic competition. It's much more natural to fight than it is to play football or hockey. A caveman or an alien from another planet would understand boxing, but he sure as hell wouldn't understand golf or tennis.

– Heavyweight boxer George Chuvalo[2]

Boxers are highly trained athletes, tuned up to a degree not known in other sports. They ply their trade alone, and there is nowhere to hide. It is a marriage of top physical conditioning with unrelenting bravery. *In my years in the fight game I have found that the professional boxers who successfully carve out a name for themselves are highly sensitive and complicated people.* It is no wonder that boxing champions react in so many different ways to the pressures that fame and wealth bring. If you take the endurance of a tennis player, the courage of a racing driver, the sensibility of an actor, the continued discipline of a long distance runner, and mix those ingredients, you are on the way to knowing what it takes to be a professional boxer.

> – Angelo Dundee, trainer of Muhammad Ali and
> Sugar Ray Leonard, among others[3]

The Boxer as Hipster

In order to understand boxing, and the chapters that comprise this book, it is important to consider its complexity and sociology as a performance art. Yes, it is an art! And a long-standing theatrical tradition. Nothing illustrates this better than the career of the great German fighter of the 1920s and 1930s, Max Schmeling, who managed to be a star in two distinctly different phases of German political and social history.

Max Schmeling's autobiography reminds the reader how much boxing was in vogue among German artists and intellectuals during the Weimar Republic of Schmeling's youth and young manhood. He became a professional fighter in 1924. Part of the mystique of the boxer was the pull of the primitive: the sport was obvious in its intentions and goals, in the nature of its performance and spectacle, administering and enduring physical punishment of the plainest kind, conquering the will of one's opponent, disconnecting one's opponent from reality by knocking him out cold. The German Smart Set appreciated the backwards purity of the sport, its anti-bourgeois essence, if you will, something modern society produced that was meant to celebrate something that transcended or preceded the modern, adored how it symbolized and re-enacted the Darwinian or Spencerian morality of survival as endless struggle. As Schmeling quotes Austrian actor and director Fritz Kortner, to whom he gives boxing lessons, "'What happens in the ring is a reflection of life. Merciless, raging – the way you go after each other – it's the way we all fight for our existence.'"[4] As Canadian fighter George Chuvalo avers, boxing is natural, natural to the point of seeming transparent and depthless. But even as the German artistic community took up Schmeling as a sort of exotic, a representation of a myth, some of them appreciated the technical aspects of the sport, the enormous sacrifice that was required to learn to throw punches properly while minimizing damage to one's hands and wrists; to duck, block, and slip punches by turning one's head, hunching the shoulders, using one's forearms and elbows; to move in the ring in the best way to give one's punches the greatest leverage and to take advantage of one's height, arm reach, and leg strength. Modern prizefighting was not just fighting in any ordinary, street corner sense, but a highly refined, restricted (no kicking, knee strikes, elbow strikes, or wrestling), and disciplined use of the body as a particularly stylized striking and blocking weapon. The enormous training that professional boxing demanded made the boxer in some ways something like an artist in devotion to craft but in some ways better, as the boxer seemed the perfect marriage of the scripted and the spontaneous. Also, the truly knowing fan could possess a form of secret knowledge in understanding the technique of a boxing match, knowing that what was going on in the ring was not a brawl but an extraordinary combination of something artful and something mechanical, something memorized and something innovated in the moment. Combining this complexity of technical accomplishment, the necessity to master a prescribed but endlessly variable choreography, with the myth of Darwinian survival and the palpable social realism of poverty as a motivator that drives someone to perform in this strange theater of personal but highly regulated violence would make the boxer something special perhaps in relation to other athletes. Thus, the boxer, in Schmeling's glamor world of the creative elite, was a kind of hipster.

There are three points of clarification to be made here: first, when Schmeling began to be criticized for the company he was keeping, being called "arrogant" and "a social climber," it brought to his mind American heavyweight champion Gene Tunney, who "had been criticized because he read the classics, corresponded with George Bernard Shaw, and modeled for the Swiss sculptor Hermann Haller."[5] But Schmeling was different from Tunney in that Schmeling did not really cultivate the Smart Set so that he could become a part of it as Tunney did, but rather he allowed himself to be taken up by them. Schmeling was not interested in affecting being a man of letters, someone who could lecture about Shakespeare in a college class, as Tunney once did. Tunney wanted to be a squire. He was not a hipster figure in the way that Schmeling was among the German bohemian crowd. (In this book, Carlo Rotella provides a detailed look at the glamor world that emerged around professional boxing in 1920s America by examining Tunney, Jack Dempsey, and the lesser known tough middleweight Harry Greb and the cultural implications of their fights for the era.)

Second, Schmeling's association with the German Smart Set was not quite the same as black American heavyweight champion Jack Johnson's (championship reign 1908–15) association with the black sporting life of the turn of the twentieth century. Johnson hung around songwriter/novelist/poet James Weldon Johnson (who knew the fighter very well),[6] poet/novelist Paul Laurence Dunbar, comedians George Walker and Bert Williams, Ernest Hogan, Sissieretta Jones, and other black entertainers and artists of the day, as well as the leading black athletes of the day, such as cyclist Major Taylor and jockey Isaac Burns Murphy. The intense racial segregation in America made this association possible, necessary, and even desirable in some respects, but it was not an arrangement in which Johnson was being cultivated or taken up with salons and the like by intellectual and artistic types who were fascinated by the fact he was a boxer. Johnson hung around with other black entertainers and artists because they ran in the same social circles.

Third, Schmeling took on another kind of symbolic role as a successful German fighter when the Nazi regime took over. If Schmeling was a hipster type to the bohemian and artistic set of the liberal regime, for Hitler he was an example of Aryan superiority (the fact that Schmeling resembled American heavyweight champion of the 1920s Jack Dempsey added to his star quality). At least, he represented Aryan superiority until he ignominiously lost his rematch to Joe Louis in 1938 (he beat Louis all around the ring in their first encounter in 1936, which in fact built up his Aryan "super fighter" image). The American public saw the 1938 rematch, one of the biggest fights of the twentieth century, as democracy versus fascism, but Germans saw it as a racial inferior versus a racial superior. By 1936, Schmeling, who had been world heavyweight champion from 1930 to 1932, was the most famous German athlete plying his trade in America, and was the benign face of Nazi Germany in its quest to host the Summer Olympics that year. In a sense, once Schmeling's identity as star athlete was coopted by the Nazi state, Schmeling became a complex mixture of being both the insider and the outsider: the Aryan boxer with the Jewish American manager and Jewish friends; the voice guaranteeing the safety of black and Jewish athletes in Berlin before the International Olympic Committee.[7] He became, however reluctantly, a member of an ideological elite with the Nazis rather than a creative one when he was a hipster among the artists and intellectuals.

It must be remembered that champion boxers are more than survivors; (in the profession, mediocre fighters are called survivors); champions are more than resilient. They are, to borrow Nassim Nicholas Taleb's term, "antifragile," something that gains strength and thrives from the adversity and resistance it encounters. Sylvester Stallone's "Rocky" films are, by and large, mythical examples of this: Rocky grows stronger from the beatings he takes as a challenger and champion. Fight manager Irving Cohen once laughingly put it, "The best tip who to bet on in a movie fight is the guy who loses the first fourteen rounds."[8]

In his book, *Antifragile*, Taleb lists "street fights" as antifragile.[9] If I understand his classifications and their justifications correctly, Taleb might list modern boxing merely as "robust" and possible even "fragile" compared with, say, its ancestor, bare-knuckle fighting, or to today's ultimate fighting or mixed martial arts, because the latter forms are much closer to street fighting in the theatricality and intensity of the risks and the range and unpredictability of the variables they offer. All high-performance athletes are asked to withstand and overcome pain and resistance; only a few, like fighters, are expected to show they thrive on the risk of pain, brain damage, and sudden death.

It is this sense of the antifragile that makes the champion boxer a unique brand of hipster particularly, but bestows this aura, for many (especially intellectuals), even on the average boxer. What sort of personality lives so casually on the edge of this strange way of measuring success by taking and giving physical punishment? This might explain why certain ethnic boxers captured the public imagination in ways that made them larger than life, that made their fights national, even international, epics – heavyweight boxing champion Jack Johnson and his struggle against the racism and imperialism of the early twentieth century; Joe Louis and his rise as an American patriotic hero; Rocky Graziano as an influence for 1950s hipster actors like Marlon Brando, James Dean, Steve McQueen, and Paul Newman;[10] Muhammad Ali and his rise as the American dissident hero; and Robert Duran as the ferocious Central American war machine.

Tales Told at Ringside

Boxing is a sport, but not a game. A physical contest of wills based on the most primitive expression of violence, boxing is mythical and absurd, anarchic and designed, heroic and depraved, uplifting and decadent. The weight of its contradictions – being inhumane yet profoundly human in the various needs it satisfies – is what gives boxing its enduring power, its cultural relevance despite its persistent marginality. And make no mistake, even during its halcyon days when certain championship fights were front-page news, when the glory or despair of a nation seemed to hinge on a fight's outcome, when certain boxers were iconic heroes or villains (or, in the case of Muhammad Ali, both), boxing was always a sport on the margins of respectability, of legitimacy, of authenticity, even of morality. For a good portion of its history it was illegal, and even today there are many who advocate that it be banned.

Boxing was a sport that was invented in eighteenth-century England by the urge to bet, has always had connections to the criminal underworld and what is called "the sporting life," and has frequently been accused and sometimes guilty of fraud in its performance or in its refereeing and judging. It is the world of boxing that popularized the expression "the set-up." Boxing has had its moments of intense bourgeois interest, especially amateur boxing, which has had both collegiate and aristocratic connections, and certain

5

professional boxing champions who were especially charismatic or larger than life, but it has largely been a sport, especially professional boxing, that has generated mixed feelings at best in the bourgeoisie and high society that have attended big-time championship fights with fascination but also been repulsed by the sport. For the bourgeoisie, boxing was always a form of slumming. (Recently, boxing training methods have become a form of fitness, and suburban gyms have opened for the middle-class hipster; jazz trumpeter Miles Davis is among the most famous devotees of boxing as a regimen of virtue, fitness, and hipness.[11]) For the slum-dwellers and the working class, boxing was always the alloy of honor and hustling, where the moguls of this "show business with blood" tried to fleece all varieties of suckers, including the boxers themselves, who on more than one occasion have been referred to as little better than "two-dollar whores."[12]

Boxing has been a sport in constant flux, at times almost resembling disarray. In the eighteenth through the mid-nineteenth century, boxers fought without gloves, wrestling as much as they punched; in many instances, gouging, butting, and biting were permitted, although the London Prize Ring Rules, established in 1838 but based on Jack Broughton's Rules that were established in 1743, eliminated much of the most gruesome aspects of the sport. Bouts were fought to the finish – that is, until one of the combatants quit or was unable to continue. Rounds were untimed and lasted until one of the opponents went down. A round could be as short as ten seconds or as long as ten minutes. Each man then had thirty seconds to get back to the scratch mark in the middle of the ring to continue the bout. Gloves were introduced in the latter part of the nineteenth century in regular bouts (gloves of a sort had been used in sparring and training during the bare-knuckle era) to protect the hands and enable the combatants to throw more punches. As more fighters wore gloves, and as the gloves began to resemble mittens, reducing one's ability to use one's hands for anything but striking, wrestling and holds were eventually banned from the sport. Under the Marquess of Queensberry Rules, published in 1867, rounds were timed, three minutes in duration. Breaks between rounds were expanded to one minute. The length of a fight became fixed, under ten rounds for fighters with less experience, ten rounds for a normal fight, fifteen or twenty rounds for a championship fight. However, at the turn of the twentieth century, fights could last forty or more rounds. (Today, championship fights are twelve rounds. Nonchampionship fights are ten. Less experienced or novice professional boxers have bouts of four, six, or eight rounds, depending on their experience.) Judges became more important in the gloved era, with a fixed number of rounds, as there was no guarantee that a fighter would be knocked out or would quit before the end of the fight.

As the epicenter of boxing shifted from England to the United States by the early twentieth century, more states legalized the sport (which had always been condemned by reformers as being brutal and inhumane, utterly shameful); for instance, New York finally legalized boxing in 1920 with the Walker Law, and established a boxing commission to regulate bouts in the state. Boxing is a state-controlled enterprise, which has made it difficult to regulate. Boxers were and still are required to be licensed, in part for their own welfare, although this does not prevent fixed fights or mismatches and the manufacture of dubious credentials on the part of promoters and managers. Nor does the existence of boxing commissions prevent fighters from being cheated by managers or promoters, but the commissions have generally been an aid to the sport. But the wild capitalistic spirit of professional boxing (its heyday in England was the early days of capitalism as a new system of relations between people and markets) is why it emphasizes individualism, is constantly at war with itself over how to regulate itself, constantly seeks new markets and opportunities (despite the rampant and strenuous racism looming large over the considerable period of its development, boxing was always a racially integrated sport – at least in a limited way early on – and also, because of its weight divisions, a sport that did not discriminate on the basis of size. Today, for instance, boxing, professional and amateur, has ceased to discriminate against women, who seriously contest in the sport. On this last head, Cathy van Ingen offers for this book an overview of women in the sport in her essay, "Women's Boxing: Bout Time.") Its origins and its tendency to generate competitive governing private regimes like the World Boxing Council, the World Boxing Association, the International Boxing Federation, and the World Boxing Organization, none of which try to regulate anything in boxing but championship fights, in addition to the half-hearted, barely enforced intervention of the federal government, the inability of boxers to form a union as a counterweight to the power of promoters, managers, and boxing commissions, and the abiding interest of organized crime, have made professional boxing nearly impossible to govern rationally. Today, the sport is balkanized not only by too many weight divisions, somewhere between sixteen and eighteen, but also by a number of "sanctioning" bodies, starting with the World Boxing Council and the World Boxing Association, which have their origins in the legalization of boxing in New York, that recognize their own champion and their own ranking of contenders. Any given weight division may have four or five "official" champions, each representing a different sanctioning authority. This proliferation began to mar the sport's coherence in the 1970s and 1980s but continued to grow steadily worse. Clearly, promoters and television executives may have thought that more champions would mean more championship fights and a greater number of viewers and revenue, but boxing has lost the casual sports fan in recent years, has lost its space in many of newspapers' sports sections, in part because the sport seems too confusing and disordered.

Another reason many Americans may have lost interest is that so many competitive boxers fighting in the United States these days are foreigners from Latin America, Eastern Europe, Asia, and Africa. Professional boxing has always been global, but during its glory days in the United States, it was largely dominated by American boxers. This is no longer the case. If it were not for the large immigrant populations in America, boxing would be an even more marginal sport than it is. Finally, boxing has taken a back seat as a combat sport to mixed martial arts and ultimate fighting where the contestants combine wrestling, boxing, judo, and karate, completely weaponizing the entire body and thus permitting bouts with fewer restrictions about where to strike or how to fight. Professional boxing, to many younger sports fans, may seem almost, for lack of a better term, Victorian.

"Watching a fight on television has always seemed to me a poor substitute for being there," writes boxing essayist A. J. Liebling.[13] Nonetheless, television transformed boxing in the 1950s when it was, in the medium's early days, the most popular sports programming by far, reducing the number of local gyms and fight clubs. According to old timers, television developed boxers too quickly, pushing them prematurely up the ladder of competition. As Liebling put it, "The clients of the television companies, by putting on a free boxing show almost every night of the week, have knocked out of business the hundreds of small-city and neighborhood boxing clubs where youngsters had a chance to learn their trade and journeymen to mature their skills … [N]either advertising agencies nor brewers, and least of all the networks, give a hoot if they push the Sweet Science back into a period of genre painting." Liebling's *The Sweet Science*, the famous collection of his *New Yorker* essays, is the classic account of boxing during the early television age, 1951–55, "the last heroic cycle" in boxing, before television's dominance completely wrecked the sport.[14] Television certainly radically changed boxing culture and how the public perceived boxing. To be sure, it gave the public more boxing than the public needed or ultimately wanted. Boxers wound up playing for the television cameras in a way that was distinctly different from when fight footage could only be seen in movie theaters. If there was pressure for boxers to slug and knock out opponents before television in order to enhance the entertainment factor of the sport, this pressure increased after television became the main medium through which the public interacted with the sport. Television nearly destroyed boxing in the 1950s by overexposing it because it was so easy and cheap to program, airing too many questionable fights, and particularly airing deadly fights such as the 1962 welterweight championship fight between Emile Griffith and Benny "Kid" Paret that resulted in Paret's death.[15] (In this book, Troy Rondinone's chapter "Prime (and Crime) Time: Boxing in the 1950s" gives an overview of the era, including an account of the impact of television; Mark Scott has a chapter on welterweight and middleweight fighter Emile Griffith, who has become a subject of interest in recent years because of the controversy surrounding his sexuality and his bout with Paret; and finally Rosalind Early's chapter on an opera about Griffith shows how much he has become a figure of the moment in our culture.)

But television also revolutionized the sport, especially in presenting new types of black male personalities like heavyweight champion Floyd Patterson, who represented a Medium Cool, television-friendly, black boxer in the early days of integration, a cross-over figure for the age of the Negro as striver and mainstream liberal. Sonny Liston, in image, was almost the polar opposite of Patterson. As African American playwright and poet LeRoi Jones (Amiri Baraka) described him: "Sonny Liston is the big black Negro in every white man's hallway, waiting to do him in, deal him under for all the hurts white men, through their arbitrary order, have been able to inflict on the world ... Sonny Liston is 'the huge Negro,' the 'bad nigger,' a heavy-faced replica of every whipped up woogie in the world." Liston was a convicted felon, a bruiser with mob connections, with poor southern roots, a menacing look and a big punch, who was, more or less, a test for the liberal belief of the day that environment, not genes, made the man in the ongoing discussion about whether he deserved a crack at Patterson's title. His life was the stuff of sociological theory in a sociological age. He, too, was a product of television and despite Jones's feverish political interpretation was a man who wound up more sinned against than sinning, used and misused by the whites who controlled him, he hardly was able, as Jones asserts, "to collect his pound of flesh" in retribution.[16] Liston was the fighter extracting his pound of flesh from other black men as a form of employment. In fact, Liston's testimony during the Senate Antitrust and Monopoly Subcommittee hearings in 1960 revealed an illiterate man who knew no math (he could count) and who knew little about the machinations going on around him as a rising professional fighter except that he knew he was being used. The police leaned on him because he was a black ex-convict who was associated with white gangsters, not necessarily because it was possible that he might commit a crime. By 1960, he was the best heavyweight in the world, even though he did not have the title. His goals were modest: "As long as I'm fighting and making money and driving a good car and eating regular, nothing much is bothering me," he once said.[17] But Patterson and

Liston did, in a crude way, represent the good black man and bad black man, the worthy black man and the man of questionable worth. They were the Negro Morality Play of the age of television.

But it was Muhammad Ali who transformed the sport and television in the 1960s with his style as a boxer, his demeanor, his personality, and his political religion that challenged the government:[18] he was a new type to form a sort of racial typological triad with Patterson and Liston: the Negro as dissenting rebel and as the child of the "permissive society." Ali was a revolution and revelation for television sports, but television also made Ali possible. His combination of humor, exaggeration, political commentary, anger, petulance, and charm was unique for a black public personality and was best suited to television that could exploit his good looks and his gregariousness almost as if he were the lead in a television sitcom. Ali would attract blacks because they so admired him, but he would also attract whites because, whether they liked or despised him, they were fascinated by him. Moreover, Ali had the glories, the energy, the pure charisma of youth in an age that was dedicated to the baby boomers and in a medium that ever increasingly wanted to both serve and reflect that generation.

Congress has investigated boxing for its ties to organized crime.[19] The sport has been called a menace to public health because of the brain trauma, deaths, and mental deterioration that it frequently causes. (Wilfred Benitez, Meldrick Taylor, the late Jerry Quarry, Gerald McClellan, the late Greg Page, the late Matthew Saad Muhammad, the late Floyd Patterson, and Freddie Roach are just a few of the noted brain-damage cases, although the most shocking, distressing, and guilt-inducing for the public was Muhammad Ali, who had been severely impaired by Parkinson's, which many believed had been caused by boxing.) Boxing stands unique in the sports world as the only sport in which the object is to physically harm your opponent. (Mixed martial arts, ultimate fighting, and other combat sport – also unregulated by the federal government – simply mimic, intensify, and broaden this aspect of boxing.)

Television brought all of this about the sport to the public as well in a startling way. Television, first network then cable, in essence glamorized, romanticized, and mythologized boxing as it also aired its dirty laundry and denigrated its corruption, sleaze, and grotesqueness. Television wound up being boxing's enabler, even its main financial support, as it also wanted to be some sort of muckraking exhibitor serving the public good. Boxing defined television's contradictions.

There are two major cultural subtexts to professional boxing: race and individualism. Boxing has always been a story about race, has long been seen as a contest between the races, which race was stronger, more fit to survive. While this interpretative feeling about boxing was especially strong during the age of social Darwinism of the late nineteenth and early twentieth centuries, when it was commonly believed that the dark races would eventually die out in their feeble competition against the Anglo-Saxon, even today, fans tend to identify with a fighter as an emblem or symbol of their particular nationality, ethnicity, or culture.

Race, of course, affects other sports, but boxing, in complex ways, is about mass identity that differs somewhat from other sports. The professional boxer does not fight for an institution or a club or a team that represents a geographical location. And he does not represent a kind of social status as the tennis player or the golfer might in being part of a sport that symbolizes leisure. Boxing as an athletic practice symbolizes a sort of sociological necessity: the pressures of poverty, the need to physically fight in a world where fighting is common and such skill is respected, the importance of both the quest for honor and the masculine credentials of succeeding at hustling and grinding. The boxer represents something uncluttered, pure as an individual, lionized in some circles, but stoic, even dimly tragic, in the acceptance of his fate. Promoters, from the earliest days of professional fighting, exploited this tendency of identification in audiences by underscoring differences between fighters. Jews, Irish, Italians, Filipinos, Mexicans – all were underclass, persecuted tribes with their heroic boxers. Black and white, of course, marked the most obvious and dramatic difference, the most epic difference between men of the modern age. Blacks had been fighters since the late eighteenth and early nineteenth centuries, when American ex-slaves Bill Richmond and Tom Molyneaux fought in England. By the end of the nineteenth century, despite a color line being drawn against interracial heavyweight championship fights – American champion John L. Sullivan refused to fight a black and so did Jack Dempsey; although Dempsey never openly said he opposed interracial championship fights, he always refused to fight the leading black heavyweight of the day, Harry Wills ("The Black Panther") – black men held championships in several lighter divisions and a black American – Jack Johnson – would win the heavyweight title in 1908, becoming one of the most controversial athletes in the history of American sports. His sexual affairs with and marriages to white women were not necessarily unique at the time for an African American man in the sporting life, but Johnson not only flaunted his affairs, he showed little interest in being humble, retiring, or reticent around white men. Johnson's assertive personality led to the cry among whites for a "Great White Hope" to defeat him and return the championship to the white race. In the highly fraught issue of interracial sex, Johnson was involved in three incidents that were outrageous to most whites: first, Etta, his first white wife, committed suicide at his Chicago nightclub in September 1912; second, under indictment for violation of the Mann Act, federal anti-prostitution legislation that made it a crime for a man to take a woman other than his wife across state lines for sexual relations, Johnson married Lucille Cameron, one of the state's key witnesses against him, in December 1912, just weeks after Etta's suicide; third, after being convicted of violation of the Mann Act in 1913, Johnson fled the country rather than serve his sentence. He would not return until July 1920, when he served his sentence of a year and a day.[20] Women Studies specialist Rebecca Wanzo provides a cultural and historical interpretation of the Mann Act for this book.

Johnson was so thoroughly disliked by the white public that after he lost the title in 1915 in Havana, Cuba, another black would not fight for the heavyweight championship for twenty-two years. But Johnson had captured the public's imagination in a way few other black athletes have. He became the measure – example or cautionary tale – by which other great black heavyweight champions were seen: Joe Louis, champion from 1937 to 1949, was the anti-Johnson, not nearly so brash, his interracial love affairs hidden, his studied indifference to his white opponents a source of calm, unlike Johnson's outspoken confidence which proved so provocative. Muhammad Ali, on the other hand, was the anti-Louis, noisy where Louis was quiet, anti-American where Louis was a patriotic figure during the Second World War, militantly racial where Louis was quietly so. In fact, in his fight with the white establishment, Ali saw himself as a sort of reincarnation of Johnson, publicly saying so on several occasions. It was during Ali's reign as champion that Johnson was revived in American popular culture, with Howard Sackler's 1967 play, *The Great White Hope*, made into a film in 1970.[21] Historian Benjamin Cawthra's chapter in this book takes on another aspect of Johnson's continuing claim on the culture as it deals with two Jack Johnson documentaries – a 1970 film produced by Bill Cayton, boxing promoter, and directed by Jimmy Jacobs, a handball champion and boxing manager,[22] and Ken Burns's 2004 film, *Unforgiveable Blackness: The Rise and Fall of Jack Johnson* – and their soundtracks, the earlier one by trumpeter Miles Davis and the other by Wynton Marsalis.

To be sure, the greatest racial dramas in boxing were between black and white fighters, whether it was Jack Johnson versus Jim Jefferies in 1910, the outcome of which (Johnson's victory) caused race riots across the country, or Joe Louis versus Primo Carnera in 1935, in which Louis was seen as fighting for Ethiopia and Carnera for Italy, or Larry Holmes versus Gerry Cooney in 1982, in which Cooney represented "Rocky" and Holmes "Apollo Creed." Great black fighters have virtually defined an epoch in twentieth-century boxing: Johnson, Louis, Ali, Mike Tyson, Larry Holmes, Floyd Mayweather, Sugar Ray Robinson, Sugar Ray Leonard, Marvelous Marvin Hagler.

It is worthy of note that Republican presidential nominee Donald J. Trump was criticized by two highly popular ethnic champions of the past during his presidential run. First, Ali, who was one of the world's most famous Muslims, castigated Trump in a statement reported in the *Washington Post* on December 10, 2015, which said, in part, "We as Muslims have to stand up to those who use Islam to advance their own personal agenda. They have alienated many from learning about Islam. True Muslims know or should know that it goes against our religion to try and force Islam on anyone." This was in response to the candidate's proposed temporary ban on Muslim immigration to the United States as a response to Islamist attacks in the West. More recently, former lightweight, welterweight, and junior middle-weight champion Roberto Duran of Panama challenged Trump to a fight because of Trump's proposal to stop illegal immigration of Latinos to the United States and to deport many illegals already here.[23]

The Muslim presence in boxing increased considerably in the 1980s and 1990s when noted American boxers like Matthew Saad Muhammad, Dwight Muhammad Qawi, Eddie Mustafa Muhammad, and Mike Tyson all converted to Islam, in addition to the rise of boxers from the Middle East and from Britain who were Muslims. What is curious about Islam among African Americans is that its reputation was generally not that of a religion of peace but rather as a militant, highly anti-pacifist faith, especially when Nation of Islam leaders like Malcolm X crowed about his faith in criticizing the pacifism of Martin Luther King's Christian nonviolence civil rights marches. In his 1963 "Message to the Grassroots," Malcolm X stated: "There is nothing in our book, the Koran, that teaches us to suffer peacefully. Our religion teaches us to be intelligent. Be peaceful, be courteous, obey the law, respect everyone; but if someone puts his hands on you, send him to the cemetery. That's a good religion. In fact, that's that old-time religion. That's the one that Ma and Pa used to talk about: an eye for an eye, and a tooth for a tooth, and a head for a head, and a life for a life. That's a good religion. And nobody resents that kind of religion being taught but a wolf; who intends to make you his meal."[24] He further elaborated about the nature of revolution: "You don't have a peaceful revolution. You don't have a turn-the-other-cheek revolution. There's no such thing as a non-violent revolution ... Revolution is bloody, revolution is hostile, revolution knows no compromise, revolution overturns and destroys everything that gets in its way ... Whoever heard of a revolution where they lock arms ... singing 'We Shall Overcome'? You don't do that in a revolution. You don't do any singing, you're too busy swinging. It's based on land. A revolutionary wants land so he can set up his own nation."[25]

The message here is not simply that the religion believes in self-defense and the primitive justice of equal retribution but that Islam is the religion of black revolution, of dramatic, traumatic, anti-Western challenge and change. In this portion of his speech, Malcolm X brilliantly conflated Marxist politics and Islam. The NOI would not quite follow him to this extent, but it is important to note the association many young black people at the time had of the religion and militant, violent political change.

But it was the aura of close-knit, protective, almost cultish violence that surrounded the Nation of Islam, which Ali joined in 1964, that made the so-called Black Muslims seem so frightening to many, black and white. The group had many ex-convicts among its ranks, including Malcolm X, and certain mosques did indeed become involved with violent crime in the early 1970s.[26] Did Ali join the Muslims because he felt he needed "muscle" to negotiate the boxing world? Was Mark Kram right that Ali feared the Muslims? Ali's relationship with the group was made more complicated by the fact that he was a boxer which Elijah Muhammad, the group's leader, strongly disliked, seeing boxers as little more than puppets for their white managers, as blacks fighting blacks for the entertainment of whites, a somewhat simplistic reading of the sport.[27] Moreover, Muhammad only became interested in Ali when he beat Liston, as he saw the young fighter as a possible foil to an increasingly troublesome Malcolm X. As Muhammad biographer Claude Andrew Clegg III writes, "To Muhammad, Clay was possibly that missing transitional link between a Nation mesmerized by Malcolm X and a new paradise in which the fallen minister played no role whatsoever. Conceivably, Clay could help the Muslim leader retain the loyalties of at least a significant portion of the young, activist element that would almost surely leave the movement if Malcolm revolted or was killed. The key would be to package the boxer in a way that accentuated his racial consciousness and loyalty to Muhammad while minimizing his boxing career and ties to the white world of entertainment. Easily enthralled by the Muslim message, Clay proved pliant in the hands of Elijah Muhammad and was amenable to playing whatever role in the movement was delegated to him. He freely allowed the Muslim leader to use him as a diversion for believers who were dismayed by some of the things that were going on with the Nation."[28]

It is interesting to note that Ali objected to the draft on the grounds of being a Muslim minister, but this was not at all a claim of being a pacifist, which he clearly was not. Ali left the Nation of Islam behind after Elijah Muhammad died in 1975, joining the more mainstream Islamic sect of Muhammad's son, Wallace D. Ali condemned the Islamist attack at San

Bernardino, which was the occasion for his statement about Trump. But there is no public statement from Ali condemning the fatwa against Salman Rushdie or the terrorist attack against the staff of *Charlie Hebdo*, which may mean that his attitude about insulting Islam did not differ from most of his co-religionists. In short, understanding Ali as a Muslim, and how this shaped his racial politics and spiritual aspirations, is difficult.

Latino boxers have made up a considerable contingent of the boxers in America for decades, dating back to Panama Al Brown, bantamweight champion from 1929 to 1935 and the first Latino champion. Duran was arguably the most famous, the most lionized, Latino fighter of the twentieth century. He would have been even more popular had he learned English, which he refused to do, perhaps out of pride. Whether he made his comic or silly (take your pick) remark in an effort to promote the Hollywood biopic about him, *Hands of Stone*, that came out a few weeks later is hard to say. But what these critiques of Trump may suggest is that the rise of certain ethnic elements in boxing may signal both a new political self-consciousness among boxers (at least retired ones) and a new sort of narrative of meaning arising around the sport.

Individualism is the other major facet of boxing. It is true, of course, that the professional boxer works with a team – a trainer, a manager, a team of sparring partners in the gym, a close set of friends and relatives who serve as supporters and an entourage. But the boxer's drama is carried out in solitude. (Most boxing movies strongly emphasize this, making the boxer an isolato, something between a rebel and relic.) He is alone in the ring, pitting himself against his opposite, his doppelganger and his adversary. This ontological aspect of boxing, the individual confronting his moment of truth, the absurdity of his fate, the triumph of his dominance over adversity, the fatalism of his helplessness before adversity, are the mythological and psychological elements that have made boxing so engaging for many writers, novelists and journalists, and filmmakers. The boxer is such a rich emblem of both the glory and futility of existence.

The chapters of *The Cambridge Companion to Boxing* examine boxing from a variety of perspectives: as a reflection of social and political history, for its role in professional sports history, and for its impact on popular and pulp culture. In addition to the chapters mentioned above, there are chapters on ethno-national boxers: Steve Reiss on Jews in twentieth-century boxing, Tony Gee on Jewish fighters in the bare-knuckle era, Benita Heiskanen on Latino boxers, and Adeyinka Makinde on Africans and boxing. There are historical overviews of the sport: Byron Nakamura's "Boxing in the Ancient World" and Elliott Gorn's "The Bare-Knuckle Era." Boxing's cultural reach is wide; it has produced first-class journalism:

(Liebling, George Plimpton, Norman Mailer, Joyce Carol Oates, Thomas Hauser, Kram, John Lardner, et al.), important literature: (fiction like W. C. Heinz's *The Professional* [1958]; Leonard's Gardner's *Fat City* [1969]; Jim Tully's *The Bruiser* [1936]; F. X. Toole's [Jerry Boyd's] "Million Dollar Baby," from his collection *Rope Burns: Stories from the Corner* [2000]; Ernest Hemingway's Nick Adams story, "The Battler," from *In Our Time* [1925], about a punch-drunk, half-crazed ex-fighter turned hobo, looked after by a black man who must club the disturbed ex-fighter on the head to quell him; and Nelson Algren's "Million-Dollar Brainstorm," from *The Neon Wilderness* [1947], about the delusional, punch-drunk "Big Jew" fighter, on his odyssey home, who keeps asking people to "save his life" by giving him a loan), famous films: (*The Champ* [1931], with Wallace Beery [remade in 1979 with Jon Voight], a tearjerker about a washed-up fighter and his young son; *Champion* [1949], with Kirk Douglas as the boxer with a temper; *Rocky*, the 1967 film about the lovable Italian American boxer from South Philadelphia and the first boxing film to win a Best Picture Oscar; *Raging Bull*, Martin Scorsese's critically acclaimed biopic of middleweight Italian American Jake LaMotta, whose life after boxing was as interesting as his time in the ring; *Play It to the Bone*, Ron Shelton's 1999 boxing film with Woody Harrelson and Antonio Banderas; *The Greatest*, the 1977 forgettable biopic of Muhammad Ali, with Ali playing himself and joining such athletes as Bob Mathias and Jackie Robinson, who played themselves in biopics, but the movie produced the hit song "The Greatest Love of All"; *The Set Up*, Robert Wise's 1949 gritty film noir about the fight game, with Robert Ryan as the fighter who is up against it; *Ali*, Michael Mann's 2001 biopic of Ali, with Will Smith in the title role and made with the assumption that every viewer will already know the story; *Requiem for a Heavyweight*, the socially conscious boxing film of 1962, with Anthony Quinn as the washed-up, exploited Mountain Rivera, written by Rod Serling with cameos by a young Cassius Clay and several other noted fighters, including Jack Dempsey, replete with slick managers, lesbian gangsters, and a social worker who seems a candidate for a Miss Lonelyhearts club; *Fat City*, John Huston's 1972 gritty adaptation of Gardner's novel, with a very young Jeff Bridges; *Body and Soul*, John Garfield stars in this 1948 Hollywood take on the Jewish fighter, very loosely based on the life of the great Jewish lightweight and welterweight Barney Ross; *Right Cross*, John Sturges's 1950 Hollywood take on the Mexican fighter, with Ricardo Montelban; *Million Dollar Baby*, Clint Eastwood's 2004 film is the second boxing film to win the Best Picture Oscar, and one of Hollywood's takes on women and boxing, the other being the woman as fight manager in films like *The Big Timer*, in 1932, with Constance Cummings as her husband's manager, who knows more about surviving in the game than he does, and Meg Ryan as a fictionalized version of Jackie Kallen in *Against the Ropes* [2004]; *The Square Jungle*, a 1955 film that stars Tony Curtis as the boxer who rises and falls and Ernest Borgnine as the wise trainer who reads the Talmud; *Ringside,* a 1949 film about a fighter who is blinded in the ring and how his brother takes up the trade seeking revenge; *Kid Galahad*, two versions – 1937 with Edward G. Robinson and Bette Davis and 1962 with Elvis Presley in the title role as the nice boy with the big punch; and many others). Interestingly, as unlikely an actor as Sammy Davis, Jr., played a boxer in the stage musical drama *Golden Boy* [1964], which featured him kissing his character's girlfriend, Paula Wayne, a white actress, to gasps from the audience.

Scott D. Emmert's "Jack London and the Great White Hopes of Boxing Literature" provides an overview of boxing fiction through the prism of the career of Jack London, one of the most famous and important of all American boxing writers. Leger Grindon's "Body and Soul of the Screen Boxer" deals with the Hollywood film and boxing, the sport that has arguably fascinated filmmakers more than any other. Kasia Boddy's "'Well, what was it really like?' George Plimpton, Norman Mailer, and the Heavyweights" examines two of the leading boxing journalists of the twentieth century. Shelley Fisher Fishkin weighs in on her friend, the late black sports writer Ralph Wiley, and his memoir about boxing, *Serenity*. And Adeyinka Makinde offers a chapter on light heavyweight champion and boxing writer Jose Torres.

Other chapters spotlight particular boxers: biographer Wil Haygood on middleweight legend Sugar Ray Robinson, Louis Moore looks at the color line in boxing of the late twentieth and early twentieth centuries through the lives of black boxers Peter Jackson and George Dixon, and Colleen Aycock's companion piece on the great black American boxer of the same period, Joe Gans, as part of an era that produced Dixon and the other great black champion, Joe Walcott. Sports biographer Randy Roberts takes on Joe Louis; Lewis Erenberg writes about Muhammad Ali in the 1970s – particularly the fight against George Foreman in Zaire – as the unfinished business of the 1960s; my chapter on Muhammad Ali as an inauthentic hero is meant to complement Erenberg's chapter and offer particular insights on the problematic nature of Ali as a Muslim, Ali as an innovative boxer, and Ali as a dissenter; Michael Ezra writes about Sonny Liston and Larry Holmes as African American champions no one wanted; and Adam Chill tells us how Jem Mace created modern boxing.

The collection is rounded out with Adam Chill's chapter on the great boxing journalist of the eighteenth century and muse for A. J. Liebling, Pierce Egan, and Colleen Aycock's history of the voices that broadcast fights.

Nearly all of the writers are among the top boxing writers and academics in the world.

NOTES

1 Max Schmeling, *Max Schmeling: An Autobiography*, translated and edited by George B. von der Lippe (Chicago, IL: Bonus Books, Inc., 1998, originally published in German in 1977), p. 22, emphasis mine.

2 George Chuvalo with Murray Greig, *Chuvalo, A Fighter's Life: The Story of Boxing's Last Gladiator* (New York: HarperCollins, 2013, EPub Edition), Loc 73, Loc 109, emphasis mine.

3 Angelo Dundee with Mike Winters, *I Only Talk Winning* (Chicago, IL: Contemporary Books, 1985), p. 160, emphasis mine.

4 Schmeling, *Max Schmeling: An Autobiography*, p. 33.

5 Schmeling, *Max Schmeling: An Autobiography*, p. 40.

6 James Weldon Johnson, *Along This Way: The Autobiography of James Weldon Johnson* (New York: Penguin Books, 1990), p. 208.

7 Schmeling, *Max Schmeling: An Autobiography*, pp. 109–10.

8 A. J. Liebling, *The Sweet Science* (New York: Penguin Books, 1982), p. 257.

9 Nassim Nicholas Taleb, *Antifragile: Things That Gain From Disorder* (New York: Random House Trade Paperback, 2014), pp. 26, 27.

10 See Nathan Ward, "How Rocky Graziano Became Boxing's Greatest Muse," *The Stacks*, January 18, 2016, http://thestacks.deadspin.com/how-rocky-graziano-became-boxings-greatest-muse-1753223035.

11 Gerald Early, "Miles Davis in the Ring: The Boxer as Black Male Hero" in *Miles Davis: The Complete Illustrated History* (Minneapolis, MN: Voyageur Press, 2012), pp. 188–91.

12 "My philosophy is that all fighters are two-dollar whores. Never fall in love with your fighter. My rule is fuck the fighter before the fighter can fuck you." Quote attributed to boxing promoter Don King in Jack Newfield, *Only in America: The Life and Crimes of Don King* (New York: William Morrow and Company, 1995), p. 143–44.

13 Liebling, *The Sweet Science*, p. 15.

14 Liebling, *The Sweet Science*, pp. 3, 5.

15 For other accounts of television, boxing, and the 1960s, see Barney Nagler, *James Norris and the Decline of Boxing* (Indianapolis, IN: Bobbs-Merrill, 1964); Truman K. Gibson with Steve Huntley, *Knocking Down Barriers: My Fight For Black America* (Evanston, IL: Northwestern University Press, 2005); Jeffrey Sammons, *Beyond the Ring: The Role of Boxing in American Society* (Champaign-Urbana, IL: University of Illinois Press, 1990); and Troy Rondinone, *Friday Night Fighter: Gaspar "Indio" Ortega and the Golden Age of Television Boxing* (Champaign-Urbana, IL: University of Illinois Press, 2013). For more on Emile Griffith, his life, and his fight with Paret, see Ron Ross, *Nine Ten and Out! The Two Worlds of Emile Griffith* (New York: DiBella Entertainment, 2008); Donald McRae, *A Man's World: the Double Life of Emile Griffith* (New York: Simon and Schuster, 2015); and the 2005 documentary *Ring of Fire – The Emile Griffith Story*.

16 LeRoi Jones, "The Dempsey–Liston Fight" (1963) in *Home: Social Essays* (New York: William Morrow and Company, 1966), pp. 155–56. For more on the unhappy life of Liston, see Rob Steen, *Sonny Liston: His Life, Strife, and the Phantom Punch* (London: JR books, 2008); Paul Gallender, *Sonny Liston: The Real Story Behind the Ali/Liston Fights* (Pacific Grove, CA: Park Place Publications, 2012); Nick Tosches, *The Devil and Sonny Liston* (New York: Little Brown, 2000); and Rob Sneddon, *The Phantom Punch: The Story Behind Boxing's Most Controversial Fight* (Rockport, ME: Down East Books, 2015).

17 Quoted in Gallender, *Sonny Liston: The Real Story Behind the Ali/Liston Fights*, p. 37.

18 For more on Ali's impact on television, see Randy Roberts, "The Wide World of Muhammad Ali: The Politics and Economics of Televised Boxing," in Elliott J. Gorn (ed.), *Muhammad Ali: The People's Champ* (Urbana-Champaign, IL: University of Illinois Press, 1995), pp. 24–53.

19 Democrat Senator Estes Kefauver of Tennessee chaired the Antitrust and Monopoly Subcommittee hearings of the early 1960s that investigated boxing and that offered the possibility of a federal commissioner overseeing the sport. Kefauver died in 1963, and no one else took up the cause of federalizing boxing. No such commissioner ever materialized. In the 1955 case *United States* v. *The International Boxing Club of New York*, the Supreme Court held that the special antitrust exemption afforded baseball did not extend to boxing. Ever since this case, there have been periodic calls from members of Congress to federally regulate the sport. (If boxing's lack of regulation has resulted in a helter-skelter sport, the regulation brought on by the strongmen of organized crime, such as the sport had under the International Boxing Club in the 1950s, although organized crime's influence in the sport preceded the 1950s, was equally destructive, even if it made the sport seemingly more orderly.) Boxing was investigated by Congress again in 1977 after the ABC/Don King US Boxing Championships scandal. Hearings were held in 1979 as well. No legislation resulted from either of these interventions. In 1983, legislation was introduced to improve the conditions under which boxers plied their trade. This was done again in 1985. No legislation was passed. In 1992, the Professional Boxing Corporation bill was introduced but many legislators balked at the idea of the federal government playing a big role in managing professional boxing. Republican senator of Arizona John McCain was finally able to put together a bill called The Professional Boxing Safety Act of 1995 that was less intrusive on the part of the federal government, requiring state commissions to share information about fights and fighters. The bill was signed by President Bill Clinton in 1997, the first federal legislation providing any regulation of boxing. This was followed by the Muhammad Ali Boxing Reform Act of 2000 that amended the 1997 bill by attacking rigged matches, fake rankings, and the abuse of undereducated, financially inexperienced, easily fooled fighters by managers and promoters. For more on the history of federal boxing regulation, see Melissa Neiman, "Protecting Professional Boxers: Federal Regulations with More Punch," University Houston Law Center, 2007, at http://papers.ssrn.com/sol3/papers.cfm?abstract_id=1006002, and Jonathan S. McElroy, "Current and Proposed Federal Regulation of Professional Boxing," Volume 9, *Seton Hall Journal of Sport Law*, pp. 463–519.

20 For more on Johnson, see Finis Farr, *Black Champion; The Life and Times of Jack Johnson* (New York: Charles Scribner's Sons, 1964); Geoffrey C. Ward, *Unforgivable Blackness: The Rise and Fall of Jack Johnson* (New York: Knopf, 2004); Randy Roberts, *Papa Jack: Jack Johnson and the Era of White Hopes* (New York: Free Press, 1983); Al-Tony Gilmore, *Bad Nigger: The National Impact of Jack Johnson* (Port Washington, New York: Kennikat Press, 1975); Theresa Runstedler, *Jack Johnson, Rebel Sojourner: Boxing in the Shadow of the Global Color Line* (Berkeley, CA: University of California Press, 2012); Nat Fleischer, *Black Dynamite: The Story of the Negro in the Prize Ring from 1782–1938 – Volume IV, "Fighting Furies," Story of the Golden Era of Jack Johnson, Sam Langford, and their Negro Contemporaries* (New York: C. J. O'Brien, 1939); Robert H. deCoy, *Jack Johnson: The Big Black Fire* (Los Angeles, CA: Holloway House, 1991). Also see Jack Johnson, *In the Ring – And Out* (Chicago, IL: National Sports Publishing Company, 1927); and Jack Johnson and Christopher Rivers (trans.), *My Life and Battles* (Westport, CT: Praeger, 2007).

21 Johnson is now the subject of another play, television writer Marco Ramirez's *The Royale: A Play in Six Rounds*, which opened in 2016 to good notices. The play takes an entirely different approach to Johnson than *The Great White Hope*, which focuses on his relationship with his first white wife, who commits suicide. Ramirez's play looks at Johnson through his black trainer, black sparring partner, and white manager (the only white in the play). The gender conflict is Johnson's confrontation with his sister, who opposes his upcoming championship fight against the white former champion as causing more harm to the race than good. Some of the interaction between the Johnson character and his sister seems a bit strained and contrived, and the bit about black women being denigrated by straightening their hair is clumsy and possibly offensive, but on the whole the play was very well received when I saw it in St. Louis in March 2017.

22 This film at be seen at www.youtube.com/watch?v=IWHpEUelQzs.

23 "Boxing Legend Roberto Duran 'would like to step into the ring with Donald Trump,'" *Daily Mirror,* August 5, 2016 www.mirror.co.uk/news/world-news/boxing-legend-roberto-duran-would-8569561, "Boxing great Roberto Duran wants to fight Donald Trump to see 'how many Latinos he's going to deport,'" *New York Daily News*, August 5, 2016, www.nydailynews.com/news/politics/boxing-great-roberto-duran-fight-donald-trump-article-1.2739276, "Roberto Duran challenges Donald Trump on Twitter," *Orlando Sentinel*, August 5, 2016, www.orlandosentinel.com/sports/george-diaz-en-fuego/os-roberto-duran-donald-trump-twitter-20160805-story.html; "Muhammad Ali on Donald Trump: 'Muslims have to stand up' to anti-Islamic speech," *Washington Post*, December 10, 2015, www.washingtonpost.com/news/acts-of-faith/wp/2015/12/10/muhammad-ali-on-donald-trump-muslims-have-to-stand-up-to-anti-islamic-speech/.

24 George Breitman (ed.), *Malcolm X Speaks: Selected Speeches and Statements* (New York: Grove Weidenfeld, 1990), pp. 12–13.

25 Breitman (ed.), *Malcolm X Speaks*, p. 9.

26 Sean Patrick Griffin, *Black Brothers, Inc.: The Violent Rise and Fall of Philadelphia's Black Mafia* (Wrea Green, UK: Milo Books, 2007). Also see Sean

Patrick Griffin, "Muhammad Ali and the Philadelphia Black Mafia" at http://seanpatrickgriffin.net/muhammad-ali-philadelphias-black-mafia/.

27 Mark Kram, *Ghosts of Manila: The Fateful Blood Feud Between Muhammad Ali and Joe Frazier* (New York: HarperCollins, 2001), pp. 37–44. "With the arrival of the Black Panthers and their street sweepers, the Black Muslims by 1968 had become a revolutionary antique. Worse, the Muslims' businesses, shops, newspapers, bakeries, were failing through systematic self-looting and bad management. Membership began to wane; they had always looked for confused kids, small-time thieves and whores; they were strong in prison, where inmates took a correspondence course from Chicago. There were rigid rules: Never eat pig, dress right, and pull your own weight; never forget the devil white man. They wanted contribution of man hours and money. If you sold their paper, *Muhammad Speaks*, on the streets and didn't make your quota, or if you were a backslider, they took you back to the temple, and worked you over. Women were reduced to chattel." Kram, *Ghosts of Manila*, p. 40. For more on Ali and the Nation of Islam, see Thomas Hauser, *Muhammad Ali: His Life and Times* (New York: Simon and Schuster, 1991), pp. 81–112; Randy Roberts and Johnny Smith, *Blood Brothers: The Fatal Friendship Between Muhammad Ali and Malcolm X* (New York: Basic Books, 2016); Jack Olsen, *Black is Best: The Riddle of Cassius Clay* (New York: Putnam, 1967); and David Remnick, *King of the World: Muhammad Ali and the Rise of an American Hero* (New York: Random House, 1998). Also see Muhammad Ali with Richard Durham, *The Greatest: My Own Story* (New York: Random House, 1975), not the most reliable autobiography but still of value.

28 Claude Andrew Clegg III, *An Original Man: The Life and Times of Elijah Muhammad* (New York: St Martin's Press, 1997), p. 211.

I

BYRON J. NAKAMURA

Boxing in the Ancient World

In the National Museum of Rome sits the bronze masterpiece *The Boxer at Rest*, a statue of an ancient Greek boxer considered to be the most famous sculpture of a fighter ever made and a national treasure.[1] The boxer is seated with his gloved hands resting on his thighs, and his head is turned to his right as if responding to something that has caught his attention, perhaps the adulation of the crowd. He is clearly a veteran of the ring and a middle-aged fighter, whose face bears testimony to the cuts, scars, and abrasions of a long, violent boxing career. Although his open mouth with lips drawn inward displays his weariness, the boxer's muscles are tense, ready to spring and engage his next opponent. Like the contours of a map, the boxer's features bring to relief the origins of his sport, from its murky beginnings and its inevitable connection to the rise of ancient civilization itself.

Early Evidence

There is little doubt that boxing traces its origins to the earliest civilizations of the ancient Near East and Mediterranean. Terracotta reliefs dating from 2400 BC to 2000 BC found in ancient Mesopotamia (modern-day Iraq) depict unarmed combatants using their fists. Details are sparse as to whether the participants employed any covering on their hands or fought bare-knuckled. An Egyptian tomb relief from Thebes dating to the mid-fourteenth century BC features boxers fighting in front of spectators and perhaps the Pharaoh himself. Hieroglyphic captions on the relief have been translated as "Hit" and "You have no opponent," indicating a set of organized rules to the fight.[2]

It is during the late Bronze Age that we encounter the first definitive evidence of glove use by early pugilists. The "Boxer Vase" from Hagia Triada (1600–1500 BC) on the island of Crete clearly shows boxers using a wrist strap securing some material that protects the hand. We do not know if the material consisted of softer padding or a harder substance like leather or even metal, but due to the fact that the fighters are wearing military-style helmets with eye and cheek protection, we may infer that the headgear was intended to provide protection from gloves made of material capable of substantial damage. The most well-known evidence for boxing in the Bronze Age Aegean, however, is the charming fresco of the "Boxing Boys," found on the island of Thera (modern Santorini) at Akrotiri. Although heavily reconstructed from fragments, the painting clearly shows two youths wearing belted loincloths standing toe to toe, engaged in fisticuffs. Each appears to wear a soft glove or covering on his right hand. Because the fresco was found at a shrine, the boys' fighting seemingly is connected to a religious ritual.[3]

Homeric Greece

With the emergence of Greece and the epic poems of Homer during the eighth century B C, we begin to see a more detailed picture of boxing in early Greek society. The *Iliad* and the *Odyssey* provide us with two depictions of boxing among the upper and lower classes. In Book 23 (23.679–728) of the *Iliad*, aristocratic Greek heroes hold a boxing contest as part of the funeral games for their comrade, Patroclus, killed in battle by the Trojan hero Hector. Achilles, the mightiest of the Greek heroes, sponsors the events and furnishes the prizes: a valuable mule for the victor and a two-handed goblet for the runner-up. The match is a showdown between Epeius, the best boxer among the Greeks (and the first boxer known for boasting "I am the greatest!"), and a fellow hero named Euryalus. Both men wear oxhide leather straps or thongs (*himantes*) around their wrists and girdled loincloths around their waists. The bout ends with Epeius piercing Euryalus' defense with a knockout blow that sends his opponent reeling. In a show of good sportsmanship, Epeius catches Euryalus and holds him upright, preventing his opponent from ignominiously hitting the ground. In this example, these elite boxers demonstrate the Greek ideal of excellence (*arête*) as they honor the fallen Patroclus. The status-conscious heroes of Homer would have been eager to compete with honor and win prizes to enhance their reputation (*kleos*).

Homer's *Odyssey* provides a less glorious, but nonetheless instructive, demonstration of ancient Greek boxing. In this section of the *Odyssey* (18.31-107), the hero Odysseus has returned to Ithaca disguised as an old beggar and finds himself in a street fight against a vagrant named Irus. The suitors of Odysseus' wife, Penelope, set the two beggars against each other in a bare-fisted brawl as a low form of sport, with a stuffed goat's stomach as the contestant's reward. Irus, a brawny but cowardly lout, lashes out wildly, hoping his strength might end the bout quickly. But Odysseus, the thinking man's boxer, measures his foe and connects with a perfectly timed counterpunch to the neck. With Irus summarily dispatched, Odysseus enjoys a hot meal and a small measure of self-respect. In this brutal contest there is no heroic *kleos* to be earned or *arête* to be demonstrated. The stakes were more basic: food in one's belly and some street cred in Ithaca.

Also revealed in Odysseus' contest with Irus is a theme that becomes prominent in the portrayal of boxing in classical mythology: the triumph of technique over brute force. In wily Odysseus we have a skilled fighter who calculates whether to strike Irus with a killing blow or simply go for a knockout, whereas Irus relies on his apparent advantage in strength and size and punches with wild and thoughtless abandon.

Boxing in Greek Mythology

Greek mythology reflects ancient Greek values, beliefs, and cultural idioms. The contrast between boxing styles, i.e. boxer versus brawler, is reflected in the stories of the Greek gods that are associated with the sport. On the one hand, we have Apollo, the cool, rational sun god, who was worshipped in some regions of Greece as Apollo *Pyktes* (the boxer). This form of Apollo, as legend has it, defeated the war god Ares (a god of irrational violence) in a boxing match at Olympia (Paus. 5.7.10). He also wrested control of the road leading to Delphi from the bully Phorbas by pummeling him into submission (Philostratus, *Imagines* 2. 19). Hercules, on the other hand, while better known for his wrestling and almost limitless strength, is reported by some traditions to have defeated the Sicilian King Eryx, a renowned boxer, in a contest over Geryon's cattle (Seneca, *Hercules Furens* 480). One imagines no matter how skilled Eryx might have been, his jaw would have not endured a chin check from Hercules.

Finally, the boxing match between King Amycus and Polydeuces (Pollux) from the story of Jason and the Argonauts (the *Argonautica*) brings together some of the major themes associated with boxing found in Greek mythology (Theocritus, *Idylls* 22.27–135). Each fighter embodies characteristics of the brawler and boxer, respectively. King Amycus is a physically imposing bully, complete with cauliflower ears, who disregards the common laws of hospitality. Like Phorbas, he is little more than a street corner thug who challenges visitors to his territory to fight. Polydeuces, on the other hand, is a rational hero who attempts diplomacy to avoid a confrontation with the belligerent king. Only when given no alternative does Polydeuces agree to fight.

The contest between Amycus and Polydeuces echoes Odysseus' fight with Irus. Polydeuces uses superior ring generalship to his advantage by maneuvering to get the sun to his back. He easily slips Amycus' punches and lands vicious counterpunches and jabs, cutting his opponent's face with the sharp edges of his dried ox-hide wrappings. Amycus is a pressure fighter but eventually tires from the sheer volume of punches he throws. Attempting to end the fight with one blow, Amycus makes a crucial error. He tries to pin Polydeuces' left hand while going for a crushing downward blow but is outmaneuvered and caught on the temple with an overhand right counter, which ends the fight, leaving Amycus dazed and defenseless. Amycus' brawling style is no match for Polydeuces' craft and skillful defense.[4]

Boxing and the Panhellenic Games

With the rise of the Greek *polis* (city-state) during the seventh century BC, boxing undergoes a change from an event linked to aristocratic funerals and individual duels between gods and heroes to competitions that celebrated the honor and glory of the community of the *polis* itself. Greek boxing proper, the *pxy*, emerged as one of the events in the four sacred Panhellenic games: the Olympic, Delphic, Nemean, and Pythian. The Olympic Festival dedicated to Zeus in Olympia was the most prestigious. Boxing (along with wrestling and the *pankration*, a form of no-holds-barred wrestling) was considered a heavy event (*alegeinos*) in contrast to the light events, which included track and field. According to the writer Philostratus (*On Gymnastics* 9–10), the Spartans originated boxing (Polydeuces was a noted pugilist and Spartan by birth) but soon abandoned it because bouts were often decided by submission, which would give critics ample opportunity to accuse the Spartans of a lack of spirit.

The earliest recorded Olympic victor was Onomastus of Smyrna, who in 688 BC also instituted the first set of formal rules of ancient Olympic boxing. Unlike modern boxing, ancient Greek boxing had no weight classes (an advantage for larger and stronger competitors) or time limit. The boxing match ended with a knockout or a submission, indicated by raising one's finger to the referee. Greek vase paintings, which provide most of the evidence for ancient boxing, show referees with long canes used to break clinching and punish infractions (i.e. biting and scratching) during the match. There was no roped off ring per se, but some vase paintings depict designated areas for boxers separate from spectators, and the use of a long pole to restrict the size of the ring itself.[5]

In the Panhellenic games, the boxers fought in the nude, abandoning the earlier custom of the girdled loincloth mentioned in Homer. Early "gloves" consisted of ten- to twelve-foot-long leather thongs (*himantes*) wrapped around the hands and the forearms giving support for the wrist (Philostratus, *On*

Gymnastics 10; Eustathius 1324.18). In the fourth century BC, harder and heavier thongs (*oxeis*) were employed and often reinforced with a hard leather insert, which improved the use of one's hands for defense while increasing the potential for damage as well. These evolved into a one-piece glove, which left the fingertips free but covered the entire upper arm. Leather straps enclosed the glove, which held a knuckleduster insert of hard leather. Soft gloves (*spairai* or *episphairai*) (Plato, *Laws* 8.830B) along with ear guards (*amphotides*) (Plutarch, *Moralia* 38B) soon followed, perhaps because the use of regular boxing equipment inflicted too many injuries during practice and sparing sessions.

Despite such precautions, boxing remained a brutal sport. The historical record provides evidence that the faces of some boxers were unrecognizable from injuries they had suffered (Lucillus, *Greek Anthology* 11.75). Moving physical evidence of this is provided by the fourth-century BC Greek *Boxer at Rest* bronze statue mentioned earlier in this chapter. His scarred brow, broken nose, lacerated cheeks, and cauliflower ears are a grim testament to a lifetime of fighting. The ideal boxer remained stoic in the ring. Plutarch writes that the crowd, not the boxer, should respond with emotion inspired by the fight. Murmurs and gasps from the spectators should punctuate a well-delivered blow, while the boxer remains silent, focused on his task at hand.[6]

The rewards of victory, though "gained in blood" as one inscription attests, were great.[7] The Panhellenic games bestowed crowns of olive (Olympian), pine (Isthmian), wild celery (Neamean), and laurel (Pythian/Delphi), whereas at other festivals winners could expect a crown of palm leaves or a palm branch to be held in the right hand (Lucian, *Anacharisis* 9; Paus. 8.48.2–3). In addition to these trophies, valuable commodities such as olive oil were often awarded as prizes. At Athens' Pan-Athenaic festival during the first half of the fourth century BC, the winner of the boxing event received sixty amphoras of olive oil, worth around $40,000.[8] Roughly a single amphora held thirty-nine liters. So we're looking at 2,340 liters of olive oil total as the prize. The monetary value is not the point, but rather the utility of the oil itself in the ancient Greek world and the prestige. Winners of Panhellenic crowns could also earn tidy sums of money from their home *polis* (Plutarch, *Solon* 23.3) or a lifetime of free room and board supplied at public expense.[9]

Beyond such material rewards, however, the most gratifying of prizes was the recognition and fame won by the victorious boxer. The Athenian sage Solon once said that the tokens of victory were less important than the reputation of the victor. This, according to Solon, was of far greater value than any prize, and the winners (at the moment of victory) were thought to be equal to the gods (Lucian, *Anarcharis* 9–14). The most famous and successful of boxers won a kind of immortality. With their victories preserved in verse and their bodies immortalized in marble and bronze, these fighters attained the status of athlete-heroes, whose legendary fame continued beyond their deaths. Let us look at two noteworthy examples: Theagenes of Thasos and the family of Diagoras of Rhodes.

Theagenes of Thasos

The ancient writer Pausanias (6.11.2–9) noted that among the hundreds of statues of Olympic victors decorating the city of Olympia, few were as famous as that of the boxer Theagenes from the island of Thasos. A two-time Olympic champion (his first victory came in 480 BC), he is reported to have won over 1,300 events in both boxing and *pankration*. During the fifth century BC, Theagenes dominated his opponents at the Panhellenic games, winning thrice at Delphi, nine times at Nemea, and also nine times at the Isthmian games, including a double victory in both boxing and *pankration*. Given such great strength and stamina, which he had allegedly displayed even as a child, Theagenes' father was rumored to have been Hercules himself.

Theagenes' arrogance and gluttony were also Herculean in scope. To commemorate his double-victory at Olympia, he named his son Diolympios ("twice at Olympia"). He consumed an entire bull on a bet and was reported to have challenged guests to wrestling matches and feats of strength at the dinner table. Growing weary of his victories in his two chosen sports, Theagenes trained for and won the long-distance running event in Thessaly, the home of the swift-footed Achilles. Doubtless his successes in the ring and immense ego outside of it made Theagenes many enemies, one of whom attempted to take his revenge not while the boxing champion was living but after his death. Pausanias wrote that after the champion had died, a man had attacked and flogged Theagenes' commemorative statue at Olympia as if it were the boxer himself. To the man's surprise, the statue fell, crushing him to death. Taking advantage of Athenian law, his sons prosecuted the statue for murder, won their case, and threw the fighter's effigy into the sea. The citizens of Thasos recovered Theagenes' statue in their fishing nets and brought it back to Olympia, consecrating the image as a divine hero imbued with healing powers (Paus. 6.11.2–9). On the island of Thasos today there are remains of a shrine to the heroic, if loutish, boxer with a hollow marble block made into an offering box.[10]

The Family of Diagoras

In 464 BC, the poet Pindar immortalized Diagoras of Rhodes in his seventh *Olympian Ode*. An accomplished boxer, Diagoras was a *periodonikes,* or circuit winner, at the Panhellenic games. He won once at Olympia, twice at Delphi, four times at the Isthmian games, and earned several victories at Nemea. He was credited with numerous wins at lesser events throughout Greece including events at Athens, Arcadia, Thebes, Arcadia, Argos, Pellana, Megara, and Aegina. A man of great size and impeccable fighting form, Diagoras (unlike Theagenes) did not engender ill will and was beloved by both the Rhodians and others outside his home community.

But while Diagoras was a champion boxer worthy of Pindar's verses, it was the athletic accomplishments of his children that solidified his legacy. His three sons continued the family tradition of athletic excellence earning statues of their own beside their father as Olympic champions. Diagoras' two elder sons, Akousilaus and Damagetus, won at Olympia in boxing and *pankration*, respectively. But Dorieus, the youngest son, proved to be the star of the Diagorean athletic dynasty with three Olympic, four Delphic, eight Isthmian, and seven Nemean crowns in boxing and *pankration*. Diagoras' daughters Kallipatira and Pherenike each bore him grandsons who became Olympic boxing champions.[11]

Under the Shadow of Rome

During the second century BC, the Greeks fell under Roman rule and as the Roman poet Horace wrote, "Captive Greece ensnared her wild conqueror" (Horace, *Letters* 2.1.156). Greek boxing was transformed under Roman rule. The sacred Greek games, which featured boxing events that celebrated the glory of the individual Greek *polis*, would now serve new Roman masters and become intertwined with Roman traditions. Roman boxing (*pugilatus*) had long been part of the athletic events in the *ludi* (state-funded games) and *munera* (privately funded spectacles) since the sixth century BC, perhaps deriving from early Etruscan examples.[12]

Though the evidence is sparse, Roman boxing was similar to Greek save for the type of boxing glove used. The Romans originally adopted the heavier gloves of the Greeks but soon replaced it with the *caestus*, a glove with a semi-cylindrical bronze reinforcement capable of causing horrific wounds.[13] The Romans considered their *pugilatus* to be more violent and deadly than Greek boxing and certainly more dangerous than wrestling and the *pankration*. These two forms of boxing, however, began to merge with the Romans holding Greek style games in Italy for the first time in 186 BC.[14]

During the imperial period in the first century AD, Roman boxing stood alongside the gladiator matches and arena beast hunts that emphasized Rome's power and dominance over man and nature. Rome's first emperor, Augustus, was an avid follower of boxing and enjoyed contests between

Roman and Greek pugilists. In AD 14 Tiberius, Augustus' successor, introduced in his honor the first set of regularly held celebratory games, in Naples, called the *Ludi Augustales*.[15] In Greece, boxing was still firmly entrenched in the sacred Panhellenic games, but their function had turned from the celebration of the *polis* itself to the aggrandizement of Roman rulers. Ironically, venues for games increased under Roman emperors who introduced Greek-style events into the city of Rome itself, including the Neronian games and the Emperor Domitian's Capitoline games.

Yet the Romans held a deep ambivalence toward Greek culture, including athletics, which were considered to be both exciting and decadent. Romans as spectators admired Greek boxers and athletes. Wealthier Romans even enjoyed training in gymnasiums or within the privacy of villas decorated with statues and murals of Greek athletes and sporting events. But to engage in athletic performance in public was shameful and unacceptable for a Roman citizen. Likewise, Greek games in Italy and abroad were safe and nonthreatening to Roman identity only when they honored the emperor. For the Greeks, the traditional Panhellenic games maintained an important link to the past (and its glories) and provided a way to attain prestige in the new political order. Imperial generosity supported Greek culture so long as it was controlled and proved beneficial to the empire. As one insightful study puts it, "Yet in the majority of cases it probably suited all parties to sign up to an image of Greek cultural prestige preserved and enabled by Roman power."[16]

Despite the enormous popularity of the games, some Roman intellectuals argued that the voyeuristic nature of athletic events had a corrupting influence. Tacitus bemoaned that due to boxing's popularity, Roman youths might strip down and take up boxing gloves instead of pursuing more practical martial arts (*Annales* 14.20.4), whereas Cicero thought nudity in the games was a shameful distraction (*Tusc. Disp.* 4.70). Other writers complained that the inflamed emotions caused by sporting events clouded reasoning and prevented spectators from striving for higher and nobler pursuits.[17] Seneca stated that any physical exertion as practiced in athletics dulled the mind (*Letters* 15.3). However, some Roman writers portrayed the rigors of athletics, boxing in particular, as a metaphor for the attainment of virtue through training and competitive struggle.[18]

Melankomas of Caria

Dio Chrysostom, a sophist in the Roman Empire during the second century AD, wrote of a famous boxer, Melankomas of Caria, whose unblemished record was a result of his unsurpassed defense (*Orations* 28 & 29). Melankomas earned his victories, which included numerous crowns, by never permitting his opponents to land a single blow while never himself landing a punch. Through his superior stamina, Melankomas outlasted his foes, forcing their capitulation once their inability to connect with their own punches had exhausted them. Due to his rigorous training and dedication to his craft, Melankomas was reportedly able to hold up his hands in defense for two consecutive days.

For Dio, Melankomas was the ultimate example of a man who attained virtue through physical contest. He had overcome the temptations of lust, sloth, and gluttony through his almost ascetic training and preparation. While in the ring, Melankomas demonstrated supreme courage, self-discipline, and temperance, never succumbing to the promise of an easy win by striking his opponent. And because his foes gave up in defeat, Melankomas earned the purest form of victory by breaking his opponents' will without causing them physical harm. Though his description of Melankomas rings with hyperbole, Dio found philosophic virtue within the brutal and violent world of boxing.

End Game: Late Antiquity

Boxing, along with the *ludi* of the Romans and the Greek games in the East, would fade during the fifth century AD. The emerging Christian ethos of the Roman world would weaken the popularity of the more violent athletic events, which had strong pagan religious connections. Though growing imperial restriction played a factor in the demise of combat sports, a more important cause was the economic decline of the Roman city, in the face of Germanic incursions, that prevented local elites from funding public games. Boxing and its associated sporting events were never revenue-makers in the conventional sense. Rather, they played an important role in the generation of political capital for its sponsors and were used as a form of social control linked to urban life in the classical city. The end of combat sports such as boxing as popular spectacles, in a way, mirrored the end of the ancient city and thus marked an important transition from the world of classical antiquity to the Middle Ages.

NOTES

1   This bronze sculpture is also known as *The Terme Boxer* or *The Boxer of the Quirinal*. See R.R.R. Smith, *Hellenistic Sculpture* (London: Thames and Hudson, 1991), 54–55, for background and context. Recently, this statue was the centerpiece of a major exhibit celebrating Italian art at the Metropolitan Museum of Art during the summer of 2013. For details, see Seán Hemingway, "The Boxer: An Ancient Masterpiece Comes to the Met," *Metropolitan Museum of*

Art, June 17, 2013, www.metmuseum.org/about-the-museum/now-at-the-met/features/2013/the-boxer.

2 For the Near Eastern evidence, see the Terracotta plaque of wrestlers and boxers, Iraq Museum, Bagdad, nos. 32 and 10039. Concerning Egypt, see M. Poliakoff, *Combat Sports in the Ancient World* (New Haven, CT: Yale University Press, 1987), 68 and fig. 64.

3 For the Hagia Triada vase see, Peter Warren, *Minoan Stone Vessels* (Cambridge: Cambridge University Press, 1969), no. 469; On the Santorini fresco see, A.J. Papalas, "The Development of Greek Boxing," *Ancient World* 9.3–4 (1984): 67–69, and N. Crowther, *Sport in Ancient Times* (Westport, CT: Praeger, 2007), 38–39.

4 The boxer versus brawler theme can be found in I. Weiler, *Der Agon im Mythos* (Darmstadt: Wissenschaftliche Buchgesellschaft, 1974), 173–174, and Plutarch, *Moralia* 724C. The fight between Polydeuces and Amycus is retold in Apollonius Rhodius, *Argonautica* 2.30–97 and later by Valerius Flaccus, *Argonautica* 4.141–293.

5 For Onomastus, see Philostratus, *On Gymnastics*, 12 and the Olympic Victors List (22nd Olympiad) cf. Paul Christensen and Zara Martirosova-Torlone, "The Olympic Victor List of Eusebius: Background, Text and Translation," *Traditio* 61 (2006): 31–93, and P. Christensen, *Olympic Victor Lists and Ancient Greek History* (Cambridge: Cambridge University Press, 2007); for kicking in boxing, see N. Crowther, "The Evidence for Kicking in Greek Boxing," *American Journal of Philology* 111 (1990): 176–181; use of a pole or ladder to restrict the movements of boxers is argued by M. Poliakoff, "Melankomas, *ek klimakos*, and Greek Boxing," *American Journal of Philology* 108 (1987): 511–518.

6 *Moralia* 79E.

7 G. Kaibel, *Epigrammata Graeca* (Berlin: Berolini Apud G. Reimer, 1878), no. 942.

8 *IG* II² 2311; The monetary value of the amphorae of olive oil is calculated by S.G. Miller, *Arete: Greek Sports from Ancient Sources*, 2nd edn, (Berkeley, CA: University of California Press, 1991) no. 84, 81, adjusted for twenty-first-century inflation.

9 *IG* I² 77.11–17. For payment of Greek athletes see, David C. Young, *The Olympic Myth of Greek Amateur Athletics* (Chicago, IL: University of Chicago Press 1984), 131.

10 *BCH* 64–65 (1940–41); 175.

11 Pausanias 6.7.1–5.

12 J.-P. Thuillier, *Les Jeux athlétiques dans la civilization étrusque* (Rome: Ecole Française de Rome, 1985), 181–286.

13 M. Junkelmann, "Greek Athletics in Rome," in *Gladiators and Caesars*, eds. E. Köhne and C. Ewigleben (Berkeley, CA: University of California Press, 2000), 75–78, and for a contrary view of the *caestus* being constructed of only leather, see H. Lee, "The Later Greek Boxing Glove and the 'Roman' *Caestus*: A Centennial Reevaluation of Jünther's Über Antike Turngeräthe," *Nikephoros* 10.9 (1997): 168–178.

14 Livy 39.22.1–2; I. R. Arnold, "Agonistic Festivals in Italy and Sicily," *American Journal of Archaeology* 64 (1960): 245–251; N. Crowther, "Greek Games in Republican Rome," *L'Antiquité classique* 52 (1983): 268–273.

15 Suetonius, *Augustus*, 45.2. Cf. R. M. Greer, "The Greek Games at Naples," *Transactions of the American Philological Association* 66 (1935): 208–221.

16 Zahra Newby, *Greek Athletics in the Roman World* (Oxford: Oxford University Press, 2005), 280.

17 Tacitus, *Dialogus de oratibus* 29.2.

18 For the spiritual and philosophic benefits of the rigors of combat sports, see Poliakoff, *Combat Sports*, 134–147. A pertinent example would include the well-known boxing match between Entellus and Dares in Virgil, *Aeneid* 5.362–484. See M. Poliakoff, "Entellus and Amycus: Virgil, *Aen.* 5. 362–484," *Illinois Classical Studies* 10 (1985): 227–231.

WORKS FOR FURTHER READING

Christensen, P. *Olympic Victor Lists and Ancient Greek History*. Cambridge: Cambridge University Press, 2007.

Christensen, P. and Martirosova-Torlone, Z. "The Olympic Victor List of Eusebius: Background, Text and Translation." *Traditio* 61 (2006): 31–93.

Crowther, N. *Sport in Ancient Times*. Westport, CT: Praeger, 2007.

Crowther, N. "The Evidence for Kicking in Greek Boxing." *American Journal of Philology* 111 (1990): 176–181.

Golden, M. *Sport and Society in Ancient Greece*. Cambridge: Cambridge University Press, 1988.

Greer, R. M. "The Greek Games at Naples." *Transactions of the American Philological Association* 66 (1935): 208–221.

Hemingway, S. "The Boxer: An Ancient Masterpiece Comes to the Met." Metropolitan Museum of Art. June 17, 2013. www.metmuseum.org/about-the-museum/now-at-the-met/features/2013/the-boxer.

Junkelman, M. "Greek Athletics in Rome: Boxing, Wrestling and the Pancration." In *Gladiators and Caesars*, edited by E. Köhne and C. Ewigleben, 75–85. Berkeley, CA: University of California Press, 2000.

Kaibel, G. *Epigrammata Graeca*. Berlin: Berolini Apud G. Reimer, 1878.

Köhne, E. and Ewigleben, C. *Gladiators and Caesars*. Berkeley, CA: University of California Press, 2000.

König, J. *Athletics and Literature in the Roman Empire*. Cambridge: Cambridge University Press, 2005.

Lee, H. "The Later Boxing Glove and the 'Roman' *Caestus*: A Centennial Reevaluation of Jünther's Über Antike Turngeräthe." *Nikephoros* 10.9 (1997): 168–178.

Miller, S.G. *Arete: Greek Sports from Ancient Sources*, 2nd edn, Berkeley, CA: University of California Press, 1991.

Newby, Z. *Greek Athletics in the Roman World*. Oxford: Oxford University Press, 2005.

Nicholson, N. *Aristocracy and Athletics in Archaic and Classical Greece*. Cambridge: Cambridge University Press, 2005.

Papalas, A. J. "The Development of Greek Boxing." *Ancient World* 9.3–4 (1984): 67–69.

Poliakoff, M. "Melankomas, *ek klimakos*, and Greek Boxing." *American Journal of Philology* 108 (1987): 511–518.

Poliakoff, M. *Combat Sports in the Ancient World*. New Haven, CT: Yale University Press, 1987.

Poliakoff, M. *Studies in the Terminology of the Greek Combat Sports*. Frankfurt, 1987.

Poliakoff, M. "Entellus and Amycus: Virgil, *Aen.* 5.362–484." *Illinois Classical Studies* 10 (1985): 227–231.

Potter, D. *The Victor's Crown: A History of Ancient Sport from Homer to Byzantium*. Oxford: Oxford University Press, 2011.

Smith, R. R. R. *Hellenistic Sculpture*. London: Thames and Hudson, 1991.

Sweet, W. *Sport and Recreation in Ancient Greece: A Sourcebook with Translations*. New York: Oxford University Press, 1987.

Thuillier, J.-P. *Les Jeux athlétiques dans la civilization étrusque*. Rome: Ecole Française de Rome, 1985.

Warren, P. *Minoan Stone Vessels*. Cambridge: Cambridge University Press, 1969.

Weiler, I. *Der Agon im Mythos*. Darmstadt: Wissenschaftliche Buchgesellschaft, 1974.

Young, D. C. *The Olympic Myth of Greek Amateur Athletics*. Chicago, IL: Ares Publishers, 1984.

2

ELLIOTT J. GORN

The Bare-Knuckle Era

Origins of the Ring

Fistic combat goes back at least as far as ancient Greece and Rome. Pindar, in 474 BC, celebrated Diagoras' victory in the Greek Olympiad: "But do thou, O father Zeus, that rulest over the height of Atabyrium, grant honour to the hymn ordained in praise of an Olympian victor, and to the hero who hath found fame for his prowess as a boxer; and do though give him grace and reverence in the eyes of citizens and of strangers too. For he goeth in a straight course along a path that hateth insolence." Worthy of Zeus' blessing, the successful boxer was a man of moral as well as physical excellence. Successful fighters were exalted heroes, showered with prizes. They, like other athletes, exemplified discipline, as well as ideals of grace and beauty. Boxing was good preparation for warfare, and the successful boxer upheld honor, demonstrated virility, paid homage to the dead. Great boxers embodied the goal of unified mental, physical, and spiritual cultivation.[1]

The Greeks passed the idea of fistic combat onto the Romans, who gave us the Latin word *pugilism*. Boxing, however, became ever more brutal under the Roman Empire, part of the fascination with bloody gladiatorial games. Fighters wore the caestus – a thong wound round the hand, protecting it and making it a much more dangerous weapon. Virgil wrote in *The Aeneid*:

> From somewhere he produced the gloves of Eryx
> And tossed them into the ring, all stiff and heavy,
> Seven layers of hide and insewn lead and iron ...
> You can still see the blood and a splash of brains
> That stained them long ago ...

Virgil described an epic match between the old champion Entellus and a young challenger, young Dares, who left the ring vanquished, spitting blood and teeth.[2]

Perhaps boxing was introduced to England during the Roman occupation, but if that was the case, the sport disappeared shortly after the Christian era and did not return until the seventeenth century. Probably Englishmen revived the ring when they rediscovered the classics, through Virgil and Homer, for example. The Restoration of the mid-1600s witnessed generally a loosening of mores from the more stringent Puritan ways. Drinking and gambling accompanied an efflorescence of rowdy sports like cockfighting and bullbaiting. Especially in the cities, boxing was part of a raucous early-modern culture.[3]

James Fig was considered the father of the English ring. He opened Fig's Amphitheater in London, and there he taught boxing, as well as swordsmanship and cudgeling. He also fought early prizefights, boxing matches fought for a purse. Jack Broughton was the next great teacher of the sport in his London Academy. Broughton received the patronage of the Duke of Cumberland, and by promulgating the famous "Broughton's Rules," he brought a more refined tone to the prize ring beginning in 1743. Broughton's Rules banned strangling an opponent, hitting him below the belt, or striking him when he was down. Matches were held outdoors on turf in a roped-off square. The rules specified that a round ended when either man was punched or thrown down, that a new round began thirty seconds later with both men toeing a mark called "the scratch" in the middle of the ring. Each boxer appointed seconds to assist between rounds, umpires to settle disputes, and the umpires in turn appointed a referee whose decisions were final.[4]

With some minor modifications, Broughton's Rules governed the English Prize Ring for a century, and the American Ring for nearly 150 years. By the late eighteenth century, boxing was considered the "National Sport of England." There were several reasons for its ascendency. The ring was part of a larger commercialized leisure culture that included sports like cricket and horse racing, which had their own formal rules, sophisticated betting, and powerful clubs comprising wealthy patrons. Moreover, several charismatic champions emerged in this era, such as Daniel Mendoza, the first Jewish champion; Bill Richmond, an African American who pioneered counterpunching; and Gentleman John Jackson, who taught the manly art to a generation of English aristocrats.[5]

Two of the most spectacular fights of this era took place in 1810 and 1811, as the English champion Tom Crib fought an African American challenger, Tom Molineaux. Crib won their first battle, but just barely, so when they came together again at a place called Thistleton Gap outside London, upwards of 20,000 Englishmen followed them – lords and knights and military officers and gamblers and publicans and pickpockets and young dandies and weavers and butchers. Crib won the second match too, and together they were interpreted as a great triumph for the English nation and English manhood; the issue of race was not nearly so important at this particular historical moment, whereas later in the century white champions like John L. Sullivan refused to fight black boxers.[6]

Above all, the ring in this era was part of a culture that embraced writers like Pierce Egan and William Hazlitt, artists such as Robert Isaac Cruikshank, young aristocrats at Eton and Harrow, even the Prince Regent of England. Prizefighters were mostly working-class men, but some among the rich, powerful and educated gave them protection as well as cultural cache. And boxing was just one popular recreation in an era that saw alliances of the rich and poor.

But English society was changing, and rapidly. In the early decades of the nineteenth century, a new bourgeois class was on the rise, rich with profits from new industries like spinning and weaving, deeply earnest in its allegiance to productivity and sober self-control, and often affiliated with powerful new evangelical organizations. This new nexus of power and culture was impatient of the sloppy ways of the old aristocracy and gentry. Improving each bright and shining hour was the way forward, not the bloody popular recreations of old, with their attendant drinking, gambling, and carousing. Just when industry called for increasingly self-controlled behavior, old sports and recreations threatened to undermine working-class discipline. In this atmosphere, prizefights were not only illegal but local magistrates and constables enforced the laws, arrested the fighters and their backers. Boxing went into a steep decline.[7]

The First American Fights

Britain continued to produce some great champions, and occasionally the fancy, as boxing aficionados were called, pulled off a big bout. But in coming decades, English and Irish fighters increasingly ventured across the Atlantic to the United States. When Bill Richmond and Tom Molineaux, both African Americans, headed to England in the late eighteenth and early nineteenth centuries, there was no extensive culture of the ring in America. Molineaux, it was said, was a slave whose master freed him after he'd won a big bout. This might or might not be true, but there is very little solid evidence that boxing matches between slaves were common. Boxing just was not well known in North America before the mid-nineteenth century, less so in the south than the north, less still in rural areas than in cities. Richmond and Molineaux went to England – to London – precisely because opportunities were so meager here.[8]

There was one odd exception to this rule, a detour in this story really. The word "boxing" came to be used for violent fights in the southern backcountry from the late eighteenth through the early nineteenth century. As in the

London Prize Ring, two men squared off and spectators gathered. But there the similarity ended. Most commonly called gouging matches or rough-and-tumbles, the goal was to disfigure an opponent, bite off his nose or ears, and if at all possible, gouge out his eyes. Great battles were celebrated in legend, and champion eye-gougers were mostly men on the fringes of "civilization," hunters and trappers, riverboat handlers, roustabouts, the sorts of men who lived largely apart from families, churches, cities. But these were not fights for a purse, as in the prize ring. Rather, they were affairs of honor – one man refused to drink with another, or belittled his fighting prowess or called him a name. Male honor was a cornerstone of white Southern culture, and eye gouging can be thought of as a backwoods version of dueling.[9]

Rough-and-tumbling aside, by the 1820s stray newspaper stories indicate that boxing matches with some of the trappings of the English ring came off sporadically in American cities. The earliest full report came from the *New York Evening Post*:

> On Tuesday the 8th July, at half past 6 P.M. being near the Ferry at Grand Street, I observed a large number of men, women and children collecting, and like others, I followed to Gardner's wharf, at the upper end of Cherry Street, where I saw a large ring forming, and on enquiry found a lad about 18 years old, a butcher, and a man whom they called the champion of Hickory Street, both stripped, and each had a second. After the proper arrangements, the seconds drew back a little, and the word was given for battle.

A round-by-round description of the forty-minute battle followed, including praise for the young butcher who possessed "the boldness and courage of a bulldog." This report established a literary convention: because boxing was illegal and considered to be immoral by the middle class, the writer, as others would in coming decades, said that he just happened upon the battle.[10]

Through the 1830s and 1840s, the ring continued to develop in America. Because of its declining fortunes in England, several notable fighters came to the United States. Men like Ned Hammond, originally from Dublin, and George Kensett of Liverpool staged bouts with increasing attention to the ring's conventions; Champion James "Deaf" Burke came to the United States after an opponent in England died in the ring, and emigration seemed like his best option; and English immigrant William Fuller founded the tradition of giving sparring lessons to well-off young men. The few regular bouts of this era took place mostly in and around New York City, and the ring began to receive consistent coverage from the gentlemanly *Spirit of the Times*, and also from the *New York Herald*, a workingman's penny-daily. As boxing grew, so did its opposition. Thomas Jefferson scorned it, along with horse racing, as an English aristocratic dissipation that had no place in democratic

America. Others condemned boxing as violent, crass, corrupting of youth. In an age that increasingly prized bourgeois values like sober self-control, the ring encouraged dissipations like gambling, swearing, and drinking. Reformers, clergymen, and journalists condemned the corruptions of the ring, yet many working-class men came to see boxing as emblematic of their way of life. "Burke presented an iron frame, in which all superfluous flesh seemed excluded," and the writer went on to describe in detail "The Deaf 'Un's" body. Here were the beginnings of a male aesthetic that appealed deeply to working-class men.[11]

Beginning in the late 1840s and lasting until the Civil War, boxing experienced a golden age in American cities. Part of the reason was the growth of a substantial working class, based on the rise of new manufacturing businesses. Simply put, there was now a critical mass of men with enough income, a little spare time, and a desire to find "manly" sports. And one other thing: there was a growing immigrant presence on urban streets. For English and Irish men, boxing was an ancestral sport; by the mid nineteenth century, it had long been associated with national pride and personal virility. The immigrant presence fed rivalries, English versus Irish, Irish versus native born, native born versus English, and these were played out in the ring, and generated unprecedented spectator interest.[12]

But before this golden age could flourish, one bout nearly killed the ring. On September 13, 1842, Chris Lilly and Tom McCoy met in Hastings, just above New York City. In this era before weight classes, both were mid-sized men, a little under 140 pounds, but 2,000 spectators jammed a dozen boats for the trip up the Hudson. Of course the bout, like all prizefights, was illegal, so the boxers, their seconds, and even the fans might be arrested, should constables choose to challenge such a tough crowd. The new 1838 rules of the London Prize Ring were in force – they would continue in the United States for another fifty years – and they explicitly outlawed the hair-pulling, head-butting, eye-gouging, gut-kneeing, and neck-throttling so often on display under Broughton's Rules. As always, a round ended when a man was punched, tripped, or thrown down, and a new round began thirty seconds later. Journalists gave the fight considerable ink, and boxing's homoeroticism, the emphasis on masculine beauty, emerged in descriptions of boxers' bodies: "[McCoy's] swelling breast curved out like a cuirass: his shoulders were deep, with a bold curved blade, and the muscular development of the arm large and finely brought out."[13]

The fight lasted over two and a half hours, 119 rounds. McCoy refused to concede the match, even though he was defenseless for the last fifty. The battle ended with his death; the coroner said he drowned in his own blood.

This was the first fatality in the American prize ring, and it prompted an outburst of rage. The grand jury sitting in Westchester County indicted eighteen men on charges ranging from riot to manslaughter. Boxers George Kensett, John McCleester, and Yankee Sullivan stood trial, and all were convicted. In his charge to the jury, the judge described the ringside crowd: "the gamblers, and the bullies, and the swearers, and the blacklegs, and the pickpockets and the thieves, and the burglars ... the idle, disorderly, vicious, dissolute people – people who live by violence – people who live by crime." The judges words expressed the fear that cities had become dens of vice, that youth there hardened into idle, drunken, bloodthirsty ruffians, that a corrupt, aggressive, alien underclass now prevailed and threatened the wellsprings of American virtue.[14]

Boxing all but disappeared for five years after the Lilly–McCoy match, but the conditions that fed the ring actually improved. Cities continued to grow rapidly, fed by a growing number of immigrant men. Most of them labored at working-class jobs, so they were eager for rough amusements. And too, ethnic conflict deepened between Englishmen and Irishmen, Americans and immigrants. Maybe most important, prizefighting rode into mid-century on the backs of several charismatic fighters.[15]

Political influence got Yankee Sullivan out of legal difficulties after the Lilly–McCoy fight, and he lay low for a few years, tending bar at his saloon in lower Manhattan. But he longed to fight, and, in 1847, he began publicly sparring at "Sportsman's Hall" and other venues where the fancy gathered. Sparring exhibitions were restrained boxing; fighters wore gloves, fought indoors for a limited number of rounds, refrained from punching too hard. It was all mostly legal, as men demonstrated the manly art but without the violence and passion of the prize ring. But Sullivan itched for a real fight and apparently so did his fans. As had become the custom before the Lilly–McCoy fight, Robert Caunt, brother of the former English champion Benjamin Caunt, published a letter in the *Spirit of the Times*: "I have received numerous challenges from Yankee Sullivan, but have never been able to bring him up to the chalk ... If he means business, I am already to fight him for one thousand dollars, and if he will not accept this challenge, I hope he will not annoy me anymore with his bounces." Their seconds arranged the match, and they fought at Harper's Ferry, Virginia, before 700 members of the fancy on May 11, 1847. Sullivan easily defeated Caunt in twelve minutes, but the fight did its work; it not only reintroduced the ring to an American audience after the Lilly–McCoy debacle, it brought back ethnic conflict, larger-than-life fighters, and high stakes ($1,000 was roughly three years of a working-class man's salary).[16]

The Golden Age

"We do not remember," the *New York Herald* declared a year and a half after the Sullivan–Caunt fight, "ever to have seen so great an excitement among certain classes of society, as has been developed during the last few days in relation to the approaching prizefight between Yankee Sullivan and Tom Hyer. It is similar in some respects to the agitation produced in the public mind by the first accounts of the Mexican War." Each side wagered $5,000, with total betting estimated at upwards of $300,000. A man could scarcely enter a saloon six months before the bout without giving his opinion of Sullivan and Hyer.[17]

And those opinions were marked by the abilities of the two fighters, but just as much by their ethnic backgrounds. The 1840s was a decade of unprecedented immigration to the United States and especially to the eastern cities. For the first time, in 1845, over 100,000 immigrants entered the country; in 1847, 200,000; in 1850, 300,000. The Irish were overrepresented because of the potato blight, or more precisely, because when the crops died beginning in 1845, England's policies failed to meet the emergency. During the 1830s, 200,000 Irish came to America; four times that number arrived in the 1840s. The English and Irish had their own long-simmering enmities; native-born Americans and the English were not fond of each other; American Protestants accused Catholics of idolatry and subservience to the pope; American workers often blamed the Irish for taking their jobs, while the Irish looked on Americans as cold-hearted, selfish, and arrogant. The prize ring, of course, was always a stage for playing out such conflicts.[18]

Tom Hyer made his reputation as a street brawler. He was a butcher, a trade long dominated by American-born workers. Hyer demanded a stake of $5,000, an amount Sullivan's backers struggled to raise. Daily fights broke out between their friends, and one night, Hyer and Sullivan chanced on each other in a downtown oyster bar, and almost instantly the former had the latter in a headlock and punched away at his leisure. Police broke up the fight, but tensions ran high in the streets for weeks, until Sullivan formally challenged Hyer, as had become customary, with an advertisement in the *New York Herald*. Sullivan claimed Hyer assaulted him without cause, accused him of cowardice, and declared, "I can 'flax him out' without any exertion." Hyer responded with an equally inflammatory card of his own. They signed "Articles of Agreement" on August 7, 1848.[19]

The Hyer–Sullivan fight marked the full maturity of the American ring. All of the rituals were in place, the challenges, the legalistic Articles of Agreement – "the said James Sullivan agrees to fight the said Thomas Hyer a fair stand up fight, half minute time, in a twenty-four feet roped ring, according to the new rules as laid down in the *Fistiana* for 1848" – the very dimensions of the ring and the tying of each man's colors to the ropes. During the six months between signing articles and the battle itself, fights constantly threatened to break out on the streets and in the saloons. Opponents of the ring argued that boxing encouraged violence, while proponents claimed that the ring allowed men to set aside pistols and knives for civilized combat, an argument that would go on for decades without resolution. The boxers' preparation, however, was surprisingly disciplined. Two months before the battle, both men went into intense training, including running, punching the heavy bag, workouts with light dumbells, a rigid diet consisting mostly of meat; and sex was absolutely forbidden. Hyer, one account concluded, lead "a perfectly chaste and abstemious life"; he was a model "to many who claim to lead up middle aisles, and to sound the key note in sacred psalmistry." One of the great paradoxes of boxing is how men in training embraced rigid self-discipline in the name of violence. Indeed, the attraction of the sport, its very aesthetic, depended on the balance between bloody passion and refined technique.[20]

Of course prizefighting itself was illegal, and as thousands prepared to disembark from Baltimore for a secret location, local magistrates decided to break up the fight. They descended on Poole's Island in Chesapeake Bay, where Hyer and Sullivan were ready for battle. However, the boxers' friends arrived before the law, rescued the two heroes, and in a final humiliation, the boat carrying the constables ran aground. So two vessels with about 100 passengers each headed for Still Pond Heights, Kent County, Maryland, where a ring was quickly raised. The sun was going down and light snow covered the ground, but at ten minutes after four, Yankee Sullivan threw his hat in the ring, followed moments later by Hyer's. Both men had their hair cropped close to avoid having it pulled, and each tied his colors to the ropes, the stars and stripes for Hyer, emerald green with white spots for Sullivan. Sullivan won the coin toss and he chose to have his back to the sun, Hyer looking straight into the light. In an age before weight classifications, the disparity in their size was striking, Sullivan giving away four inches and thirty pounds. But both were impressive, and one newspaper declared, "They were as finely developed in every muscle as their physical capacity could reach, and the bounding confidence which sparkled fiercely in their eyes, showed that their spirits and courage were at their highest mark."[21]

Size and youth won. Sullivan depended on his wrestling craft to weaken the larger man, but he simply was not able to handle Hyer. The fight lasted a little over seventeen minutes, just ten of it actual fighting, with both men well bloodied, Sullivan's face "clotted with gore," Hyer's chest covered with his own blood from having the skin under his right eye lanced by his cornermen to prevent it from closing. In the end, "Hyer let fly both right and left in Sullivan's face, who, though he could not return it, took it without wincing in the least. Hyer then rushed him to the ropes again, and after a short struggle there, threw him and fell heavily upon him ... When he was taken off, Sullivan was found to be entirely exhausted." "The Great $10,000 Match" was over, but the celebrations and news coverage lasted for days, and was unlike anything seen before. Above all, boxing had come of age, and a series of great matches would follow. Still, prizefighting remained almost entirely a sport for working-class men, roundly condemned by respectable bourgeois Victorians.[22]

For the next decade, the ring thrived in big American cities. A series of notable champions and exciting matches kept boxing in the news. In an era of heavy immigration, especially in the wake of the Irish Famine, the fights were often billed as having ethnic enmities at their core. But equally important, a group of great fighters emerged. Yankee Sullivan and Tom Hyer – the acknowledged "Champion of America" – continued to command attention, and new men like John Morrissey from Troy, New York, and John C. Heenan, the "Benicia Boy," fought spectacular matches. And too, the border between street fighting and the ring remained vague, as toughs like "Butcher" Bill Poole, whose reputation was earned entirely in brawls, challenged regular ring fighters like Morrissey to street battles. Poole was a notorious nativist, and when he was murdered on the streets of New York, it was easy for partisans to portray it as an assassination of a patriot by Irish zealots, led by Morrissey. "Good-bye, boys, I die a true American," Poole allegedly gasped, then died. His life and violent end were both emblematic of the turbulent male subculture of the urban streets that nurtured the ring.[23]

The culture of boxing continued to expand, with saloons opening where the fancy could gather in East Coast and Great Lakes cities, and all the way to San Francisco. More and more newspapers gave the ring ink, and a new compendium of ring history, *The American Fistiana* saw the light of day. And new professors of pugilism gave lessons and presented sparring exhibitions, introducing young fans to the "manly art." But to thrive, boxing needed real prize ring bouts, championship matches, and a newcomer, John Morrissey, was eager to oblige. The son of Irish immigrants, raised in Troy, New York, a veteran of brutal street fights, he became a logical opponent for Tom Hyer. But Hyer wanted a match for far more money than Morrissey's backers could raise, so the next logical opponent was Yankee Sullivan. Sullivan was old enough to be Morrissey's father, and he also gave away twenty-five pounds to the young man. They met on September 1, 1853, in the tiny town of Boston Corners, where New York, Massachusetts, and Connecticut all bordered each other, ideal because legal jurisdiction was easily muddled.[24]

Roughly 6,000 fans made their way to the secret venue. From the outset, Yankee Sullivan pummeled Morrissey, leaving him a bloody mess, but Old Smoke was renowned for his "bottom," his sheer ability to take punishment and keep going. In round forty-two, long into their second hour of fighting, chaos broke loose. Some say it began with Morrissey choking Sullivan on the ropes; others claimed that Old Smoke's seconds broke the ring to create a diversion and save their man. In any event, Sullivan found himself fighting Orville "Awful" Gardiner, and thus too busy to come up to scratch at the call of time. Morrissey was awarded the fight by default. The *New York Times* thundered,

> With the benefits of a diffused education; with a press strong in upholding the moral amenities of life; with a clergy devout, sincere and energetic in the discharge of their duties, and a public sentiment opposed to animal brutality in any shape; with these and similar influences at work, it is inexplicable, deplorable, humiliating that an exhibition such as the contest between Morrissey and Sullivan could have occurred …

Sullivan spent a week in the Lennox, Massachusetts, jail; Morrissey paid a $1,200 fine to stay out of prison.[25]

Several big matches followed the Morrissey–Sullivan battle, but it was Old Smoke the fancy wanted to see, since his victory over Yankee Sullivan (and Hyer's refusal to fight) made him champion. A young challenger emerged in California, John C. Heenan, originally from Morrissey's hometown of Troy, New York, but long since employed by the Pacific Steamship Company in Benicia, California. In recent non-championship fights, Buffalo, New York, had become a favorite staging ground. Fans came by rail, and from there took steamers to secret locations in Canada. Morrissey and Heenan signed articles of agreement, did their training, and finally, thousands of fans purchased tickets marked "excursion" or "picnic." On October 20, 1858, they made the journey to Long Point, Canada West. Morrissey was the heavy favorite, not only because Heenan was younger and less experienced, but also because Heenan had developed an ugly abscess on his leg. The fight in some ways resembled Sullivan and Morrissey. For ten rounds, Heenan punched and threw Morrissey, making an ugly red mask of the older man's face. But finally, in his weakened condition, Heenan ran out of steam, and Morrissey, despite the beating he took, had enough left to finish off the challenger. "Probably no human eye will ever look upon so much rowdyism, villainy, scoundrelism and boiled-down viciousness, concentrated upon so small a space," thundered the *New York Herald Tribune*. Yet that city gave Heenan and Morrissey an unmatched reception.[26]

The international acme of bare knuckle fighting came in 1861, with the "Great Contest for the Championship of the World." Benecia Boy Heenan signed articles to fight the Champion of England, Tom Sayers, near London. When Tom Molineaux fought Tom Crib, the American reaction was all but nonexistent. But now there was an explosion of excitement. That Heenan was white and of Irish parentage mattered. But that wasn't all. Many Americans were now familiar with the ring. The sport no longer seemed outlandish, foreign; it had been domesticated, though stigmatized as a lower-class dissipation. Besides, this was a great match. Tom Sayers, small at five foot eight, about 155 pounds, had beaten every conceivable challenger. Heenan was the perfect foil, young, aggressive, and big, 200 pounds on a six foot two inch frame. They fought forty-two rounds, over two hours; one of Sayer's arms was broken, and Heenan was nearly blind from blows around his eyes. It was not really possible to say that either fighter was ahead, but it was a moot point anyway. A contingent of Hampshire constables marched in to break up the fight, and the battle ended in chaos, the referee declaring it a draw. With time Americans came to believe that Heenan was robbed, but in the immediate aftermath, the fight was a touchstone of American nationalism at the very moment the American nation fell apart with secession and civil war.[27]

The dozen years between the Sullivan–Hyer fight in 1849 and Heenan–Sayers in 1861 was the golden age of American bare-knuckle fighting. The ring became an emblem of working-class masculinity. Far from the steady habits and sober self-control of the Victorian middle class, the prize ring with its attendant culture of gambling, drinking, and carousing represented an anti-Victorian world. The great boxers were avatars of masculine toughness, their pictures hung in countless saloons in Northern cities. The ring was part of a web of male institutions, including volunteer fire companies, ethnic gangs, urban political wards, unions, fraternal organizations, brothels, saloons, and gambling dens. Boxing, with its emphasis on violence, toughness, physical skill, and bloody competition, was at the heart of this male subculture.[28]

The fate of three of the great champions of the era gives a sense of the possibilities and dangers of this world. After losing to John Morrissey, Yankee Sullivan left New York for San Francisco. There he again practiced his skills at electoral abuse – intimidating voters, ballot box stuffing with fake returns. But Sullivan was unlucky. A group of businessmen organized a vigilance committee. They deported several political opponents (including a few other pugilists who had moved out from New York), hanged others, and arrested Yankee Sullivan. A few days later, he was found dead in his cell; his life bled out from a gash on his arm. Tom Hyer stayed in New York, engaged in various nativist causes, got into some street battles, and generally played the role of a great man in local saloons. But soon his health broke down; in his mid-forties, he died of heart failure. John Morrissey, on the other hand, became involved in politics and forged connections with Tammany Hall. Always interested in gambling, Morrissey opened one then another Faro parlor. Before long, he organized several very wealthy businessmen in turning Saratoga, New York, into a gambling mecca, including opening Saratoga racetrack. Late in life, Morrissey became a United States congressman. Never quite regarded as a "gentleman," he was nonetheless a successful man.[29]

Decline and Rebirth

The years following the Sayers–Heenan battle were mixed ones for the prize ring. On the positive side, the Civil War turned out to be a crucible of American sports. Bringing hundreds of thousands of men together in camp and field allowed sporting ideals to spread. Officers often encouraged men to keep in shape with competitive games, so baseball, cricket, and "football" grew enormously in popularity. Boxing too gained converts, and stories were told of violent conflicts between men settled amicably with the gloves. In the aftermath of war, new fans deepened boxing's appeal.[30]

But much as in England forty years earlier, the ring's problems multiplied. The old Victorian suspicion of men apart from families, drinking, gambling, and carousing did not go away. And increasing disorder inside and outside the ropes gave boxing's enemies new opportunities to police the ring. Fixed fights became common in the 1860s and 1870s. The violence that the ring supposedly tamed and contained often broke loose, as factionalism led to increasing numbers of battles ending in free-for-alls. "The referee failed to be killed" was a euphemism for the rare battle that came off without extramural bloodletting. Many fights ended with the principals and even fans in jail. Then, too, boxing always depended on great champions, charismatic, larger-than-life figures, and for whatever reason, few seemed to be around in the 1860s and 1870s.[31]

Tom Sayers was one of the last English bare-knucklers. In 1867, the Marquess of Queensberry Rules were published in London, and soon ran the English ring. The Queensberry Rules forbade wrestling and mandated three-minute rounds with one minute of rest between them, a ten-second knock-down rule, and gloved fists. Claims of order and safety notwithstanding, the new rules arguably made the sport more dangerous, since gloves protected the hands against broken bones, allowing far more punches to the head. Twenty more years would pass in America before the Queensberry

Rules became the norm for championship fights. But the new rules were prizefighting's route to semi-respectability. While matches increasingly came under suspicion for being fixed – that is, if they weren't stopped by the police before they even got going – the Queensberry Rules offered a way forward, first in "exhibitions" on indoor stages, then finally for championship bouts. The key figure in the transformation would emerge in the late 1870s, a charismatic young Bostonian of Irish parentage. John L. Sullivan possessed enormous strength, stamina, and athletic talent. He also had a knack for self-promotion. Before he was done, he was arguably America's first modern athlete, earning over a million dollars along the way and becoming one of the most famous men in America.[32]

Sullivan originally hoped to be a professional baseball player, but while still in his teens his fistic talents emerged along with his temper. Soon he was challenging local heroes in glove affairs on Boston stages and winning. He went on tour, offering to pay any man $50, then $100, who could stay in the ring with him for three rounds. Sullivan also fought a couple of battles under bare-knuckle rules, but his first big fight came in 1882. Champion Paddy Ryan, having first admonished the youth to "go and get a reputation," now took on Sullivan. They fought in Mississippi City on the Gulf Coast, thousands of men finding their way to the hastily built risers surrounding the ring. The "Boston Strong Boy" surprised everyone. "When Sullivan struck me," Ryan said after the fight, "I thought that a telegraph pole had been shoved against me endways." The fight lasted about ten minutes in nine rounds. Sullivan pressed Ryan relentlessly, and knocked him around the ring. For the next ten years the Strong Boy was the toast of the ring. More, he transformed the sport.[33]

With his fame as champion secure, Sullivan realized that there was far more money to be made fighting with gloves than in bare-knuckle battles. In fact, he challenged all comers after defeating Ryan, but he insisted he would wear gloves so as to not be arrested. More important, Sullivan began touring the country in traveling shows and circuses. Night after night, he came on stage, challenged anyone in the house to fight him for three or four or six rounds under the Queensberry Rules, and of course he never met anything like his match. He made thousands of dollars a week, and before his career ended, he was the first American athlete to earn one million dollars.[34]

Local police rarely broke up Queensberry fights. Part of the reason was that for the first time, prominent American men had begun advocating rough sports. Games like college football where boys died with alarming frequency, for example, became metaphors for the stern self-testing needed in an era that extolled social Darwinism. Men of means like young Theodore Roosevelt and the psychologist G. Stanley Hall spoke openly of their fascination with the ring. Even some men of faith joined the chorus for "Muscular Christianity." In other words, Sullivan entered the pugilistic world when many of the old Victorian strictures against the ring were loosening, even as the means to stage and promote his "Knocking-Out-Tours" – railroads, telegraphs, and cheap newspaper coverage – proliferated. And he understood that glove fights could attract a richer, more prestigious clientele – "gentlemen," as he put it – rather than the old fancy crowd.[35]

There was one more reason beyond Sullivan's charismatic personality and athletic ability that he was so successful. He was assisted by his archenemy, Richard Kyle Fox. In truth, it is unclear if the two really disliked each other, but they clearly understood that their enmity was profitable. Richard Kyle Fox was a Scotch immigrant, a journalist, who, after knocking around New York's newspaper world for a while, purchased the old *National Police Gazette*. The *Gazette* had been around since the 1850s and mostly covered news of crime and police work. When Fox purchased it at the end of the 1870s, he saw an opportunity to market something new – a weekly journal printed on shocking pink paper and aimed at working-class men, filled with outrageous stories and sketches. Fox invented crazy competitions like haircutting and water-drinking contests; he covered the scandals of the theater world (the stage of course was still considered disreputable); he reprinted lurid pictures and descriptions of lynchings from the South and Midwest, gory murders filled the *Gazette*'s pages, sexual improprieties with pictures of scantily clad women, and all sorts of images and stories tilting toward sexual sadism and masochism appeared, and sports, too, especially rough sports like boxing. The *Police Gazette* became known as "the barber's bible" because places where men gathered – pool halls, saloons, barbershops – went out of their way to subscribe and to keep back copies on file. Past the turn of the century, the *Gazette* was the source for all that was tawdry and scandalous, and newspaper moguls like William Randolph Hurst and Joseph Pulitzer learned much about shaping and marketing news from Richard Kyle Fox.[36]

So of course the *Gazette* became the leading organ for stories about the ring. But far more than just disseminate fight results and ring gossip, Fox effectively was now America's boxing promoter. Because boxing remained illegal until the 1890s, there was no easy way to rationalize the sport. But the *Gazette* became the ring's trusted authority above all others, so that Fox could simply declare particular fighters to be champions then arrange new matches and publicize them. More, he created six weight classifications. These did not exist in the earlier bare-knuckle era, as witnessed by Yankee Sullivan and Tom Sayers fighting men who outweighed them by thirty or forty pounds. But beginning about 1890, as the bare-knuckle era ended and the Queensberry Rules took hold, boxing men recognized the categories of flyweight, bantamweight, lightweight, welterweight, middleweight, and heavyweight, mainly because the *Gazette* legitimated them. More, Fox used his money to promote the ring, offering up stakes money for particular boxers, conferring championship belts, turning the *Gazette* offices into the central location where fights were arranged, drumming up interest in matches.[37]

Early in John L. Sullivan's career, as the story goes, Fox was at an elegant saloon and he called the Strong Boy over to his table. "Let Fox come to me" was Sullivan's reply. Years later, in the last great bare-knuckle battle, the 1889 fight between Sullivan and Jake Kilrain, their public antagonism boiled over. Fox designed a new heavyweight championship belt in 1887, with diamonds and gold and 200 ounces of silver. He would award it to the next title holder, but he insisted that the *Gazette* offices arrange all fights for the belt, that he, Fox, be stakeholder, and that the *Gazette* have a reporter at ringside. Meanwhile, Kilrain, whose career had risen swiftly, published a challenge to Sullivan for $5,000 a side. Sullivan was still healing from a broken arm, so he rejected the challenge. With that Fox declared Kilrain the new champion, and on June 4 awarded him the belt in a public ceremony. Sullivan said that when he won it from Kilrain, he would offer it as a trophy to the bootblacks of New York. Then several of Sullivan's friends and backers had an even larger and more elegant belt made, and they presented it to him in Boston.[38]

The End of the Bare-Knuckle Era

Sullivan saw little reason to fight another bare-knuckle match. No one believed, at least not yet, that Kilrain was his match, and the Boston Strong Boy continued to make a fortune fighting brief glove fights against local chumps. He went out on another "knocking-out tour," but within a few months, England's Charley Mitchell humiliated him in a glove fight. Worse, Sullivan's drinking and lack of training made it obvious that he was overweight and out of shape. Derided by critics for his long absence from the prize ring, Sullivan and Kilrain finally agreed to a bare-knuckle match on July 8, 1889, in Richburg, Mississippi. After months of ballyhoo in the press, they met on a sweltering day. The sun blistered their backs as they fought for three hours. Sullivan had trained hard and worked himself back into shape; reporters said he looked like the champion of old. Midway through, drinking a concoction of tea and whiskey between rounds, Sullivan began to vomit. Word around the ring was that his stomach retained the whiskey but rejected the tea. He won in seventy-five rounds, handily. His return north was a triumph as he stopped in town after town to receive the plaudits of fans.[39]

No one knew for sure at the time, but the bare-knuckle era had just ended. Sullivan would not fight a championship battle again for three years, and when he finally published a challenge to all comers, he insisted on the Queensberry Rules. So confident was he that such a fight would be legal that he openly named the venue – New Orleans, at the new Olympic Club. Wealthy men in tuxedoes sat at ringside on September 24, 1892. Sullivan lost his title to James J. Corbett from San Francisco that night, part of a festival of championships of various weight classes, all fought under the new rules. The glove era had begun – no more running from the law, or at least not as much. Boxing certainly never lost the taint of corruption, but finally the prize ring had emerged from the underworld into semi-respectability.[40]

NOTES

1 Pindar, *The Odes of Pindar*, translated by Sir John Sandys (Cambridge, MA: Harvard University Press, 1978), pp. 79–80.

2 *The Aeneid of Virgil*, translated by Rolfe Humphries (New York: Scribner, 1951), pp. 125–29.

3 Dennis Brailsford, *Sport and Society, Elizabeth to Anne* (Toronto: Routledge & K. Paul, 1969), pp. 198–216; Robert W. Malcolmson, *Popular Recreations in English Society, 1700–1850* (Cambridge: Cambridge University Press, 1973), chapter 1.

4 Pierce Egan, *Boxiana, Or Sketches of Ancient and Modern Pugilism* (London: Sherwood, Neely and Jones, 1829), pp. 8–23; John Ford, *Prize Fighting, The Age of Regency Boximania* (South Brunswick, NJ: Great Albion Books, 1971), chapter 6.

5 Malcolmson, pp. 42–43, 145–46; Ford, pp. 131–36.

6 Egan, pp. 360–71, 386–420.

7 Elliott J. Gorn, *The Manly Art: Bare-Knuckle Prize Fighting in America* (Ithaca NY: Cornell University Press, 1986), pp. 24–33.

8 Gorn, pp. 34–36.

9 Elliott J. Gorn, "'Gouge and Bite, Pull Hair and Scratch': The Social Significance of Fighting in the Southern Backcountry," *American Historical Review* 90(1) (Feb. 1985), pp. 18–43.

10 *New York Evening Post*, July 10, 1923; Gorn, *Manly Art*, pp. 36–40.

11 Gorn, *Manly Art*, pp. 40–47; *American Fistiana* (New York, 1860), pp. 6–9; Anon, *The Life and Battles of Yankee Sullivan* (New York, 1854), pp. 88–89.

12 *American Fistiana*, pp. 8–11; *Life and Battles of Yankee Sullivan*, pp. 16–24; Gorn *Manly Art*, pp. 69–73.

13 Gorn, *Manly Art*, pp. 73–81; Thomas McDade, "Death in the Afternoon," *Westchester Historian*, 46 (Winter 1970), pp. 1–6.

14 Gorn, *Manly Art*, pp. 76–79; *New York Herald*, extra edition, November 28, 1842.

15 Gorn, *Manly Art*, pp. 76–80.

16 *Life and Battles of Yankee Sullivan*, pp. 29–33; *American Fistiana*, pp. 16–17.

17 *New York Herald*, February 6, 1849.

18 Gorn, *Manly Art*, pp. 83–85, 136–38. Also see Gorn, "'Good-Bye Boys, I Die a True American': Homicide, Nativism, and Working-Class Culture in Antebellum New York City," *Journal of American History*, 74(2) (Sept. 1987), pp. 388–410.

19 *American Fistiana* (1849 edition), pp. 2–4; Ed James, *The Life and Battles of Yankee Sullivan* (New York, n.d.), pp. 33–36, 63–64; Ed James, *The Life of Tom Hyer* (New York, 1849), p. 1.

20 Gorn, *Manly Art*, pp. 86–91.

21 *American Fistiana* (1849), pp. 22–28; *Life and Battles of Yankee Sullivan*, pp. 50–60; Gorn, *Manly Art*, pp. 90–92.

22 Gorn, *Manly Art*, pp. 92–97.

23 Gorn, *The Manly Art*, chapter 3; Gorn, "Good-Bye Boys."

24 Ed James, *The Life and Battles of John Morrissey* (New York, 1879), pp. 3–10.

25 *Life and Battles of Yankee Sullivan*, pp. 64–71; James, *Life of Morrissey*, pp. 6–12; *American Fistiana* (1860), pp. 20–22.

26 *American Fistiana*, pp. 58–61; James, *Life of Morrissey*, pp. 13–19; Anon, *The Lives and Battles of Tom Sayers and John C. Heenan, "The Benicia Boy,"* (New York, 1860), pp. 63–67.

27 *Lives of Sayers and Heenan*, pp. 69–71, 77–86, 91–94; Ed James, *The Life and Battles of John C. Heenan: The Hero of Farnborough* (New York, 1879), pp. 6–18.

28 Gorn, *Manly Art*, chapter 4.

29 Ibid.

30 Ibid, pp. 159–64.

31 Ibid, pp. 164–78.

32 Duffield Osborn, "A Defense of Pugilism," *North American Review*, v46, April 1888, pp. 434–35; John Boyle O'Reilly, *Ethics of Boxing and Manly Sports* (Boston, MA: Ticknor, 1888).

33 On the Ryan fight, see Michael T. Isenberg, *John L. Sullivan and His America* (Urbana, IL: University of Illinois Press, 1988), pp. 102–13; for Sullivan's life and times, see his autobiography, *John L. Sullivan, The Life and Reminiscences of a 19th Century Gladiator* (Boston, 1892).

34 Isenberg, chapters 5–7.

35 Gorn, *Manly Art*, chapter 6; Elliott Gorn and Warren Goldstein, *A Brief History of American Sports* (New York: University of Illinois Press, 1993), chapter 3.

36 Elliott Gorn, "The Wicked World: The *National Police Gazette* and Gilded Age America," *Media Studies Journal*, v 6, Winter 1992, pp. 1–15.

37 Gorn, *Manly Art*, pp. 207–29.

38 Ibid., pp. 230–32.

39 William Edgar Harding, *Life and Battles of Jake Kilrain* (New York: R.K. Fox, 1888), pp. 5–29; Sullivan, *Life and Reminiscences*, chapters 9, 10; Isenberg, pp. 257–80; Gorn, *Manly Art*, pp. 207–37.

40 Gorn, *Manly Art*, pp. 237–54; Isenberg, chapters 11, 12.

SELECT BIBLIOGRAPHY

Anon, *American Fistiana*, New York: H. Johnson, 1849, 1860, 1873.

Egan, P., *Boxiana, Or Sketches of Ancient and Modern Pugilism*, London: Sherwood, Neely and Jones, 1829.

Ford, J., *Prize Fighting: The Age of Regency Boximania*, Newton Abbot, UK: David and Charles, 1971.

Gorn, E. J., *The Manly Art: Bare-Knuckle Fighting in America*, Ithaca, NY: Cornell University Press, 1986.

Isenberg, M. T., *John L. Sullivan and His America*, Urbana, IL: University of Illinois Press, 1988.

Mee, B., *Bare Fists: The History of Bare-Knuckle Prize Fighting*, New York: Overlook Press, 2001.

White, P., *The Legends of Bare-Knuckle Boxing*, New York: Overlook Press, 2015.

3

ADAM CHILL

Jem Mace and the Making of Modern Boxing

In the news media and in popular histories of boxing, James "Jem" Mace is often called "the father of modern boxing."[1] As the first world champion and pioneer of a new style focused on speed and skill rather than stamina, Mace's place in the pantheon of boxing seems assured. In contrast to popular histories, however, academic discussions of boxing in the late nineteenth century have tended to obscure or diminish Mace's role in the transformation of the sport. Instead, scholars have debated whether the new "code" of boxing – with the order provided by timed and limited rounds – succeeded because of a downward diffusion of bourgeois values or because of workers' attraction to a less violent sport.[2] These academic histories have also tended to downplay the role of flamboyant and highly visible individual figures like Mace in spreading boxing's popularity worldwide and have instead attributed it to local conditions in the individual nations where it spread. Sometimes lost in these accounts of the sport's development is the role of innovative boxers such as Mace.

Jem Mace was a pivotal figure in the late nineteenth-century transformation of boxing, which included the widespread adoption of the Queensberry Rules and the sport's growing popularity in the United States and Australia. Mace was a product of the London Prize Ring, but, as the old Prize Ring began to collapse, he took advantage of new commercial opportunities and became an innovator in the development of a new form of boxing that encouraged spectators to appreciate speed and defensive fighting rather than stamina and brute force. When he traveled to the United States and Australia, he took with him this new approach.

Jem Mace was born in 1831, the son of a Norfolk blacksmith and a tenant of the Windham family, descendants of William Windham, an early nineteenth-century defender of boxing. After a brief career as a local boxer, Mace in 1850 joined the traveling boxing booth of Nat Langham, the only fighter to defeat the great English champion Tom Sayers. For a fixed wage of £2 per week, he fought "all comers" at stops around the country.

He proved a great success on tour, and so Langham brought him to his London pub with the intention of, as Mace put it, "giving exhibitions of my skill before his aristocratic patrons." In addition to exhibitions, Mace and other young boxers served as bodyguards for Langham's aristocratic customers when they ventured out to enjoy the pleasures of the old West End.[3] He also fought several times in the Prize Ring in the late 1850s and, despite being briefly ostracized by the boxing community after missing a match with Mike Madden, won the English championship from Sam Hurst on June 18, 1861. Like champions since the late eighteenth century, Mace's rise had relied on the patronage of an established boxer, a connection with a pugilism pub, and service to aristocrats.

While Mace was a product of the old London Prize Ring, he also operated in new ways that anticipated the mass entertainment spectacles of the late nineteenth and early twentieth centuries. As historian of sport Neil Tranter has argued, urbanization and a gradual rise in wages in the second half of the nineteenth century opened up commercial opportunities for popular amusements in Britain. Circuses were among the more successful of these.[4] Mace had experience with the circus and as a traveling performer even before joining with Langham's boxing booth and used these to great effect throughout his career. He had left home at age fifteen, playing a violin for money as he traveled with a Romany group into which his uncle had married. This was the source for the persistent – and unsubstantiated – rumor that Mace was Romany. More significantly, this early familiarity and comfort with the life of a traveling performer helped position him to take advantage of new opportunities for popular amusements.[5] Several months before his fight with Hurst in 1861, Mace signed a contract to join Pablo Fanque's well-known Circus Royal, earning £70 per week for a six-week tour.[6] After winning a tough bout with Tom King in January of the following year, Mace joined Frederick Ginnett's circus for six months, earning the enormous sum of £1,300 while staying in first-class accommodation. In August, he opened the Jem Mace Circus at Brighton. The circus featured the "Jem Mace Brass Band" and such diversions as "the Cannon King," a man who could catch a ball fired from a cannon. It was successful enough that Mace ultimately decided to give up his public house, the King John.[7]

Mace continued to fight bouts in the early 1860s but the long decline of the London Prize Ring was accelerating. The expansion of the railway network had briefly buoyed the sport as railway companies chartered special trains for large parties of fight-goers, but the corruption and criminality that had plagued the Prize Ring since the 1820s undermined this outlet as well. As journalist Henry Downes Miles lamented, "it had become the practice of the floating fraternity of thieves, mobsmen, and 'roughs' … to stream to the railway station whenever they got a hint of a Ring 'excursion.' "⁸ This remark was prompted by the appearance of a mob at a railway station before a fight between Mace and Joe Goss in September 1863. The following year, authorities in Ireland prevented a scheduled bout between Mace and American champion Tom Coburn and attempted to take the two fighters into custody. After Mace escaped arrest, Coburn dishonestly tried to seize the stakes. Finally, in 1867, Mace was followed by agents of the London Metropolitan Police and arrested before a fight with Ned O'Baldwin.⁹

While the London Prize Ring was experiencing its "death-knell" and Mace was evading the authorities, he continued to diversify his interests. His pursuits outside the Prize Ring were part of the transformation of sport in the last third of the nineteenth century. In 1865, he was contracted to serve as an "instructor in boxing" at the Myrtle Street Gymnasium in Liverpool.¹⁰ This new facility and the National Olympian Association formed there in November 1865 were part of a growing movement in Britain and elsewhere to promote athletic activity to revive the "health" of the nation.¹¹ The growth of support for such amateur athletic competition would become an important part of the transformation of boxing.

In addition to helping popularize the new amateur athletic culture, Mace also played a key role in the development of the rules that would govern amateur, and then professional, boxing. Among the more popular attractions of the "Jem Mace Circus" were sparring contests in which Mace announced that he would pay £5 to a local challenger who fought him with gloves and could survive three timed rounds without being knocked out. Since the eighteenth-century origins of English boxing, pugilists had frequently fought local toughs for money and, in other cases, often sparred with gloves, but Mace's combination of these elements with timed rounds was, as he described it, "a bit of a novelty."¹² Mace's sparring contests at his circus preceded the publication of the Marquess of Queensberry rules and, as his biographer notes, "only in his willingness to countenance wrestling did Mace fail to anticipate the Queensberry Rules."¹³ While John Chambers, the author of the Queensberry Rules, did not seek advice from Mace, it seems likely that he would have been aware of Mace's well-publicized sparring contests.

Part of the reason Mace developed this new form of exhibition was that it showcased his particular talents: speed, technique, and punching accuracy. As Mace noted in his memoir, he often "would play with [his opponent] till half-way through the second round." Then, he dropped the unlucky novice by "feinting with the right, and then landing the left upon ... 'the mark.' "¹⁴ Mace's contemporaries frequently remarked on his speed and technique in prizefights as well. In his account of Mace's championship bout with Sam Hurst in 1861, journalist Henry Downes Miles wrote that Mace "delivered both hands with the quickness of lightning, and with tremendous force [while his] attack and defense ... were in every respect indicative of the master."[15] Whereas earlier fighters such as Daniel Mendoza and Jem Belcher had been known for speed and science, Mace used this skill to help transform boxing in the late nineteenth century as "finesse" became more valued.[16] As historian Dennis Brailsford has noted, Mace's style had a profound influence on a generation of accomplished Australian boxers and, through them (and his own tours), in the United States.[17] Mace developed his boxing exhibitions as a showcase for this new style. The basic form of the exhibition – timed rounds with gloves and a defined endpoint – highlighted his speed and skill. These were the elements of the "briefer" and "less painful" contests that transformed first amateur and then professional boxing in the 1890s and 1900s.[18]

Mace's popular moniker, "the father of modern boxing," owes less to his skill or innovations in exhibitions than to his role in developing the sport in Australia and the United States. With the London Prize Ring virtually moribund by the late 1860s, Mace, like many preeminent English fighters, decided to travel to the United States, where a vibrant sporting scene flourished. In 1869 he arrived in New York City.[19] He spent several months at Harry Hill's famous pub, one of the new centers of American sporting culture, giving exhibitions of Greek statuary (a popular diversion in which an exhibitor displayed his body for an audience) and playing his violin. In May 1870, Mace – now aged thirty-eight – fought English boxer Tom Allen in New Orleans for $2,500. Mace won decisively, showcasing his movement and speed.[20]

Allen had been acknowledged as the Champion of America, and so Mace now claimed to be the Champion of the World. As an English champion, however, Mace was threatened repeatedly and therefore escaped to the American West. In California and Nevada, he participated in innovative matches that prefigured key elements of twentieth-century fights. In Virginia City, Nevada, millionaire John W. Mackay arranged a match between Mace and Bill Davis in December 1876, for $1,000 and a gold trophy belt. This was a new kind of professional fight: the bout was contested for eight timed rounds with gloves in an indoor arena that was lit electrically. Advanced tickets were sold for $5, and a large crowd witnessed Mace defeat Davis.[21] Although Mace did not organize it, the fact that it was fought in timed rounds and with gloves meant that the match was much like Mace's sparring exhibitions. These elements, and a referee counting landed punches, suggested new possibilities for the sport of boxing. Mace continued to enjoy success on the West Coast, touring in California and even fighting Bill Davis again in San Francisco. After winning this second match, he was presented with a "solid silver brick" from "the Miners of California."[22]

Despite his successes in the American West, Mace decided to travel to Australia, where he arrived in March of 1877.[23] In Australia, which produced some of the most outstanding boxers of the late nineteenth and early twentieth centuries, Mace achieved great success in training gloved fighters to use speed and technique to defeat their foes. His innovations as a showman and as a boxer, which were so important to the transformation of the sport, helped him succeed in Australia. By 1881, as several American newspapers reported, Mace was "one of the wealthiest settlers in Australia."[24]

There were few experienced pugilists living in Australia at the time of Mace's arrival. A fighter from Sydney named Larry Foley was his first pupil. Mace trained Foley for a match against Abe Hicken, who claimed to be the Champion of Australia and cannily avoided challenges for his title. When Foley defeated him in early 1879, the way was open for Mace, as the recognized trainer of the new champion, to revive and dominate boxing in Australia.[25] As Bob Petersen has argued, the Australian boxing "scene became a little organized" after Mace's arrival. Mace "converted" Foley, who became an influential trainer in Sydney, "to the use of gloves and the Queensberry Rules" and to Mace's style, emphasizing speed and technique.[26] Foley's pub in Sydney, the White Horse, became a center for training in this new style and produced some of the best fighters in the world in the late nineteenth and early twentieth centuries. While ceding Sydney to Foley, Mace continued to train boxers in Melbourne and, in March 1882, traveled to New Zealand to scout for boxing talent. In Timaru, he organized boxing and wrestling competitions. The matches in the boxing competition stipulated twelve rounds, with the winner determined by Mace if there was not a knockout. The winner of the middleweight competition was an unknown local named Bob Fitzsimmons.[27]

Fitzsimmons, the future heavyweight champion of the world, was Mace's most famous discovery and one of the biggest contributing factors to his being labeled "the father of modern boxing." Although his discovery of Fitzsimmons was undoubtedly important, Mace's real legacy is that he was the successful and highly visible champion of a new style of fighting. He was not the only boxer of his era to promote gloved and timed boxing that emphasized skill over brute force, but his career provides particularly clear and compelling evidence that the revolution in boxing was driven by individuals as much as by structural forces. For that reason, Mace deserves a central place in academic accounts of the revolution in modern sports that characterized the late nineteenth century.

NOTES

1 For a recent example, see Harry Pearson, "Ring of romance surrounding the hardmen of the boxing booths," *Guardian*, August 5, 2010; accessed August 15, 2013, at www.theguardian.com/sport/blog/2010/aug/06/boxing-booths-romance-harry-pearson.

2 This debate is summarized in Neil Tranter, *Sport, Economy and Society in Britain 1750–1914* (Cambridge: Cambridge University Press, 1998), 13–31.

3 Jem Mace, *Fifty Years a Fighter: The Life Story of Jem Mace (retired Champion of the World) Told by Himself* (London: C. Arthur Peterson, Limited, 1908), 42, 46, 50–51.

4 Tranter, *Sport in Britain*, 7.

5 Mace, *Fifty Years a Fighter*, 22–23.

6 Graham Gordon, *Master of the Ring: The Extraordinary Life of Jem Mace Father of Boxing and the First Worldwide Sports Star* (Wrea Green, UK: Milo Books, 2007), 65.

7 Ibid., 89, 98. Mace, *Fifty Years a Fighter*, 92–94. An advertisement from May 3, 1863, still named the house as "Jem Mace's Old King John's," but apologized for "the unavoidable absence of the gallant Jem." *Bell's Life in London*, May 3, 1863.

8 Henry Downes Miles, *Pugilistica: the history of British boxing containing lives of the most celebrated pugilists; full reports of their battles from contemporary newspapers, with authentic portraits, personal anecdotes, and sketches of the principal patrons of the prize ring, forming a complete history of the ring from Fig and Broughton, 1719–40, to the last championship battle between King and Heenan, in December 1863*, vol. 3 (London: Weldon, 1880–81; reprint, Edinburgh: John Grant, 1906), 471.

9 Mace, *Fifty Years a Fighter*, 156–58, 187–93; Gordon, *Master of the Ring*, 132–33, 172.

10 Gordon, *Master of the Ring*, 146.

11 Debbie Challis, *Archealogy of Race: The Eugenic Ideas of Francis Galton and Flinders Petrie* (London: Bloombury Academic, 2013), 63–64.

12 Mace, *Fifty Years a Fighter*, 94.

13 Gordon, *Master of the Ring*, 190.

14 "The mark" was "a spot … about where the third button of the waistcoat falls." Mace, *Fifty Years a Fighter*, 96.

15 Miles, *Puglistica*, vol. 3, 461–62.

16 Dennis Brailsford, *British Sport: A Social History* (Cambridge: Lutterworth Press, 1997), 88.

17 Dennis Brailsford, *Bareknuckles: A Social History of Prize-fighting* (Cambridge: Lutterworth Press, 1988), 153.

18 Stan Shipley, "Boxing," in Tony Mason, ed., *Sport in Britain: A Social History* (Cambridge: Cambridge University Press, 1989), 90.

19 Mace, *Fifty Years a Fighter*, 194.

20 Gordon, *Master of the Ring*, 219.

21 *Reno Evening Gazette*, December 12 and 18, 1876; Mace, *Fifty Years a Fighter*, 200–207; Gordon, *Master of the Ring*, 208.

22 Mace, *Fifty Years a Fighter*, 211.

23 Gordon, *Master of the Ring*, 284.
24 For instance, the *Salt Lake Daily Tribune*, May 19, 1881.
25 Gordon, *Master of the Ring*, 287–97. Before the match, *Bell's Life in London and Sporting Chronicle* noted that Foley would "of course benefit from [Mace's] vast skill," *Bell's Life in London and Sporting Chronicle*, March 29, 1879.
26 Bob Petersen, "Boxing, Australia," in John Nauright and Charles Parrish, eds, *Sports around the World: History, Culture, and Practice*, volume 1 (Santa Barbara, California: ABC-CLIO, LLC, 2012), 363.
27 Gordon, *Master of the Ring*, 316.

4

LOUIS MOORE

Race and Boxing in the Nineteenth Century

The two splendid sluggers stood stripped and ready to battle. On one side stood George Godfrey, also known as "Old Chocolate," a 170-pound heavyweight with the skills of a lightweight, trained in the manly art of self-defense by the renowned black boxing master John B. Bailey. His opponent, the massive John L. Sullivan, an Irish American known as the "Boston Strong Boy," honed his skills in battles in Boston's bars and could knock any man down with one violent punch.[1] This was to be a bare-knuckle battle for boasting rights in Boston, the sweet scientist versus the slugger. Styles make fights. But beyond bragging rights and a clash of styles, this bout represented a test of racial superiority, black versus white. This was always the case when two men of a different hue sparred. How could it not be? White men put so much stock in the sport. Domination in the ring, so they thought, was part of their racial rights. "This contest of men with padded gloves on their hands is a sport that belongs unequally to the English-speaking race," the American novelist Jack London once observed. "No genius or philosopher devised it and persuaded the race to adopt it as the racial sport of sports. It is as deep as our consciousness and is woven into the fibers of our being. It grew as our very language grew. It is an instinctive passion of race."[2] At $2 a head – a high price in 1880 – the room was jam-packed with men ready to see ferocious fisticuffs. But something odd happened. One of Sullivan's friends left the room and came back with a police officer. Why would he retrieve the police? Before states sanctioned prizefighting, fighters always made sure the law wasn't near. A stopped bout meant no money. Nevertheless, the officer arrived and straight away sought Sullivan. He reportedly told the Boston Strong Boy, "I know you, you are a South end fellow, and if I were you would not spar." With that, Sullivan got up, left the room, and demanded everyone get their money back. But Sullivan's actions were not about following the law; this was about adhering to a social custom. Someone did not want the two men of a different hue to mix.

Godfrey could not understand this slight. "If I had quit like that," Godfrey claimed, "it would have been a crime." True. A black man could not leave a white audience hanging. Besides, if boxing represented manhood, how could a man refuse to fight a person on the account of skin color? Godfrey pondered this question for the next twenty years of his life. Every time he thought of Sullivan, the man who won the heavyweight crown in 1882 and declared he would not fight a black man, Godfrey could not come to terms with Sullivan's racist stance. For ten years, Sullivan denied Godfrey an opportunity to battle. Sullivan went as far as reportedly telling Godfrey, "George, when I get ready to fight rats, dogs, pigs and niggers, I'll give you the first chance."[3] Sullivan, a staunch racist, never fought a black man. Godfrey, however, showed no fear. He preferred fighting white men. "I am satisfied to fight white men," he said. "They are easier whipped."[4] Sullivan was the only white fighter to permanently draw the color line against Godfrey. Usually, money and pride were enough to force a man to drop his personal Jim Crow. Despite a willingness to concede to a white man's color line, fans, both black and white, would much rather see contests of racial superiority than to see two men of the same hue duke it out, especially two black fighters. Why? What explains a need for a color line and a desire to see interracial battles for superiority? I will explore the meaning of race in the ring during the nineteenth century by examining John L. Sullivan's color line and the reaction of the black press to black fighter George Dixon's featherweight championship.

The boxing ring represented an arena for racial dialogue, and interracial fights both challenged and proved ideologies about manliness and racial superiority. In brief, whites looked at the ring as a symbol of superiority, and blacks viewed the ring as a sign of equality. But with so much at stake, and so much to prove, mixed bouts became the great paradox of the prize ring. People wanted to see interracial contests but did not want to deal with the reality of their outcomes. In 1902, a white writer announced, "The recent agitation against the matching of white pugilists against colored pugilist is no novelty, as the practice has been the cause of much ill feeling and controversy ever since boxing secured a firm foothold in this country." He continued, "Despite the hatred of the colored boxer when pitted against a white man fight promoters and managers continue matching them, and undoubtedly, will continue doing so as long as the sport remains alive." "Human nature," the writer reasoned, "is a peculiar thing, especially with reference to race prejudice in pugilism ... When a crackerjack color fighter challenges a white man and the latter does not accept, the den cry will immediately be raised that the white man is afraid to fight. That is, the public abuses him for dodging the colored man, and when finally he is sandbagged into meeting the colored man the latter falls heir to the abuse previously heaped upon the head of the white fighter."[5] Whites hated the implication of social equality in the ring, but wanted to prove superiority.

What did the color line mean? The color line in boxing indicated who had and did not have racial privileges, and no fighter better understood that reality than John L. Sullivan. In 1882, when Sullivan won the heavyweight championship, he knew enough about race, power, and privilege to proclaim that he would never fight a black man.[6] In July 1883, for example, when he heard people making a fuss about C.A.C. Smith, a black fighter from Port Huron, Michigan ("The Michigan Thunderbolt"), Sullivan told a newspaper, "I won't fight a darky for there is no credit in licking a coon." Sullivan's color line, however, was not good enough for some white writers. The *Cincinnati Enquirer*'s John B. McCormick ("Macon") argued that Sullivan had to establish the "superiority of the Caucasian race over the negro [sic] race." McCormick also remarked, "By the way, if Sullivan's reply to the darky Smith who wants to fight him for the championship is correctly reported John L has queer ideas on the subject of his 'rights and privileges.' "[7] As a white champion, Sullivan knew exactly what his "rights and privileges" were. He did not have to face a black man to prove superiority; he need only keep them from fighting for the championship. This extended to men who had questionable whiteness. In 1884, for example, Sullivan declined to fight Mervine Thompson – Thompson was an octoroon passing as a white man in order to fight Sullivan – because he heard a rumor Thompson had black blood. Although Thompson came close to tricking Sullivan into a fight, the champion did his racial research. After three months of investigation – he asked his friends in Boston to confirm rumors of Thompson's race – Sullivan told a Louisville reporter, "I've never seen him, but one of the boys seen him in Boston when he was wrestling there and they say he's a nigger. He's been charged with it and never denied it. In Boston he went by the name of O'Donnell, but they say his real name's Thompson."[8] Why the need for a staunch color line? Racial pride. As one writer in 1889 put it, "Suppose John should go down before black fists – but that cannot be thought of. The American eagle would go off and starve itself to death."[9] In short, the heavyweight championship stood for white supremacy, and if a white fighter lost the title, it would cause a racial upheaval to social order. Throughout Sullivan's reign as champion, he continued to deny other worthy black fighters a claim to the title, including Peter Jackson, the greatest heavyweight of his generation.

For four years Peter Jackson, the West Indian-born black heavyweight who won the Australian championship in 1886, tried to get Sullivan in the ring.[10] Jackson, surprisingly, even had members of the white press supporting his cause. A writer for the *New York Sun* argued, "there must be no bigotry in champions' methods. They cannot be choosers anymore than can beggars. There can therefore be no professional tolerance of Mr. SULLIVAN'S refusal to contest the fistic palm with the Australian black man, Jackson, who has just wiped the Pacific Slope with JOSEPHUS McAULIFFE." He continued with his rant, reminding readers, "the Constitution forbids any discrimination against the dark skin."[11] Why did whites seem comfortable with a potential Jackson victory over Sullivan? Jackson, as scholar Gerald Early notes, was a "spiritual mulatto."[12] In other words, although he had black skin, the white press liked to think Jackson had a white soul. He had supposed middle-class mannerism, he dressed respectable, spoke the King's English, and did not brag or boast. The *San Francisco Call* remembered, "Jackson was one of the most popular men that ever entered the ring. He could not be induced to discuss his own prowess and never belittled an opponent. Although not well educated he mixed so much with men of the world that he has acquired a polished manner."[13] In 1923, boxing writer Trevor Wignall added, "Even to-day he is frequently called the whitest black man who ever lived." Wignall also observed, "Jackson's main assets were his excellent behaviour and his sportsmanlike qualities. He was never known to boast." On another occasion Wignall concluded that Jackson "was black only in hue; otherwise he was as white as snow."[14] But a white soul was not a white skin, and character did not count more than color. The only way he would fight Jackson, Sullivan remarked, was if he could "fight the nigger with nothing but a baseball bat."[15]

Sullivan's overt racism toward Jackson irritated the respectable sensibilites of the black press. In comparing Jackson to Sullivan, the *Indianapolis Freeman* remarked, "Peter Jackson, unlike our country's blowhard and 'ham' actor, John L. Sullivan, is a gentleman and a fighter." The editor also argued, "MR. JOHN L. SULLIVAN, the 'bean eating' gladiator, of Boston, objects to standing up before a Negro. All right, nobody objects but coming from a man instead of an animal, how silly and purile [sic] such an objection would seem."[16] They saw Jackson as a middle-class black hero, and the black press hoped that one day their own class would trump their race. If Jackson could get over, so could they. But Sullivan's ardent racism reinforced to the black middle class the unbendable power of the color line.

In hopes of enticing Sullivan into the ring, Jackson kept fighting the best white fighters.[17] In May 1891, Jackson fought one of the most important fights of his career when he battled San Francisco native Jim Corbett for $10,000. But things did not go as planned for Jackson. The sixty-one-round no-contest – the club stopped the fight because neither man had enough energy to finish off his opponent – convinced white fans that Corbett was worthy of a title shot with Sullivan. In September 1892, Corbett outclassed Sullivan to win the championship. Jackson wasted very little time in challenging the new champion, because he believed that Corbett had forfeited his racial privileges when he fought him the first time. Jackson told a London reporter, "If Sullivan had worsted Corbett I would have nothing to say, for I know that Sullivan declines to meet colored men. But it is not so with Corbett ... I am willing to fight anywhere except in towns where the color line is drawn."[18] In July 1893, Jackson's manager, Parson Davies, signed articles of agreement with Corbett for a match to take place after Corbett's battle with white contender Charles Mitchell. The articles also stipulated the fight had to take place above the Mason–Dixon line.[19] The following January, Corbett knocked out Mitchell, opening the gate for the Jackson bout.

A few months after Corbett defeated Mitchell, however, Corbett closed the door on a fight with Jackson. The champion claimed he would fight Jackson, but insisted on battling in Jacksonville, Florida. Corbett knew that Jackson feared the possibility of southern racial violence, and even if Jackson agreed to fight in the South, Jim Crow would constantly embarrass the proud black man. In the end, on account of his racial pride, Jackson refused to fight. He told a reporter, "It is pretty plain that all this is merely an advertising dodge of Corbett's. I am tired of being a party to it, and I quit right here."[20] Waiting for Corbett to fight, however, effectively ended Jackson's career. The distraught Jackson did not engage in a prizefight until 1898. He died in 1901 of tuberculosis.

To be sure, there were not too many places in America where a black man could get a fair shake in the ring. Most clubs had white ownership and white fans that created a hostile work environment for black fighters. At arenas across America, white fans called black fighters "Niggers," "coons," and even threatened to kill black fighters, especially in interracial contests. One reporter noted, "On the night of the fight as soon as the colored boxer puts up his hands voices from all parts of the house can be heard advising the white man to knock the negro's [sic] head off."[21] In 1888, for example, George Godfrey declined a $1,000 offer to fight a white opponent in New York, and cited, "I do not recall an instance of where a colored man went up against a white man in Gotham and was fairly treated. There is a prejudice there among the sporting people against the colored race, and I firmly believe that they would 'kick' against me on principle."[22] On another occasion, after Godfrey read that Jack Ashton (white) wanted to fight in Providence, Rhode Island, Godfrey asked, "How long is it since they had a good old-fashioned lynching down in Providence?" "Don't you think they are itching for one now?" In 1891, champion George Dixon recalled that in Boston, "it is not many years ago since I first stepped into a ring in this city, but even then a colored man would be considered crazy if he went to fight a white man outside of a club-room. He would surely have been killed, or brutally injured, if he made the least attempt to win."[23] Despite the racism in the ring, the arena, and the press, the black fighter triumphed.

By 1884, the *Boston Globe* observed, "Colored pugs are prevalent all over the country, the latest addition to the [Baltimore] Black Stars and [Cincinnati] Black Diamonds being [Boston] George Godfrey, who wants to do battle with Jake Kilrain, [Port Huron] C.A.C. Smith, the Western Terror who was used as a shuttlecock by that other colored gentleman [Rochester] Mervin Thompson, and a "Pop" Lewis of Chicago."[24] Soon, black participation became black domination, and in 1890 a well-known New York sporting man observed, "It looks as if the pugilistic fever which has raged so fiercely in this country for the past ten years is abating. The prominence darky fighters have assumed in the ring is contributing to this effect ... The shadow of the black man's fist is over the ring."[25] In 1890, featherweight George Dixon became the first and only black fighter to win a championship during the nineteenth century.

Born in 1870, in Halifax, Dixon – he moved to Boston as a teenager – was the greatest fighter of his generation. From the moment he turned pro at seventeen, it was clear that the teenager was the best bantamweight in Boston. Within three years of turning pro, he fought 115-pound Cal McCarthy for the American featherweight championship. Although he did not defeat McCarthy in their epic seventy-round draw, Dixon's showing in that fight earned him a title shot in London against England's bantamweight champion, Nunc Wallace (105 pounds). At the age of twenty, in a battle for the championship and $2,500, Dixon defeated his foe, becoming the first black world champion. The following year, Dixon beat McCarthy for the American featherweight title and also Australian featherweight champion, Abe Willis. Three championships, on three continents, the best boxer in the world. Why allow the diminutive Dixon to fight for a championship but exclude black heavyweights? There is no clear-cut answer, but money might explain some of the reason. Ultimately, Sullivan could deny a black challenger a fight and lose a lucrative payday, because he made most of his money through charging admission at his exhibitions across the country. As one writer explained in 1888, "It was he [Sullivan] who developed the knock out blow, and by making four, six, and ten rounds contests as full of uncertainly and danger as the old finish fights made pugilism the remunerative profession that it is now."[26] Without the power of heavyweights, white featherweight fighters could do no such thing. A fight with Dixon made financial sense.

Instead of openly lamenting that Dixon's championship status challenged white superiority, some white writers wondered if Dixon could help advance the black race. After discussing the prowess of Dixon and Jackson, one white writer openly questioned, "Is the colored race to step in and steal the laurels from us white folk in this way? If so, perhaps those to whom only brute force can appeal as an argument may begin to respect the negro [sic] as a man and brother."[27] In his 1897 book *The Squared Circle*, John B. McCormick wrote, "The Negroes of America should be staunch upholders of the ring, for it has done more toward enabling them to command the respect of the masses than even the ballot." He also believed that through boxing, blacks "found that 'equality' that is so much harped about in political platforms and speeches, but is so seldom in the ordinary walks and avocations of life."[28] McCormick asserted a common belief within the white middle class that the brawny athletic achievements of the individual had social and political capital.

In a sport-crazed America that looked to boxing battles to represent ideas about racial superiority and authority, Dixon was a perfect example of black advancement. A number of black newspapermen also bought into the belief that sports could lead to change in society. After Dixon won his first championship, an editorial in the *Cleveland Gazette* quipped, "Will someone tell us what this country is coming to? Young Afro-Americans are winning prizes at colleges, riding winning horses in leading races and winning world's championships in the pugilistic arena. There are other avenues in which we have excelled in the past year. Isn't all this an indication of progress?"[29] In the *New York Age*, in an articled entitled "In the College and the Prize Ring," the editorialist argued that through boxer's victories, "We shall yet convince the Anglo-Saxons that they are not the monopolized salt of the earth and sea." He closed his thought by saying, "may the best man win."[30]

For the black middle class, the most powerful symbol of Dixon's ability to change the race question occurred in 1892, when, just a few months after Homer Plessey filed his famous anti-Jim Crow case against segregated street cars, Dixon momentarily knocked out Jim Crow in New Orleans.[31] As a stipulation of his contract for the $7,500 championship fight against Jack Skelly – he also had a $5,000 side bet – Dixon required the New Orleans Olympic Club to integrate the stadium and reserve seating for black fans. With Dixon's threat to boycott, the club desegregated and set aside 1,000 seats for blacks. Roughly 300 black men supported their champion and screamed loudly when Dixon knocked out Skelly in the eighth round.[32] After Dixon won the fight, a *Cleveland Gazette* writer cheered, "Dixon has given a favorite Dixie prejudice a terrible black eye." He also boasted, "It is all right to see one white man whip another in the south, but to pay one's dollars and a number of them, too, to see a Hamite 'whip the stuffing out of' a white man, even if he is a northerner, and then give the former an ovation, is something more than the average southerner can or will stand."[33] Due to the violent nature of Dixon's victory, and its potential racial implications, the white New Orleans press urged white clubs to bar interracial matches. The *Times-Democrat* reasoned it "a mistake to match a negro [sic] and a white man, a mistake to bring the races together on any terms of equality, even in the prize ring."[34] The *Cleveland Gazette*, however, retorted, "We thought the sight of one of our race pummeling the face and body of even a northern white pugilist would be more than they could stand, and our readers can now see how correct our estimate was."[35] Indeed, the writer was correct. New Orleans was the last holdout to draw the color line in the Deep South.

The more black men won interracial fights, however, the more white fighters, managers, and politicians across the country drew the color line. Neither Dixon's victories, nor the black championships after him – Joe Gans, Joe Walcott, Al Brown ("Dixie Kid"), and Jack Johnson won championships between 1902 and 1908 – helped race relations in America or advance black equality. In fact, during the Progressive Era, whites tried their best to end interracial fights. By the beginning of the twentieth century, most major cities drew the color line in the ring. Between 1900 and 1908, for example, St. Louis, Milwaukee, Baltimore, Louisville, Los Angeles, Pittsburgh, and Chicago drew the color line.[36] Why did lawmakers in cities and states outside of the Deep South stop mixed bouts? Lawmakers wanted to protect white superiority. Before Baltimore banned mixed bouts in 1902 – lightweight champion Joe Gans had just defeated a white fighter – a local police officer said that "the sight of the negro [sic] defeating a white man in the prize ring had a most unwholesome effect upon the rough colored element and tended to make that element unruly and disorderly."[37] Each black victory in the ring against white opponents stripped away at the notion of white male social and political authority, a confidence that partly hinged on whites' racial belief in physical superiority. In other words, in the nineteenth and into the early twentieth century, race ruled the ring.

NOTES

1 For the best biographic treatment of Sullivan and manhood, see Michael T. Isenberg, *John L. Sullivan and His America* (Chicago, IL: University of Illinois Press, 1994).
2 Jack London, "Thirst for Prize Fighting Deep-Seated in Human Race," *The Los Angeles Times*, June 29, 1910.
3 "Mack's Melange," *New Orleans Picayune*, January 5, 1902.

4 "Latest Sporting Topics," *National Police Gazette*, January 31, 1891.

5 "The Color Line with Pugilists," *Baltimore American*, December 2, 1902.

6 See Isenberg, *John L. Sullivan and His America.*

7 Macon, "Pugilistic Points," *Cincinnati Enquirer*, July 22, 1883. He also noted, "If Sullivan is a true Bostonian he will not persist in a determination not to slug a man merely because of his color."

8 "A Talk With the Best Man," *Louisville Courier Journal*, May 4, 1884. In the interview he added, "They won't let us spar in Ohio; I'll do this: Chicago is about 800 miles from Cleveland and I'll pay Thompson's expenses there and give him $1,000 and the gate receipts if he will stand up in front of me. He wants the right to use wrestling powers. Well, I'll give him that too. I'll fight by the London rules and lick him."

9 "John L. Sullivan," *Philadelphia Inquirer*, December 1, 1889.

10 David Wiggins, "Peter Jackson and the Elusive Heavyweight Championship: A Black Athlete's Struggle Against the Late Nineteenth-Century Color Line," in *Glory Bound: Black Athletes in a White America* (Syracuse, NY: Syracuse University Press, 1997), 34–57.

11 "Black Cloud on the Pacific," *New York Sun*, January 4, 1889.

12 Gerald Early, *The Culture of Bruising: Essays on Prizefighting, Literature, and Modern American Culture* (Hopewell, NJ: The Ecco Press, 1994), 15.

13 "Peter Jackson Returns to his Former Home, *San Francisco Call*, March 22, 1900.

14 Trevor Wignall, *The Story of Boxing* (London: Hutchinson and Co, 1923), 253, 257; Trevor Wignall, *The Sweet Science* (London: Chapman and Hall), 195.

15 "New Orleans Notes," *Indianapolis Freeman*, July 5, 1890.

16 "Editorial," *Indianapolis Freeman*, June 11, 1892; "Editorial," *Indianapolis Freeman*, January 5, 1889.

17 Wiggins, 44–46.

18 "Jackson and Corbett," *New York Herald*, October 16, 1892.

19 "Corbett Caught Up," *Chicago Tribune*, July 11, 1892.

20 "Corbett Signs Articles," *New York Herald*, September 9, 1894.

21 George Siler, "Color Line in Prizefighting," *Chicago Tribune*, November 4, 1900.

22 "Godfrey's Decision," *Boston Globe*, April 13, 1888.

23 "The Colored Man in the Ring," *Boston Globe*, April 19, 1891.

24 "Sporting Notes," *Boston Globe*, May 4, 1884.

25 "Arenic," *San Francisco Chronicle*, March 3, 1890.

26 "Prodigal Pugilists," *New York Herald*, December 23, 1888.

27 Quoted in "The Negro as a Prize Fighter," *Indianapolis Freeman*, July 19, 1890.

28 Macon, 52, 230.

29 "Pugilism and Progress," *Cleveland Gazette*, July 5, 1890.

30 "In the College and the Prize Ring," *New York Age*, December 20, 1890.

31 "Dixon and Prejudice," *Cleveland Gazette*, March 12, 1892. In March of that year, a hotel in Buffalo, New York, drew the color line on the champion and refused him service in their restaurant. Dixon vigorously protested until the hotel served the champ with white guests.

32 Dale A. Somers, *The Rise of Sport in New Orleans, 1850–1900* (Baton Rouge, LA: Louisiana State University Press, 1972), 179–83.

33 "Dixon and Jim Crow," *Cleveland Gazette*, September 10, 1892.

34 Somers, 181.

35 "Editorial," *Cleveland Gazette*, September 17, 1892.

36 "Negro Boxers Barred," *Trenton Times*, March 2, 1902; "Barring the Black Boxer," *Boston Globe*, February 5, 1904; "Black Boxers May Sue," *Chicago Tribune*, February 11, 1904; "Colored Boxers Becoming Scarce," *National Police Gazette*, November 3, 1906; "Seconds Often Save Fights," *Springfield Republican*, January 30, 1910; "Jack Johnson Cannot Fight in New York," *Salt Lake Herald*, August 23, 1912; "Negro Pugilists Barred Hereafter," *New Orleans Picayune*, January 19, 1913.

37 "Is Boxing Doomed Here?," *Baltimore Sun*, November 18, 1902.

5

COLLEEN AYCOCK

Joe Gans and His Contemporaries

Joe Gans fought for almost twenty years during the 1890s and 1900s, in an era when his contemporaries included such fistic luminaries as Jim Corbett, George Dixon, Bob Fitzsimmons, Joe Walcott, Sam Langford, and Jack Johnson. Among these greats, it was Joe Gans who earned the moniker the "Old Master" and who was recognized well into the twentieth century as one of the best fighters who ever lived. In the book *Black Dynamite*, ring historian Nat Fleischer referred to Dixon, Walcott, and Gans as the "Three Colored Aces," recognizing them not only for their incomparable skills but also for their achievements as firsts of their race to be crowned world champions: featherweight, welterweight, and lightweight. Not to be overlooked would be the fourth Ace: heavyweight champion Jack Johnson. These boxers were so enormously talented that their likes would not be seen again until Joe Louis' heyday and later, with the elite fighters of the last half of the twentieth century. These early champions were innovative and tough as nails. They seemed to possess superhuman endurance. They could take on back-to-back opponents or endure finish fights scheduled for forty-five rounds under harsh elements. While Dixon's and Gans's lives were short – Dixon died at the age of thirty-nine and Gans at thirty-five – their careers were long. The most telling difference between the "Aces" and their white contemporaries was the number of their bouts: Stanley Ketchel, who died in 1910, had a total of sixty-four; Jim Corbett and Jim Jeffries each had less than twenty-five. Dixon, Walcott, and Gans each had over 150; Langford over 300. By comparison to modern boxers, Sugar Ray Leonard had forty professional fights; Joe Frazier, thirty-seven; Muhammad Ali, sixty-one; and Floyd Mayweather, Jr., fifty. As will be seen, black boxers had to fight continually as they invariably received smaller paydays.

The era after the Civil War was one of uncertain promise for the first generation of free black men born on American soil and for the flood of immigrants into the war-free country. Ethnic enclaves urbanized, ensuring social relief and fostering a cultural pride tested on the ring stage.

Although boxing had generally operated on the fringe of society, boxers were now able to climb the social and economic ladders in ways unimagined before the 1890s. Most men entering the workforce toiled as laborers, clocking in ten- to twelve-hour days, six days a week. Boxers went from town to town, making and accepting challenges, building up their reputations and earning their livings as prizefighters. They were wildly popular, fit specimens of manhood in a new age celebrating physical culture. They were attractive and intelligent and earned in their prize winnings above-average incomes. Although the language used to report interracial matches was still full of slurs and insults, front-page photographs of the decorated black champions in 1901 and 1902 brought old social notions of racial superiority and new, practical issues of fair play into question. Was a particular race naturally superior? Could interracial contests be held "on the level"? What was to be the division of the spoils? The ring mixed the races and churned out champions who challenged the status quo.

For boxers publicity and mobility were necessary for advancement. The development of the railroad moved people of all socioeconomic groups around the country, and boxers spent much of their time riding the rails. Once boxers had beaten their local competitors, they traveled to sporting venues in Baltimore, Philly, Boston, New York, Chicago, New Orleans, Louisville, Denver, Butte, Portland, and San Francisco in search of fights of regional and national importance.

George Pullman of Chicago, builder of luxury sleeper cars, created one of the largest all-black employee pools, drawing workers from the rural south to the industrial north. During Gans' professional life, the highly esteemed Pullman's Porters earned an average monthly pay of $34, less than a night's pay for a working pugilist. Like the professional boxers who were also highly esteemed, porters bore the cost of their gear (a uniform cost $15), their meals on the road, and the loss of their income if they were injured on the job.[1] Railroad jobs were segregated; but as these worker-travelers crossed the country, they interacted with all segments of society, bringing stories of the day home to family and friends. News of the "Aces" and their championship wins, first about George Dixon, then Joe Walcott and Joe Gans, was sensational.

Canadian-born George "Little Chocolate" Dixon began fighting in Nova Scotia in 1886. When the family moved to Boston, Dixon began his climb to boxing's upper rank with manager Tom O'Rourke. Dixon's best fighting weight was between 110 and 115 pounds, but he generally fought anyone 135 and below. Dixon's star was already bright when Joe Gans began boxing. In 1890, Dixon's first challenge for America's top honor resulted in a seventy-round, four-hour and forty-minute draw in Boston with Cal McCarthy. In the summer Dixon beat British champion Nunc Wallace in England. In 1891 he came back to beat Cal McCarthy and Australia's Abe Willis. After these victories, O'Rourke declared Dixon world champion. Richard K. Fox, owner-publisher of the *Police Gazette*, concurred and awarded Dixon a featherweight belt in March 1893.

Although Dixon was a popular fighter, he didn't grab national media attention until the 1892 Carnival of Champions in New Orleans for a winner-take-all purse of an astounding (for that time) $17,500. His opponent Jack Skelly fared poorly in the battle, and the image coming out of New Orleans that a black man had beaten a white man to a pulp, and to the humiliating applause of the crowd, disturbed some news editors.[2] Papers announced it "a mistake to bring the races together on any terms of equality, even in the prize ring."[3]

Like many good fighters, Dixon was forced to make disadvantageous deals in order to get work. In 1893 George Siddons was originally matched with Jack Skelly for a $1,500 fight. (Siddons is remembered for his epic seventy-seven and fifty-five-round battles in 1889 with Kid Lavigne.) When Skelly bowed out, Dixon filled in. George Siddons would only fight the new opponent for a prearranged draw for twelve rounds, demanding that he (Siddons) be left on his feet at the end. It is important to keep in mind when examining the records that many such "arrangements" may have been made with these early fighters known for their speed, powerful punch, clever defense, ring generalship, and minority status.

Also important for boxing history is the fact that Dixon's contests would prepare a slate of fighters for Joe Gans. Dixon fought Siddons in 1893; Gans would fight Siddons (also to a draw) in 1895. Dixon fought Walter Edgerton, the "Kentucky Rosebud" five times from 1892 through 1894. Gans would kick-start his career fighting the Rosebud in 1895. Dixon fought Young Griffo three times in 1894 and 1895; Gans fought him in 1895 and 1897. Dixon fought Martin Flaherty in 1891 and 1896; Flaherty was past his prime when Gans fought him in 1901. Dixon fought Mike Leonard in 1895; Gans fought him in 1897. Like Gans, Dixon would first lose to Frank Erne and then win, in 1895 and 1897 respectively. Gans would fight Erne for the lightweight title and lose in 1900 and fight again and win in 1902 in Canada. Dixon fought Terry McGovern and Dal Hawkins, both opponents who would see significant ring action later with Joe Gans.

After a string of wins and big-moneyed fights, Dixon lost his featherweight title to Terry McGovern in 1900, and continued with a string of losses. That same year Joe Gans fought McGovern in a fixed fight, and Walcott "quit" in a fixed fight against Tommy West at Madison Square Garden when boxing's mafia showed its unpleasant face, demanding that Walcott lose in the eleventh round.

While waiting for opportunities and making ends meet, Dixon formed a vaudeville and athletic company that toured the country, allowing locals to challenge the champion in four-round bouts. During these tours Dixon mentored Joe Walcott into ring fame.

Nat Fleischer called Walcott the greatest welterweight in history. The "Barbados Demon" fought from 1890 to 1911. Walcott sailed from the West Indies as a cabin boy to Boston when he was fifteen. There Walcott met talent and opportunity in Dixon and his manager Tom O'Rourke. A natural welter at 145 pounds, but only 5'1½", Walcott battled for the lightweight crown, twice unsuccessfully against George "Kid" Lavigne. In the first battle in New York in 1895, the contract specified that Walcott could win only by a KO. In 1897 in San Francisco, Walcott's stamina was compromised when forced to reduce his weight to meet the champion below 135 pounds. Walcott would move up to the welter class and win the championship in Ft. Erie, Ontario in December 1901. Six months later, Joe Gans would beat Frank Erne there to become the first American-born black to win a world championship title.

At the height of their careers, Gans and his band of brothers were called the most powerful and clever boxers who ever fought. Gans called Dixon the best fighter he ever saw, and Dixon said the same about Gans. After watching Walcott, lightweight champion Jack McAuliffe said he never could have beaten Walcott in his prime. These fighters would be revered later by Joe Louis and mentioned in the literature of Ernest Hemingway. They were the early masters of the science of boxing, and they were so superior that when they lost, it was assumed that the referee gave their opponents the advantage (which often happened) or that the fights were fixed.

In 1903, Dixon, America's Napoleon of the ring, went to England to look for paying fights. Independence Day that year found Gans and Walcott in copper-mine rich Butte, Montana defending their titles in a triple-crown event (middleweight, welterweight, and lightweight). With them were stable mates Young Peter Jackson and Jack Johnson. Middleweight Tommy Ryan would successfully defend his crown against John Willy of England, July 3. Welterweight Walcott, who had been fighting at 150 pounds, weighed in at 142 to meet the local Mose LaFontise on July 4. LaFontise had trained with another Butte local, Stanley Ketchel. It appeared that LaFontise was evenly matched with Walcott in the first two rounds; but in the third round, LaFontise was knocked out with such lightning speed that few saw the punch. When asked about the knockout blow in the dressing room, Walcott said it was a left followed by a right cross that landed as LaFontise was going down. LaFontise was retching in his dressing room and could not recall the blow.

The week's festivities culminated in Joe Gans' lightweight title defense with Buddy King of Denver on July 5, in the old ball park where seats had been built for the Jimmy Britt–Jack O'Keefe fight three weeks earlier. The day was spoiled by rain and by the failure of the preliminary fight to materialize between Young Peter Jackson and Ike Hayes when Hayes' manager failed to post the guarantee money to ensure his fighter's appearance. Spectators sat in the rain from 1.30 to 3.00 before Gans and King appeared. King tried to fight at long range but could not land a punch to Gans's head, and he was helpless when it came to in-fighting. Gans drew first blood, landing a straight right to King's mouth in the second round. The match sputtered along until a spectator yelled, "Fake!" which caused Gans to stop and invite the hooligan into the ring where he would show him something about fakes; and Walcott followed up, offering to "lick" any man in the crowd. The crowd hushed, and Gans went back to business, trying for a knockout in the fourth. King hung on. Gans won in the fifth by putting his opponent down three times with hard rights to the jaw and left uppercuts to the face.

Gans would finish out 1903 losing to future heavyweight great Sam Langford, in Philly.[4] Gans had fought the day before in Baltimore and it seemed that his energy was spent. After the fight Gans explained to Langford how he could have won more decisively. Like Dixon, Langford maintained that Gans was the greatest fighter he had ever seen. Walcott would fight Langford to a draw in 1904. Walcott, Gans, and Langford fought each other only once each.

In 1904, Gans fought Walcott for the welterweight crown. The battle at Woodward's Pavilion, Valencia Street, San Francisco, was considered one of the best old-time fights, going the distance of twenty action-packed rounds. The referee declared it a draw due to Walcott's aggressiveness, but gave more rounds to Gans. The next day, Spider Kelly wrote about the fight saying that Gans had it all: a hard punch, extreme cleverness, and courage. "Did you ever see a terrier play with a rat? That's the way Gans operated that night with Wolcott [sic]," wrote Kelly.[5]

While newsmen and editors wrote about "fair-minded sportsmen," few comments addressed the subject of fair pay. After saying that he would never fight a Negro, Jimmy Britt of San Francisco decided that the only way he could be called a world champion was to fight Joe Gans. The contract was signed in San Francisco on October 8, 1904, for a fight to be held on October 31, with Gans set to receive the lesser share. The contract stipulated: "the fighters are to receive sixty percent of the gross receipts as follows: Britt is to receive seventy-five percent if he wins, fifty percent if it is a draw and fifty percent if he loses; Gans to receive fifty percent if he wins, fifty percent if it is a draw, and twenty-five percent if he loses."[6] When it came to paying the black boxers, even their white managers cut them short. The same unequal pay would be demanded by Battling Nelson for fighting Gans.

It would take three gladiatorial bouts for Oscar Nelson to finally beat Joe Gans and end the Master's career. Gans won their first bout in 1906 after forty-two grueling rounds, and Nelson won their last two bouts in 1908, when Gans was in the late stages of tuberculosis.

The September 3, 1906, forty-two-round Gans–Nelson lightweight title bout is one of the most notable fights in boxing history for many reasons. It was the first "Great Fight of the Century" and Tex Rickard's first of many colossal promotions. The Texas cattle drover turned sheriff would go on to promote the Jack Johnson–Jim Jeffries fight, to guide Jack Dempsey into the million-dollar stratosphere, and to establish Madison Square Garden as the premier boxing arena in the United States.[7] Tex Rickard generated such hype for the 1906 match that news editors admitted that nothing but a presidential election could garner more sustained interest than the Labor Day fight. It helped that Rickard posted the largest purse of its time: $30,000 in gold.

The Gans–Nelson fight was the first "Great White Hope" fight. Newspapers caricatured Nelson with a grin, wild straw hair and square jaw, a good-looking Viking-type with manly resolve to wrest the title away from Joe Gans. Nelson bragged of his "coon graveyard," pointing to a list of black boxers he had defeated.[8] Illustrators depicted Gans with a sloping forehead, bug eyes, and thick white lips, a demeaning caricature of a handsome man. The parodies were the reverse of reality. Gans was known as a gentleman his entire life; Nelson was labeled famously as a classic "brute" by Jack London in his literary coverage of an earlier Nelson–Britt fight in California.[9]

Like Johnson in 1910, Oscar "Battling" Nelson had youth and stamina on his side in 1906. Nelson was a rugged brawler, like Elbows McFadden, another tough lightweight who fought Gans in long, memorable battles. Nelson was known for his brutal head butts and his superhuman ability to shake off punishing blows to his own head. However, Nelson had never faced a boxer with a punch as hard as Gans's. When Gans knocked out an opponent, it often looked as if he had been shot dead. In the fight following the first Nelson bout, Gans would be filmed knocking out Kid Herman with the hand he had broken four months earlier. Herman remained unconscious for five minutes.

The 1906 Gans bout was remarkable in that it highlighted the acceptance of a black man who was one of the first to assert his full rights and expect equal treatment. Thus the Rev. Francis Grimke, one of the founders of the National Association for the Advancement of Colored People, said that Gans had done more to help "the cause" than Booker T. Washington.[10] The

San Francisco Examiner noted that Gans was the "first Negro ever allowed to take a drink in a Goldfield saloon."[11] Newspapers singled out Gans for his popularity with the Goldfield miners, who saw him as a man of their own ilk. In the haggling over details in the Articles of Agreement regarding division of the purse, Gans told the press that he expected Nelson's manager to follow "the rules of the game." He stated emphatically, "I know what I am entitled to and I will not let such a fellow as Nolan do me out of my just rights."[12] These are words of strength and conviction coming from a public figure at the top of the sport he dominated. Gans even said to Nolan, "I wish I could get you in the ring instead of Nelson."[13] Publicity of the contest in and out of the ring put the entire country on edge.

The day before combat, trains from San Francisco and Chicago hauled Pullman coaches full of high-roller spectators into Goldfield on new track laid specifically for the match. The betting odds favored Gans. But the examining physician said that although both fighters were ready, Nelson was in better shape, in that Gans was feverish.

Those favoring Gans to win thought the fight would be over in fewer than ten rounds. Both men, however, would be tested if the fight went the forty-five-round limit. While Gans had fought many twenty- and twenty-five-round battles with formidable opponents, none had gone over twenty-five rounds. Nelson had only gone twenty rounds on three occasions. Although both fighters had scored plenty of knockouts, this match would see none. Was Gans still at his prime? Or would Nelson's desire to take the meat from the lion's mouth and his ability to absorb punishment tip the scale?

The three-hour fight was brutal.[14] By mid-point both fighters and the canvas were covered in blood. In the early rounds, Gans tried to box, but the Battler's tactic was to bore in with his head to fight at close range. Gans landed any number of straight rights and lefts to pummel Nelson and used multiple uppercuts and short arm jabs in the in-fighting to bloody Batt's face and ears. By the twentieth round, Batt's face, said one correspondent, looked as if it had taken a beating hard enough to kill twenty Jimmy Britts. Gans's gloves were soaked in blood from Nelson's face, but his own face was relatively unmarked. Whenever Gans landed one of his battle-ending blows, Nelson appeared dazed and wobbly, but the bell inevitably saved him from the ten-count. In the one-minute interludes, Nelson was miraculously refreshed.

By the twenty-fifth round, when Nelson bore in, Gans seemed to lay his head listlessly on Nelson's shoulder allowing Nelson to punch his stomach. But after the momentary rest, Gans pushed Nelson away and hit him on the jaw so hard that Nelson staggered and seemed like he was going down. But again, Nelson was saved by the bell. At one point in the fight when Nelson fell through the ropes and Gans tried to help him up, he kicked at Gans. Referee George Siler overlooked many of Nelson's fouls, later saying that the spectators had come to see a fight. It would be several hours before the crowd would tire of Nelson's tactics. So the battle went, back and forth, Gans landing combinations on Batt's head, and Batt boring in, landing punishing blows to Gans's body.

By round thirty-three, Gans had completely shut Nelson's left eye with a flurry of blows, and had broken a bone in his right hand during the action. While Gans used his damaged hand in the remaining rounds, he could not put Nelson out with his left. By round forty-two, both men were war-weary, and Nelson knew that he was not likely to win a decision. When they were locked in a clinch, Nelson punched Gans repeatedly below the belt with his left mitt searching for the target. Then he struck Gans solidly in the groin, sending Gans to the floor, writhing in pain. Referee Siler witnessed the low blow and disqualified Nelson on a foul in the forty-second round, giving the win to Gans. The crowd roared its approval.

Outside Nevada, pro-Gans sentiments were not shared, especially in the South. On September 5, 1906, the *Atlanta Constitution* headline reported: "Race War is Provoked by Gans–Nelson Fight."[15] In Chicago, as the returns of the fight were coming in over the wire, one black man was shot and killed, another wounded in the levee district; and on the south side, five blacks were beaten. Atlanta would be at war, in one of the largest race riots in American history, where as many as 10,000 whites attacked and killed as many as forty blacks. The Atlanta race riot began September 22, 1906. The report of the Gans–Nelson fight may have been one of the turning points that gave strength to black civil rights advocates; but it brought fear from the whites, given the outcome of the most important contest in the fistic world to date. Thus, on September 23, 1906, police stopped the welterweight championship between Joe Walcott and his challenger, Billy Rhodes, in Leavenworth, Kansas.

Gans, suffering from tuberculosis and in need of money, promised Nelson a rematch, and then there was a third – all fights to the finish. The last two bouts were held in Colma, California, on July 4 and September 9, 1908. Nelson won their second match in the seventeenth round, and the third match in the twenty-first round. Gans and Nelson fought a total of eighty rounds.

While Gans was celebrating his greatest victory in 1906, Dixon was hanging up the gloves. Dixon died alone and impoverished in New York in 1908.

In 1910, the Old Master was dying. His last time in the ring was as a second to Sam Langford in his fight with Stanley Ketchel in Philadelphia in

April. Six weeks later, the storied Ketchel would be shot and killed. Gans would be in Arizona in a last-ditch effort to cure his advanced stage of tuberculosis, still hoping to be in Reno, Nevada, to serve Jack Johnson as his chief second for the Independence Day Fight with Jim Jeffries. But by July, Gans was too ill to attend. He died in August, following the famous bout where Jack Johnson soundly thrashed the supposedly invincible former champion Jeffries, who reluctantly emerged from a five-year retirement to calls of returning the title to the white race. Jack Johnson would say that none of the heavyweights compared in skill to three men he knew in the lighter weight categories: George "Little Chocolate" Dixon, "Barbados" Joe Walcott, and Joe Gans, the "Old Master."

By 1911 the golden age was over for the three Aces. Walcott spent his final days working as a custodian at Madison Square Garden, a place where he could share the stories with a new generation eager to engage in the good fight.[16] By 1935, Walcott was dead.

Today a bronze statue of Joe Gans stands in Madison Square Garden, the only statue of a boxer in the famous Garden that Tex Rickard built for the sport. Long gone are the days when boxers entering the ring before their bouts touched Gans's glove for luck. Few know these dedicated gladiators or the impact they had on American social and sports history, breaking the color line against great odds and managing to be competitive and successful in a sport during savage racial times in the United States when blacks were trying to maintain their precarious hold on their highly compromised freedom. Only by knowing their rich history can spectators and participants today more fully appreciate the science and art developed by these early technicians and strive to sustain what they struggled and fought for in sportsmanship and fair play.

NOTES

1 A well-researched history of the Pullman Porters and their salaries and duties during this period when they came into contact with the boxers can be found in Larry Tye's book *Rising from the Rails*.

2 For a round-by-round report of the fight, see Colleen Aycock and Mark Scott, eds, *The First Black Boxing Champions*, Appendix, "George Dixon vs. Jack Skelly," pp. 260–64. See also, Mike Glenn, "George Dixon: World Bantamweight and Featherweight Champion," pp. 48–59.

3 See the *Chicago Tribune*, *New Orleans Times Picayune*, and the *New Orleans Time-Democrat* reports of the fight, Sept. 7, 1892.

4 See Clay Moyle, *Sam Langford: Boxing's Greatest Uncrowned Champion*.

5 Spider Kelly, *San Francisco Chronicle*, Sept. 30, 1904.

6 *Police Gazette*, Oct. 22, 1904.

7 See Colleen Aycock and Mark Scott, *Tex Rickard: Boxing's Greatest Promoter*.

8 Battling Nelson, *Life, Battles and Career of Battling Nelson, Lightweight Champion of the World.*

9 Journalist Jack London was hired by William R. Hearst to cover the Jimmy Britt–Battling Nelson fight Sept. 9, 1905 for the *San Francisco Examiner*. In that article, he called Nelson the "abysmal brute," a concept he would use again in his literature when discussing "the game." For a discussion of this, see Aycock and Scott, *Tex Rickard*, pp. 51–54.

10 Francis J. Grimke, "The Atlanta Riot: A Discourse Published by Request," Washington, DC, Oct. 7, 1906.

11 "Fight Articles Will Be Signed Today," *San Francisco Examiner*, Aug. 11, 1906.

12 "Gans and Nelson," *San Francisco Examiner*, Aug. 10, 1906.

13 *San Francisco, Examiner*, Aug. 11, 1906.

14 For a complete round-by-round summary of the fight, see Colleen Aycock and Mark Scott, "Epic Battle in the Nevada Desert," *Joe Gans: A Biography of the First African American World Boxing Champion*, or Colleen Aycock and Mark Scott, eds, *The First Black Boxing Champions*, Appendix, "Joe Gans vs. Oscar 'Battling' Nelson (The Fight of the Century, September 3, 1906)," pp. 264–77.

15 "Race War is Provoked by Gans–Nelson Fight," *Atlanta Constitution,* Sept. 5, 1906. The article detailed what had occurred in Chicago as a result of the Gans–Nelson fight.

16 See Michael J. Schmidt, "Joe Walcott, the Barbados Demon: World Welterweight Champion," *The First Black Boxing Champions*, pp. 109–28.

BIBLIOGRAPHY

Aycock, Colleen and Mark Scott. *Joe Gans: A Biography of the First African American World Boxing Champion.* Jefferson, NC and London: McFarland & Company, 2008.

(eds) *The First Black Boxing Champions: Essays on Fighters of the 1800s to the 1920s.* Jefferson, NC and London: McFarland & Company, 2011.

Tex Rickard: Boxing's Greatest Promoter. Jefferson, NC and London: McFarland & Company, 2012.

Fleischer, Nat, *Black Dynamite: The Story of the Negro in the Prize Ring from 1782–1938, vol. 3, Three Colored Aces.* New York: C. J. O'Brien, 1938.

Grimké, Francis J. "The Atlanta Riot: A Discourse Published by Request." Washington, DC, Oct. 7, 1906. A facsimile of the first edition, Georgia Room, Main library, University of Georgia: http://fax.libs.uga.edu/F294xA8xG8/#.

Moyle, Clay. *Sam Langford: Boxing's Greatest Uncrowned Champion.* Seattle, WA: Bennet and Hastings, 2006.

Nelson, Battling. *Life, Battles and Career of Battling Nelson, Lightweight Champion of the World.* Hegewisch, IL, 1908.

Tye, Larry. *Rising From the Rails: Pullman Porters and the Making of the Black Middle Class.* New York: Henry Holt and Company, 2004.

6

CARLO ROTELLA

Harry Greb, Gene Tunney, Jack Dempsey, and the Roaring Twenties

The celebrated pair of heavyweight title fights between Jack Dempsey and Gene Tunney have long played a familiar part in accounts of the Roaring Twenties. They mark the triumphant arrival of boxing in the emerging mass-culture mainstream, culminating its progress from criminal marginality to legal and social legitimacy. Boxing and baseball were the sports that mattered most in the 1920s, often called the Golden Age of Sport, when sports became big business and rose to new prominence in symbiotic partnership with newspapers, magazines, radio, and film. The maturing celebrity industry popularized not only movie stars and musical idols and quasi-sporting heroes, like the aviator Charles Lindbergh, but also sports figures like Benny Leonard, Babe Ruth, Ty Cobb, Lou Gehrig, Knute Rockne, Red Grange, the long-distance swimmer Gertrude Ederle, the tennis players Helen Wills and Bill Tilden, and the golfer Bobby Jones. Dempsey, marketed as a broodingly handsome Western man of violence, was perhaps the biggest star of them all.

Dempsey's two defeats at the hands of Tunney bracketed Lindbergh's transatlantic solo flight, and they rival its status as the signature popular-culture event of the decade. The first fight, on September 23, 1926, set the pattern for the period's major media spectacles, with 130,000 spectators jamming Philadelphia's Sesquicentennial Stadium in soaking rain; 39 million listening to the fight on the radio; large crowds gathering in taverns, hotel lobbies, athletic clubs, parks, and the streets outside newspaper and wire offices all across the nation to receive live updates; and newspapers achieving record sales with special Dempsey–Tunney editions. Talk of a $2 million gate and similarly enormous purses (it was observed that Dempsey's $700,000 take was ten times President Coolidge's salary) underscored the economic potential of boxing – and of sports and popular entertainment in general. The mix of ringside notables included everyone from the songwriter Irving Berlin to the young Franklin Delano Roosevelt, the newspaper baron William Randolph Hearst to Babe Ruth, Gertrude Ederle to the conductor Leopold

Stokowski, the automaker Walter Chrysler to the notorious actress Mae West, Charlie Chaplin to Al Smith, governor of New York. It was estimated that 10,000 women were present, and 2,000 millionaires. Elmer Smith wrote in the *New York Times* that "almost everybody who professes to be a person of prominence and who was able to get down to Philadelphia at this particular time was on the premises."

The rematch, held in Chicago on September 22, 1927, was, if possible, an even bigger deal. The live crowd, radio audience, gate, and purses reached even more astonishing numbers. Tunney, now the defending champion, made the bigger share this time, $990,445.54, and gave the promoter, Tex Rickard, a personal check for $9,554.46 so that he could receive in return the first million-dollar paycheck in sports history. Another illustrious roster of ringsiders was conveyed to Soldier Field by an unprecedented convergence of automobiles, special trains, and, in the aftermath of Lucky Lindy's feat, about fifty private planes, including a trimotor bearing Princess Xenia of Greece. Al Capone was said to have put down a big bet on Dempsey. Boxing, having crossed over into respectability without losing its frisson of lowlife and danger, was the ideal Prohibition-era spectacle.

The protagonists were well suited to bear the freight of meanings assigned to their contest. The regional contrast pitted a Western brute from the once-wild frontier against an immigrant-ethnic Eastern city boy. The two men also embodied opposed styles of working-class manliness: the lusty, hardhanded roustabout who treated social convention with the easy laxity of a man who had grown up riding the rods; the ascetic shipping clerk-turned-marine who dutifully played by the rules of society and aspired to upward class mobility. And as men who were good with their hands, both Dempsey the sexy beast and Tunney the clean-cut paladin represented in their different ways the resonant structural connections between boxing and the America shaped by industrialization, urbanization, and immigration. Dempsey, whose parents were said to have come out to Colorado in a covered wagon, had learned to fight by scrapping on the Western tank-town circuit of mining camps, cowboy saloons, and other places defined by hard physical labor. Tunney, the American-born son of a longshoreman from Ireland, had apprenticed himself to the sweet science in the gyms and sporting clubs of New York City, institutional outposts of the fight-world network that was as deeply ingrained in the life of the urban village as were the factory, union hall, saloon, and parish church.

So the Dempsey–Tunney bouts, awash in gushers of ballyhoo and capital, were ripe for exploitation as repositories of cultural significance. If only the actual fights had been better.

We ask heavyweight title fights, and especially rivalries that develop beyond an initial confrontation through one or more rematches, to perform all sorts of meaning-making work. Beyond using them to do the essential fight-world business of assessing boxers' relative individual merit and analyzing the contest of styles, we rely on them when we frame periods in boxing history in relation to broader movements in culture and society. That's certainly what we do – what newspapers of the time were already doing – with the Dempsey–Tunney fights, turning the confrontation between mauler and technician into a snowglobe microcosm of the Roaring Twenties. Similarly, the Ali–Frazier trilogy is not just an exemplary struggle between swarming aggressor and inspired stylist, it's also used to trace the arc that carried Ali from his supercharged dissent of the late 1960s to consorting with Third World despots for profit in the 1970s on the way to being rebranded in the 1980s and 1990s as America's loved-to-pieces fuzzy bunny. The Louis–Schmeling diptych, not just the story of a maturing heavyweight who took care of business in his rematch with a dangerous veteran, became a world-historical fable in which to read the possibilities and limits of racialized nationhood. And we can extract a rich account of early twentieth-century race relations and popular culture from the extensive cycles that set Sam Langford, Harry Wills, Joe Jeanette, Sam McVey, and other black heavyweights against each other for the unofficial colored title, because they were prevented from securing a shot at the official world title.

It makes cultural sense to ask leading heavyweights, the most widely known and celebrated boxers, to carry these loads of meaning. And it even makes boxing sense to the extent that, following the foundational fight-world principle that a good big man beats a good little man, premier heavyweights are the best of the best. But if you look at it from a pound-for-pound perspective, they don't deserve the distinction. The heavyweight division is usually the shallowest in talent, heavyweights tend to be the least active and to lack the resiliency that produces lasting rivalries of high quality, and pound-for-pound the heavies are the worst, not the best. If you could somehow blow up a typical good lightweight to 6′ 2″ and 200 pounds, his advantage in skill over heavyweights would make him unbeatable, but if you could somehow shrink a typical good heavyweight to 5′ 6″ and 135, he would find himself outclassed by even average lightweights. The most complimentary superlative that commentators could find to attach to the young Ali was that he fought like a welterweight.

Moreover, a heavyweight matchup regarded as culturally important does not necessarily produce a good fight or cycle of fights. The Ali–Liston bouts, for example, for all their epochal importance in helping to kick off the canonical 1960s, are pretty disappointing as a rivalry between heavyweight all-timers. And, conversely, the best heavyweight matchups often fail to catch on as culturally important. Both Ali and Foreman had some of their finest moments in terrific encounters with the extremely tough and hard-hitting Ron Lyle, for instance, but it's Ali–Foreman, a lower-quality fight in which Ali showed improvisational flair and psychological acumen but Foreman fought like a sulky child, that gets treated as historically important.

In the case of Dempsey–Tunney, while as events the two fights may provide excellent occasions for exploring the Roaring Twenties, they proved less compelling as boxing match-ups. Tunney did some of his finest work against Dempsey, but the reverse is not true. The two men in their primes might have elicited each other's best, but Dempsey was no longer close to his prime when they fought. After three years out of the ring, much of it spent in showbiz as a full-time celebrity, he was very rusty and clearly in decline, showing only in brief spurts the surging energy with which he overwhelmed Jess Willard and Luis Angel Firpo in wildly exciting contests that reeled from one knockdown to the next. The veteran trainer Ray Arcel once said that when Dempsey entered the ring "you could see smoke rising from the canvas," but Tunney defused what was left of that explosive intensity by thoroughly outboxing him. In their first bout, Tunney did pretty much what he pleased on the way to a virtual shutout – moving and scoring easily, in command at long range and controlling Dempsey's balance in the clinches. He made Dempsey pay for his rushes with jabs and a sharp right hand, and when forced to retreat he expertly shifted his charging opponent so that it was Dempsey who ended up with his back to the ropes.

Tunney also schooled Dempsey in the rematch, but the one-sidedness was temporarily relieved when, in the seventh round, Dempsey finally reached Tunney with a series of blows that put him down in deep distress, one leg bent awkwardly under him. The confusion that followed has gone down in history as the Long Count. Dempsey, who was used to standing over a fallen man to pounce on him as soon as he got up, failed to immediately heed the new knockdown rule that required him to go to a neutral corner before the count could begin. The referee, Dave Barry, took five seconds to shoo him away and then returned to initiate his count. Tunney came out of a daze to pick up Barry's count at around three (about eight by the timekeeper's count) and then, as he had been taught by orthodox mentors, gathered himself and waited to rise until Barry had reached nine. Tunney was down for fourteen seconds in all, although on film it appears that probably he could have gotten up after eight or nine, and the extra five seconds are most fairly seen as Dempsey's, not Barry's, gift to him. In any case, the reversal of fortunes didn't last long. Tunney retreated and clinched to make it out of the seventh round, and in the eighth resumed patiently outboxing Dempsey, scoring a knockdown of his own with a crisp one-two.

It's not at all clear that the outcome would have been different if Dempsey had gone straight to a neutral corner, although he probably would have finished Tunney if they were fighting by the old rules that allowed him to jump on a downed opponent as he got up, as he had done repeatedly in beating Willard to a pulp. But the excitement and possibility associated with the Long Count tends to obscure the fact that – like Earnie Shavers's crushing knockdown of Larry Holmes in 1979, which also briefly turned the tables in the seventh round of a rematch – it was a fearsome hitter's one glorious moment during two otherwise unequal encounters with a master boxer.

So, staying within the same period, let's replace the Dempsey–Tunney cycle with a better one: for instance, the five-bout series that matched Tunney as a light heavyweight against the middleweight Harry Greb. Tunney ranks higher on the all-time rolls as a heavy-hitting light heavyweight than as a willowy heavyweight, and the prodigious Greb has to be regarded as a significant upgrade over the faded Dempsey who fought Tunney.

It can be a little disorienting to take Greb's measure from the vantage point of the twenty-first century. He fought well over 300 times, 299 of them official bouts, in a thirteen-year professional career. He fought thirty-seven times in 1917 and forty-five times in 1919, none of them losses. That means he managed to compress into a single year the equivalent of Floyd Mayweather, Jr.'s entire first-ballot Hall of Fame career, and faced stiffer competition to boot. Greb went through extended stretches in which he fought every few days, and he routinely gave away fifteen or more pounds, sometimes a lot more, to his opponent. At 5′ 8″ and a prime fighting weight around 160 pounds, he indiscriminately fought men of all sizes: he held the world middleweight championship from 1923 to 1926, he took the American light heavyweight championship from Tunney in 1922, and he beat every heavyweight and each of the eleven members of the International Boxing Hall of Fame that he fought. And, unlike Dempsey and Tunney, Greb regularly fought across the color line, a practice he extended to title fights.

The who's who of his conquests, many of them in multi-bout cycles, includes George Chip, Al McCoy, Jeff Smith, Mike McTigue, Eddie McGoorty, Tiger Flowers, Gunboat Smith, Battling Levinsky, Leo Houck, Jimmy Slattery, Maxie Rosenbloom, Tommy Gibbons, Mike Gibbons, Tommy Loughran, Bill Brennan, Jack Dillon, Kid Norfolk, Johnny Wilson, Mickey Walker, and Tunney. Greb, the quintessential good little man, also campaigned for a fight with Dempsey, who showed no enthusiasm for taking up the challenge, especially after Greb made him look like a fool in a series of sparring exhibitions in 1920 that left Dempsey banged up, winded, and bewildered. Greb managed to assemble this catalogue of accomplishments before dying at the age of thirty-two in 1926, during an operation after a car accident. In addition, just to add another degree of unlikeliness to this already unlikely curriculum vitae, for his last 100 or so bouts (including all five with Tunney) Greb fought with a major handicap that he kept secret: he was effectively blind in his right eye, which was probably damaged beyond repair during a nasty exchange of thumbing fouls with Kid Norfolk in 1921.

Greb is justly ranked among the best middleweights of all time, and at the top of all-time pound-for-pound lists along with Sugar Ray Robinson, Henry Armstrong, Sam Langford, and a handful of other elite-of-the-elite peers. Robinson was the more complete stylist, and he and others in this select company had the advantage of longer life spans in which to pile up late-career accomplishments, but Greb has the edge over just about everyone when it comes to the range and quality of his opposition and his success against bigger men.

In the absence of any known film of Greb's fights, we have had to rely on eyewitness descriptions of him in action, which are not always precise. (This situation may yet change: as of this writing, a collector is trying to authenticate a recently discovered videotape made from what appears to be twelve minutes of film footage of a bout between Greb and Allentown Joe Gans in 1926.) Frequent comparisons to a windmill, wildcat, kangaroo, or octopus don't do justice to Greb's impossibly high work rate, his skill at throwing punches and feinting from many angles while moving in and out, his perplexing speed and rhythm, and the improbable leaps, twists, and bends he employed to deliver and avoid blows. Dempsey said, "He makes you think you're in a glove factory, and shelves of them are tumbling down on you." Bill Paxton, Greb's biographer, has done a good job of clearing away the mythologized image of Greb as a wild man, a dirty brawler who eschewed training in favor of boozing and womanizing – an image promulgated in the memoirs of Mickey Walker, who lost a hard-fought title bout to Greb in 1925, and Jack Kearns, who managed both Walker and Dempsey. In fact, Greb kept himself in permanently superb fighting trim, drank sparingly, was apparently devoted to his wife, and fouled judiciously. And he was a remarkably skilled boxer, particularly in the advanced art of punching while moving sideways or backwards. One defeated opponent, Pal Reed, remarked wonderingly on Greb's "great faculty for starting a blow and stopping in midair, but countering with another blow." Greb pointed out that he could have hit much harder if he set his feet and sat down on his punches, but his ceaseless movement gave him an advantage on both offense and defense, and he made up in volume and speed for the power it cost him.

Tunney first faced this uniquely forbidding opponent on May 23, 1922, in Madison Square Garden, with the American light heavyweight title on the line. Tunney, who had twelve pounds and four inches of height and five inches of reach on Greb, had beaten some good men in his fifty-three fights, but Greb had already beaten the best of them, Battling Levinsky and Leo Houck, six times and three times, respectively. Tunney wasn't ready for Greb, who broke his nose with a furious assault at the opening bell and proceeded to administer a soup-to-nuts thrashing. Tunney revealed previously undiscovered reserves of heart and chin in managing to last the entire fifteen rounds, bleeding so freely from the nose, mouth, and eyebrows that his corner ran out of adrenalin chloride and switched to brandy-and-orange juice. Tunney lost two quarts of blood; both fighters and the referee were slathered with it. It was the kind of asswhipping in front of a hometown crowd that could easily have broken or at least discouraged a developing fighter, marking an upper limit in the class of opponents he could handle. Instead, Tunney felt that the experience of being mauled by Greb had taught him – had, indeed, intimately imprinted on his suffering body and mind – what he needed to know to do better in a rematch.

The Tunney–Greb cycle offers us a deeper, faster, meaner, tauter non-heavyweight rendition of the stylistic drama presented by Dempsey-Tunney: a technical boxer rising to the challenge presented by a pressure fighter. Greb kept after the bigger man with his usual manic rigor – round after round, fight after fight, year after year – and reckoning with him forced Tunney to mature as both boxer and fighter. In addition to discovering just how much pressure and punishment he could withstand, Tunney had to become more self-possessed and resourceful on both defense and offense. Coached by the great lightweight champion Benny Leonard, among others, he learned to resist the temptation to aim for Greb's elusive head and to go to the body instead. "Going for the heart" was more likely to result in clean shots that drove Greb back and slowed him down.

The sixty-five-round Tunney–Greb series (versus twenty rounds for Dempsey–Tunney) was brutally and evenly contested. Tunney, going to the body, won a controversial split decision in the second bout, which many observers either considered a draw or awarded to Greb for making the fight throughout. The third was also close but seen as more clearly Tunney's, a victory by unanimous decision. In the fourth, a ten-rounder held in Cleveland, the two men went at it with particular gusto. Tunney seized the initiative for brief periods, Greb inevitably reclaimed it, and the final round built to a climax as they exchanged punches in the center of the ring and then along the ropes. This was a no-decision, non-title bout unofficially adjudicated by the newspapermen in attendance, who called it a satisfying draw. The fifth fight, also a ten-round newspaper-decision bout, was held in St. Paul on March 27, 1925, eighteen months before Tunney's first fight with Dempsey. Tunney, who at the age of twenty-eight was filling out, weighed 181 pounds for this one, and through hard experience he had figured out how to keep Greb mostly at bay. His success in doing this made their final meeting the least eventful of the five, and the papers awarded him the victory.

So Greb decisively won the first bout, Tunney less decisively won the last and had a slight edge in the third, and the other two could have gone either way. That Tunney shaded Greb on the decisions in the second and third (both held in Tunney's hometown) gives him the official laurels in their series, although once the size differential is taken into account, the whole cycle becomes another pound-for-pound all-timer credential for Greb, the only man ever to beat Tunney. One of the most difficult problems for an aggressive fighter is to take on a technically sophisticated defender who's bigger than he is and familiar with his style.

What about the big picture? Does replacing Dempsey–Tunney with Tunney–Greb alter our perspective on the 1920s?

Tunney–Greb lacks Dempsey's heavyweight glamor and star power, of course. Although the five bouts were significant occasions in the fight world and duly reported in the papers, they didn't make the jump to become major national events in the culture at large, and as far as we know Princess Xenia and the Roosevelts were not at ringside in Cleveland yelling at Tunney to stick the jab. But it's still instructive, and in some ways more illuminating of the period, to see how big a deal even a non-heavyweight, non-title fight could be in the Golden Age of Sport. Take, for instance, Greb's victory over Tommy Gibbons in New York in March 1922. This was just a precursor to determine which of them would take on Tunney for the title, but there were movie and opera stars at ringside along with Dempsey, Leonard, and other fight-world dignitaries, and Mrs. William Randolph Hearst, founder of the Milk Fund, sponsored the bout. After Greb beat Gibbons, his reception in his hometown of Pittsburgh featured a parade that drew "the greatest turnout ever in the history of the city," a mayoral welcome, a week-long starring role for Greb in vaudeville shows at the Gayety Theater, and a radio address broadcast across the Americas.

Tunney–Greb also lacks an intensely scrutinized and argued-over Long Count episode, the kind of resonant dramatic turn that invites larger meanings to accrue around the event. Beyond stirring the usual speculation about a fix, the Long Count excited imaginations by opening up the possibility of metaphorically reversing the flow of civilizing progress. Especially while Tunney was down, and for the rest of the seventh round as he fled from the hotly pursuing Dempsey, it seemed as if the atavistic disorder associated with Dempsey – and other period figures, like Capone, Tarzan of the Apes, and the melancholic sack of appetites known as the Babe – might still have enough potency to stand its ground and even rally against the militantly advancing forces of modern order represented by Tunney. Greb's boxing style did inspire observers to miscast him as a Dempsey-like embodiment of elemental savagery that Tunney had to contain, but the Tunney–Greb cycle offers no Long Count moment to conjure with. One might argue, though, that it offers an equally vivid tableau that shows why the forces of atavistic disorder were in big trouble: the broken-nosed Tunney, a bone-deep cut in one eyebrow and a severed vein pumping blood from the other, coolly parsing and filing away for later review the lessons imparted by the beating that Greb was even then visiting upon him.

We can read the same major historical developments in Tunney–Greb as in Dempsey–Tunney: the mainstreaming of boxing, the rise of celebrity culture, the boom in sports and other leisure industries, the symbiosis between these growing sectors and the media, the depth of connection between the fight world and industrial America. But Tunney–Greb gives us a different picture of how these developments played out as part of the texture of life in a rapidly transforming country. Both Tunney and Greb (whose father emigrated from Germany and whose mother was second-generation German) represented the streams of immigrants and their children who had remade America's cities, shop floors, and fight world. Both men came up through the urban networks that increasingly constituted that fight world's core – Tunney in the waterfront milieu of stevedores and athletic clubs in Manhattan's West Village, and Greb in Pittsburgh, where he apprenticed as an electrician at the Westinghouse plant and found his way into local gyms. The Western frontier circuit on which Dempsey learned the trade had enjoyed its heyday during the bare-knuckle and early gloved eras of boxing's marginality. By the 1920s it was in eclipse, superseded by the networks of gyms, clubs, local venues, and other institutions embedded in urban neighborhoods that formed the heartland of boxing as a legitimate enterprise. It was this heartland in its various forms – not only immigrant-ethnic urban villages like those that produced Tunney and Greb, but also the Black Metropolis and the industrial-era barrio – that would provide most of the infrastructure and talent for American boxing during its era of greatest sporting and cultural prominence. The subsequent contraction of boxing's institutional base and its decline in importance after midcentury would follow upon the breakup of this world, part of the larger decline and fall of the industrial city.

It's easier in some ways to see the grain of the era's fight world in Tunney–Greb than in Dempsey–Tunney. What's most golden about the golden age is not that you might join Charlie Chaplin and the Vanderbilts at ringside to watch Tunney anticlimactically whitewash a shot Dempsey in an event billed as the biggest thing ever, but that you could sit in the cheap seats of Cleveland's Olympic Arena on a Saturday night in late September to watch, along with 10,000 other fans, a well-matched Tunney and Greb give of their best in fighting to a rousing draw that you felt confident would lead to yet another installment in their long-running series. And then you could follow Greb back through Pennsylvania during subsequent weeks as he took on Tommy Loughran in Philadelphia, Ray Nelson in Philipsburg, Jimmy Delaney in Pittsburgh, and Frankie Ritz in Wheeling, West Virginia. And then you could switch to Tunney, getting down to New Orleans in December to see him go fifteen rounds with Jeff Smith.

In support of the notion that the week-to-week business-as-usual of an era can offer a better snapshot of it than its epochal marquee fights, look at Greb's schedule for February and March 1919: Len Rowlands, Southside Market House, Pittsburgh; Bill Brennan, Olympian Arena, Syracuse; Battling Levinsky, Broadway Auditorium, Buffalo; Chuck Wiggins, Coliseum, Toledo; Wiggins again, Elks Club, Detroit; Leo Houck, Fulton Opera House, Lancaster; Brennan again, Duquesne Gardens, Pittsburgh. Yes, it's a remarkably demanding itinerary, but, beyond that, the roll call of names and venues and cities, representing just a portion of the nation's pattern of overlapping regional circuits, suggests how deeply the fight world's root system worked itself into the fabric of urbanized, industrialized, immigrant-rich America in the early twentieth century.

Together, Dempsey, Tunney, and Greb remind us that the business of assigning greatness to boxers, like the perversely imperfect process of deciding who belongs in the International Boxing Hall of Fame, entails at least three strands of analysis. One strand considers pure fighting ability: compare styles, consider the visual evidence, look at common and analogous opponents, and decide who wins if you match boxers in their primes. One strand considers accomplishment: look at wins and losses, quality of opposition, career arc, and a fighter's stature in his time, and decide who racked up more merit. And one strand considers significance, which takes us into the realm of culture: who carries the biggest charge of historical meaning, who most potently embodied or even changed the fight world and the society around it – who mattered more, in other words, or, at the third strand's most banal extreme, who was more famous. As fearsome a heavyweight as Dempsey was, and there's a strong case for his having been one of the very best ever, it's the third strand that sets him apart from Tunney and Greb and puts him in the company of Ali, Louis, and Jack

Johnson (and Mike Tyson, whose case for greatness is almost entirely a cultural one, since as a fighter he doesn't deserve to keep company with the great heavyweights). It takes an act of analytical will to set aside star power for a moment and remind ourselves that greatness for a boxer should begin and end with ability and accomplishment. Tunney's fights with Dempsey made him famous beyond all fantasy, and rich, too, but it was five very hard days at the office against Greb that turned Tunney from a promising up-and-comer into the great fighter who put Dempsey out to pasture. And it was punishingly ordinary cycles like Tunney–Greb, more than extraordinary extravaganzas like Dempsey–Tunney, that defined the greatness of boxing in its golden age.

A note on sources. The best account of Dempsey–Tunney in its historical context is Bruce J. Evensen's *When Dempsey Fought Tunney: Heroes, Hokum, and Storytelling in the Jazz Age* (University of Tennessee Press, 1996). Bill Paxton's obsessively thorough *The Fearless Harry Greb: Biography of a Tragic Hero of Boxing* (MacFarland, 2009) does a great service by dispersing the fog of myth that has long surrounded Greb. Stephen Compton's compendiously detailed *Live Fast, Die Young: The Life and Times of Harry Greb* (Windmill Writing Publications, 2013) is even more obsessively thorough. Jack Cavanaugh's *Tunney: Boxing's Brainiest Champ and His Upset of the Great Jack Dempsey* (Random House, 2006) is a solid biography that also offers an extensive treatment of Dempsey, whose own versions of his life and career are charmingly unreliable. I am grateful to Charles Farrell and Mike Ezra, who were, as always, generous with their critical acuity and knowledge of boxing.

7

TROY RONDINONE

Prime (and Crime) Time:
Boxing in the 1950s

In the 1950s, boxing was family entertainment, thanks to television and *la cosa nostra*. The plunging price and rapid improvement of TV technology helped spread the device across the country. The rise of the International Boxing Club (IBC), an organization both well-capitalized and well-connected to the mob, provided the on-screen talent. It was a glorious run, and while its demise now can be seen as clearly as an amateur's telescoped punch, 1950s prizefighting held an unrivaled, if rarely mentioned, power over American culture.

The Idiot Box

TV made its public debut at the 1939 World's Fair, but the technology was so primitive and expensive that it simply could not compete with radio. Improvements were on the way, however, and by the end of the 1940s it was apparent that a hostile takeover was in the works. As TV ascended, not only radios but libraries, movie theaters, and bookstores saw declining fortunes. Televisions even made a conquest of the American domicile: a new phrase, the "family-television room," was coined by *Better Homes and Gardens* in 1950.[1] By 1960, almost 90 percent of homes had a TV that the average person watched five hours a day. One study by Westinghouse Electric reported that by the end of the 1950s more person-hours were spent watching television than working for a wage. Some elites complained that the boob tube was rotting America's collective brain, but these people were ignored. Americans happily supped at the trough of visual electronic entertainment. They were taught that TV was a binding agent for families, even an educational tool. Boxing provided a violent sort of education.

Boxing translated well to the new medium. Two men – one in white shorts, the other in dark shorts – faced off in a brightly lit white cube in finite space. The rules were simple; it was a contest of brute strength and ring science. Would people watch? Gillette Razor cut a deal with Madison

Square Garden and began broadcasting shows in 1944, and within a decade it had become clear that as the coaxial cable inched its way West, so too did increasing Gillette sales. In 1952, Gillette added a jaunty march composed by Mahlon Merrick, along with cartoon spokesbird Sharpie, who screeched, "Look sharp, feel sharp!" to the delight of the home audience. The popularity of the fight shows even inspired storekeepers to place large magnifiers in front of their TVs and face them out windows so street traffic might be tempted to enter their shops. *The Gillette Cavalcade of Sports Friday Night Fights* on NBC would be the most durable of the early boxing programs, occasionally garnering upwards of 50 million viewers. After NBC, other networks caught on. The now-defunct Dumont network had a fight show, and starting in 1948 the *Pabst Blue Ribbon Wednesday Night Fights* on CBS kept people happy midweek.

Boxing did not just take advantage of the new medium. In a culture that already celebrated the sport (witness the numerous boxing gyms, school teams, and backyard rings), boxing formed a symbiotic relationship with the rising small screen. The cost of the shows was minimal, often fully incurred by a single sponsor. The talent was ready to go, and ready to work cheap. For a short time, boxing shows made up a shocking 40 percent of all programming.[2] By the early 1950s, although other shows were rapidly being added to network rosters, you could watch fight shows six days a week in New York City and its environs.[3] This was reality TV that sold sets, pure and simple.

But it was a reality show that exacted a great cost. Unlike the folks on *Survivor*, TV boxers were highly trained pugilists who required years of cultivation, starting with youth organizations, moving up via the club circuit, and always putting in thousands of hours training. TV ate these kids alive. As Truman Gibson (an IBC President) explained in his autobiography, "Television ruled us ... 100 fights a year required us to come up with 400 fighters ... two for each main event and two waiting in the wings in case of fast knockout."[4] TV also bent the nature of the sport. Home viewers were less interested in a defensive, scientific counterpuncher than in a fellow who charged right in and took as much as he gave. This led to a near-constant critique among the boxing crowd that the idiot box was "ruining" the sport. In 1953 John Lardner bitterly noted that "the fine old art of fisticuffs is rapidly being replaced by pugilistic soap opera – more blood, more violence, less skill."[5] A couple years later Nat Fleischer, editor of *The Ring*, lamented that the TV had turned the Garden into a glorified TV studio, and that the clubs were dying. He said, "We have no men of real ability coming up now. Today's fighter is primarily a slugger. The boxer, the hitter, the combination man – we don't see him. The sponsor wants a man who'll sell his product. Somebody popular, somebody colorful. The sponsor is not looking for ability."[6]

So, ironically, just as it was helping make boxing more popular than ever, TV seemed to be eroding the foundations of the sport. As TV searched insatiably for warm bodies to put in the ring, the local boxing clubs emptied out, and once a fighter did poorly onscreen, TV dropped him like a hot potato. Plus, attendance in the local clubs plummeted because it was cheaper to watch good fighters from home. As early as 1951, Fleischer told *Newsweek*, "Our records show that the fighter population of this country has dropped nearly 50 per cent in one year. In 1950 we had well over 6,000 professional boxers. Right now we've got maybe 3,500." TV was moving kids up too fast, and fans who used to watch fights in the clubs now watched from their La-Z-Boys. In 1956 *Harper's* ran a piece saying straight out that "television has decimated boxing as a business and all but ruined it as a sport."[7]

This argument might be true, but it underestimates other factors at work. For example, boxing numbers were in decline long before TV. Also, the population shift to the suburbs, which in part produced the middle-class TV viewers sponsors adored, helped empty the urban cores of fight fans and witnessed the replacement of grungy boxing gyms with pretty baseball diamonds in leafy postwar neighborhoods. TV, in fact, might even be seen less as a killer than as a side-effect of the real assassin: affluence. Folks who could afford TVs might be lifting themselves out of poverty, and poverty, so the saying goes, is the nursery of boxing.

The increasing globalization of the sport in this period tells us that when American ghettos produced fewer fighters, ghettos in the so-called Third World were only too happy to make up the slack. And as more foreigners filled out the ranks, some viewers began to complain that the sport was becoming un-American. But let's not get ahead of ourselves. For the 1950s were golden years.

Friday's Heroes

Within the Boxing-TV Complex, fighters became, in the words of the immortal Willie Pep, "Friday's Heroes." Friday Night Fighters like Dick Tiger, Emile Griffith, Carmen Basilio, Gaspar Ortega, Tony DeMarco, Kid Gavilan, Isaac Logart, and many others became household names, much discussed around water coolers and in bars, on street corners and in the backs of classrooms. A generation of Baby Boomers remembers watching the fights with Dad (and sometimes Mom). They remember the smell of Dad's cigar, or the stuffed animal they clung to while sitting in his lap. They remember keeping their own score of the fight, listening to Dad discourse on the fineries of uppercuts and overhand rights. For many folks, the fights meant bonding. The fighters slugged it out and kept parents and kids hooked together.

As Friday's Heroes found themselves ensconced in a love affair with viewers, they started emphasizing personas to cultivate the at-home audience. What Hollywood called "human interest" entered the boxing world. Gaspar "Indio" Ortega, fighting out of Tijuana, Mexico, wore an Indian headdress (when not donning a garish sombrero) and wielded a tomahawk in publicity stills. Jake LaMotta was only too happy to give the press the kind of copy that painted him as the rough, tough (and mobbed up?) Bronx Bull. Chico Vejar's dreamy looks would be parlayed into a nascent movie career. Chuck Davey's "blonde curls" received much comment, only adding to the shock when he was floored four times by the much better (and decidedly non-blonde) Kid Gavilan in 1953. Still, looks weren't everything. The culture seemed to celebrate the caveman in the 1950s, too, brow-ridge and all. Those who did not have James Dean's face or Fred Astaire's grace could at least have the prehistoric man's will to power. Even the *Flintstones* would riff the allure of "Rocky Rockciano." The popular cartoon (it aired from 1960 to 1966, but it was rooted in the 1950s in many respects) reflected the culture by showing Barney and Fred as inveterate fight fans, watching on TV in several episodes or going out to see fights at the Bedrock arena. Indeed, there were some plots that were built around Barney and Fred trying to sneak out to a boxing match without their wives knowing.

Perhaps because of the decline of the American clubs, boxing was an increasingly global sport in the 1950s. Friday's Heroes came not only from New York and the rural hinterlands of the Midwest and South, but also from the ghettos and backwoods of Mexico, Puerto Rico, Cuba, Italy, France, and Nigeria. So many fighters came from Cuba in the 1950s that *The Ring* reflected on the Cuban "Invasion" in 1959.[8] One of the stunning things about the TV fights is the fact that in an age when most of TV offerings were lily white, boxing offered a racial amalgam seen rarely in the mass media. As Henry Louis Gates would remember, "What interracial sex was to the seventies, interracial sports were to the 1950s. Except for sports, we rarely saw a colored person on TV."[9] Though the thrill of interracial fights was a primary attractant, and while boxing certainly represented no fix to the nation's racial strife, it did offer middle-class white America an alternative model of masculinity to the pasty sort found on the dusty Hollywood backlots of TV Westerns. And for African Americans and Latinos, non-white fighters became heroes of a new sort.

The Marriage Made in Hell

The simplicity of the sport was also deceiving. Behind the scenes, a conjuncture of business, boxing, and the mafia created a marriage made in hell. Dating this blessed event takes us to New York City in the late 1940s. Madison Square Garden promoter Mike Jacobs, who had struck the initial deal to put boxing on regular television programming back in the Second World War, found himself in a tough spot in 1947. The Garden was beginning to lose money (in part due to the TV cameras that encouraged folks to stay home and watch for free), and his most prized possession, the heavyweight champion Joe Louis, was aging and slowing down. By December 1947 Louis knew his career had met trail's end, and he sought an exit strategy. With the help of some friends, he created Joe Louis Enterprises, Inc., and promoted a plan to create a tournament to find the next champion, providing the Brown Bomber with a graceful departure. What this meant for Jacobs (who was also experiencing a marked health decline at the time) was that his influence was at an end. Enter James Dougan Norris, millionaire playboy, sports aficionado, and friend of the mob.

Jim Norris already owned two hockey teams (Detroit Red Wings and Chicago Black Hawks), a number of thoroughbred racehorses, and held controlling interests in Madison Square Garden, the Detroit Olympia, and the St. Louis Arena.[10] He liked to say that he never needed the money that boxing generated. This was true. Nevertheless, for reasons that he took with him to the grave, Jim liked to both have a hand in boxing and to hang out with mobsters. The organization that he helmed, along with his partner Arthur Wirtz (the International Boxing Club), proceeded to control the sport in monopoly fashion. Red Smith rightly dubbed the IBC "the Octopus." And its tentacles stretched into living rooms.

Much ink would be spilled then and since regarding the influence of organized crime on boxing in the 1950s. The best way to understand the mob's influence is to connect the mob with the larger story of American business enterprise. As other entrepreneurs long understood, unregulated competition breeds anarchy, and anarchy begets low profit margins and economic instability. It would be up to business to self-regulate, divide the spoils, merge, and monopolize. Following a ruinous internecine conflict known as the Castellammarese War in the 1930s, a group of mobsters under the leadership of an entrepreneurial genius named Charles "Lucky" Luciano came up with a plan. In what might be called the Great Mafia Merger Movement, a governing body emerged that, in the words of Selwyn Raab, functioned as "the equivalent of a national board of directors [in order to] establish general policies and regulations for all families in the country and … settle all disputes that might arise." Each crime family received a single vote, and the majority ruled.[11] Such centralization is what granted Frankie Carbo, a man associated with the Lucchese crime family, the unhampered ability to control access to the boxing ring. They called him the "Commissioner."

The reach of mafia influence via the IBC was incredible. Carbo worked with Norris, and together they controlled the show. Carbo would be involved with managements of welterweights Chuck Davey and Johnny Saxton, middleweights Rocky Graziano and Jake LaMotta, heavyweights Charles "Sonny" Liston and Rocky Marciano, and who knows who else. Carbo did this typically through an organization called the Boxing Managers Guild. As Thomas Myler explains, "If you want to get fights that matter, join the guild; otherwise, you're out."[12] Getting your man in the ring meant dealing with the IBC and the Managers Guild. Cut in the mob, you can get on the show. This was great economics for the criminals. Whoever won in the ring, the mob got its cut. As with any business monopoly, finding a safe, regular revenue stream was key. The mob was happier with a steady stream of cash than with the hit-and-miss that came with unregulated anarchy. The IBC facilitated a mob tax.

As a bonus, Carbo helped Norris keep up the supply of boxers, which was great, due to the constant demand for new, exciting TV pugilists. Recalled Truman Gibson, "With a set amount of time booked on network TV, the show had to go on even in the event of knockouts, which of course were much desired to arouse fan enthusiasm. Therefore, a main event pitted two fighters against each other, with two more boxers waiting in the wings should one of the participants in the main event knock the other one out. That meant we had to have four fighters ready on fight nights fifty one weeks of the year."[13] According to one witness, at one point Carbo drew his finger across a map of America and literally assigned Norris the top half and himself the bottom half.

So the mob put fighters in the ring, dipping its long fingers into their pocket before they climbed through the ropes. But does this mean that the mob had a say in the outcome? This is much harder to prove. After the IBC was finally dragged before the US Senate, Truman Gibson tried to explain that fights were never fixed for the simple reason that it would ruin betting, thus destroying the golden egg-laying goose: "[I]f there were fixed fights, we would be out of business, so we try to protect ourselves in every way against the possibility of a fixed fight ... you only need one or two and you have no more boxing."[14] Carbo's profits – a shocking 50 percent of the take, according to some[15] – did not mean that the audience was not treated to a real sport. The mob took its "vig," but so what? I've spoken with lots of fighters, and believe me, this was not vaudeville. This was gladiatorial combat. Gloved fists crushed delicate cartilage, mushed eyelids shut, split lips, and throttled brains. The fighters understood that they needed to destroy their opponents in order to stay gainfully employed. This was real. And the audience knew it.

This makes the story of 1950s boxing as slippery as a wet glove. Friday's Heroes gave America a model of Cold War masculinity that bonded families and showed white executives that all TV need not be safe and Anglo. The fighters challenged not only each other but also America's racial order. And the mob wasn't quite the devil the moralists would have us think. It provided the kind of organization that gave structure (basically one belt in each division) and stability to a sport long associated with chaos and boodle. It fed boxers into rings at a time when TV demanded a steady flow of top-quality fistic practitioners. It worked well with a money man (Norris) who permitted the kind of monopoly that, say, keeps professional baseball big and America's favorite sport. Yet the mob also stained boxing, putting hard-working fighters in bed with assassins and grafters. And it took so much that, after the criminals and the IRS got their cut, boxers were left hollow, damaged, unwanted. Willie Pep would wistfully write, "Maybe there should have been a boxing union!" Instead, the fighter's "pension" was only "a pocket full of memories."[16] Given the tragic effects of brain trauma, even these memories could be compromised.

The End

The last regular TV fight took place on September 11, 1964. The first and greatest boxing TV show, *Gillette Cavalcade of Sports Friday Night Fights*, begun during the Second World War and featuring some truly impressive ring talent over the years, fizzled out ignominiously after being shifted from Friday to Saturday and back to Friday night, and from one network to another. When the end came, it was in the form of a whimper – a dud of a match between Dick Tiger and Don Fullmer. The press didn't pay particular notice, though the *New York Times* saw fit to connect the end with rising wealth, ethnic "assimilation," and the ascent of new, more appropriate family fare.[17]

Considering all of the problems besetting TV boxing, it is amazing that it lasted as long as it did. Beyond mobsters and monopolies, there was the problem of serious injury. The first televised ring death was back in 1950, when ex-Marine Laverne Roach met his demise at the hands of Georgie Small. The most infamous TV ring death, the pummeling of Benny "Kid" Paret by Emile Griffith in 1962, created an even greater uproar, but no cease in TV matches. As the medical community slowly became aware of brain damage in the ring, perhaps more viewers became concerned, but not enough to do anything major.

Similarly, the common knowledge that boxing was plagued by criminals did not seem to be sharply detrimental to ratings. Newspapers and magazines throughout the 1950s pointed to Carbo and his cronies as manipulating the IBC. The *New York Sun* called Carbo "a secret power in the prizefight world" as early as 1947.[18] Carbo's imprisonment in 1959 did not stop the show. The breakup of the IBC by the Supreme Court in 1957, following a series of high-profile Senate investigations, did not stop the show. TV boxing survived it all – the corruption, the monopoly, the death, everything.

It was ratings that killed the show. Folks changed the channel.

The end finally came when networks decided more viewers would watch other programs.[19] There were rising sports like football, new TV genres like spy shows and space shows. The old fight shows increasingly became something that only Dad watched, and sponsors recognized it was smarter to cater to youngsters and women, with their disposable income, than to the aging veteran sipping his Pabst on his recliner.

But of course, September 11, 1964, was not the end at all. Boxing would rise again. There would be new stars, men like Muhammad Ali, himself a former Friday Night Fighter. There would also be new rules. With the demise of the IBC and its tight mob connections, anarchy was reintroduced. New sanctioning bodies made for a variety of simultaneous title holders. The World Boxing Association came into existence in 1962. In 1963 came the World Boxing Council. Then came the International Boxing Federation and the World Boxing Organization. Add to this more weight classes and the simultaneous end of regular TV boxing programming, and the sport began its march toward unwieldy obscurity.

The IBC and the mob brought boxing to families and spread the sport to the widest audience it has ever known. Monopoly and crime – two American devils – created something yet to be repeated: a golden age of boxing.

NOTES

1 Lynn Spigel, *Make Room for TV: Television and the Family Ideal in Postwar America* (Chicago, IL: University of Chicago Press, 1992), 39–40.

2 Jeff Neal-Lunsford, "Sport in the Land of Television: The Use of Sport in Network Prime-time Schedules 1946–1950," *Journal of Sports History* 19:1 (Spring 1992), 61.

3 Neal-Lunsford, "Sport in the Land of Television," 58–61; see also television listings section of *New York Times* ca. 1952–55.

4 Truman K. Gibson with Steve Huntley, *Knocking Down Barriers: My Fight for Black America* (Evanston, IL: Northwestern University Press, 2005), 251.

5   John Lardner, "So You Think You See the Fights on TV!" *Saturday Evening Post*, April 5, 1953.

6   Charles Einstein, "TV Slugs the Boxers," *Harper's Magazine*, August 1956.

7   "Prizefighting: Quantity is Down but Some Quality is Coming Up," *Newsweek*, December 10, 1951; Einstein, "TV Slugs the Boxers."

8   Jersey Jones, "Successful Invasion by Cubans," *The Ring*, December 1959.

9   Henry Louis Gates, *Colored People: A Memoir* (New York: Knopf, 1994), 20.

10 Thomas Myler, *The Sweet Science Goes Sour: How Scandal Brought Boxing to Its Knees* (Vancouver: Greystone Books, 2006), 28.

11 Selwyn Raab, *Five Families: The Rise, Decline, and Resurgence of America's most Powerful Mafia Empires* (New York: St. Martin's Press, 2006), 23–34, viii, ix.

12 Myler, *The Sweet Science Goes Sour*, 22.

13 Gibson with Huntley, *Knocking Down Barriers*, 251.

14 US Senate, Hearings before the Subcommittee on Antitrust and Monopoly of the Committee of the Judiciary, "Professional Boxing," 86th Cong., 2nd sess., *Congressional Record* (December 5–6, 1960), 417.

15 Ferdie Pacheco, *Blood in My Coffee: The Life of the Fight Doctor* (Champaign, IL: Sports Publishing, 2005), 100.

16 Willie Pep with Robert Sacchi, *Willie Pep Remembers Friday's Heroes* (New York: Friday's Heroes, Inc., 1973), 184.

17 Robert Lipsyte, "Sports of the Times: What's Next in Boxing?" *New York Times*, September 21, 1964.

18 Nick Tosches, *The Devil and Sonny Liston* (Boston, MA: Little, Brown and Company, 2000), 113–14.

19 See Randy Roberts, "The Wide World of Muhammad Ali: The Politics and Economics of Televised Boxing," in Elliot J. Gorn, ed., *Muhammad Ali, the People's Champ* (Urbana, IL: University of Illinois Press, 1995), 28–37; Troy Rondinone, *Friday Night Fighter: Gaspar "Indio" Ortega and the Golden Age of Television Boxing* (Urbana, IL: University of Illinois Press, 2013), 218.

8

ADEYINKA MAKINDE

The Africans: Boxing and Africa

The history of the sport of boxing is one that is replete with the saga of competing races and nationalities. The story of the African-descended American pugilist is of course intimately bound with the history of the sport in its American epicenter. The contributions of the greats: Joe Gans, Jack Johnson, Joe Louis, Muhammad Ali, and the one reputed to be the greatest ever, Sugar Ray Robinson, are incalculable.

But what of those fighters from the "Mother Continent"? The names which stand out appear to be few and far in between: "Siki," "Tiger," and "Azumah" nonetheless would surely feature prominently in any creditable rendition of the history of boxing.

The contests in which they fought as world champions and against top contenders within American and European locations are recorded for posterity. Less well known – if at all known – are the stories of these fighters in their native lands and as immigrants in the established nations of boxing.

It is an often neglected aspect in the overall narrative of the history of the sport.

As is the case with much of the history of boxers, these men came from the lower orders of society. Africa has produced fighters who migrated from villages to the teeming urban areas built around colonial centers of commerce and administration. They were and still are of the urban proletariat; growing up scraping for survival on the margins of the community; more often than not the societal riff-raff.

The attraction to boxing in any society at any time and in any cultural environment is often bolstered by notions of masculine identity as well as the attraction to lucre.

In Africa, these factors have been present too. For instance, a boy who lost a traditional boxing contest in Ga-land was liable to have his food ration reduced by his mother,[1] whereas the skill of warding off troublemakers during disputes occurring while waiting at temper-infested communal water pumps became part of the molding process for Hogan "Kid" Bassey.

The sport has been viewed as a means of economic advancement by many a budding pugilist: from the petty-trading Nigerian, Dick Tiger, to the Ugandan child-soldier Kassim Ouma.

The vast and complex landscape of the land mass saddled with the unfortunate reputation as the "Dark Continent" has a boxing narrative as engaging as any other. The development of the sport in Africa is one which juxtaposes the colliding forces of pre-colonial culture with that of the succeeding colonial order and further on, was influenced by burgeoning nationalism and anti-colonial movements, and is shaped for better and for ill by the contemporary currents of social and economic development.

Before the advent of boxing, African societies had developed traditional forms of fighting. The Yoruba had the martial arts system of *Gidigbo*, whereas the Igbo, another West African people, practiced *Mgba*, a form of wrestling alluded to in passages of Chinua Achebe's seminal novel, *Things Fall Apart*. The wrestling techniques practiced by the Nuba are recorded in depictions on ancient Egyptian art, and among the Bantu tribes of south-western Africa, the fighting spirit of these communities embodied in the term *Kapwera* was distilled into a system evolved by African slaves in Brazil, which came to be known as *Capoeira*.

But the connection between the myriad traditional African fighting styles and boxing is not as tenuous as may often appear. While the sport of boxing, along with other Western-developed sports, came to Africa largely through the institutions of colonialism: the education system, missionaries, and the military, the ensuing dialectic of Western and indigenous values produced a particular synthesis in the former British colony of the Gold Coast, now known as Ghana, which has succeeded in producing a steady stream of champion fighters – some of them at world level.[2]

Among the Ga people, the genesis of a boxing culture was the result of the outlawing of traditional forms of martial warfare by the British-imposed colonial order. *Asafo atwele*, a form of group fighting among the urban poor of the city of Accra, emerged in the early part of the twentieth century. It pitted age-graded combatants among the largely fishing communities in contests which featured the exchange of bare-knuckled blows and kicks which utilized the soles of the feet.

Whereas the British and American narrative of the beginnings of modern boxing often depict fights occurring in rural open fields, inside dockside warehouses and on barges, for Ghanaians it is the beach. The lead-up to the contests held during "Saturday Beach Boxing" would begin early in the morning, with a lengthy period of "sea bathing," which would be followed by the issuing of challenges. The combatants would then do battle according to the appropriate age groups: children, youths, young men, and older men.[3]

It is from these origins that *asafo atwele* was transformed into organized forms of amateur and professional boxing. And while from the 1930s a host of boxing clubs would develop across the colony, from coastal cities like Accra to Kumasi in the center and Tamale in the north, it is Accra and specifically the area of Bukom that has produced the overwhelming numbers of Ghana's champions.

These include Roy Ankrah, the British Empire (later styled "Commonwealth") featherweight champion in the 1950s, and Floyd Robertson, a Commonwealth champion of the 1960s who unsuccessfully challenged for Sugar Ramos's world featherweight title.

In 1972, Attuquaye Clottey, a national champion, established the Akotoku Academy in Bukom. It is this fight factory, while building upon the historical legacy and tapping into the omnipresent fighting spirit of the Ga culture, that produced Ghana's first world boxing champion, David "Poison" Kotei who defeated Ruben Olivares for the WBC version of the featherweight title at California's Inglewood Forum in 1975. It also spawned the legendary Azumah Nelson who reigned as a world featherweight and super featherweight champion for most of the period between 1985 and 1997.

"Master boxer" would be a suitable appellation for Nelson, who combined boxing finesse with brutal knockout power. Born on July 19, 1958, his gold medal win at the Commonwealth Games of 1978 provided the icing on a stellar amateur career during which he compiled a record of fifty wins against two losses. Nelson won the Ghanaian featherweight title in only his third professional bout, adding the African title ten months later in December 1980 and then the vacant Commonwealth crown in September the following year by defeating the Australian Brian Roberts by a fifth-round stoppage.

His America debut in July 1982 was as a late substitute challenger for the WBC featherweight title held by the Mexican Salvador Sanchez. Nelson was unsuccessful, being stopped in the fifteenth and final round by a supremely gifted champion who would die tragically in a car accident the following month. He won the world title in December 1984 via an eleventh-round knockout of Wilfredo Gomez in San Juan, Puerto Rico, and made six successful defenses before stepping up to win the vacated super featherweight title in a match with Mario Martinez, a Mexican. He would make nine successful defenses until he lost the title to Jesse James Leija.

Nelson won his third world title in December 1995 before losing it by split decision to Gernardo Hernandez in March 1997. He did not win any of the three comeback attempts he would make over the next decade. Nonetheless, these failures do not diminish the stature or the accomplishments of the man who bore the moniker "The Professor."[4]

It was remarked back in the 1960s, at a time when Nigeria could boast of having had two boxers take up the mantle of world champion, how ironic it was that Ghana, with a far better system of organization, had none.

But it was no surprise that African champions would have emanated from either nation, both being former colonies of the British, whose colonial administrations across the continent had consistently promoted the idea of organized games and sports, which had the explicit objectives of harmonizing the different ethnic communities they had conquered.[5]

The requirement of sports as a part of the academic curricula, that ideal of developing the body alongside the mind, was pursued in a manner not pursued by rival French and Portuguese colonists.[6]

Organized boxing through a system of clubs controlled by local promoters were common enough around the urban centers of Nigeria that by the late 1940s, the country's boxing board of control was established. The sport had been brought there by colonists and developed by their successors, a host of sports enthusiasts within the expatriate community.[7]

Much of the inspiration to lace up the gloves came from the descendants of Africans in the diaspora.

The tales of Jack Jackson's feat in defeating Tommy Burns in 1908 to become the first black heavyweight champion were passed down to budding Nigerian fighters. When the rising black American heavyweight Joe Louis took on the Italian Primo Carnera in New York City in 1935, that contest became in the eyes of American blacks and their African cousins a symbol of Abyssinian (Ethiopian) resistance to an invasion of that nation by the fascist forces of Italy. The rise of black American fighters such as Archie Moore and Sugar Ray Robinson to the elite levels of the sport inspired many.[8]

The improvements in standards of administration as well as what would turn out to be a great migration of Nigerian and other fighters of West African origin to the United Kingdom would pave the way for the emergence of the first Nigerian fighters to make a mark on a world level: Hogan "Kid" Bassey and Dick Tiger.

The circumstances that led to this "great migration" involved a combination of mainly economic factors: the United Kingdom's parlous financial position and a recession in the boxing industry.

Britain at the end of the Second World War, while still at the helm of an empire and officially the "Mother Nation" of vast swathes of the globe, was effectively bankrupt.

The British Nationality Act passed by Parliament in 1948 granted citizenship to all members of the colonies and enabled those who traveled to Britain the right to stay for an indefinite period of time.

Among the migrants were boxers who came to seek gainful employment in industry and aspirant workers who ended up as boxers. But given that most could not earn a living solely from prizefighting, many straddled both worlds; working daylight hours in menial jobs and training during the evenings in gymnasiums in readiness for bouts scheduled to occur either during the week or at the weekend.

A significant development in focusing the sights of ambitious African fighters was the decision in 1950 to form the British Empire Championships Committee. This enabled each British-ruled African nation to appoint a representative steward who would participate in determining the rankings of boxers in the different weight divisions.

The British Empire boxing title system had been inaugurated in 1908 and, although technically open to boxers from any part of the empire, was effectively limited to those from the "white" nations: Britain, Australia, New Zealand, Canada, and South Africa.

The issue of race was of course never far away.

A black South African welterweight, one Andrew Jeptha, had in fact won the British title in that division back in 1907, but the "color bar," an adopted policy measure which imposed a rule restricting the ability to fight for mainstream titles on the grounds of racial origin, proved not to be only an American phenomenon.

The British authorities had been alarmed by the outbreaks of violence between the races in America in the aftermath of the victory of Jack Johnson over James J. Jeffries in 1910 and were keen to avoid such occurrences in the territories over which they ruled a large amount of black and brown peoples.

The body that controlled boxing, the National Sporting Club, would in the 1920s prevent not only Africans from attempting to repeat the feat of Jeptha, but also ban British-born blacks from contesting for British titles.

"It is only right," said Charles Donmall, the general-secretary of the NSC's successor, the British Boxing Board of Control, "that a small country such as ours should have championships restricted to boxers of white parents – otherwise we might be faced with a situation where all our British titles are held by coloured empire boxers."

The board formally abrogated its position in 1947 in the face of a great deal of pressure provided not least by the progress up the ranks of the fabulously talented mixed-race Turpin brothers, Randolph and Dick.[9]

This was progress. When Battling Siki ripped through Georges Carpentier, stopping the Frenchman in the sixth round to claim the world's light heavyweight championship in 1922, he had initially been denied the championship on the grounds of a manufactured foul disqualification decision.

He was, afterward, effectively denied the right to earn a living by being banned from European boxing jurisdictions. Holland, Belgium, and England all prevented matches being made so that in the following year he was forced to make a circuitous journey to Dublin where, in the midst of the Irish Civil War and ill-prepared, he lost to Mike McTigue.

There was much more to Siki, the man and the boxer, than the mythology constructed by contemporary reportage that was immersed in the racially biased standards of the age and which was dutifully transmitted over the years as gospel truth by scribes of the sport.

Born Amadou Fall at the turn of the twentieth century in Saint-Louis, a town situated in the north of French-ruled Senegal, to a Wolof family, the boy who became the first African to win a world boxing title was taken to France by an expatriate benefactor only to be abandoned. He worked in a succession of menial jobs in the south of the country while acquainting himself with the boxing clubs and boxing booths situated in the cities of Marseille, Toulon, Nice, and Bordeaux.

He was fighting professionally just before the outbreak of the First World War. After the United States' entry into the war he would, according to the recollection of an American soldier, tour the camps of the American Expeditionary Force (AEF) based in the South of France, meeting "the best heavyweights of the American Army."

During the war, Siki served in Toulon's Eighth Colonial regiment. Beginning with an assault in the Champagne sector of the Western front and, later, a ferociously fought landing and subsequent trench-based fighting in Gallipoli, he would go on to participate in battles in most of the fronts. He was decorated with the *Croix de Guerre* and *Medaille Militaire* before being demobilized in 1919.

After the war, his record of forty-three wins in forty-six bouts earned him a shot at Carpentier's world title. Relocating himself to the United States after the loss of his title, Siki found little success, losing key bouts to Kid Norfolk and Paul Berlenbach. He was shot and killed in the Hell's Kitchen area of New York on December 15, 1925, in what may have been a gangland execution.

It was an inglorious end and one that gave credence to frequent tales of Siki the barely civilized "Jungle-child."

The real Siki, although no paragon of virtue and decorum, was a sensitive man who spoke several languages fluently. He had grown up in a colonial garrison town that bordered the Atlantic Ocean. As a fighter, he spoke out against the racism that often constricted his career, and he also defied the gangsters who ran the sport of boxing by refusing to go along with fight fixes, acts which may have led to the termination of his life.[10]

For Africans, boxing competitively in 1950s Britain would be a far cry from earlier times when common chants of "Don't let the nigger win" echoed around match venues. When suspicious decisions went against an African fighter, audiences were often fair enough to slow-clap the verdict.

The first African boxer to take advantage of the opportunities presented by the removal of travel and other restrictions was a son of Bukom. Roy Ankrah's nickname among British fight fans, the "Black Flash," alluded to a style he had developed within the fighting culture of *asafo atwele*.

His nonstop attacking style, which consisted of rapidly moving, windmill-like fists, were an adaptation of the *Kla* method by which practitioners of *asafo atwele* sought to overwhelm their opponents. Ankrah won the British Empire featherweight title in April 1951 when he defeated Ronnie Clayton at the Empress Hall in London's Earls Court district.

Although Ankrah's landmark victory would serve as a model of achievement for his people back home in the Gold Coast and would inspire more African fighters to seriously take up boxing, his success was met with displeasure in certain quarters. The presence of growing numbers of blacks in the sport and in wider society worried some, including one journalist who effectively called for an ethnic cleansing of blacks in the sport.[11]

But the steady stream of boxers among the general ranks of immigrants would continue. In fact, developments in the health of the sport of boxing would contribute to an ever-increasing number of transatlantic travelers.

While the trajectory of boxing as a mass audience spectacle as well as a participatory sport was inevitably headed on a downward curve, the recession the sport suffered in Britain from the early 1950s was due to the impact of the imposition of a taxation measure, which led to the closure of many small and medium-scale fight promoters as well as a steep decline in the figures of licensed boxers.[12]

The migrant fighters of West African origin would thus become cheap labor for the struggling managers and promoters within the game, and they played a major role in keeping the British game afloat during the ensuing depression.

They fought in the halls and arenas up and down the British Isles, and within the confines of the squared ring they earned the reputation as earnest if not particularly skilful scrappers.[13] That was not particularly surprising given that the environments from which they had been transplanted had not been immersed in any substantive traditions of the sport. Organized boxing in their homelands could be traced back to a period not exceeding two decades.

That they always appeared to be in training spoke not only of their capacity for hard work, but also of their readiness to be co-opted onto the bills of promoters. For most, boxing would be the life of the "substitute fighter," that is, a fighter who was available to perform at short notice.

It was a state of affairs that reeked of exploitation.

One fighter who was not prepared to succumb to the life of a journeyman boxer and who displayed a level of skill far in excess of that typically offered by the West African fighters was the Nigerian, Hogan "Kid" Bassey, who made it a rule never to take a substitute fight.

He was born Okon Bassey Asuquo on June 3, 1932 in Creek Town, situated on the banks of the Cross River in what was the British-ruled southern protectorate of Nigeria. A product of Nap Peregrino's Imperial Boxing Club, Bassey had become the West African flyweight champion when barely out of secondary school. He fought behind a forceful left jab, was fleet of foot, and commanded the ring with an intelligence that belied his tender years.

To his first English manager, Peter Banasko, a former boxer of Ghanaian ancestry, Bassey, who arrived in Liverpool in November 1951 as a nineteen-year-old, was "the finished article."

He was also personable and good looking, a package that would easily make him the most bankable of the migrant fighters. Interviewed by the *Liverpool Echo* in 1954, Johnny Best Jr., the proprietor of the famous Liverpool Stadium, said the following:

> If you could hear the reception Hogan Bassey gets from the crowd in the (Liverpool) Stadium, you would think that he was a white boy. The whole crowd just rises to him ... In my opinion, boxing has deteriorated since before the war, but Hogan Bassey as a fighter is as good, if not better than pre-war English boxers.[14]

Bassey's inexorable rise began after his debut victory, a stoppage, at the Liverpool Stadium against Ray Hillyard in January 1952. The single-mindedness which ensured that he did not take on substitute fights informed his action in ruthlessly discarding Banasko in favor of George Biddles, a manager based in Leicester.

After winning the British Empire featherweight title with a devastating eighth-round knockout of Billy "Spider" Kelly in November 1955, Bassey linked up with the American duo of Lew Burston and Wilfred "Jersey" Jones, the former an international agent who had developed a habit of importing non-American fighters to the United States, and the latter a boxing insider who had taken to managing and had useful contacts within the Madison Square Garden organization.

These contacts ensured that he was well placed to be put in line as one of the candidates to succeed Sandy Saddler as world champion in a series of elimination contests. In Paris, on June 24, 1957, he defeated Cherif Hamia by a tenth-round technical knockout to become the world champion.

During a twenty-one-month reign, Bassey fought frequently. Most were nontitle bouts against European opposition on British soil and American-based fighters including a stoppage win over featherweight great Willie Pep. His first defense in April 1958, against the Mexican Ricardo Moreno, ended with a third-round knockout of the challenger. He lost his title against the American Davey Moore, in March 1959, when his corner threw in the towel at the end of the thirteenth round. Bassey failed in an attempt to regain his title six months later and soon after announced his retirement.[15]

He was appointed Nigeria's chief amateur boxing coach and guided the national teams to a succession of international tournaments including the Commonwealth and Olympic Games. He died in January 1998.

Bassey laid the groundwork for his compatriot, Richard Ihetu, who fought under the *nomme de guerre* Dick Tiger. Unlike Bassey, he was a late bloomer who did not display finesse but possessed a willingness to learn and displayed sheer doggedness to recover from a debut of four consecutive losses after relocating to Liverpool in late 1955.

He went on to take the British Empire middleweight title from Patrick McAteer in March 1958 and soon after relocated to the United States with the same team that had handled Bassey and would wrest the NBC version of the world middleweight title from Gene Fullmer.

Tiger, whose popularity owed a lot to fighting during the waning years of regularly televised boxing, sponsored by the Gillette Corporation, would become a crowd-attracting figure at New York City's Madison Square Garden in the last phase of the halcyon era of the venue often referred to as the "Mecca of Boxing."

Born on August 14, 1929, in Amaigbo in the Southern Nigeria Protectorate of the British Empire, Tiger's life and career as a boxer was replete with setbacks. Yet, time and again, he would dig into an immense set of internal resources that enabled him to overcome these difficulties. He had learned to be self-reliant when barely into adolescence; his father's death had compelled him to head to the city to work alongside his brothers as a petty trader.

His outlook was doubtlessly shaped during his formative years by the spirit of the times in many Igbo communities, such as that found in the city of Aba, where he lived and worked. They were consumed by a sense of unbridled optimism and a marked sentiment of aspiration, undergirded by Christian and entrepreneurial precepts. The titles of the chapbooks that sold voluminously in market places and the inscriptions etched prominently on a multitude of commercial vehicles distilled a simple and persuasive philosophy for even the barely literate: a life of sobriety and determination would inevitably grant one the blessings of success in life's endeavors.

Dick Tiger may have walked the well-trodden path of the down-trodden African journeyman fighter common in the British fight game in the 1950s and 1960s, but an inner resolution to achieve prevented this. His accomplishment in obtaining the British Empire championship, and indeed, the later feat of becoming a two-division world champion is better appreciated when acquainted with the facts of his early career.

Tiger was on the verge of being stripped of his boxing license by the British Boxing Board of Control after his initial losses, a near disaster that would have led to his quitting the game. Then eschewing what would have been his lot as just another ne'er-do-well African boxer, he won bouts even when selected at short notice as a substitute fighter. When Mickey Duff earmarked him as a trial horse for the up-and-coming Terry Downes, Tiger upset the odds and created a pathway that led to the Empire title.

His path to world championship glory was not easy in the United States, where he would compete against arguably the most formidable array of middleweight talent in the history of the division. Among those who he came up against and defeated were the likes of Gene Fullmer, Joey Giardello, Rubin Carter, Jose Gonzalez, Florentino Fernanadez, and Henry Hank.[16]

For a time the oldest world champion at thirty-six, he confounded the boxing world when, after losing his middleweight title to Emile Griffith, he stepped up to the light heavyweight division and in December 1966 defeated the champion Jose Torres. Torres, who only had one loss in forty-one bouts, was six years younger and had marked advantages over Tiger in both height and reach.

Tiger's reign came to an end in May 1968 when a powerful combination by Bob Foster knocked him out. It was no disgrace to lose to a man who for many is the greatest light heavyweight in history. A passionate spokesman for the cause of Biafran secession from Nigeria during an extremely bloody thirty-month civil war, Tiger boxed for a few more years and officially retired after being diagnosed with terminal liver cancer. He died on December 14, 1971.[17]

After Tiger's success as a two-time world middleweight champion and a light heavyweight titleholder until his dethronement by Bob Foster, there would be no further champions from Nigeria, until the heavyweight Samuel Peter won a version of a world title in the 2000s.[18]

In the aftermath of the Nigerian Civil War, during which the secessionist state of Biafra sought independent status, the Nigerian government instituted a policy of encouraging boxers not to turn professional. Success within the amateur ranks brought rewards of cars, apartments, and government jobs.

The professional sport was neglected at the expense of the amateur game. It meant that talented fighters, such as the featherweight Eddie Ndukwu, a Commonwealth gold medallist in 1966, would not turn professional until over a decade later, by which time, perhaps, he was unable to make as great an impact as he could have.[19]

In the 1970s a crop of boxers from another English-speaking outpost would begin making an impression in the amateur and then the professional ranks of world boxing. As was the case with Ghana and Nigeria, organized boxing in the East African nation of Uganda took root via the institutions of the British education system, the military, and a merging of interests of both expatriate and indigenous sports enthusiasts.

A key mark in the development of the sport there was the winning of a silver medal at the Commonwealth Games in Perth in 1962 by a light middleweight boxer, Francis Were Nyangweso.

Three strong contingents of fighters were sent to the Olympic Games in Mexico in 1968, to the 1970 Commonwealth Games held in Scotland, as well as to the Munich Olympics of 1972. Leo Rwabwogo made his mark as a bronze medallist at the Mexico City games and as a silver medallist in Munich. In 1973, Uganda was crowned the amateur boxing champion nation of Africa.

The upward trajectory of the sport was shaken but not destroyed by the political turmoil brought about by the tyrannical reign of General Idi Amin, himself a former light heavyweight champion of the nation.

Boxers formed part of the statistics of disappeared ones, which included cabinet ministers and the archbishop of the nation.

Ayub Kalule, who won the welterweight gold medal at the inaugural world amateur championships, was forced to flee to Denmark to start his professional career, and John Mugabi, a silver medallist at the 1980 Moscow Olympics, went to London where he earned a contract fighting out of Mickey Duff's stable before relocating to Florida in the United States.

Kalule eventually won the WBA version of the junior middleweight world title which he lost to Sugar Ray Leonard at Houston's Astrodome in 1981, and Mugabi also won a title at that division after stepping up to the middleweight division to challenge and lose to Marvelous Marvin Hagler in 1986.[20]

The continental powerhouse of boxing is arguably South Africa, where international-level competition was stifled for decades by the sporting isolation imposed in protest against the state policy of apartheid: the institutionalized separation of the races. Between 1927 and 2001, thirty-five South African fighters won a total of forty-nine world boxing titles.[21]

The story of the development of the game in South Africa hinges on the migration of black Africans to the urban population centers including those around Durban, Cape Town, Pietermaritzburg, and Bloemfontein.

Not unlike in other parts of the world, boxing was touted as a crime-preventative activity through which restless youth could be occupied by a form of physical activity which would enable them to develop discipline and self-respect. It was also a useful skill to have in the rough townships.[22]

It also became associated with notions of cosmopolitanism and egalitarianism: the game attracted both plebeians and the elite in African society, such as the budding lawyer, Nelson Mandela.

The racially based separation of boxing titles was already established in South Africa long before the formal establishment of the system of apartheid by the National Party in 1949.

The emergence of Willie "Baby Jake" Mbatha in winning the Non-European welterweight title in 1938 triggered a revolution among black fighters, which a decade later would prompt a promoter, J.B. Panday, to make the prescient observation that "they will be right on top and there may come a time when South Africa will capture the world titles."[23]

The world championship victories of "Baby Jake" Matlala, "Sugar Boy" Malinga and others in recent decades attest to this. But long before this, a first dose of international achievement came in 1952 when Jake Ntuli won the British Empire flyweight title during a year-long tour of the British Isles.

This success among others, however, posed a threat to the hegemonic aspirations of apartheid, prompting the Nationalist government to pass the Boxing and Wrestling Control Act of 1954.[24]

White privilege had afforded the South African boxer of European ancestry opportunities to compete internationally for British Empire and world championship belts as well as in the Olympic Games.

The lot of his black counterpart was much different.

"Shackled," as he put it, "by the twin handicaps of poverty and racism," Nelson Mandela observed the travails of the typical black African boxer whose income went primarily toward "food, rent, and clothing with whatever was left meeting the cost of training and equipment."[25]

The black boxer did not have the luxury of belonging to the white boxing clubs, which were better equipped than the clubs to which blacks belonged. They had to make do without quality sparring and high-grade trainers as they attempted to make it in the boxing world while holding down full-time jobs.[26]

As was the case in the United States, changes to the system of racial separation began occurring in the field of sport long before its formal dismantling. In South Africa, interracial bouts were made legal in October 1976, but the practice of separating boxers on racial grounds was firmly dispensed with only after the abolition of "white," "black," and "supreme" titles two years later, in January 1979.[27]

The narrated history of Africa tends to characterize Europeans as a "settler" community lacking the credentials of an indigenous people. Yet, if the designation of Marcel Cerdan, a "Pied Noir" born in French Algeria, as an "African" fighter has a ring of tenuousness surrounding it, such an appellation in the case of white South Africans does not seem as forced.

The "white tribe" of *voetrekker* Afrikaners arguably have such a claim, even more than their English co-nationals. Afrikaner sporting identity, is of course inextricably entwined in the sport of rugby, but many have laced the gloves and made an impact on the sport.

Gerry Coetzee holds the distinction of being the first boxer from the African continent to have fought for a world heavyweight title. When in 1983 he won a version at his third attempt by knocking out the American Michael Dokes, he not only became Africa's first ever world heavyweight champion, but, as was prominently noted at the time, he happened to be the first white man to hold a title since the Swede Ingemar Johansson, twenty-three years earlier.[28]

Coetzee was born on April 8, 1955, in Boksburg, a city in what was then the Transvaal Province. After an amateur career during which he maintained a keen rivalry with Kallie Knoetze, a fighter who would come to national and international attention at the same time as him, Coetzee turned professional in 1974.

He became South African heavyweight champion in August 1976 after his opponent, Mike "The Tank" Schutte, was disqualified in the sixth round. A first-round stoppage of former world champion Leon Spinks in Monte Carlo in June 1979 set up his first tilt at a world title, which he lost (on home soil) to the American John Tate. A year later he lost to Mike Weaver, Tate's successor, via a thirteenth-round technical knockout.[29]

Coetzee did not hold on to the title for long after his victory over Michael Dokes whom he knocked out in the tenth round. Fifteen months later, in his first defense, Coetzee was himself knocked out by Greg Page.

After Coetzee, Francois Botha won the IBF World Heavyweight title in 1995 but was soon afterward stripped of it after failing a drug test. The last South African to hold a version of the title was Corrie Sanders, when on March 8, 2003, he upset WBO heavyweight champion Wladimir Klitschko in two rounds.[30]

The black African fighters nonetheless have come to dominate South African boxing and emerge on to the world stage, among them the super middleweight Thulani "Sugar Boy" Malinga, flyweight "Baby Jake" Jacob

Matlala, and lightweight Dingaan Thobela, all title holders. It is therefore somewhat ironic that the man widely believed to be the greatest South African boxer is white, albeit that he was often referred to by his compatriots as a "black fighter in white skin."

Brian Mitchell, a high-volume aggressive puncher, learned his trade and earned his laurels the hard way. He took on the best fighters in the black townships and won the national title at junior lightweight before defeating the Panamanian Alfredo Layne for the WBA super featherweight title, which he would go on to defend a record eleven times.[31]

He would never lose a title fight.

As the twentieth century transitioned into the twenty-first, the ebony-hewed, sinewy muscled figure of the African boxer continued to ply his trade from the Cape to Cairo and to the far ends of the globe. Bukom continues to churn out world-level talent through the likes of Ike Quartey and Joshua Clottey. The Ugandan, Kassim Ouma, like Quartey and Clottey, for a time became the holder of a version of a world title.[32] However, the constructed reputation of a dominant fighter – the closest of which was the reign of Ghana's Azumah – is one which has continually eluded fighters of African origin.

Casting a gaze back to a time when Nigeria boasted of two world champions in relatively quick succession and with world title bouts being staged first in Ibadan[33] and then Accra, it would have been forgivable to predict a future in which the African component of the sport would achieve a measure of prominence, if not outright dominance.

This is not to imbue Africans with an exaggerated set of qualities by which they are predisposed to perform better, but rather is an acknowledgement of the turn in the wheels of history.

As a route to economic advancement, prizefighting is naturally dominated by those from poorer backgrounds, so that the emergent African boxer along with his South American and Central American counterparts were expected to increase their participation as the more prosperous bastions in North America and Western Europe decreased theirs.

The sense of promise engendered by the achievements of the 1950s and 1960s has not been fulfilled. The lack of infrastructure in most African countries serves as a continuing impediment to the growth and development of the sport. As in the past, fighters need to migrate to America and to Europe to make an impact. There they have access to trainers, managers, and promoters to put them on a path toward building a career that would not be possible in their local habitat.

The story of African boxing is nonetheless an expansive one. African boxing and boxers merged into the consciousness of the different societies fighting for liberation from colonial control and as such the careers of the most successful ones became entwined with the nationalist sentiments of the day as the connection between Roy Ankrah's British Empire title win and Kwame Nkrumah's release from British detention showed.[34]

Both Hogan Bassey[35] and Dick Tiger represented an emergent nationalism in a conglomerate nation indelicately weaved together by imperial draughtsmen. The leaders of the major political factions in Nigeria were in Paris to witness Bassey's world title victory as the political elite were on hand to sponsor Dick Tiger's 1963 middleweight title defense against Gene Fullmer in the city of Ibadan, black Africa's first world title bout.[36]

That their achievements intensified the pan-Africanist spirit of the times is attested to by Bassey's popularity in 1950s South Africa[37] and Nkrumah's congratulatory letter to Dick Tiger on the occasion of his victory over Fullmer.[38]

Boxers also served as components in the tribally motivated revolts that wracked the continent. It was the national torchbearer Tiger – to one American journalist, a "pugilistic plenipotentiary" – who renounced Nigeria and became a propagandist in the cause of Biafran secession.[39] And as purveyors of a politically active youth subculture referred to as "Tokyo Joes," many Ga boxers of the late 1950s and the early 1960s, with their distinctive military haircuts, represented an ethnicized resistance against the ruling political party in Ghana.[40]

The financial emancipation promised by boxing is often illusory. The attraction of society elites to the sport never camouflages the sport's attraction to the exploiters: the hard-nosed promoter, organized criminals, and the hangers-on who bleed the boxer dry.

The migrant West African boxers who relocated to Britain in the 1950s were for the most part an expendable commodity to be chewed over and spat out by an industry that was in need of cheap labor. They were willing victims in a game they were all too familiar with back home and practiced by promoters who paid them even less than they received in Britain.

The twin forces of capital exploitation and racism pervade the development of the sport in South Africa, where the story of the tragic Jacob "Dancing Shoes" Morake, an earnest professional short of money and in need of providing for his family, was hustled into an ill-advised comeback on a bill at Sun City, where, weight-drained, his body succumbed to the heat and the blows of his opponent.[41]

The African boxer, as with all boxers, consents to dice with death every time he steps into the ring;[42] the fate of Young Ali, the Nigerian featherweight who died after a bout with Barry McGuigan, being one example of this ultimate sacrifice.[43]

And it is to the shades of each departed protagonist and his present and future successors – the village migrant, the urban street urchin, the Western-bound stowaway who dreamed and still dreams the good pugilist's dream – that this story is dedicated.

NOTES

1 *Sunday Mirror* (Ghana), September 26, 1954, 15. Referred to by Dunzendorfer, Jan (2013). "Ethnicized Boxing: The Tale of Ghana's Boxing Roots in Local Martial Art." *Sport in Society: Cultures, Commerce, Media, Politics* 17 (8).

2 Examined in the following paper: Akyeampong, Emmanuel (2002). "Bukom and the Social History of Boxing in Accra: Warfare and Citizenship in Pre-colonial Ga Society." *The International Journal of African Historical Studies*, 35 (1), Special Issue: Leisure in African History.

3 The organizing and the rituals of the issuing challenges associated with *asafo atwele* are described by Akyeampong in his paper, pp. 49–52.

4 See Morrison, Ashley (2014). *The Professor: The Life Story of Azumah Nelson*, Houston, TX: Strategic Book Publishing & Rights Agency.

5 Turner, Victor (ed.) (1971). *Colonialism in Africa 1870–1960. Vol. III: Profiles of Change: African Society and Colonial Rule*. London: Cambridge University Press.

6 Mazrui, Ali (1986). *The Africans: A Triple Heritage*, 1st edn, London: BBC Publications, p. 130.

7 See Makinde, Adeyinka (2005). "Boxing: Rousing the Nigerian Giant." *African Renaissance*, 2 (2), p. 69.

8 Dick Tiger claimed to have been inspired to box after reading about the exploits of the likes of "Henry Armstrong, Joe Louis, and Ray Robinson." See Makinde, Adeyinka (2005). *Dick Tiger: The Life and Times of a Boxing Immortal*, Tarentum: Word Association, p.11. Hogan Bassey often alluded to Joe Louis as his role model. See Hogan Bassey's piece, "My Fighting Life", in the October 1957 edition of *Drum* magazine.

9 The impact on black and African fighters through the policies and initiatives of first the National Sporting Club and the British Boxing Board of Control is covered in depth in John Harding's *Lonsdale's Belt: Story of Boxing's Greatest Prize*, published by Robson Books in 1994.

10 For an in-depth reassessment of Siki's life and times, see Benson, Peter (2006). *Battling Siki: A Tale of Ring Fixes, Race and Murder in the 1920s*, Fayetteville, AR: University of Arkansas Press.

11 A 1951 article in the *Sunday Dispatch* by Tony Horstead referred to by Makinde in *Dick Tiger*, p. 37.

12 See Harding, *Lonsdale's Belt*. Also Makinde's *Dick Tiger*, which makes references to the changing conditions as conveyed by contemporary reports in *Boxing News*, the *Liverpool Echo* and columns written for the Nigerian *Daily Times* by Douglas Collister, an expatriate English boxing enthusiast who became the first chairman of the Nigerian Boxing Board of Control, relocating to England after his retirement where he became a steward for the British Boxing Board of Control.

13 A discussion of the generally "unscientific style" of African fighters and the racialized analysis of the day can be found in Michael Gennero's unpublished dissertation, "'Empire Boxers are the Goods': Race, Boxing, and Nigerians in the Black Atlantic," University of Florida, 2016, p. 5.

14 Interviewed by the *Liverpool Echo* in 1954. Reproduced by Makinde in *Dick Tiger*, p. 24.

15 See Bassey, Hogan (1963). *Bassey on Boxing*, London: Thomas Nelson & Sons.

16 See Makinde, Adeyinka (Dec. 12 2012). "Dick Tiger vs. Henry Hank: A Golden Era of Middleweight Boxers," *Boxing.com*.

17 Tiger's life and career is comprehensively covered by Makinde in *Dick Tiger*.

18 Albeit that Henry Akinwande, a Briton born of Nigerian parents, won the WBO heavyweight title in 1996.

19 Ndukwu failed in his attempt to wrest the world title from Wilfredo Gomez in April 1980.

20 Cornelius Boza Edwards, like Mugabi a migrant to England, won the WBC super featherweight championship in 1981.

21 www.boxingsa.co.za/sa_boxing_champs.html (accessed September 20, 2017) "South Africa's Boxing Champs" from *Boxing South Africa*. Midway through 2016, the figure had risen to seventy-nine boxers winning 136 titles recognized by one or more of boxing's sanctioning organizations. See Jackson, Ron (July 11, 2016). "Colourful History of SA Boxing." *Supersport.com*. Vic Toweel, who won the world batamweight title in 1950, remains the only South African to win an undisputed world title.

22 Fleming, Tyler (2011). "Now the African Reigns Supreme: The Rise of African Boxing on the Witwatersrand, 1924–1959," *International Journal of the History of Sport*.

23 Untitled article in the *Natal Daily News*, June 4, 1947, quoted from Singh, Benny (1947) *My Baby and Me: A Story of Non-European Boxing in South Africa*, Durban: Central News Agency, p. 87.

24 This piece of legislation, alongside the broader-based Group Areas Act (1950), which restricted the number of blacks who could settle in urban areas, affected the development of black African boxing.

25 Mandela, Nelson (1995). *Long Road to Freedom: The Autobiography of Nelson Mandela*, 1st edn, London: Little, Brown and Company, p.194.

26 Ibid.

27 Nauright, John and Parrish, Charles (eds) (2012). *Sports Around the World. Vol. I: History, Culture and Practice*, Santa Barbara, CA: ABC-CLIO), p. 110.

28 Coetzee won the WBA version of the world heavyweight title.

29 The dates of his losses were, respectively, October 20, 1979 (to Tate) and October 25, 1980 (to Weaver).

30 Sanders vacated his title to challenge Klitschko's elder brother Vitali for the vacant WBC belt. He was stopped in the eighth round.

31 Mitchell defeated Layne on September 27, 1986.

32 Both Clottey and Quartey won titles in the welterweight division whereas Ouma succeeded at light middleweight.

33 See Makinde, Adeyinka (2013). "A Night to Remember but ...," *Africa Today*, 19 (0809), 31–34. Also, Gennaro, Michael (2013). "The Whole Place is in

Pandemonium": Dick Tiger Versus Gene Fullmer III, and the Consumption of Boxing in Nigeria," *International Journal of the History of Sport*, 30 (16), 1903–1914.

34 Nkrumah was released on February 12, 1951, while Ankrah won his title on April 30 of the same year.

35 Bassey's triumphs "became an emblem of what Nigeria could achieve." See Anene Ejikeme, "Hogan 'Kid' Bassey: Nigerian Icon." In Toyin Falola and Adam Paddock (eds), *Emerging Themes and Methods in African Studies* (Trenton: African World Press, 2008), p. 444.

36 Ibid. Makinde and Gennaro.

37 Efforts to bring Bassey to fight in South Africa were unsuccessful because of a government ban on foreign fighters when he was active in the 1950s. See Fleming, ibid.

38 Nkrumah's cable to Tiger, reproduced in Makinde, *Dick Tiger*, p. 130, lauds the boxer's achievement as "testimony to the ability of the African to scale the highest ladder of human achievement." He went on to mention his hope that his example would "inspire the youth of Africa and give fillip to the quest to assert the African personality not only in sport but in all fields of human endeavour."

39 Makinde, ibid. Tiger also made a stance against apartheid by refusing to participate in a three-bout tour against black opponents scheduled for September 1970. Ibid. pp. 247–48.

40 Referred to by Dunzendorfer in "Ethnicized Boxing: The Tale of Ghana's Boxing Roots in Local Martial Art." *Sport in Society: Cultures, Commerce, Media, Politics* 17 (8), 11–12.

41 Detailed in Gavin Evans's biography *Dancing Shoes is Dead: A Tale of Fighting Men in South Africa*, London: Doubleday.

42 Boxing deaths in Africa, as in other jurisdictions, are invariably followed by emotive public discourse. For instance, in 1953, in Nigeria, the death of a fighter and a five-day long coma endured by another boxer knocked unconscious on the same fight card, spurred an animated debate, conducted in the press columns, between Bishop S.C. Phillips, a former boxer turned critic of the sport, and Horatio Agedah, a well-known journalist. Examined in the following paper: Gennaro, Michael (2016), "Ban This Cruel Sport Boxing: Death in the Ring and the Legitimacy of Boxing in Colonial Nigeria," *Nigeria in the Ring: Boxing, Masculinity, and Empire in Nigeria, 1930–1957*, unpublished dissertation, University of Florida.

43 The fight was held on June 14, 1982. See McGuigan, Barry (2011). *Cyclone: My Story*, 1st edn, London: Virgin, pp. 95–106.

SOURCES

Books

Bassey, Hogan. *Bassey on Boxing*. London: Thomas Nelson & Sons, 1963.

Benson, Peter. *Battling Siki: A Tale of Ring Fixes, Race and Murder in the 1920s*. Fayetteville, AR: University of Arkansas Press, 2006.

Evans, Gavin. *Dancing Shoes is Dead: A Tale of Fighting Men in South Africa*. London: Doubleday, 2002.

Harding, John. *Lonsdale's Belt: Story of Boxing's Greatest Prize*. London: Robson Books, 1994.

Makinde, Adeyinka. *Dick Tiger: The Life and Times of a Boxing Immortal*. Tarentum, PA: Word Association, 2005.

Mandela, Nelson. *Long Road to Freedom: The Autobiography of Nelson Mandela*, 1st edn. London: Little, Brown and Company, 1995.

Morrison, Ashley. *The Professor: The Life Story of Azumah Nelson*. Houston, TX: Strategic Book Publishing & Rights Agency, 2014.

Journals

Akyeampong, Emmanuel (2002). "Bukom and the Social History of Boxing in Accra: Warfare and Citizenship in Pre-colonial Ga Society." *The International Journal of African Historical Studies*, 35 (1), Special Issue: Leisure in African History, 39–60.

Dunzendorfer, Jan (2013). "Ethnicized Boxing: The Tale of Ghana's Boxing Roots in Local Martial Art." *Sport in Society: Cultures, Commerce, Media, Politics*, 17 (8), 1015–1029.

Fleming, Tyler (2011). "Now the African Reigns Supreme: The Rise of African Boxing on the Witwatersrand, 1924–1959." *The International Journal of the History of Sport*, 28 (1), 47–62.

Gennaro, Michael (2013). "The Whole Place is in Pandemonium: Dick Tiger Versus Gene Fullmer III, and the Consumption of Boxing in Nigeria." *The International Journal of the History of Sport*, 30 (16), 1903–1914.

Makinde, Adeyinka (2005). "Boxing: Rousing the Nigerian Giant." *African Renaissance*, 2 (2), 68–71.

Unpublished Work

Gennaro, Michael, "Empire Boxers are the Goods: Race, Boxing, and Nigerians in the Black Atlantic", *Nigeria in the Ring: Boxing, Masculinity, and Empire in Nigeria, 1930–1957*, unpublished dissertation, University of Florida, 2016.

9

BENITA HEISKANEN

A Century of Fighting Latinos: From the Margins to the Mainstream

In December 1914, the *Morning Oregonian* published an article lamenting that boxing was "practically unknown" in Latin America. Although "Americans of Spanish descent" had been accused of "being too prone to settle their quarrels with the knife," the article claimed, there was no reason why they should "not take kindly to the 'noble art.' "[1] In fact, the "great game of give and take" would not only be beneficial to trade and commerce between North and South America, but it would replace other "dangerous pastimes" – such as bullfighting – that made the locals "bloodthirsty and barbarous."[2] Also in 1914, the *Trenton Evening Times* lambasted Mexicans for steering clear of "honorable" fighting: "Give a Mexican a gun and he can go out and do a pretty bloody job of fighting, but ask him to put up his fists and mix things in Anglo-Saxon style and – carramba! [sic] – he will fade away."[3] Some fifteen years later, in June 1929, an article entitled "El Boxeador Popular Guy in Land of Chili Con Carne" in the *Reading Eagle* claimed exactly the opposite: "Everywhere 'boxeadores' flourish. Each country of Latin America boasts its 'campeones' in the various classes."[4] While demonstrating the nascent popularity of Latin American boxing, these excerpts also speak to changing stereotypes about Latinos.[5] A century ago, a widespread belief held that "the Latin race is incapable of producing good pugilists."[6] Yet during the course of the century, the toughest Latino fighters across the Americas came to epitomize the display of honor, courage, and heart in the ring. As they emerged from the margins to mainstream limelight, from abject poverty and the most ascetic training conditions, Latinos came to stand for national pride as much as personal heroism.

In the United States, prizefighting was banned in most states in the early 1900s, but despite its illegality, it was particularly popular in California. Although largely forgotten in the annals of pugilistic history, there were a number of Latino boxers who claimed fame in the prize ring in these early days, and many of them accumulated sizable ring records. As early as 1893, Solly Smith (Solomon Garcia Smith, 1871–1933) of Los Angeles, California, was the first Latino to win the world championship in the featherweight division, against Johnny Griffin of Braintree, Massachusetts. Hailing from half Mexican, half Irish background, newspapers habitually referred to Smith as a "Western pugilist" or a "Los Angeles lad" rather than a boxer of Mexican descent. It is unclear whether Smith's Mexican heritage would have been disadvantageous to his boxing career at a time when Irish and Jewish fighters were particularly popular, but emphasizing his Irishness likely boosted his ring credibility. Whatever the rationale to downplay his Mexican origins, Smith's career was an example of the ways in which boxers' marketability for crossover audiences was as crucial as their athletic ability, one which could make or break pugilistic careers.

Smith is best known for his two championship bouts with Canadian George "Little Chocolate" Dixon (1870–1908), the first black fighter to win the world championship in 1890, and the first Canadian world champion. Dixon, who fought both as a bantamweight and a featherweight, held the featherweight title between 1891 and 1897, before losing it to Smith, but reclaimed the belt in 1898. Two weeks before the first Smith–Dixon meeting in 1893, the *Philadelphia Inquirer* predicted the fight to be the "grandest fistic struggle which has ever occurred in this country between midget monarchs of the ring."[7] Although Smith had lost their first encounter, he came back to win the world featherweight title in his rematch against Dixon in 1897. These two overlooked Smith–Dixon boxing matches were effectively the first times a championship between North American fighters of African and Mexican descent was fought in the prize ring, long before African American and Latino match-ups would become the most exciting drama the sport had to offer in the late twentieth century. Other star-caliber Latino path-breakers of the early twentieth century included lightweight Aurelio Hererra, lightweight "Mexican" Joe Rivers (José Ybarra), bantamweight Ad Zotte, heavyweight "Mexican Pete" Everett, and featherweight Benny Chávez.[8] In the 1920s, Luis "El Toro Salvaje de las Pampas" [Wild Bull of the Pampas] Firpo of Argentina claimed worldwide fame not for his boxing record (39–24–2), but for being the first heavyweight Latino challenger for the world championship title in 1923. Firpo fought Jack Dempsey, who had built his reputation for fighting foreign nationals, all the while refusing to fight African American challengers in the ring, and managed to knock Dempsey down, even as he lost a controversial decision.

The most famous mainstream superstar Afro-Latino boxer of the early twentieth century was featherweight Kid Chocolate (1910–88), who grew up as Eligio Sardiñas Montalvo in Cerro, Cuba, and began his professional boxing career in Havana in 1927. Only a year later, in 1928, Chocolate made his debut in New York, where he lived for ten years. North American crossover audiences were dazzled by the Cuban sensation's physical ability: "He was a veritable will-o'-the wisp in speed," wrote the *New York Times* in 1930, "a strategical wizard and a rushing, crushing, destructive hitter."[9] Wherever the "Cuban Bon Bon" appeared, he created buzz: "They were so enthusiastic, I felt, they must be exaggerating. About one in fifty of these phenoms lines up to his billing. But as far as giving me a real bang is concerned, Kid Chocolate was all they said."[10] Moreover, Chocolate was praised for his sportsmanship, albeit through an odd combination of appraisal and racist insult: "Kid Chocolate is an amiable gentleman who conducts himself like a sportsman every minute he is in the ring. For one of his age and race, he is a remarkably cool performer."[11]

The overwhelming majority of Kid Chocolate's fights were fought on the East Coast, initially in front of crowds of thousands, and later to jam-packed audiences of tens of thousands. According to a *New York Times* report, seeing the Cuban perform, "50,000 fans were whipped into a wild holocaust of emotion."[12] Chocolate won his first world championship title in the junior lightweight division against Benny Bass in 1931 as the first Cuban to do so. Also in 1931, he challenged Tony Canzoneri for his light-weight and junior welterweight titles but was narrowly defeated in the score cards; in their rematch two years later, Canzoneri served Chocolate his first knockout loss. In 1933, Chocolate engaged in a series of overseas fights in France, Spain, Venezuela, and Cuba, after which he fought over twenty more victorious fights in New York before returning to Cuba for his final five bouts. On December 20, 1938, Chocolate's managers, Pincho Gutierrez and Jess Lasado, announced his retirement from boxing; the final record of his 151 bouts stands as 135 wins, ten losses, and six draws.

Although hugely popular, Kid Chocolate did not escape criticism, sporting as he did "fancy canes, spats, cravats and two-button suits" at a time when the nation was grappling with economic upheavals and general uncertainty.[13] Nor did he escape scandal. In December 1931, Chocolate was imprisoned for two weeks when the US State Department received a request from the Cuban government to extradite him. He was wanted on a charge of "seduction," one which in today's parlance translates into statutory rape. The father of seventeen-year-old Rosario Martínez accused Chocolate of deserting his daughter after having promised to marry her.[14] The charges were dropped after the fighter, accompanied by two Cuban police officers, legalized the marriage by proxy in New York, with the bride taking the vows in Havana.[15] After returning to Cuba, Chocolate started his own boxing gym, the Sala Polivalente Kid Chocolate, which is still used for boxing matches in Havana today. At a time when boxing was in dire straits because of economic turmoil in the United States, the "Cuban Bon Bon" managed to fill boxing arenas, disproving the notion that only heavyweight champions produced crossover interest in the ring. Another exciting fighter of the era was Alfonso Teófilo Brown (1902–51), aka "Panama" Al Brown, the first Panamanian to win the bantamweight championship, in 1929.

Sixto "El Gallito" [Little Rooster] Escobar (1913–79), the first Puerto Rican world champion, was a hugely popular fighter in the Caribbean, South America, and Spanish Harlem in New York. Escobar began his career in Puerto Rico in 1930 at age seventeen, but a year later went to explore his opportunities in Venezuela, fighting a total of seventeen fights in South America. After another series of bouts in Puerto Rico, he settled in Spanish Harlem to begin his North American career. Fighting in his adopted hometown, "El Gallito" was "hailed by a crowd of 9,000," the *New York Times* reported, "most of whom were rabid supporters of Escobar."[16] Escobar won the world bantamweight title against Mexican Rodolfo "Baby" Casanova in Montreal in 1934. Visiting San Juan after his victory, he received a hero's welcome by the Governor General and a crowd of 15,000 meeting him in the San Juan Harbor.[17] Schools were ordered closed, and government offices opened an hour late so that employees could go to the dock to see the parade welcoming the champion, and his hometown of Barceloneta declared a week of festivities in his honor. In 1936, a stadium in San Juan was named after Sixto Escobar; that year he was also featured in the December issue of *The Ring*.[18]

Despite a somewhat suspect ring record of thirty-nine wins, twenty-three losses, and three draws, Escobar claimed the bantamweight championship three times. Visitors to San Juan will sense the tremendous pride the island still holds for its first pugilistic hero, with two statues and a park boasting his name in San Juan County. In Puerto Rican classrooms, Escobar is used to discuss topics as varied as the socioeconomic conditions of Puerto Rico, his significance to Puerto Rican society, and his relationship to the Puerto Rican community in the United States. Escobar's posthumous popularity is explained not only by his ability to put Puerto Rican boxing on the world map, but, as a commentator in a documentary about his life story puts it, because it was the first time Puerto Ricans felt that the international community recognized small Puerto Rico "as the best in anything."[19] Escobar's legacy, then, signifies not only his sporting prowess, but also the ways in which Puerto Rico was responding to its troubled colonial history under the aegis of the United States.

José Florez Pérez (1910–94), better known as Battling Shaw or Benny Kid Roy, was the first boxer from Mexico to win the world championship in the light welterweight division, against Johnny Jadick in Philadelphia in February 1933, but he only held it briefly, losing it to Tony Canzoneri in

May of the same year.[20] Despite being the first Mexican world champion in the record books, Perez's career pales to that of "Kid Azteca" (born Luis Villanueva Paramo in 1913), whose career extended from 1932 to 1961, with a total of 252 fights (192 wins [114 knockouts], 46 losses, and 12 draws). A year and eight months into his career, Jack Singer of the *Los Angeles Times* marveled: "Who is this modern Galahad who may one day secure a fistic Holy Grail for pugilistically ambitious Mexico?"[21] After winning the Mexican welterweight title against David Velasco in 1932, the Spanish-language newspaper *La Prensa* deemed him the best fighter Mexico had ever produced.[22] Kid Azteca held the Mexican welterweight championship from 1934 until 1949. He fought Kid Chocolate to a draw in 1930 but won their rematch by TKO a year later, and he beat Battling Shaw by points in 1932. In 1934, the *Los Angeles Times* described "the lethal-dealing right hand of Kid Azteca" flashing out with "the lightning speed of a cobra," which brought him a victory over Young Peter Jackson, a popular African American fighter from Los Angeles.[23] The same year, Azteca got a decision over the popular "Baby" Joe Gans. Despite his victories over the crème de la crème fighters of his division, the Spanish-language press maintained that Azteca was being discriminated against in the rankings of the National Boxing Association (NBA) as well as the New York State Athletic Commission (NYSAC), notorious for its questionable business practices.[24] Kid Azteca also claimed popularity on the Mexican silver screen, featuring in such boxing films as *El Gran Campeon* [The Great Champion] (1949), *Kid Tabaco* (1955), *Guantes de Oro* [Golden Gloves] (1961), and *Buscando un Campeón* [In Search of a Champion] (1980).

Gerardo González (1926–2003), who claimed fame as Kid Gavilán and the "Cuban Hawk," launched his career in Cuba in 1943, but moved to the United States in 1947. His crowd-pleasing style and technical ability won him fans in both nations. Gavilán's trademark punch was the bolo punch, a combination of the hook and the uppercut, which he allegedly developed in his childhood cutting sugar cane with a machete. Gavilán claimed the welterweight title against Johnny Bratton of Chicago in May 1951 as the first Cuban since Kid Chocolate's championship two decades earlier.[25] He held the title for four years, with seven successful defenses and victories against the likes of Billy Graham, Carmen Basilio, Tony Janiro, Ike Williams, and Chuck Davey; however, he twice lost to "Sugar" Ray Robinson. Gavilán's career coincided with the birth of televised boxing, a time when as many as five different networks broadcast fight cards; he had a total of forty-six nationally televised bouts.[26] Although a crossover celebrity in both the United States and Cuba, it was in the latter where Gavilán was embraced as a national hero. Visiting his native island, "hundreds of fans, sports writers, and a legion of followers," the *New York Times* reported, met him at the airport, chanting, "Viva Gavilán."[27] Cuban dictator Fulgencio Batista, an ardent sports fan himself, sponsored Gavilán's fight with Billy Graham in Havana in 1952, with 40,000 showing up for the fight.[28]

The 1950s was a time when boxing promotions were dominated by the notoriously corrupt International Boxing Club (IBC), while managers and matchmakers often came from criminal organizations. Fight fixing, coercion, and bribery were common features of the day, and few boxers could escape their influence.[29] Gávilan was no exception. His first of four fights with Billy Graham, for example, was shrouded in controversy, with frequent allegations of foul play. According to a *New York Times* report from 1981, Artie Schwartz, the referee of the bout, admitted on his deathbed that the fight was a fix and that he gave it to Gavilán only because the "boys ordered me to do it."[30] Gavilán could never quite escape the rumors of the mob influence in his career; on the other hand, his integrity as a fighter was sustained by the fact that he was never knocked out. He retired from boxing in 1958.

Gávilan's post-retirement return to his native Cuba, where professional boxing was outlawed after the Revolution of 1959, was a struggle, and the former national hero became a prime example of prizefighters climbing from rags to riches, but ending up even worse than they had started. A converted Jehovah's Witness of meager means, Gavilán was jailed by the Castro regime for preaching the Bible. After a decade on his native island, he returned to the United States in 1968 at age forty-two, "broke and in poor health," as the *Los Angeles Times* put it, and settled in Florida.[31] His death in poverty in February 1993 created uproar among contemporary boxing insiders, some of whom found out that the champion's remains had been placed in a pauper's grave in Miami. A group of boxers – including Mike Tyson, Roberto Durán, Leon Spinks, Buddy McGirt, and Emile Griffith – and the legendary trainer Angelo Dundee paid for his exhumation and a placement of his remains in a more respectable part of the cemetery, complete with a new memorial headstone erected in his memory.[32] Kid Gávilan's career is an unfortunate case in point of the ways in which the prizefighting industry celebrated boxers at the peak of their careers, but provided no infrastructure or measures with which to protect their post-retirement financial security. The problems beleaguering boxing stem from its structural deficiencies, as the sport does not have a centralized national governing body or the equivalent of a players' union. Boxers do not have health benefits, life insurance, or basic pension plans. The Professional Boxing Safety Act of 1996 and the Muhammad Ali Boxing Reform Act of 2000 were initiated to tackle some of the health and business grievances of the sport, but many of them remain unenforced.

The 1960s saw several Latino boxers claim fame in the ring. Among them were Puerto Ricans José "Chegüí" Torres, one of only five Latino light heavyweight champions of all time, and Carlos Ortiz, who claimed the junior welterweight title in 1959 and the lightweight title in 1962. Brazilian Éder Jofre won the world bantamweight title in 1962. Cuban Bernardo "Benny the Kid" Paret won the welterweight championship in 1960, but tragically died two years later in front of a national television audience while defending his title.[33] José "Mantequilla" Nápoles, who claimed the welterweight crown in 1969, had a tremendous following in Cuba, Mexico, and the United States.[34] Nápoles left his native island in 1961 to escape Castro's regime and sought asylum in Mexico; from then on, he referred to his ethnic identity as a "Cuban-Mexican." After winning the welterweight crown against Curtis Cokes in 1969, he wore a sombrero in appreciation of his adopted homeland. The low point of Nápoles's career came in 1974, when he moved up in weight class to challenge Argentine Carlos Monzón, the middleweight champion of the world, but was unable to respond to the punishment delivered by his opponent and was forced to quit in the sixth round. Argentine writer Julio Cortazar published a short story *La Noche de Mantequilla* of the fight in 1992. Despite this crushing defeat, Nápoles had an outstanding record of eighty-eight fights, with eighty-one victories (fifty-four by knockout) and only seven losses. Another superb welterweight emerging from the 1970s was Wilfred "El Radar" Benitez of Puerto Rico, who at age seventeen earned the world championship as the youngest world champion in the history of boxing. During his career (53–8–1), Benitez won three world championship titles.

Carlos "Escopeta" [Shotgun] Monzón (1942–95), from San Javier, Argentina, was one of the most gifted superstars of the 1970s. Monzón gained the middleweight title in a stunning upset by a twelfth-round knockout against Nino Benvuti in Rome in November 1970.[35] In their second meeting in Monte Carlo, Monaco, in May 1971, Benvuti's manager threw in the towel in the third round of a bout scheduled for fifteen rounds.[36] The Argentinian held the title for seven years, with a total of fourteen title defenses. Monzón attracted as much attention for his skill as a fighter as for his volatile temperament. Dave Anderson of the *New York Times* characterized him inside the ring as "a boxing machine, likened by some to 'Sugar' Ray Robinson," while outside the ring he had "the smoldering appearance of a volcano about to erupt."[37] Monzón fought only once in the United States, at the Madison Square Garden in 1975, winning the bout against Tony Licata by a tenth-round stoppage by the referee. Monzón retired in 1977 with a record of 100 fights, of which he won eighty-seven and lost only three, with nine draws and one no contest.

Outside the ring, Monzón's life was steeped in scandal, with frequent headlines alleging domestic violence, adultery, and shooting incidents. After starring in several popular movies, *La Mary* (1974), *Soñar, Soñar* [To Dream, to Dream] (1976), *El Macho* [Macho Killers] (1977), and *Amigos para la Aventura* [Friends for the Adventure] (1978), his popularity – and extramarital affairs – only intensified: "Although he's married and the father of two boys, Monzon is usually seen together with Susana Jimenez [sic], an Argentinian actress. At his last fight, Susana sat on one side of the ring rooting for him. His wife sat on the other side. It was never determined whether she was rooting for him or against him, and in a way that's understandable."[38] Giménez and Monzón had met at the set of *La Mary*, after which they had no qualms about flaunting their romance in public. After the two separated, Monzón got in another tumultuous relationship with Alicia Muñíz, and tragedy ensued. In a physical altercation, Mónzon strangled Muñíz and threw her from the balcony. He was convicted of murder and sentenced to eleven years' imprisonment in 1988.[39] Monzón's own life came to a tragic ending in an auto accident on his way back to prison after a one-day furlough, at age fifty-two.[40] Monzón's contradictory legacy is commemorated in folk singer León Giego's song "*Puño Loco*" [Crazy Fist], which celebrates the rollercoaster life of the legendary but troubled pugilist.[41]

Alexis Argüello (1952–2009), "*El Flaco Explosivo*" [The Explosive Thin Man], hailed from the slums in Managua, Nicaragua. The sinewy and lanky fighter, who began his career as a flyweight, had remarkable height (5′10″) and reach (72″) advantages over his opponents, and he also became known for his superb technical skill. A documentary about the greatest Latino fighters eloquently describes his style: "Rembrandt must have painted like Alexis Argüello fought ... Watching him fight is like enjoying the subtleties of a great masterpiece. There's rich color and detail in his performance: his jabs are straight, strong, and accurate; his body punches are delivered with care; his right crosses and left hooks are issued with awesome potency."[42] In November 1974, Argüello claimed the WBA featherweight title by a thirteenth-round knockout of Mexican Ruben "*El Púas*" [Spikes] Olivares. In an emotional plea after the fight, Argüello assured the dethroned champion of the continuation of his pugilistic legacy: "Ruben, I'll defend this belt with the last drop of my blood."[43]

During his career, Argüello won three championships in the flyweight, junior lightweight, and lightweight divisions against the likes of Rafael "Bazooka" Limón, Bobby "Schoolboy" Chacon, and Ray "Boom Boom" Mancini. Attempting his fourth title in the super lightweight division in November 1982, he lost to Aaron "The Hawk" Pryor by fourteenth-round knockout in a bout that *The Ring* labeled the "Fight of the Decade." Their rematch a year later ended up in Pryor's tenth-round knockout victory, causing Argüello to announce his retirement. However, he came out of retirement two years later, fighting two more fights in the 1980s and two in the 1990s, before finally calling it a day in 1995.[44] His final record stands as seventy-seven wins, eight defeats. In 1999, the Associated Press deemed him the top junior lightweight of the twentieth century.

After his retirement, Argüello entered Nicaraguan politics and briefly fought with the counter-revolutionaries – also known as *contras* – against the Sandinistas, who had overthrown the right-wing dictator Anastasio Somoza, but later changed his position.[45] After the Sandinistas confiscated Argüello's fortune, he grappled with unpaid taxes, unscrupulous managers, and a lavish lifestyle. Argüello was hugely popular throughout the Americas and was often praised for his sportsmanly behavior toward his opponents before and after a fight.[46] In Nicaragua, the *New York Times* wrote, "Alexis is the biggest sports idol and the Pope is the biggest religious idol. That is the company he keeps."[47] Despite his integrity, the ex-champion had difficulties adjusting to his life after retirement, candidly describing his substance abuse problems and suicidal thoughts in the media.[48] Even so, Argüello continued his involvement in Nicaraguan politics and was elected mayor of Managua in 2008. His political career was fraught with tensions because of the widespread corruption that beleaguered the local political system, rendering his de facto power minimal. Before his death in 2009,which occurred under dubious circumstances and was officially ruled a suicide, Argüello was allegedly highly disillusioned with Nicaraguan politics, and local commentators have questioned the official version of the cause of his death.[49] The Nicaraguan icon's untimely death at age fifty-seven marked the end of his life, but his legacy as among the best and the brightest of the ring lived on in the minds of fight fans the world over.

Roberto Durán (b. 1951), "*Manos de Piedra*" [Hands of Stone], of Panama City, Panama, was a ferocious warrior who won championships in the lightweight, welterweight, light middleweight, and middleweight divisions, with a career covering five decades. Durán won his first lightweight title against Ken Buchanan of Scotland at Madison Square Garden in 1972; had a total of thirteen title fights as a lightweight, twelve of them ending in knockout. In his first seventy-three fights, his only loss came against Esteban de Jesús of Puerto Rico. At the peak of his career in the 1970s and 1980s, the "Hands of Stone" epitomized the fighting Latino spirit. The *New York Times* described his status in the sport in 1980: "[T]he great name in boxing is Roberto Durán, nobody else. When people talk about the best prizefighter around now, the conversation starts and ends with that name."[50] Akin to many prizefighters who represented small island nations with complex power relations with the United States, Durán's career was tied to the Panamanian government and the Panamanian military, which was heavily involved in dictating whom, when, and where he fought.[51]

The most (in)famous fights of Durán's career were his three title bouts against African American "Sugar" Ray Leonard. The *New York Times* described the anticipation before their first welterweight matchup in this way: "Sugar Ray Leonard, smooth and stylish and smiling, once an Olympic gold medal winner and now a corporation unto himself, going against Roberto Duran, the sneering street-fighter from Panama, punch-for-punch the world's most respected boxer."[52] Durán, who won the bout by unanimous decision in front of an audience of 46,317 at the Olympic Stadium in Montreal in June 1980, was transported home via the executive jet of President Aristides Royo."[53] Victory celebrations complete with parades, a Roberto Durán Day, and the Amador Guerrero Medal, the nation's highest decoration, followed. In the United States, one newspaper pitted the two fighters against each other as "A Man vs. a Boy, two different specimens": "[Durán] has gone through the mill. He has dodged knives, bullets, and baseball bats and iron chains. He has butted, kneed, clawed and slugged his way through an adolescent jungle to emerge a champion with raw fighting skills."[54]

During the 1980s, when championship boxing was largely a black-and-brown affair, promoters capitalized on ethnic and racial characterization of the fighters. A particularly popular strategy for generating publicity and boosting ticket sales was to pit African American and Latino boxers against each other. Leonard and Durán's welterweight championship bouts in the 1980s epitomized what boxing aficionados would start referring to as black and brown fighting styles. Gerald Early describes the meeting of the rivals as follows: "Here was the monumental encounter between the hot and the cool, between the classical order of technique and the romantic impulse of improvisation ... Duran becomes the stereotypical fiery, macho Latin and Leonard becomes the stereotypical cool, slick boxing black."[55] The shock could not have been greater, then, when five months later during their rematch in New Orleans, after eight rounds of boxing, Durán walked up to his corner, uttering the now notorious words "*no más*" [no more] while raising his arms up as a signal of his wish to quit the fight.[56] Newspaper headlines in Panama declared the day after the loss a "Day of Mourning," and some disillusioned fans expressed their anger with "Durán Traitor" graffiti on the walls of Panama City.[57] Durán's trainer, Ray Arcel, would never work his corner again.

After a bout of depression and a fourteen-month hiatus from boxing, Durán reentered the ring in January 1982 to challenge Wilfred Benitez's title, losing by unanimous decision. The same year, *The Ring* labeled his loss to Jamaican-born Kirkland Laing of the United Kingdom "Upset of the Year." On his thirty-second birthday, on June 16, 1983, Durán was able to redeem himself by defeating African American Davey Moore, who had a recent a victory over Thomas "Hitman" Hearns, for the WBA junior middleweight title. In public, Durán has described the bout with Moore as the greatest one he ever had. After consecutive losses to African Americans Marvelous Marvin Hagler and Thomas Hearns in 1983 and 1984, it took Durán five years to claim the WBC middleweight crown against African American Iran Barkley in February 1989 in a bout that *The Ring* recognized as the "Fight of the Year." After a third, unsuccessful meeting with "Sugar" Ray Leonard in 1989, Durán retired in 2001, with a record of 119 fights, including 103 wins (seventy knockouts) and sixteen losses. Notwithstanding his tumultuous career, Durán is widely considered as one of the best lightweights of all time. His aggressive fighting style, boxing skill, and masterful defense are what fight fans cherish as his pugilistic legacy, while the low points of his career have been largely chucked to "being human."

Mexican boxing saw a remarkable boost in the 1980s, with a total of twenty-nine world champions hailing from Mexico. The king of the Mexican champions, Julio César Chávez (b. 1962), went undefeated for thirteen years of his career, with ninety straight wins. Chávez's career, with six world championships in the super featherweight, lightweight, and light welterweight divisions, went on for two decades. His first nationally televised bout against Roger Mayweather in 1985 lasted only two rounds, giving the twenty-two-year-old a chance to display his talent in front of US fans.[58] Chávez became known for his combination of technical skill and an unyielding mindset; in his bout against Edwin Rosario in 1987, the audience was, according to the *New York Times*, "mesmerized by the unrelenting, unerring attack."[59] His other notable opponents included Rafael Limón in 1988, Tony López in 1988, Meldrick Taylor in 1990, and Hector "Macho" Camacho in 1992. Chávez, who grew up poor, one of ten children in the working-class neighborhood of Culiacán, Sinaloa, became Mexico's biggest sports hero, adored equally by the common man as well as President Carlos Salinas de Gortari, with whom he had a close relationship.[60] Chávez's career is immortalized in several traditional Mexican narrative songs called *corridos*, which praise the "king of the ring" for his punching power, the heart he showed in his battles, and the glory he brought to Mexico.

Two of Chávez's major losses came against Oscar De La Hoya in 1996 and 1998, well past his prime. The first of their highly anticipated bouts marked the thirty-four-year-old Chávez's one hundredth bout as a professional, while the Golden Boy was at the peak of his career at age twenty-two. De La

Hoya, who had an image problem and was often vilified among his Latino fans as a "sell out," was a betting favorite of the fight, but Chávez, hailed as "a people's champion," was the crowd favorite.[61] Chávez suffered a cut on his eyebrow in the first round, and De La Hoya claimed a technical knockout in the fourth round.[62] Chávez's continuation of his career past his prime was largely due to his financial problems, resulting from his tumultuous business relationships with promoters Don King, Bob Arum, and Rogelio Robles; the ensuing legal run-ins were widely publicized in the media.[63] In 1995, Chávez testified against Don King in Federal Court in New York about contract abuses, mishandling of finances, and insurance fraud.[64] Toward the end of his career, Chávez's reputation was marred by allegations of alcohol and substance abuse.[65] He continued fighting until 2005, retiring with a record of 115 fights, including 107 wins (eighty-six by knockout), six losses, and two draws.

Hector "Macho" Camacho (1962–2012) of Bayamon, Puerto Rico, who grew up in Spanish Harlem in New York City, was the most flamboyant fighter of the late twentieth century. Known for his flashy outfits featuring leopard-print robes and matching loincloths, he walked, as the *New York Times* put it, "with more sequins than a Las Vegas chorus line and sometimes with less cloth."[66] Often, he entered the ring in a sequined robe of the red, white, and blue design of the Puerto Rican flag, with matching trunks and shoes, hollering his idiosyncratic rallying call: "What time is it? It's Macho Time!" Camacho won the super featherweight title against Rafael "Bazooka" Limón in 1983; the lightweight title against the tough Mexican southpaw José Luis Ramirez in 1985; and the super lightweight title against Ray "Boom Boom" Mancini in 1989. Other notable opponents whom Camacho defeated during his career consisting of a record of 79–6–3 include Freddie Roach, Edwin Rosario, Roberto Durán, and "Sugar" Ray Leonard. His major losses came against Julio César Chávez in 1992, fellow Puerto Rican Felix "Tito" Trinidad in 1994, and Oscar De La Hoya in 1997. Outside the ring, Camacho was from early on in frequent trouble with the law, with charges ranging from reckless driving and domestic violence to burglary and substance abuse. Notwithstanding his troubled background, Camacho became a huge icon in Latino popular culture, with TV appearances in such popular shows as *Super Sábados*, *El Show del Mediodía*, and *El Gordo y la Flaca*. He also starred in *It's Macho Time*, a dating show in which women competed to be his girlfriend. Camacho died in a gang-related shooting in his native Puerto Rico in 2012. His son, Hector "Machito" [Little Macho], is also a professional boxer.

While professional boxing has produced some of the most marketable Latino athletes of the past century, Cuba has produced some of the most acclaimed amateur boxers. The most famous of the Cuban champions is

Teófilo Stevenson (1952–2012), who won three Olympic medals in the heavyweight division in Munich in 1972, Montreal in 1976, and Moscow in 1980, but he never turned professional in obeisance of the Cuban ban on professional boxing. Stevenson's bid for his fourth gold medal never materialized itself because of the Cuban boycott of the Los Angeles games in 1984. Fight scribes the world over have speculated over the outcome of a hypothetical match between Muhammad Ali and Teófilo Stevenson, but in vain, as the fight was never to be. Muhammad Ali only ever fought two Latino boxers – Oscar Bonvena in 1970 and Alfredo Evangelista in 1977 – and was outspoken about his rationale to avoid them: "Don't fight a Latin fighter, because they fight for God and country."[67] On offers to turn professional, Stevenson, nicknamed "El Caballero del Ring" [Knight of the Ring], allegedly responded "The only millions that interest me are the ones that remain in Cuba with the affection of my eight million compatriots."[68] The Cuban state picks the most talented youth for its boxing schools, where the trainers have university degrees and full-time jobs as boxing professors. Until his death in 2012 at age sixty, Stevenson was hailed as a national hero in Cuba and carried tremendous symbolic value for the cause of the Cuban revolution, as a champion of the people, who never gave in to the lure of the capitalist prize ring of its northern neighbor. Stevenson fought a total of 322 bouts, with 307 wins and fifteen losses. In 1988 a *Boxing Illustrated* poll voted Stevenson as the greatest Olympic boxer of all time.

The generation of Latino boxers who matured during the 1990s and 2000s had distinctly different career paths from their predecessors. Although most fighters still came from low socioeconomic backgrounds, there were also those who came from middle-class families; some had university degrees and professional careers outside boxing, while others launched successful careers within boxing. Celebrity fighters began to take charge of the financial aspects of the sport and several champions launched their own promotional companies before their active careers were over. Oscar De La Hoya (b. 1973) was the best example of this change in Latino fighters' profile. "The Golden Boy" came from humble beginnings in the East Los Angeles *barrio*, but after his success he moved to the middle-class neighborhood of Montebello, a move which turned some of his fan base against him as a "sell out," who failed to remain true to his humble origins.[69] For his first professional fight, De La Hoya entered the ring wearing a sombrero and waving both the US and Mexican flags, with mariachis playing in the background, but later on in his career he did not focus as much on his ethnic identity. During his career, De La Hoya won world championships in six different weight classes, from super featherweight to middleweight. He retired in 2009 with a record of thirty-nine wins and six losses. Even as he gained victories over such notable fighters as Pernell Whitaker, Hector "Macho" Camacho, Jesse James Leija, John John Molina, and the aging Julio César Chávez, some disgruntled fans were unforgiving of his major losses against Manny Pacquiao, Floyd Mayweather, Jr., Bernard Hopkins, "Sugar" Shane Mosley, and Felix "Tito" Trinidad. Although De La Hoya was a main attraction for crossover and women fans, some Mexican and Mexican American fans continued to grumble about him not being true to his roots.[70] During his career, De La Hoya generated record-breaking pay-per-view sales; today, his company, Golden Boy Promotions, is one of the most successful promotional companies, particularly appealing to up-and-coming Latino fighters.[71]

Mexican Saúl "Canelo" Álvarez (b. 1990) of Guadalajara, Jalisco, is a light middleweight superstar fighter characterizing the "new" generation of Latino boxers. By age twenty-two, he had compiled a record of forty-one wins, one draw, and no losses against stand-up opposition including Austin Trout, Matthew Hatton, Josesito Lopez, Kermit Cintron, and Lovemore Ndou, and Miguel Cotto. A fighter of great talent and equally amiable personality, he seemed to be shooting for the stars, quickly winning over the hearts and minds of fight fans in the Americas. Álvarez received his nickname Canelo [Cinnamon] for his red hair, a perennial source of curiosity among TV commentators: "He is Mexican, he looks Irish, and he fights like George Foreman!"[72] Álvarez's first defeat came against the undefeated Floyd Mayweather, Jr., in 2013 in a sold-out mega-event in Las Vegas that was promoted by Mayweather Promotions, Golden Boy Promotions, and Canelo Promotions. The fight attracted 2.2 million pay-per-view sales, for total revenue of $150 million, more than the previous record of $137 million, set by Mayweather and De La Hoya's meeting in 2007.[73] Álvarez's career exemplifies the shift in the status of Latino boxers from the margins to the mainstream, especially in the lower weight divisions, and the ways in which superstar Latino boxers have begun to change the sport's age-old business practices to their advantage. Other contemporary star-caliber Latino boxers include Danny "Swift" Garcia of Pennsylvania, Leo "Terremoto" [Earthquake] Santa Cruz of California, Juan Manuel "Dinamita" [Dinamite] Marquez of Mexico, Marcos "El Chino" Maidana of Argentina, Miguel "Junito" Cotto and Roman "Rocky" Martinez of Puerto Rico, and the Cuban exiles Erislandy "The American Dream" Lara and Guillermo "El Chacal" [The Jackal] Rigondeaux.

Throughout Latin America women boxers have broadened the sport's fan base. Even if women in the United States rarely headline major fight cards on television, Mexican fighters – such as Mariana Juarez, Jackie Nava, and Ana Maria Torres – are regularly showcased on Mexican TV and have a huge fan base in the United States as well. Other women fighters of renown in Latin America include Yesica Bopp of Argentina, Hanna Gabriel of Costa Rica, Kina Malpartida of Peru, and Chanttal Martinez of Panama. Cuba is the only major boxing nation that does not sanction either women's amateur or professional boxing. Although not household names in the United States, Latina fighters Anissa "The Assassin" Zamarron, Delia "Chiquita" Gonzalez, Ada Velez, and Jackie Chávez are just some of the names that women's boxing insiders will recognize. In the amateurs, Marlene Esparza was the first US Latina boxer to participate in the women's boxing event in the London Olympics in 2012. After the inclusion of women's boxing as an Olympic event, women boxers have received more positive media publicity in the United States than they had up until then. The interest in Latina boxing is also evident in various popular culture manifestations. Two US films from 2000, *Girlfight* and *Knockout*, feature Latina boxers.[74] In Mexico a *telenovela* [soap opera], *Un Gancho Al Corazón* ([A Hook to the Heart]), featuring a woman boxer, began airing on the Canal de las Estrellas in 2008. Even if the portrayals of women boxers in popular culture mainly focus on their romantic/sexual relations, rather than their athletic ambitions and ability, they nevertheless speak to the growing popularity of the sport among mainstream audiences.

In the United States, boxing has historically been the sport of immigrants, with a direct correlation to the nation's shifting demographics. In the 2010s, Latinos represent the nation's fastest-growing population, with 65 percent of Mexican origin, 9.2 percent of Puerto Rican origin, 3.7 percent of Cuban origin, and the rest representing various South American nations.[75] Because Mexicans have the highest regional concentration in the West and Southwest of the United States, a large number of Latino fighters – and their audiences – reside in Arizona, California, Nevada, New Mexico, and Texas. Outside of these states, other Latino boxing hubs are New York, Chicago, and Florida. From curious sideshows of the early twentieth century, over the past fifty years Latino boxing has claimed the center stage of the pugilistic limelight. Its increasing popularity is evident in the number of Spanish-language broadcasts of fight cards on Telemundo, Univision, HBO Latino, and Showtime. Some recent films featuring Latino boxers include *Honeyboy* (1982), *Play It to the Bone* (1999), *Price of Glory* (2000), and *El Boxeo* (2013).[76] Mexican *corridos* dealing with boxers are popular on both sides of the US–Mexico border; on the Internet one can find songs dealing with contemporary fighters, such as Erik Morales, Juan Manuel Márquez, Canelo Álvarez, and Jackie Nava, as well as many legends from the past.[77] Whereas the most exciting boxing matches used to be between African American and Latino fighters, increasingly two Latino boxers are stepping into the ring to face each other. The selling point for the all-Latino match-ups is often based on class rivalries among the fighters as well as their representation of fighting *Latinidad* to their fans. A review of the past century of Latinos attests that theirs is not – and never has been – a singular, unchanging identity, but a much more diverse, nuanced, and subtle culture that assumes different meanings in shifting historical ambiences, in and out of the ring.

NOTES

1 "Sport Tonic Likely Remedy for Revolution Craze. South American Needs Games of Boxing and Baseball [sic] Variety," *Morning Oregonian*, December 13, 1914, p. 4.
2 Ibid.
3 "Sportography," *Trenton Evening Times*, March 19, 1914, p. 15.
4 "El Boxeador Popular Guy in Land of Chili Con Carne," *The Reading Eagle*, June 30, 1929, p. 16.
5 I am using the term "Latino" throughout this article to refer to boxers of Latin American descent in the United States, Central America, and South America.
6 "Sportography."
7 "Dixon and Smith Ready to Fight the Feather-weight Gladiators Ready to Weigh in at Coney Island," *Philadelphia Inquirer*, September 25, 1893, p. 3.
8 See "Herrera Was the First Mexican to Win Laurels in Prize Ring," *Trenton Evening Times*, June 16, 1915, p. 13. Joe Rivers was referred to as "Mexican" Joe Rivers, although he identified himself as of "Spanish-Indian descent."
9 James P. Dawson, "10,000 See Kid Chocolate Stop Petrone in Sixth Rounds at Ebbets Field," *New York Times*, July 3, 1930, p. 24.
10 Damyon Runyon, "I Think So," *Chester Times*, October 31, 1928, p. 12.
11 Frank Getty, "Speaking of Sports," *Denton Record Chronicle*, April 12, 1929, p. 3.
12 Cited in Neil Amdur, "'Kid Chocolate' in Fading but Not Forgotten," *Salina Journal*, August 22, 1971, p. 19.
13 John Kieran, "Sport of the Times: Unemployment Decreases. A Minority Report," *New York Times*, March 21, 1930, p. 39.
14 "Kid Chocolate is Jailed: Boxer Held In Extradition Action on Charge of Seduction in Cuba," *New York Times*, December 2, 1931, p. 19.
15 "Pugilist Wed by Proxy: Kid Chocolate's Manager Goes Through Ceremony in Havana," *New York Times*, December 17, 1931, p. 21.
16 Joseph C. Nichols, "Escobar Wins Bout for Bantam Title: Beats Marino When Commission Doctor Stops Dyckman Oval Contest After 13th," *New York Times*, September 1, 1936, p. 25.
17 "15,000 in Puerto Rico Greet Boxer Escobar: Bantam, Reportedly Warned by Nationalists, Carries Lone-Star Instead of American Flag," *New York Times*, December 10, 1935, p. 20.
18 See "Honor Puerto Ricans: Holiday Today in Tribute to Escobar and Trackmen," *New York Times*, February 28, 1938, p. 10, and "Escobar to be Honored: Stadium in Puerto Rico Will be Named for Champion," *New York Times*, April 14, 1938, p. 33.
19 Elliott Castro in *Autógrafo*, dir. Francisco Zamora (Angel Ramos, 1997), accessed December 13, 2013, at http://autografo.tv/sixto-escobar/.

20 "Canzoneri Drops Shaw Twice to Win Verdict; Regain Junior Title," *Los Angeles Times*, May 22, 1933, p. 9.

21 Jack Singer, "Kid Azteca New Mexican Title Threat: Conqueror of Garcia Has Been Fighting Little Over a Year," *Los Angeles Times*, July 13, 1933, p. A9.

22 "Que Kid Azteca es el mejor boxeador que México ha producido," *La Prensa*, July 27, 1933, p. 7.

23 "Negro Battler Knocked Down in Third Round: Mexican Champ Cops Verdict," *Los Angeles Times*, June 6, 1934, p. A9.

24 "Al Margen del Deporte La Catalogación Annual de la Asociación Nacional de Box," *La Prensa*, September 19, 1934, p. 7.

25 Joseph C. Nichols, "Gavilan Takes World Welterweight Title by Outpointing Bratton at the Garden: An Exchange of Blows in Title Battle Last Night," *New York Times*, May 19, 1951, p. 24.

26 "Popularity of TV Boxing Conflicting," *Los Angeles Times*, December 25, 1954, p. B4.

27 "Havana Hails Kid Gavilan: Welterweight Boxer Receives Huge Ovation in Home Town," *New York Times*, November 17, 1948, p. 35. See also Anju Reejhsinghani, "For Blood or for Glory: A History of Cuban Boxing, 1898–1962," PhD Dissertation (University of Texas-Austin, 2009).

28 "Gavilan Outpoints Graham in Havana and Keeps World Welterweight Title: Cuban Boxer Wins Unanimous Decision," *New York Times*, October 6, 1952, p. 31.

29 See Benita Heiskanen, "Boxing" in *Sports in America: From Colonial Times to the Twenty-First Century*, edited by Steven A Riess (Armonk, NY: M.E. Sharpe, 2011), 188–97.

30 Red Smith, "Sports of the Times: When Only the Ring Was Square," *New York Times*, November 8, 1981, p. S4.

31 "Kid Gavilan, Down on His Luck, Back in U.S.," *Los Angeles Times*, September 18, 1968, p. E6.

32 Vincent M. Mallozi, "No Rest Until Kid Gavilan Has Peace," *New York Times*, March 13, 2005, accessed December 13, 2013, at www.nytimes.com/2005/03/13/sports/othersports/13gavilan.html?_r=0.

33 See Christina D. Abreu, "The Story of Benny 'Kid' Paret: Cuban Boxers, the Cuban Revolution, and the US Media, 1959–1962," *Journal of Sport History* 38-1 (2011): 95–114.

34 Stephen D. Allen, "Boxing in Mexico: Masculinity, Modernity, and Nationalism, 1946–1892," PhD Dissertation (Rutgers, State University of New Jersey, 2013).

35 "Monzon Scores Knockout in 12th: Middleweight Title Won by Argentine in Rome Upset Before Crowd of 18,000," *New York Times*, November 8, 1970, 191.

36 Michael Katz, "Monzon Retains Title, Stopping Benvenuti in 3 D: Middleweight Bout is Halted after Towel is Thrown In – Loser Floored Twice," *New York Times*, May 9, 1971, p. S1.

37 Dave Anderson, "The Smoldering Middleweight Champ," *New York Times*, June 19, 1975, p. 57.

38 Ibid.

39 Milton Richman, "Monzon has Record Book on his Side," *Bucks County Courier Times*, June 19, 1975, p. C34.

40 "Carlos Monzon, Boxer, Dies at 52," *New York Times*, January 9, 1995, p. B9.

41 www.youtube.com/watch?v=XZNSmtSt9cA, January 12, 2014.

42 Lee Librado, dir., *Champions Forever: The Latin Legends!* (Liberty International, 2000).

43 Ibid.

44 Michael Katz, "Argüello Returns to Pay Debt," *New York Times*, August 11, 1985, p. S8.

45 Bruce Weber, "Alexis Argüello, 57, Boxer and Politician," *New York Times*, July 2, 2009, p. 20.

46 Michael Katz, "Arguello Reacting Like a Gentleman," *New York Times*, November 11, p. B19.

47 Ibid.

48 Weber, "Alexis Argüello, 57, Boxer and Politician."

49 José Ramon Gutiérrez, "La Muerte de Alexis Argüello no fue suicidio," *Solo Boxeo*, July 4, 2009, accessed July 15, 2015, at www.soloboxeo.com/2009/07/04/muerte-de-alexis-arguello-no-fue-suicidio/.

50 Dave Anderson, "Sports of the Times: Durán Proves He's the Best Prizefighter," *New York Times*, June 22, 1980, p. S1.

51 "Duran, the Pride of Panama, Continues to Rebuild His Career," *Syracuse Herald-Journal*, November 8, 1983, p. D4.

52 Dave Anderson, "Leonard and Duran Are on a Collision Course," *New York Times*, September 30, 1979, p. S3.

53 "Durán Gets Hero's Welcome," *New York Times*, June 24, 1980, p. C13.

54 "A Man vs. a Boy," *Annapolis Capital*, November 25, 1980, p. 18.

55 Gerald Early, "Hot Spics versus Cool Spades: Three Notes toward a Cultural Definition of Prizefighting," in *Tuxedo Junction: Essays on American Culture* (New York: The Ecco Press, 1989), pp. 115–129.

56 Mark Heisler, "Duran Quits – and Then Retires: Leonard is Stunned by Ending," *Los Angeles Times*, November 26, 1980, p. D1.

57 "Panama in Mourning Over Duran Throwing in the Towel: His Countrymen Celebrated in the Streets When He Won Title; This Time They Stayed Home," *Los Angeles Times*, November 27, 1980, p. E17.

58 Michael Katz, "Chávez, in Round 2, Stops Mayweather," *New York Times*, July 8, 1985, p. C2.

59 Phil Berger, "Chávez Faces Toughest Challenge," *New York Times*, March 17, 1990.

60 See Diego Luna, dir., *JC Chávez: El ultimo heroe mexicano* (Genius Entertainment, 2008).

61 See Fernando Delgado, "Golden But Not Brown: Oscar De La Hoya and the Complications of Culture, Manhood, and Boxing," *International Journal of the History of Sport*, 22-2 (2005), pp. 196–211.

62 Tom Friend, "De La Hoya Stops Chavez; T.K.O. in 4 Bloody Rounds," *New York Times*, June 8, 1996, p. 27.

63 "Chávez Has Plans to Spar with King," *New York Times*, November 9, 1988, p. D32; "Phil Berger, "Power Struggle to Control Chávez," *New York Times*, March 21, 1990, p. B10; "Tyson Undercard to Include Chávez," *New York Times*, January 14, 1991, p. C6.

64 James C. McKinley Jr., "Chavez Testifies Against King," *New York Times*, October 18, 1995, p. B16.

65 "Chávez Fined $5,000," *New York Times*, January 29, 1998, p. C7.

66 Michael Katz, "Camacho Wins Last Laugh," *New York Times*, August 12, 1985, p. C9.

67 Quoted in Benita Heiskanen, *The Urban Geography of Boxing: Race, Class, and Gender in the Ring* (New York: Routledge, 2012), p. 86.

68 My translation of *Los únicos millones que me interesan quedaron en Cuba con el cariño de ocho millones de compatriotas* quoted in *Monarcas Boxeo*, accessed July 20, 2015, at www.radiorebelde.cu/beijing/monarcas/boxeo-monarcas.html.

69 Tom Friend, "Why De La Hoya Refuses to Part With His Gold," *New York Times*, November 25, 1992, p. B11.

70 Gregory Rodríguez, "Saving Face, Place, and Race: Oscar De La Hoya and the 'All-American' Dreams of US Boxing," in John Bloom and Michael Nevin Willard, eds, *Sport Matters: Race, Recreation, and Culture* (New York: New York University Press, 2002), 279–98.

71 Of the growing presence of boxing in the US Southwest, see Benita Heiskanen, "The *Latinization* of Boxing: A Texas Case-Study," *Journal of Sport History* 32 (2005): 45–66.

72 www.youtube.com/watch?v=5UMQytr6pCk. Accessed January 26, 2014.

73 Kevin Iole, "Floyd Mayweather and Canelo Álvarez PPV Sales at 2.2. Million, Setting Revenue Record," September 19, 2013, accessed January 26, 2014, at http://sports.yahoo.com/blogs/boxing/floyd-mayweather-canelo-alvarez-ppv-sales-2-2-213253910--box.html.

74 Lorenzo Doumani, dir., *Knockout* (DMG Pictures, 2000); Kusama, Karyn, dir., *Girlfight* (Sony, 2000).

75 Seth Motel and Eileen Patten, "The 10 Largest Hispanic Origin Groups: Characteristics, Rankings, Top Counties," Hispanic Trends, Pew Research Center, June 27, 2012, accessed July 20, 2015, at www.pewhispanic.org/2012/06/27/the-10-largest-hispanic-origin-groups-characteristics-rankings-top-counties/.

76 John Berry, dir., *Honeyboy* (Erik Estrada Productions, 1982,) Carlos Ávila, dir., *Price of Glory* (New Line Cinema 2000), Ron Shelton, dir., *Play It to the Bone* (Play It Inc. 1999), Alan Swyer, dir., *El Boxeo* (Independent Film Production Company, 2013).

77 See "Desde El Ring," http://desdeelring.com/Nota/30/20-corridos-inspirados-en-boxeadores.

IO

CATHY VAN INGEN

Women's Boxing: Bout Time

The history of women's boxing has been traced back to the very roots of the modern sport – bare-knuckle fights in eighteenth-century England. Yet women's boxing has been outlawed for most of the sport's history. This leaves us with some rather complex history. It is impossible to write, in a single chapter, a full-length treatise on women's boxing. This chapter is ambitious in another way – it sets out to explore women's boxing, not in its wholeness or totality, but to offer a set of propositions. Writer Sarah Deming observes that "women's boxing is a small pie cut into very few slices."[1] This is true. It is also instructive and points out the ways the past is part of the present.

The Olympic debut of women's amateur boxing in 2012 was heralded as a key moment in the sport's history. Gender parity at last. Except there was not actually parity at the Games. Male boxers had ten weight classes at the London Olympics, ranging from 108 pounds to the super heavyweight division for boxers over 200 pounds. Female boxers were only granted three weight classes and had to squeeze into 112, 132, or 165 pounds. At the 2012 Games there were 250 male and 36 female pugilists. The lead-up to the London Olympics exposed another struggle – the Amateur International Boxing Association (AIBA), the international sanctioning body, proposed changes to women's uniforms that would require women to compete in skirts, rather than boxing shorts. Dr. Ching-Kuo Wu, president of the AIBA, was concerned that without skirts spectators would not be able to tell the difference between men and women.

Boxing, as Loic Waquant's work[2] thoroughly details, is a body-centered universe. The fighter's body, with its specific muscular armor, is its key resource. The elite female boxer's body threatened to destabilize normative and binary constructions of gender. The presence of skilled, physically powerful, female boxers capable of the sport's unrelenting violence became an "identification problem." As one journalist asked, "But what's wrong with women boxers resembling men? Having gained equal status in the sport at last, women are now being pushed to elide that equality and differentiate themselves; they are not boxers, but lady boxers."[3] Several prominent boxers from Western nations joined in the widespread criticism of the proposed rule change, and five months before the London Olympics the AIBA announced that women would have the choice of wearing skirts or shorts in the ring.[4] National federations could still require their female athletes to wear skirts, and a few, including Poland and Romania, did.

Boxing has always reflected broader historical and cultural narratives. As Kasia Boddy has outlined, the "sport became a focus for many competing, and often oddly intermingling, discourses," situating fighters within shifting notions of nation, race, class, religion, politics, and different versions of masculinity.[5] Boxing, it seems, to quote singer James Brown (1966), is "a man's man's man's world." Brown's lyrics were characterized by *Rolling Stone* magazine as "biblically chauvinistic." In much the same way, writing about boxing has been staggeringly masculinist. Take, for example, Joyce Carol Oates, who has famously written that "[b]oxing is a purely masculine activity and inhabits a purely masculine world … women's role in the sport has always been extremely marginal."[6] Of course, I am not disputing that men have formed the backbone of the fistic trade; rather I am interested in the marginalization of women in the sport and the disregard for their marginality as a site of oppression.

Boxing scribes and historians have played an interesting role framing and narrating women's marginality within the sport. For example, Jeffery Sammons's book *Beyond the Ring: The Role of Boxing in American Society* pays scant attention to women's boxing, highlighting a bout between two unnamed women in the 1880s as "an anomaly" and "that periods answer to contemporary, voyeuristic mud wrestling."[7] Similarly, Bob Mee, who traces the history of bare-knuckled prizefighting, claims that prior to the 1990s, women's boxing "had laid dormant for the best part of a century."[8] This type of narrative closure, so certain of itself, keeps women's boxing off the pages of history books in any meaningful way. These histories rarely highlight the efforts that were undertaken to ban women's boxing in Europe and most of North America in the nineteenth century. What also remains overlooked in these accounts are the women who did continue to box at the margins of the sport. Women's exhibitions and bouts, including fighting for financial gain, continued on both sides of the Atlantic.[9]

Black men figure prominently in the social and cultural history of boxing. As Gerald Early notes, "one could argue that the three most important black figures in twentieth-century American culture were prizefighters: Jack Johnson, Joe Louis, and Muhammad Ali."[10] While a great deal of research has been done in the area of race and boxing, it has largely focused on black, and more recently Latino, male boxers, rarely incorporating "gender" as a focus. The history of women's boxing traces all the way back to London, in 1722, with Elizabeth Wilkinson Stokes, an accomplished professional in stage combat and a rare fighter of either sex who was featured in bouts using weapons (such as the back-sword and quarterstaff) as well as fists.[11] Yet boxing historians have paid insufficient attention to the ways gender, racism, and white privilege have obscured various accounts of history within women's boxing.

In "'Seeing What Frames Our Seeing': Seeking Histories on Early Black Female Boxers" (2013),[12] I explored the role that boxing writers and historians have played in directly constructing histories on women's boxing, and highlighted, in particular, the erasure of black females from the sport. I undertook this research after noticing the earliest mention of black ringwomen was not until 1978, over 200 years after women began boxing. In 1978 Jackie Tonawanda and Marian Trimiar, along with Cathy Davis, filed suits against the New York State Athletic Commission, demanding that women be allowed to get pro boxing licenses. It is also interesting to note that the only white women in the trio, Cathy Davis, was featured on the cover of *The Ring* magazine, the self-proclaimed "Bible of Boxing." This is also the first time a woman was ever been featured on the cover since the magazine's inception in 1922, and it would be another thirty-eight years before a second female, Ronda Rousey, appeared on the cover.

In order to examine the erasure of black female combatants from boxing history, I searched mainstream and African American newspapers, US boxing periodicals, as well as scholarly and popular literature on the history of boxing. What I compiled was a partial historical account, one that highlights that there is a spectrum of critical issues that remain underexamined in women's boxing history. The earliest example of black female pugilists was in 1882; two women, Bessie Williams (290 pounds) and Josephine Green (280 pounds), both trained by their husbands, who were also noted as talented fighters, fought for a prize of $20 a side and the title of the colored lady championship. The fight, which took place in front of a large crowd, was reported as "a bloody, brutal, vicious fight," with Williams victorious after landing a right that knocked Green out.

There were a handful of other examples that surfaced, including a court case in 1885 covered in the *Brooklyn Daily Eagle*. Mary Carl was before the courts and was asked to state her employment. She claimed to be a pugilist. The court then asked her brother to confirm this assertion, and she is formally noted in the remaining case as a "colored female pugilist" who is "*one* of Mr Harry Hill's dark stars" (emphasis added). Harry Hill, the legendary owner of the nineteenth-century New York saloon, was a nationally known prizefight matchmaker and referee. Harry Hill's Variety Theatre was a popular prizefighting venue, and Hill often added women's fights to his roster of entertainers.[13] Several of the women's bouts, including world title bare-knuckle boxing matches, took place at Hill's venue and were reported in newspapers like the *National Police Gazette*. Drawing from this coverage, historians have traced out the careers of leading female pugilists, like Hattie Stewart and Libby Ross. However, many female fighters remain unnamed, and, in particular, we know virtually nothing about the black female fighters who played a role in the early New York boxing scene.

In 1890, Lizzie Somers, a 114-pound fighter based in New York, was preparing for a bout against Nellie Malloy. Somers's trainer claimed to have her walk twelve miles in the morning and again in the afternoon. He also stated that every night Somers engaged "in a four-round fight with a negress, twenty pounds heavier, and beat the negro girl every time." This brief mention of an unnamed black woman who serves as a sparring partner for Somers and who presumably takes more than she gives is an ignored and troubling aspect of boxing history. Boxing scholars have explored the lives of boxers like Joe Gans and Jack Johnson and their battle against the global color line.[14] There remains a need for more in-depth and transnational explorations of female boxers that extend the ways we understand race, sport, and history.

More press reportage exists on two African American women, Emma Maitland and Aurelia Wheeldin, than any other early black female pugilist, yet these two have been ignored within contemporary boxing histories. Maitland and Wheeldin were theatrical performers who began training as boxers in Paris under American Jack Taylor. The pair brought their ring work to the stage and booked tours in France, Belgium, Italy, Holland, Switzerland, Austria, and the United States. Emma Maitland also boxed competitively outside of the theater and traveled to compete in Cuba and Mexico, where, the black newspaper the *Pittsburgh Courier* reported, "The powerful left hand of Miss Maitland has helped her win bouts." Maitland and Wheeldin's histories speak to issues that intersect with gender, including colonialism, imperialism, race, and the global impact of sport.

There are many different stories to be told about the roles women have played in the sport as fighters, spectators, judges, managers, and trainers. Jennifer Hargraves initiated a call for a much fuller treatment of women in the fight game, including the "diverse and complex bodies of the boxers and the structures of power including gender, class, race, commercialization and politics."[15] Two of the most thorough sources available to date are Malissa Smith's (2014) *A History of Women's Boxing* and the online site *Women Boxing Archive Network* (WBAN). WBAN is the longest running and most in-depth Web site on women's boxing, created by former professional boxer turned boxing writer and archivist Sue Fox.

The legalization of women's amateur boxing in Sweden in 1988 had a cascading effect on the sport. Bettan Andersson, a Swedish boxer petitioned for and received the world's first female license for amateur boxing. Canada became the second country to lift the ban on amateur women's boxing in 1991, followed by the United States in 1993, and England in 1997. In several countries, the ban on women's amateur boxing was only lifted under the threat of lawsuits. In Canada, for example, there were numerous provincial regulations and federal laws that prevented public boxing matches for women. Prior to the 1990s there were several women who unsuccessfully tried to compete in sanctioned boxing matches. Canada's largest daily, *The Toronto Star*, reported one such attempt in a 1982 article: "She's down but not out: Suzanne Hotchkiss insists she has the right to be a lady boxer – even though Boxing Ontario says it could give her cancer."[16]

The AIBA lifted its ban on women's boxing in 1993, and held the first Women's World Championships in 2001. Fighters from thirty countries competed in the inaugural championships.[17] AIBA-sponsored international events spurred further progress and highlighted stellar athletes from around the globe including India's Mary Kom (Mangte Chungneijang Mery-kom) and Ireland's Katie Taylor, the only fighters to have won five world titles. Mary Kom's international boxing career also includes a bronze Olympic medal and a Bollywood biopic. Katie Taylor held the Irish, European, World, and Olympic championship in the 60 kg (132 lbs) division and is enormously popular in Ireland. There are now over 120 international boxing federations with registered female competitors, and the debut of women's boxing at the 2012 London Olympics placed it, at least momentarily, on an international stage.

ESPN's coverage of the London Olympics included a scathing article on the US men's boxing program, stating that it had become a "dysfunctional embarrassment."[18] The USA boxing program, which had once produced fighters like Muhammad Ali, Ray Leonard, Evander Holyfield, Pernell Whitaker, Oscar De La Hoya, and Floyd Mayweather, had won just one gold medal over the last three Olympics. The article also makes passing reference to the success of African American middleweight boxer Claressa Shields. Shields was seventeen years old at the London Olympics, where she won the United States' only gold medal in boxing. Shields started boxing as a thirteen-year-old in Flint, Michigan, one of America's most dangerous and impoverished cities. Her journey to the Olympics is captured in the 2015 documentary film *T-Rex*. Unlike American men who had previously won gold at the Games and then moved on with their boxing careers sporting lucrative endorsements or professional contracts, Shield's received no national endorsement deals. She did receive her $25,000 Olympic medal bonus. Her fellow teen Olympian, gold medal gymnast Gabby Douglas, received millions in sponsorships.[19] In an interview, Shields expressed disappointment at her lack of financial opportunities after winning the gold medal. Shields noted that Gabby Douglas is "the 41st person to win in that category, but the first African-American to do it. I was just like, 'I'm the first person to do what I did, period, no matter what race.' There will never be another first."[20] Sarah Deming, who has a critical eye for the sport, writes, "what happens outside the ring is only interesting if what happens inside the ring is beautiful."[21] Claressa Shields boxes beautifully. She throws jarring, fast punches in quick combinations. Deming explains, "Claressa Shields was the first boxer who showed me that women can be artists in the ring, like men. It was kind of like the first time I read Virginia Woolf."[22] Claressa Shields is that good and still overlooked. After the 2012 Olympics, a moment when women's sporting bodies briefly represent nations, we returned to the perennial tale of female athletes trying to make it work in an often-indifferent world. Following London, the International Olympic Committee announced that at the Rio De Janeiro 2016 Games women would still be restricted to the same three weight categories – flyweight, lightweight and middleweight – as they had been at London.

Just as the legalization of amateur boxing in the 1990s spurred further growth of the sport, the 1990s also saw a handful of female pro boxers gain prominence. Prior to this women's professional boxing was in a unique position – without boxers moving up from the amateurs, which had only recently been legally sanctioned, the pool of talent in the pro ranks was often shallow. Christy Salters Martin is credited with moving women's boxing into the mainstream. Like several other boxers who migrated to the sport from martial arts, kickboxing, or Toughwoman competitions, Christy Salters had to find a trainer willing to work with her. In 1990 when Christy walked into Jim Martin's Tennessee gym, he boasted, "I didn't think women belonged in the fight game. So there was no question I was going to have her ribs broke."[23] After a few sessions, he began to see Christy's work ethic and skill, as well as her potential to make money in the sport. He quickly became her trainer, and within a year they were married.

The 5'4", 133-pound fighter became the first woman to sign a promotional contract with Don King, the once ruling promoter of the sport. Her appearance on a Mike Tyson pay-per-view card in 1996 garnered worldwide attention. Upwards of 1.1 million viewers watched a bloodied Martin beat Ireland's Deirdre Gogarty in a hard-hitting, action-packed six rounds.[24] The Mike Tyson–Frank Bruno fight was over in three rounds, but it was the Martin–Gogarty match that stole the show. Boxing analyst Alex Wallau reflected in a televised interview, "The reason the fight captured everyone's imagination was because it displayed the one quality that boxing tests in a way that nothing else does and that is courage, and that fight turned, within a matter of seconds, from being an event that was being laughed at and ridiculed in the arena to one that absolutely thrilled the people that were watching." The fight caught the attention of people outside the ring as well. Martin was featured on the cover of *Sports Illustrated*, billed as "Boxing's New Sensation," and was soon fielding calls from numerous media sources, including *60 Minutes* and the *Late Show with David Letterman*.

The Martin–Gogarty bout was, as Malissa Smith explains, "a seminal moment pinpointing the entry of women's boxing on the world stage."[25] The exposure from the fight sparked a boom in female professional boxing. It also fostered the sport's first mainstream rivalry between Christy Martin and Mia St. John. St. John signed with Don King, then *Top Rank Boxing,* and was featured on the undercard of Oscar De La Hoya's bouts. While Christy Martin was on the cover of *Sports Illustrated*, Mia "The Knockout" St. John was on the cover of *Playboy*.[26] Christy Martin's exposure also inspired several daughters of legendary fighters – Laila Ali, Jaqui Frazier, Freeda Foreman, and Irichelle Duran. It was the ring debut of Laila Ali, daughter of three-time heavyweight champion and global boxing icon Muhammad Ali, that attracted major media attention and journalists from around the world.

At 5′10″, Laila "She Bee Stingin'" Ali eventually matured into a strong and capable fighter, winning four super middleweight titles, including the first World Boxing Council (WBC) title won by a female. With Ali as its centerpiece, women's boxing peaked fan interest and reached new heights of media coverage. The most highly anticipated fight in Ali's career was against Christy Martin on August 23, 2003, for the International Boxing Association (IBA) super middleweight title. Martin, considered by many to be the best pound-for-pound female boxer, normally fought as a welterweight but moved up three weight classes to face Ali. Martin, at 5′4″, was at a significant disadvantage against the taller and heavier Ali. The scheduled ten-round bout was stopped early in the fourth round as Ali sent Martin to the canvas. It remains Martin's only loss by knockout in fifty-eight fights and solidified Ali's status as a star in women's boxing. Ali retired as the undefeated Super Middleweight boxing champion in 2007 with a record of 24–0 (21 KO). Ali continues to face criticism from boxing insiders who argue that she avoided formidable opponents while banking on her name recognition to rack up solid purses.[27]

Boxing writer Mark Otega argues that women's boxing became taboo when Laila Ali hung up the gloves, citing that many of her bouts were "mismatches against unskilled opponents on ESPN2 televised cards," which turned people off the sport. In North America, despite the strides the sport has made in improving the level of competition in large part to the amateur system, there are now very few outlets that cover the sport closely. Boxing analyst Corey Erdman insists, "[W]e have pretty clear proof that when women's boxing is presented on equal ground with men's boxing, and treated like any other sport, it thrives."[28] Indeed, women's boxing is thriving in many parts of Europe, Asia, and South and Central America, as well as Mexico, where there are a number of female boxing stars. Argentina boasts over 100 registered professional female boxers, some of whom are immensely popular. Spanish-language television network Azteca routinely airs women's boxing. Erdman argues, "Germany's top promoter Sauerland has a handful of female fighters, something no major American promoter has even one of. All of these countries not only air women's boxing, but put their fights in the main event, and when they have they've produced the kinds of ratings US networks would lose their minds over."[29] For instance, in 2010, Filipino-American boxer Anna Julaton fought Mexican Maria Villalobos for the WBO super bantamweight title. The fight was broadcast in the Philippines, where it held a 15.3 percent share. As a comparison, the Julaton–Villalobos fight went head to head with another boxing match the same night, another Filipino boxing star, A.J. Banal, and his fight drew only a 9.2 rating. Yet Julaton, like other popular female professionals, are not on big American fight cards, and not on premium American television. Many of the sport's top American and Canadian professionals, including New Mexico's Holly Holm, arguably one of the best female boxers, have switched to mixed martial arts.

Many of the problems that plague women's professional boxing are rife within the prizefight industry globally. There is a proliferation of sanctioning bodies, some more reputable than others, that operate independently. In addition to the more established organizations, like the World Boxing Association (WBA) and the World Boxing Council (WBC), that anoint female champions, there are also several organizations specifically for women's boxing. The Women's International Boxing Federation (WIBF), established in 1989, was the first followed by several other sanctioning bodies. As a result there are numerous acronym-emblazoned "championship" belts from an "alphabet soup" of sanctioning bodies. Wacquant highlights that we are left with a "bureaucratic cacophony and regulatory ineptitude, the cost of which is born by boxers, who are assuredly the least protected of all professional athletes in the modern era."[30]

Women's boxing has long struggled to move out of the fringes of sport and into the mainstream. Prior to the 1990s, women's boxing was often less sporting and more erotic entertainment best located on the periphery of the sex industry. Foxy boxing, more burlesque than sport, put underdressed women in oversized gloves. Yet, as Carlo Rotella observes, "Even when foxy boxers are nowhere in evidence, at every fight the ring girls remind the crowd of is investment in the link between female body work and sex work."[31] Ring card girls began to appear in 1964 on promoter Bill Miller's weekly shows in Las Vegas. The May 1965 issue of *The Ring* magazine reported, "This card girl deal seems like a pretty good thing to us. At least it adds some appeal and spice to a sport this is rough and nice."[32] Miller's fight cards featured showgirls and television and film "starlets," prompting one journalist to note, "If something like this caught on around the country gate receipts automatically would fatten."[33] Ring card girls are now a fixture at professional bouts and on most amateur cards. Robert Anasi, an American journalist whose memoir details his experience as an amateur boxer, writes, "Between rounds, the ring card girls – certainly strippers from a local club – tottered around the ring on fantastic stiletto heels. The girls changed costumes between fights: miniskirts and halter top down to bikinis, down, down to silver-spangled G-string and cropped pudenda, each costume change unveiling more plucked and shaved flesh."[34] Fight promoters readily employ card girls to work in the ring. One of boxing's richest fights, the May 2, 2015, Floyd Mayweather–Manny Pacquiao bout, is estimated to have generated $500 million in revenue. There were no female fights on the undercard. The only women doing any work in the ring were the ring girls who were at the pre-fight press conference as well as the fight.

At the next colossally hyped fight with the biggest pay-per-view in history, boxing fans in over 200 countries watched four ring girls hired by Corona, the fight's official beer sponsor, but only those in the Las Vegas stadium six hours before the main event could witness a women's bout. Floyd Mayweather and mixed martial artist Connor McGregor's historic and money-spinning cross-over bout took place on August 26, 2017. One woman's bout was scheduled to open the undercard. British boxer Savannah Marshall, a former world amateur champion and the only opponent to ever beat Claressa Shields, won her professional debut after being only the second woman to sign a contract with Mayweather Promotions.

Women's boxing has changed dramatically over the past two decades. After the boom in the mid-1990s, female pros in the United States face poor promotional opportunities, a lack of media exposure, and low pay. In 2014, the World Boxing Council (WBC) held a four-day convention in Mexico to address the current state of women's boxing. The event, which brought together boxing insiders and female champions from around the globe, highlighted the need to improve salaries and discussed the length and number of rounds women fight. Men's bouts are three-minute rounds, compared with two minutes for women. Men's world title fights are twelve rounds, and women's are capped at ten. The WBC determined it would not participate in or sanction any fight for female boxers scheduled for more than ten two-minute rounds. One of the four reasons put forward by the WBC that was that the "menstrual cycle has tremendous impact on the body of a woman." A second reason was that "women's endurance has been proven to be less than men," citing the different marathon running times between men and women.[35] These reasons reflect back to a time when Victorian sportswomen were warned that an overly zealous pursuit of sport would endanger their bodies, particularly their reproductive system.

The International Boxing Hall of Fame (IBHOF) outlines that its mission is to honor and preserve boxing's rich heritage and chronicle the achievements of those who excelled. Members of the Boxing Writers Association of America and an international panel of boxing historians cast votes to determine who is inducted. After the 2014 ceremonies there were a total of 423 inductees, 422 men and one woman. Alieen Eaton, a boxing promoter for five decades, is the only woman inducted. In 2014, WBAN and Sue Fox established an International Women's Boxing Hall of Fame (IWBHF). The mission of the IWBHF is "to provide increased awareness of the contributions of both female boxers and the men and women whose outside-the-ring contributions to the sport played a significant role in the on-going growth of the sport through the creation of competitive opportunities for female boxers along with increasing the awareness of women's boxing within the sporting public."[36] The first seven inductees included Barbara Buttrick, Bonnie Canino, Christy Martin, Regina Halmich, Christy Halbert, Lucia Rijker, and Jo-Ann Hagen. The nominations for the IWBHF were open to the public worldwide, and overseen by a board of nine members.

Most often, women's boxing has worked in the shadows. Christy Salters Martin, who finished her career with forty-nine wins, five losses, three draws, and thirty-one knockouts, has witnessed the fight game dwindle, with few women being placed on major cards in the United States and receiving smaller paydays. Salters Martin, like many female pros, has seen firsthand a sport that is often cruel and exploitative as much as it is wondrous and beautiful. She was at the center of the sport during its peak and fought on the biggest cards in Las Vegas. In 2010, her husband and trainer, Jim Martin, stabbed her in the breast, back, and leg, and shot her with a 9-millimeter pistol, leaving her for dead. She survived. He was sentenced to twenty-five years in prison for attempted second-degree murder. Just over a week after the attack, with the bullet still in her back, Christy returned to the boxing gym. A journalist asked why she would want to go back to boxing after being hurt so badly. She responded, "I'm in the hurt business."[37] Women's boxing is a story of obstacles. It, as Sarah Deming writes, "gives you the blues."

NOTES

1 Deming, Sarah. "Heather Hardy Brings the Heat To Nydia Feliciano in Brooklyn." *Stiff Jab*. Web. Mar. 24, 2014.
2 Wacquant, Loic. "The Pugilistic Point of View: How Boxers Think and Feel About Their Trade." *Theory and Society* 24 (1995): 489–535.
3 Onstad, Katrina. "Do Female Athletes Have To Wear Miniskirts To Be Taken Seriously?" *The Globe and Mail*, Nov. 26, 2011, Web.
4 van Ingen, Cathy, and Nicole Kovacs. "Subverting the Skirt: Female Boxers' 'Troubling' Uniforms." *Feminist Media Studies* 12 (2012): 460–63.
5 Boddy, Kasia. *Boxing: A Cultural History*. London: Reakton, 2008, 165.
6 Oates, Joyce Carol. *On Boxing*. New York: HarperCollins, 2006, 72.
7 Sammons, Jeffrey. *Beyond the Ring: The Role of Boxing in American Society*. Chicago, IL: University of Illinois Press, 1988, 54.
8 Mee, Bob. *Bare Fists: The History of Bare Knuckle Prize Fighting*. New York: Overlook Press, 2001, 6.
9 Woodward, Kath. "MC Mary Kom Boxes Clever." BBC Sport, July 28, 2010. Web. Mar. 12, 2015.
10 Early, Gerald. *The Culture of Bruising: Essays on Prizefighting, Literature, and Modern American Culture*. New Jersey: Ecco Press, 1994, 13.
11 Gee, Tony. "Elizabeth Stokes (c.1723–1733)." *Oxford Dictionary of National Biography*. Ed. H.C.G. Matthew and Brian Harrison. Oxford: Oxford University Press, 2004, 857.
12 van Ingen, Cathy. "'Seeing What Frames Our Seeing': Seeking Histories on Early Black Female Boxers." *Journal of Sports History* 40 (2013): 93–110.
13 Smith, Malissa. *A History of Women's Boxing*. New York: Roman & Littlefield, 2014.
14 Aycock, Collen, and Mark Scott. *Joe Gans: A Biography of the First African American World Boxing Champion*. North Carolina: McFarland, 2008.
15 Hargreaves, Jennifer. "Women's Boxing and Related Activities: Introducing Images and Meanings." *Body & Society* 3 (1997): 33–49 (34).
16 Harvey, Gail. "She's Down But Not Out." *The Toronto Star*, Dec. 19, 1982, C4.
17 Smith, *A History of Women's Boxing*.
18 Wilbon, Michael. "USA Boxing Still Getting Hit" ESPN. ESPN Summer Olympics. Aug. 8, 2012. Web. Mar. 21, 2015.
19 Oatman, Maddie. "No Endorsements, No Problem: Boxing Gold Medalist Claressa Shields Keeps Fighting." *Mother Jones*, Mar. 29, 2013. Web. Mar. 13, 2015.
20 Bella, Timothy. "Claressa Explains it All: Gold Medalist Shields on Boxing, Black Activism." *Aljazeera America*, America Tonight, 20 Mar, 2015.
21 Deming, "Heather Hardy."
22 Ibid.

23 Hoffer, Richard. "Gritty Woman: Christy Martin is Knocking Down Stereotypes Even as She Refuses to Champion The Cause of Women in the Ring." *Sports Illustrated* 15 Apr. 1996.

24 Ibid.

25 Smith, *A History of Women's Boxing*, 208.

26 Ibid., 218.

27 Ortega, Mark. "Can Mikaela Mayer's Rivalry with Queen Underwood Help Take Women's Boxing to the Next Level?" *Behind The Gloves*, Jan. 25, 2014. Web. Mar. 13, 2015.

28 Erdman, Corey. "Women's Boxing Vs. North American Media," *Fighting Women: A Symposium on Women's Boxing*. Gladstone Hotel, Toronto, ON. 21 June 2013. Presentation.

29 Ibid.

30 Wacquant, Loic. "A Fleshpeddler at Work: Power, Pain and Profit in the Prizefighting Economy." *Theory and Society* 27 (1998): 1–42.

31 Rotella, Carlo. "Good With Her Hands: Women, Boxing, and Work." *Critical Inquiry* 25 (1999): 566–98 (592).

32 Banke, Bruce. "Tuesday Night Bouts Drawing Lots of Fans at Resort Hotel." *The Ring*, May 1965, 34.

33 Ibid., 33.

34 Anasi, Robert. *The Gloves: A Boxing Chronicle*. New York: North Point Press, 2003.

35 World Boxing Council. "The WBC Will Not Participate in Any Female Bout Schedule for 12 Rounds x 3 Minutes." *World Boxing Council*. Web. Oct. 15, 2014.

36 Fox, Sue. Women Boxing Archive Network. Web.

37 Walder, Joyce. "Christy Martin, Boxer, Takes Another Shot." *New York Times* 21 Jan 2011. Web. Apr. 16, 2014.

BIBLIOGRAPHY

Anasi, Robert. *The Gloves: A Boxing Chronicle*. New York: North Point Press, 2003.

Aycock, Collen, and Mark Scott. *Joe Gans: A Biography of the First African American World Boxing Champion*. North Carolina: McFarland, 2008.

Banke, Bruce. "Tuesday Night Bouts Drawing Lots of Fans at Resort Hotel." *The Ring*. May 1965.

Bella, Timothy. "Claressa Explains it All: Gold Medalist Shields on Boxing, Black Activism." *Aljazeera America*, America Tonight, Mar. 20, 2015.

Boddy, Kasia. *Boxing: A Cultural History*. London: Reakton, 2008.

Deming, Sarah. "Heather Hardy Brings the Heat To Nydia Feliciano in Brooklyn." *Stiff Jab*. Web. Mar. 24, 2014.

Early, Gerald. *The Culture of Bruising: Essays on Prizefighting, Literature, and Modern American Culture*. New Jersey: Ecco Press, 1994.

Erdman, Corey. "Women's Boxing vs. North American Media," *Fighting Women: A Symposium on Women's Boxing*. Gladstone Hotel, Toronto, ON. Jun. 21, 2013. Presentation.

Fox, Sue. Women Boxing Archive Network. Web.

Gee, Tony. "Elizabeth Stokes (c.1723–1733)." *Oxford Dictionary of National Biography*. Ed. H. C. G. Matthew and Brian Harrison. Oxford: Oxford University Press, 2004.

Hargreaves, Jennifer. "Women's Boxing and Related Activities: Introducing Images and Meanings." *Body and Society* 3 (1997): 33–49.

Harvey, Gail. "She's Down but Not Out." *The Toronto Star*, Dec. 19, 1982, C4.

Hoffer, Richard. "Gritty Woman: Christy Martin is Knocking Down Stereotypes Even as She Refuses to Champion the Cause of Women in the Ring." *Sports Illustrated*, Apr. 15, 1996.

International Women's Boxing Hall of Fame. Web. 2014.

Mee, Bob. *Bare Fists: The History of Bare Knuckle Prize Fighting*. New York: Overlook Press, 2001.

Oates, Joyce Carol. *On Boxing*. New York: HarperCollins, 2006.

Onstad, Katrina. "Do Female Athletes Have to Wear Miniskirts to Be Taken Seriously?" *The Globe and Mail*, Nov. 26, 2011, Web.

Oatman, Maddie. "No Endorsements, No Problem: Boxing Gold Medalist Claressa Shields Keeps Fighting." *Mother Jones*, Mar. 29, 2013. Web. Mar. 13, 2015.

Ortega, Mark. "Can Mikaela Mayer's Rivalry with Queen Underwood Help Take Women's Boxing to the Next Level?" *Behind The Gloves*, Jan. 25, 2014. Web. Mar. 13, 2015.

Rotella, Carlo. "Good With Her Hands: Women, Boxing, and Work." *Critical Inquiry* 25 (1999): 566–98.

Sammons, Jeffrey. *Beyond the Ring: The Role of Boxing in American Society*. Chicago, IL: University of Illinois Press, 1988.

Smith, Malissa. *A History of Women's Boxing*. New York: Roman & Littlefield, 2014.

van Ingen, Cathy. "'Seeing What Frames Our Seeing': Seeking Histories on Early Black Female Boxers." *Journal of Sport History* 40 (2013): 93–110.

van Ingen, Cathy, and Nicole Kovacs. "Subverting the Skirt: Female Boxers' 'Troubling' Uniforms." *Feminist Media Studies* 12 (2012): 460–63.

Wacquant, Loic. "The Pugilistic Point of View: How Boxers Think and Feel About Their Trade." *Theory and Society* 24 (1995): 489–535.

"A Fleshpeddler at Work: Power, Pain, and Profit in the Prizefighting Economy." *Theory and Society* 27 (1998): 1–42.

Walder, Joyce. "Christy Martin, Boxer, Takes Another Shot." *New York Times*, Jan. 21, 2011. Web. Apr. 16, 2014.

Wilbon, Michael. "USA Boxing Still Getting Hit" *ESPN*. ESPN Summer Olympics. Aug. 8, 2012. Web. Mar. 21, 2015.

Woodward, Kath. "MC Mary Kom Boxes Clever." *BBC Sport*, July 28, 2010. Web. Mar. 12, 2015.

World Boxing Council. "The WBC Will Not Participate in Any Female Bout Schedule for 12 Rounds x 3 Minutes." *World Boxing Council*. Web. Oct. 15, 2014.

11

STEVEN A. RIESS

Jews in Twentieth-Century Boxing

In the early 1900s, Jewish immigrants and their sons were derided for their presumed lack of manliness. Their fathers were impoverished Eastern European immigrants who came from a pre-modern world that lacked a sporting heritage. The newcomers hoped to maintain Old World religious institutions and traditions in their new homes in Great Britain and the United States, and opposed sports as physically dangerous, a waste of time, and an activity that could Americanize their sons. Parents particularly scorned boxing because of its brutality, immorality, and underworld connections, making pugilism an abomination, a *schande* (shame) for the community. However, the second-generation boys enjoyed sports because they were fun and signified their acculturation and manliness.[1]

Inner-city Jewish youth mainly participated in inexpensive, accessible sports that fit into their environment, like basketball, track, and boxing. Boxing was inexpensive and could be learned at neighborhood gymnasiums or settlement houses sponsored by social reformers who believed it obviated more dangerous combat and countered negative stereotypes about Jewish manliness. In addition, the art of self-defense was useful, enabling them to defend themselves and friends against rival ethnic thugs. Novices had role models like English champion Daniel Mendoza (1791–95) and American heavyweight Joe Choynski, a contender in the 1890s and early 1900s. Amateur boxing provided a means to prove one's manhood and honor, gain the attention of girls, and even make money by selling off prizes. A top amateur could dream of a professional career and escape from the ghetto.[2]

Inner-city British and American Jews achieved marked success quite quickly. In 1904, American Sam Berger won the first Olympic heavyweight gold medal; but fame came to mostly smaller men, like Joe Bernstein, "the Pride of the Ghetto," who in 1900 fought featherweight champion "Terrible" Terry McGovern. Another Lower East Side hero was lightweight Leach Cross, who "had to fight [his] way through many of the streets where the Jews were looked upon as outcasts." His Jewish fans rooted for him to beat his Irish foes.[3]

The first two Jewish world champions in the 1900s were also men of small stature. Chicagoan Harry Harris, the "Human Hairpin," at 5′ 7½″ and 105 lbs, became world bantamweight champion in 1901 by defeating British champion Pedlar Palmer in a fifteen-rounder to gain the vacated title. Harris relinquished his title one year later, having grown into a featherweight. The next Jewish title holder was San Franciscan Abe Attell, who came from a large family, and whose Russian father abandoned them. Abe grew up a neighborhood street fighter in a heavily Irish neighborhood: "I either had to hold my own with those tough Irish lads or be chased off the block." The 5′ 4″, 122 lb pugilist claimed the featherweight championship in 1904 but did not achieve universal recognition until 1906. A crafty and quick ring artist, "The Little Hebrew" successfully defended his crown twenty-one times until losing in 1912 to Johnny Kilbane by a referee's decision. He retired with a record of 92–28–45, which included several matches against much heavier men.

Boxing expert Nat Fleischer, founder and publisher of *The Ring* magazine (1922), rated Attell the third greatest featherweight of all time. At a time when pejorative images of Jewish men typically emphasized their weak and deformed bodies, Attell was applauded in 1902 by the popular *National Police Gazette*, with a photograph describing him and seven other fighters as "Splendid Specimens of Muscular Development."[4] However, the little champion's accomplishments were blemished by his lack of integrity. One journalist claimed that Attell "engaged in more crooked bouts than all the champions in the country put together." Attell earned about $300,000 in the ring but lost nearly all of it to gambling. He later worked for gambling kingpin Arnold Rothstein and had a prominent role in the Black Sox Scandal of 1919.[5]

The Age of Benny Leonard

The Jewish presence in boxing became increasingly visible in the 1910s, as they became more assimilated, and as the sport provided an alternative route to success for uneducated ghetto youth. Though in 1916 there were more Irish, German, and Italian contenders than Jews, there was a Jewish champion every year between 1910 and 1938 (except for 1913). In the 1910s, among the thirty-three undisputed world champions, four were Jewish Americans, most notably Benny Leonard, and London welterweights Matt Wells (1914–15) and Ted "Kid" Lewis (1915–16, 1917–19). Lewis, born Gershon Mendeloff, started boxing at age fifteen over the objections of his father, a cabinet maker. He had a career record of 155–24 in some 250 fights. Lewis was best known for his twenty matches, including five title bouts against Jimmy Britton, a three-time champion, in which Lewis went 3–4–2–11. Nat Fleischer rated Lewis the fourth best welterweight in history.[6]

Lightweight titlist Benny Leonard (1917–25) was the greatest Jewish fighter in history, with a career record of 183–24–8–4. Like many other Jews, he fought under a pseudonym to hide his fighting from his parents. *The Ring* magazine rated Benny as the best boxer (ring general) of all time because of his strong defense and astute decision making. Leonard was a fighting champion who brawled in over eighty contests during his championship tenure. Leonard was also admired for his manly physique, training soldiers during the First World War, and teaching physical fitness after he retired.[7]

Benny's toughest defense came in 1922 against Jewish southpaw Lew Tendler, who knocked Leonard down. Their rematch a year later at Yankee Stadium drew over 58,000 people and a gate of $453,000, then the second highest in history. Leonard's only loss while champion came in a title match that year against welterweight champion Jack Britton, whom he knocked down in the thirteenth round, but then fouled him. It eventually came out that his manager had told him to lose the fight. Leonard retired with a million dollars but went broke following the stock market crash. Despite his one black mark, Leonard was considered an outstanding sportsman, who wore a Star of David on his trunks to profess his Jewish identity. Philanthropist and Zionist Nathan Straus, the owner of Macy's, considered Leonard's ring success "a great advertisement for the Jewish people." During the Depression, Leonard raised funds for the American Committee for the Relief of Jews in Poland, and to promote sports in Palestine.[8]

New York State legalized prizefighting in 1920, which helped the sport flourish. The New York State Athletic Commission became a model for the supervision of pugilism in other states. Major fights in the decade took place at arenas like Madison Square Garden as well as outdoors in the Polo Grounds, the top venues for the sport. Tex Rickard claimed that most New York fans were Jewish or Italian. Among the sport's biggest fans were underworld figures that had often grown up with aspiring inner city boxers. Men like Rothstein and Jake Spot, the "godfather" of London's East End, bet heavily on the fights, preferably the fixed ones. In addition, gangsters gained control of gifted fighters by wining and dining them, promising to use their influence to get them big bouts, or simply employing muscle or threats to take over talented boxers, like New Yorker bootlegger Waxey Gordon did when he secured the contract of lightweight Ruby Goldstein, the "Jewel of the Ghetto."[9]

The rising Jewish success in boxing was reflected by the presence of five Americans on the 1920 Olympic team and six in 1924, including featherweight gold medalist Jackie Fields, a future professional welterweight champion. In the 1920s there were eleven Jewish American champions out of fifty-eight title holders in ten divisions (19 percent), just one behind Italian Americans and Irish Americans. Furthermore, by 1928 there were more Jewish fighters (nineteen) ranked in the "top ten" of the ten fighting divisions than any other ethnic group, followed by Italians and Irish.[10]

Jewish fighters showed solidarity with their fellow Jews and supported their causes. In 1929, five Jews, including three future champions, Jackie Berg, Maxie Rosenbloom, and Al Singer, fought gentile opponents at Madison Square Garden to raise funds for Palestinian Jews following a series of Arab attacks. Historian Stephen Norwood said the event helped support the image of tough Jews who would retaliate against future provocations.[11]

The Age of Barney Ross

During the Depression era, Jews continued to dominate among boxers and fans. Joe Gould, manager of heavyweight champion Jimmy Braddock, claimed (with considerable exaggeration), that 75 percent of spectators at title matches in 1937 were Jewish. By then, even middle-class Jews *kvelled* at Jewish boxing success, reflected in 1934 when the highly assimilated *American Hebrew* printed photographs of eight outstanding Jews, including champions Max Baer and Barney Ross.[12]

During the Depression when young men struggled to earn a living, there were reportedly some 8,000 professional boxers. In the 1930s, thirteen of the sixty-one world champions were Jews (21.3 percent), followed by Italians (eleven) African Americans (eight), and Irishmen (six). There were seven individual Jewish American champions plus English middleweight Jackie Berg, the "Whitechapel Windmill" (1930–31), and Tunisian flyweight Victor "Young" Perez (1931–32), who died in the Holocaust.[13]

In 1933, there were Jewish champions in four divisions. Their success peaked in 1934, when they reigned in six divisions. However, the number of Jewish contenders in 1936 fell to third place behind the Italians and Irish. Just seven of the top ten ranked fighters in the sport's eight divisions were Jewish, a substantial decline since 1928. Young men who might have boxed in Whitechapel or Brownsville were finding better job opportunities. The result was a sharp drop in Jewish champions.[14]

The finest Jewish fighters in the 1930s included "Slapsie Maxie" Rosenbloom, the world champion light heavyweight (1932–34), with 289 matches and 203 victories, who was a bigger hero to young Philip Roth than Albert Einstein. Another was the physically imposing heavyweight champion Max Baer (1934–35), who was 6' 2½" and 220 lbs. Baer was a powerful puncher, who had a record of 68–13, including fifty-two KOs, and killed two men in the ring, which made him a more reticent fighter. Many fans questioned Baer's Jewish identity because he had not been circumcised, did not observe the faith, and had a gentile mother at a time when intermarriage was rare. In June 1933, when he defeated former world champion Germany's Max Schmeling, with a tenth-round TKO, Baer wore a Star of David on his trunks, signifying he identified with Jews. This was particularly symbolic because the public identified Schmeling (incorrectly) with Nazism. One year later, Baer became world champion with an eleventh-round TKO of Primo Carnera, considered a representative of Italian fascism. But one year later Max lost his crown in an enormous upset to Jimmy Braddock.[15]

Barney Ross (Barnet David Rosofsky), the first pugilist to simultaneously hold three world championships, was the preeminent Jewish fighter in the 1930s. His lifetime record was 74–4–3. Never knocked off his feet, *The Ring* ranked him as one of the three gutsiest fighters of all time. Barney grew up in Chicago's impoverished Maxwell Street area, where tough Jews like "Nails" Morton and the Miller brothers were heroes for defending the community against other ethnic groups. Ross's Orthodox father, a small storekeeper, was murdered when Barney was thirteen, and Barney became a wayward youth, which led to an interest in boxing. In 1933 Barney defeated Tony Canzoneri, the lightweight and junior welterweight champion, and one year later took the welterweight championship from Jimmy McLarnin. McLarnin won their rematch, but Ross prevailed in a pivotal third fight, in 1935, and remained champion until 1938.[16]

Barney was an ardent Zionist who, like many Jewish fighters, saw himself as defender of his people against Adolf Hitler. In Newark, New Jersey, bootlegger Abner Zwillman, a major underworld kingpin, employed well-known Jewish boxers to fight anti-Semitism in northern New Jersey. His "Minutemen" broke up Nazi meetings with baseball bats, iron pipes, and fists, hindering their movement in the state. Ross's life was depicted in the films *Body and Soul* (1947), starring John Garfield, a Jewish actor, and *Monkey on My Back* (1957), starring Cameron Mitchell, a gentile actor.[17]

Boxing in Europe, 1929–1945

The Anglo-American success in boxing far surpassed Jews on the Continent, where they encountered significant anti-Semitism. Dutch flyweight Ben Bril, an Olympian in 1928, made the 1932 squad, but was barred from competing by prejudiced members of the Dutch Olympic Committee. He later survived Bergen-Belsen. In Germany, shortly after Hitler came to power in 1933, the German Boxing Federation (GBF) expelled Jewish fighters, referees, and trainers from national boxing associations. Erich Seelig lost his German middleweight and light heavyweight titles, and was told to leave the country or have his family executed. Seelig, a top ten contender, resumed his career in France and the United States. Italian featherweight champion Leone Efrati was fighting in the United States when the war broke out. He was deported in 1943 and died one year later in Auschwitz.[18]

During the Second World War, Jewish boxers like Latvian Nathan Shapow and Pole Harry Haft entertained concentration camp guards to stay alive. Middleweight Balkan professional champion Salamo Arouch of Solonika survived Auschwitz by winning over 200 bouts. His story was the basis for the 1989 movie *Triumph of the Spirit*, starring gentile actor William Dafoe.[19]

Jewish Boxing after the Second World War

By the coming of the Second World War, Jewish boxers were virtually gone in Great Britain and the United States because of alternative opportunities to get ahead. In 1950, for instance, Jewish men were twice as likely as other Americans to have a white-collar job, a product of the ethnic group's emphasis on education, and entrepreneurial experiences. The only two Jewish world champions were Algerian bantamweights Robert Cohen (1954–56) and Alphonse Halimi (1957–59, 1960–61), who fought out of France.[20]

The next Jewish champion was the American light heavyweight Mike Rossman (1978–79), who had an Italian father and a Jewish mother. Rossman was followed as a title holder by African Americans Saoul Mamby, the WBC junior welterweight champion (1980–82), and Zab Judah, who held five titles. Young Saoul had many street fights in the Bronx. "I would be walking down the street and the kids would pull my yarmulke off my head or grab at my tallis bag." Judah, one of three Jewish African American fighting brothers, was the undisputed welterweight champion (2005–06) but subsequently converted to Christianity.[21]

There has recently been a boxing revival among Jewish fighters, mainly poor youth from the former Soviet Union who emigrated to Israel. The most notable was Yuri Foreman, an Orthodox Jew, who held the WBA super welterweight championship in 2009–10. Jewish women are another new source of talent. They include Israeli Hagar Finer, the IBF bantamweight (2009–12), and Carolina Raquel "The Turk" Duer, of Buenos Aires,

WBO super flyweight champion (2010–13) and WBO bantamweight champion (2013–14, 2016–17).[22]

Jews in Boxing Outside the Squared Ring

The Jewish prominence in boxing went far beyond the boxers, encompassing trainers, managers, referees, and promoters, as well as inventors and journalists. Boxing was an occupation where there was considerable ethnic succession, and Jews were particularly successful in utilizing their knowledge of the sport to become trainers, following in the footsteps of the Irish. Jewish trainers became prominent by the 1920s. They worked with fighters from all ethnic groups, including Italians, African Americans, and Latinos as they emerged as highly respected experts. Top Jewish trainers included Whitey Bimstein, Charley Goldman, Mannie Seamon, Freddie Brown, and especially Ray Arcel, who trained twenty-two champions, from Benny Leonard to Panamanian Roberto Durán and African American Larry Holmes. They respected top boxers of all backgrounds, yet shared the same prejudices as other trainers. In 1940, for instance, Arcel claimed that Jewish fighters were the smartest; Italians, the sturdiest (among white pugilists); Irish and Poles, the most courageous and determined; and African Americans had the most stamina and thickest skulls. Arcel rated Jack Blackburn, Joe Louis's African American trainer as the best trainer of his time.[23]

Several of the leading referees from the 1920s through the 1960s were Jewish, notably Ruby Goldstein, who refereed thirty-nine championship fights, and Davey Miller, who refereed about 5,000 bouts. Miller was the scheduled referee for the 1927 "Long Count" Dempsey–Tunney heavyweight championship fight, but was replaced after he took a car ride with Al Capone, a heavy Dempsey supporter.[24]

Managers were responsible for grooming a fighter and getting him good purses and suitable matches, but often cheated them out of their money. By the early 1930s there were more than twenty prominent Jewish American fight managers, some of whom were mob connected, and by the late 1930s a high percentage of British managers were also Jewish. The top Jewish managers from the 1930s to the 1950s included Al Weill, whose fighters included champions Tony Canzoneri, Lou Ambers, and Rocky Marciano; "Leaping Lena" Levy, who managed her brother, "Kingfish" Levinsky; and Joe "Yussel the Muscle" Jacobs, who handled German heavyweight titlist Max Schmeling despite Nazi bans on Jewish managers. By 1960, there were fewer Jewish managers. That year, four of the eleven managers called before the Senate hearings on professional boxing were Jewish, all underworld fronts. Later one of the most prominent was Jim Jacobs, the world champion handball player, who co-managed Mike Tyson. One of the first women managers was Jackie Kallen, whose fighter, African American James Toney, won the IBF middleweight championship in 1991. He often fought with a Star of David on his trunks out of respect to his manager. Kallen's life was dramatized in the movies, including *Against the Ropes*, starring Meg Ryan.[25]

The historic Jewish success in entrepreneurship was reflected by their achievements as manufacturers of boxing equipment and as boxing promoters. In the 1890s Sol Levinson, a fancy glove manufacturer, invented the modern boxing glove. In 1910, tailor Jacob Golomb created the Everlast Company, still the top manufacturer of boxing gloves, trunks, and other equipment.[26]

Jews were prominent boxing promoters in London, where the Jewish East End had several boxing halls, including Wonderland (1894–1911), the Judæans Athletic and Social Club (1902–14), and Premierland (1912–31). The outstanding British matchmaker Jack Solomons got his start in the 1930s and went on to promote twenty-six world title fights.[27] In the United States there were over twenty Jewish American promoters by the 1930s, most notably Mike Jacobs, who organized the Twentieth Century Sporting Club, in 1933, and two years later landed an exclusive contract with contender Joe Louis. Jacobs, abetted by mobster Frankie Carbo, promoted sixty-one world championship bouts from 1937 to 1947. Four of the ten promoters who testified in the 1960 investigation of the sport were Jewish. The tradition of Jewish boxing promoters was later sustained by attorney Bob Arum, whose Top Rank, Inc., in the 1980s, promoted the fights of such champions as Roberto Durán; African Americans Marvin Hagler, Thomas Hearns, and Sugar Ray Leonard; and more recently, Mexican American Oscar De La Hoya and Filipino Manny Pacquiao.[28]

Finally, Jews dominated boxing journalism, going back to Nat Fleischer, Barney Nagler, who covered boxing for forty years, Bert Randolph Sugar, who wrote dozens of books about the sport, and Howard Cosell, the most important TV broadcaster. Jewish authors have also been influential, including Clifford Odets (*Golden Boy*, 1937), Budd Schulberg (*The Harder They Fall*, 1947), Norman Mailer (*The Fight*, 1975), and Rod Serling's teleplay *Requiem for a Heavyweight* (1956).[29]

Conclusion

The Jewish eminence in the ring dissipated after the 1930s, with second-generation Jewish Americans, a page of history largely now forgotten. Jews thereafter no longer lived in impoverished inner city neighborhoods where rough lives created an environment conducive to the emergence of professional pugilists. Instead, socially mobile Jews moved out of poverty by acquired skilled employment, opening small businesses and taking advantage of the group's entrepreneurial traditions or becoming professionals through higher education.[30] Jewish fighters were replaced by poor Italians, African Americans, and Latinos, though Jews continued for years to work as trainers, managers, referees, and promoters. Today there are virtually no Jewish boxers and trainers, and few managers or promoters, though they are still prominent as boxing journalists, authors, and broadcasters.

Jewish boxers were tough Jews who in the first half of the twentieth century (along with gangsters) defended fellow inner-city Jews against bullies and anti-Semitism. They were heroes to second-generation working class youth in Jewish communities around the globe who demonstrated the manliness and courage of Jewish men. The need for such heroes lessened as Jews in the 1930s, like Hank Greenberg in baseball and Sid Luckman in football, proved their masculinity in more respectable American sports, as did Jewish soldiers in the Second World War. Furthermore, after the Holocaust, whatever questions remained about Jewish manliness was answered in Israel, first by militant freedom fighters, and then the Israel Defense Forces.[31]

NOTES

1 On Jewish manliness, see Sander L. Gilman, *The Jew's Body* (New York: Routledge, 1991); Dana Mihailescu, "Jewish Men and the Early Twentieth Century American Code of Masculinity Though Ethnic Lenses," *Atenea* 28 (June 2008): 87–101; Herbert L. Sussman, *Masculine Identities: The History and Meanings of Manliness* (Santa Barbara, CA: ABC-CLIO, 2012), 119–31. On negative Jewish stereotypes about manliness and sport, see Steven A. Riess, "Tough Jews: The Jewish American Boxing Experience," in Riess, ed., *Sport and the American Jew* (Syracuse, NY: University of Syracuse Press, 1995), 60. On Jewish American sport, see Peter Levine, *Ellis Island to Ebbets Field: Sport and the American Jewish Experience* (New York: Oxford University Press, 1992); and Riess, *Sport and the American Jew*. The close relationship between boxers and their peers who became boxers is exemplified by Max Moses, a prominent contender who in the early 1900s led London's notorious Bessarabian gang, and was sentenced to ten years in prison for manslaughter. In Chicago there were the Miller brothers, whose street gang was known for its criminality and also for protecting the community. One brother was a boxer, restaurateur, and political fixer; one was a bootlegger and murderer; and one was a policeman. See Riess, "Tough Jews," 87–88; Alex Garel-Frantzen, *Gangsters & Organized Crime in Jewish Chicago* (Charleston, SC: History Press, 2013), 59–60.

2 Riess, "Tough Jews," 61–65; Stephen H. Norwood, "'American Jewish Muscle': Forging a New Masculinity in the Streets and in the Ring, 1890–1940," *Modern Judaism* 29 (May 2009): 176–77.

3 Riess, "Tough Jews," 65–68; Bernard Postal, Jesse Silver, and Roy Silver, *Encyclopedia of Jews in Sports* (New York: Bloch, 1965), 149 (hereafter *EJS*).

4 Riess, "Tough Jews," 68–72; Richard Barry, "Abe Attell – The Elusive Feather," *Pearson's Magazine* 29 (March 1913): 353–59; "Splendid Specimens of Muscular Development," *National Police Gazette*, January 11, 1902, 16, cited in Norwood, "American Jewish Muscle," 191; *EJS*, 144–46; *New York Times*, February 7, 1970; "Attell, Abe," s.v., *American National Biography*.

5 Quote appears in "Boxing Scrapbooks," 16: 38, Chicago History Museum. On Attell and the Black Sox scandal, see Harold Seymour, *Baseball*: Vol. 2, *The Golden Years* (New York: Oxford University Press, 1971), 300–3, 307–9, 325–27, 329, 336–37; Leo Katcher, *The Big Bankroll: The Life and Times of Arnold Rothstein* (New York: Harper, 1959), 142–45, 147, 148; and David Pietrusza, *Rothstein: The Life, Times, and Murder of the Criminal Genius Who Fixed the 1919 World Series* (New York: Carroll & Graf, 2003), 156–58, 160–63, 170–72.

6 Riess, "Tough Jews," 72–74; Levine, *Ellis Island to Ebbets Field*, 162; S. Kirson Weinberg, and Henry Arond, "The Occupational Culture of the Boxer," *American Journal of Sociology* 57 (March 1952): 460. On English Jewish fighters, see Edward Berkowitz, "Jewish Fighters in Britain in Historical Context: Repugnance, Requiem, Reconsideration," *Sport in History* 31 (2011): 423–43; David Dee, "'The Hefty Hebrew': Boxing and British-Jewish Identity, 1890–1960," *Sport in Society* 32(September 2012): 361–38; David Dee, *Sport and British Jewry: Integration, Ethnicity and Anti-Semitism 1890–1970* (Manchester: Manchester University Press, 2013), 80–121, 112, 114–15, 117–18; Morton Lewis, *Ted Kid Lewis: His Life and Times* (London: Robson, 1990).

7 Norwood, "American Jewish Muscle," 167; "Governor Smith Keeps Fit With Benny Leonard's Course," *Ring* (July 1925): 17; "Why Shouldn't You, Too, Have a Glowing, Healthy Body?" *Ring* (May 1925): 15, cited in Norwood, "American Jewish Muscle," 179.

8 Nat Fleischer, *Leonard the Magnificent* (New York: n.p., 1947), 30–39, 82–84; "Ray Arcel Interview," 66–67, American Jewish Committee Oral History Collection, New York Public Library; *EJS*, 164; Ken Blady, *The Jewish Boxing Hall of Fame* (New York: Sapolsky, 1988), 116–18; Ronald K. Fried, *Corner Men: The Great Boxing Trainers* (New York: 4 Walls, 8 Windows, 1991), 237–49.

9 Riess, *Sports and the American Jews*, 82–84; Norwood, "American Jewish Muscle," 175, 188; Peter Heller, *In This Corner...!: Forty World Champions Tell Their Story* (New York: Simon and Schuster, 1973), 83; Ruby Goldstein and Frank Graham, *Third Man in the Ring* (New York: Funk and Wagnalls, 1959), 56, 60, 65–66.

10 Data on consensus champions is drawn from Herbert G. Goldman, *The Ring 1985 Record Book and Boxing Encyclopedia* (New York: Ring Publishing Group, 1985). For the rankings of 1928's "top ten" fighters in ten weight divisions, see "*The Ring* Magazine's Annual Ratings: 1928," http://boxrec.com/media/index.php/The_Ring_Magazine%27s_Annual_Ratings:_1928. Accessed February 8, 2014. On Jewish fandom, see Norwood, "American Jewish Muscle," 175.

11 Norwood, "American Jewish Muscle," 181.

12 Riess, "Tough Jews," 82–84; Norwood, "American Jewish Muscle," 175, 188; Heller, *In This Corner…!*, 83; Goldstein and Graham, *Third Man in the Ring*, 56, 60, 65–66

13 The discrepancy is because Jackie Fields won the welterweight title twice, and Barney Ross held three titles himself, including twice winning the welterweight title. On Berg, see John Harding, *Jack Kid Berg: The Whitechapel Windmill* (London: Robson, 1987).

14 On consensus champions, see Goldman, *The Ring 1985 Record Book and Boxing Encyclopedia*. For the "top ten" rankings in 1936 for eight weight divisions, see "*The Ring* Magazine's Annual Ratings: 1936," http://boxrec .com/media/index.php/The_Ring_Magazine's_Annual_Ratings:_1936. Accessed February 8, 2014.

15 Philip Roth, *The Facts: A Novelist's Autobiography* (New York: Farrar, Straus & Giroux, 1988), 28; Riess, "Tough Jews," 85–86, 93, 99, 102; Jeremy Schaap, *Cinderella Man: Jams Braddock, Max Baer, and the Greatest Upset in Boxing History* (New York: Houghton Mifflin Harcourt, 2005), 144–57; Levine, *Ellis Island to Ebbets Field*, 180–83; *New York Times*, November 22, 1959, March 8, 1976. Baer was elected to the International Jewish Sports Hall of Fame in 2010. See "Max Baer," www.jewishsports.net/BioPages/Maximilian-Baer.htm. Accessed February 11, 2014.

16 Barney Ross and Martin Abrahamson, *No Man Stands Alone: The True Story of Barney Ross* (Philadelphia, PA: Lippincott, 1957), 11, 21, 41–65; Riess, "Tough Jews," 86–90; Douglas Century, *Barney Ross* (New York: Nextbook/ Schocken: 2006). On life in Maxwell Street, see Ira Berkow, *Maxwell Street: Life Survival in a Bazaar* (New York: Knopf, 1977); and Louis Wirth, *The Ghetto* (Chicago, IL: University of Chicago Press, 1928), 171–292.

17 Norwood, "Jewish American Muscle," 181. On Anglo Jewish fighters and anti-Semitism, see Dee, *Sport and British Jewry*, 199–200. On Ross and films, see Aaron Baker, *Contesting Identities: Sport in American Film* (Urbana, IL: University of Illinois Press, 2003), 25–27, 67–69, 102–4, 114–30.

18 *New York Times*, August 12, 1935, 1; Norwood, "American Jewish Muscle," 183; "A Look Back: Ben Bril and Nathan Shapow," *The Jewish Boxing Blog*, October 31, 2013. http://jewishboxing.blogspot.com/search?q=ben+bril. Accessed February 9, 2014; Ed van Opzeeland and Loet van Schellenbeek, *Ben Bril: Davidster als Ereteken* (Ben Bril: Decorated with a Star of David) (Kats, Netherlandd: De Buitenspelers, 2006); "Leone Effrati," International Jewish Sports Hall of Fame. www.jewishsports.net/PillarAchievementBios/LeoneEfrati .htm. Accessed February 8, 2014. On boxing in Poland, see Roni Gechtman, "Socialist Mass Politics Through Sport: The Bund's Morgenshtern in Poland, 1926–1939," *Journal of Sport History* 26 (1999): 338, 343, 344–45; Jack Jacobs, "Jewish Workers' Sports Movements in Interwar Poland: Shtern and Morgenshtern in Comparative Perspective," in Jack Kugelmass, ed., *Jews, Sports, and the Rites of Citizenship* (Urbana, IL: University of Illinois Press, 2007), 118–22; Diethelm Blecking, "Jews and Sports in Poland Before the Second World War," in Ezra Mendelsohn, ed., *Jews and the Sporting Life*. Studies in Contemporary Jewry: An Annual (23) (Oxford: Oxford University Press), 17, 23, 24–28. On displaced Jews and boxing after the war, see Gabriel N. Finder, "'Boxing for Everyone.' Jewish DPs, Sport and Boxing," in ibid., 36–53.

19 "Ben Bril and Nathan Shapow"; Nathan Shapow, and Bob Harris, *The Boxer's Story: Fighting for My Life in the Nazi Camps* (New York: Bieback, 2012); Alan Scott Haft, *Harry Haft: Survivor of Auschwitz, Challenger of Rocky Marciano* (Syracuse, NY: Syracuse University Press, 2006); *New York Times*, May 14, 1989, H11, December 18, 1989, C2; *Washington Post*, May 1, 2009, B5; Susan Schindehette, Jack Kelley, and Mira Avrech, "Boxer Salamo Arouch's Death Camp Bouts End in a Triumph of the Spirit," *People Magazine*, February 19, 1990. www .people.com/people/article/0,,20116862,00.html. Accessed February 9, 2014.

20 A study in 1950 of American workers found that from 75 percent to 96 percent of Jews in twelve cities had a white-collar job compared with 38 percent of other Americans. See Howard M. Sachar, *A History of the Jews in America* (New York: Knopf, 1992), 646. On the Franco-Algerian champions, see "Robert Cohen," International Jewish Sports Hall of Fame, www.jewishsports.net/ BioPages/RobertCohen.htm; "Alphonse Halimi," International Jewish Sports Hall of Fame, www.jewishsports.net/BioPages/AlphonseHalimi.htm. Accessed February 10, 2014.

21 "A Look Back: Mike Rossman," *The Jewish Boxing Blog*, September 13, 2012. http://jewishboxing.blogspot.com/2011/09/look-back-mike-rossman .html. "A Look Back: Saoul Mamby." *The Jewish Boxing Blog*, July 31, 2012. http://jewishboxing.blogspot.com/2012/07/a-look-back-saoul-mamby.html; "Zab 'Super' Judah." www.jewsinsports.org/profile.asp?sport=boxing&ID=250. Accessed February 10, 2014.

22 Thomas Hauser, "The Haifa Connection: Roman Greenberg and Yuri Foreman," *SecondsOut.com.*, www.secondsout.com/usa-boxing-news/usa-boxing-news/the- haifa-connection-roman-greenberg-and-yuri-foreman; "Hager Finer," WBAN (Women's Boxing Archive Network). www.wban.org/biog/hfiner.htm; Diego Melamed, "Argentine Jewish Boxer Defends Her Title," *Arizona Jewish Post*, November 18, 2011. http://azjewishpost.com/2011/argentine-jewish-boxer- defends-her-title. Accessed February 10, 2014.

23 Riess, "Tough Jews," 93–96; Fried, *Corner Men*, 55–112, 159–288; Dave Anderson, *In the Corner: Great Boxing Trainers Talk About Their Art* (New York: William Morrow, 1991), 119–50; "Arcel Interview," 17, 62, 71–73; *New York Times*, 8 March 1994, B8-1; Donald Dewey, *Ray Arcel: A Boxing Biography* (Jefferson City, NC: McFarland, 2012), 5–194, and esp. 101 and 122 for ethnic stereotypes; A. J. Liebling, "The University of Eighth Avenue," in James Warner and Fred Barbour, eds., *A Neutral Corner: Boxing Essays* (New York: Simon and Schuster, 1992), 40–42.

24 Randy Roberts, *The Manassa Mauler* (Baton Rouge, LA: Louisiana State University, 1979), 258–63; Goldstein and Graham, *Third Man in the Ring*, 23– 29; Bill Miller, "The Jew in Boxing," *Ring* (December 1932): 9–10; "undated article, *Chicago Herald American*," in Davey Miller Scrapbook, Chicago Jewish Historical Society, Spertus College Library, Chicago, IL.

25 Riess, "Tough Jews," 98–100; Goldstein and Graham, *Third Man in the Ring*, 23–62; John V. Grombach, *The Saga of the Fist* (South Brunswick, NJ: A.S. Barnes, 1977), 176, 178–79; Jeffrey Sammons, *Beyond the Ring: The Role of Boxing in American Society* (Urbana, IL: University of Illinois Press, 1988), 115; Norwood, "American Jewish Muscle," 180; Dave Anderson, *In This Corner: Great Boxing Trainers Talk About Their Art* (New York: William

Morrow, 1991), 119–50. On Joe "Yussel the Muscle" Jacobs, see Max Schmeling, and George B. von der Lippe, *Max Schmeling: An Autobiography* (Chicago, IL: Bonus Books, 1998); Lewis Erenberg, *The Greatest Fight of Our Generation: Louis vs. Schmeling* (New York: Oxford University Press, 2006), 19, 61, 76; David Margolick, *Beyond Glory: Joe Louis vs. Max Schmeling, and A World on the Brink* (New York: Knopf, 2005), 21–26, 31–33, 54–57, 138–39; Berkowitz, "Jewish Fighters," 425. On Jacobs, see *New York Times*, March 24, 1988, D23-3. On Kallen, see "Jackie Kallen: The First Lady of Boxing," www .clevelandwomen.com/people/jackie-kallen.htm. Accessed September 18, 2015. On the 1960 federal boxing hearings, see US Senate, Judiciary, *Professional Boxing: Hearings Before the Subcommittee on Antitrust and Monopoly of the Committee on the Judiciary, United States Senate, Eighty-sixth Congress, second session* (Washington, DC: 1961), pts. 1–4.

26 Riess, "Tough Jews," 92.

27 Dee, "Hefty Hebrew," 370, 373; Dee, *Sport and British Jewry*, 110, 118–22, 151–52.

28 Riess, "Tough Jews," 91, 101–3; Teddy Brenner and Barney Nagler, *Only the Ring was Square* (Englewood Cliffs, NJ: Prentice-Hall, 1981), 21–24; Dan Daniel, *The Mike Jacobs Story*. New York: Ring Book Shop, 1950), 18–50, 53–54, 125; Nat Fleischer, *Fifty Years at Ringside* (New York: Fleet, 1958), 50; Barney Nagler, *James Norris and the Decline of Boxing* (Indianapolis, IN: Bobbs-Merrill, 1964). The number of promoters called before the 1960 Senate boxing hearings is drawn from US Senate, Judiciary Committee, *Professional Boxing*, 288, 294, 425, 460, 542, 695, 1022.

29 Riess "Tough Jews," 93; Dave Kindred, *Sound and Fury: Two Powerful Lives: One Fateful Friendship* (New York: Simon & Schuster, 2006); John Bloom, *There You Have It: The Life, Legend, and Legacy of Howard Cosell* (Amherst, MA: University of Massachusetts Press 2010); Christopher Ross, "Cosell Backed Ali From the Start," http://espn.go.com/abcsports/wwos/ objector.html. Accessed February 10, 2014.

30 Sachar, *History of the Jews in America*, 340–76, 646–71; Stephen Thernstrom, *The Other Bostonians: Poverty and Progress in the American Metropolis, 1880–1970* (Cambridge, MA: Harvard University Press, 1973), 131, 136–37; Thomas Kessner, *The Golden Door: Italian and Jewish Immigrant Mobility in New York City, 1880–1915* (New York: Oxford University Press, 1977); Bernard Sarachek "Jewish American Entrepreneurs," *Journal of Economic History* 40 (June 1980): 359–72; Adam D. Mendelsohn, *The Rag Race: How Jews Sewed Their Way to Success in America and the British Empire* (New York: New York University Press, 2015).

31 On "tough jews," see Paul Breines, *Touch Jews: Political Fantasies and the Moral Dilemma of American Jewry* (New York: Basic Books, 1990); Rich Cohen, *Tough Jews* (New York: Simon and Schuster, 1998); and David Moscowitz, *A Culture of Tough Jews: Rhetorical Regeneration and the Politics of Identity* (New York: Peter Lang, 2015), which have virtually no mention of prizefighters. On Jewish partisans in the Holocaust, see Peter Duffy, *The Bielski Brothers* (New York: HarperCollins, 2003); Zeev Barmatz, *Heroism in the Forest: The*

Jewish Partisans of Belarus (Tel Aviv: KIP International Publishing, 2013); Allan Levine, *Fugitives of the Forest: The Heroic Story of Jewish Resistance and Survival During the Second World War* (Guilford, CT: Lyons, 2009); Tec Nechama, *Defiance: The Bielski Partisans* (New York: Oxford University Press, 1993); Edward Zwick, prod. and dir., *Defiance* (Los Angeles: Paramount Vantage, 2009).

12

TONY GEE

A Surprising Dearth of Top English-Born Jewish Fighters in the Bare-Knuckle Era

Minority boxers have always had a visible presence in fistic circles, and in the bare-knuckle period,[1] English-born Jews appear to have been one of the most prominent of the minority groups.[2] However, although it has been said that there were a significant number of Jewish combatants active in the bare-knuckle arena (despite comparatively infrequent involvement until the late eighteenth century), there were surprisingly few who could, in fact, be considered of the first rank. This lack of any substantial, proven, in-depth quality is reflected in the brevity of the list of top men given, in order of merit, below.

1. Daniel Mendoza (1765?[3]–1836)
2. Dutch Sam (Samuel Elias,[4] 1775–1816)
3. Barney Aaron (1800–59)
4. Young Barney Aaron (1833?[5]–1907)
5. Aby Belasco (1796–1859)
6. Izzy Lazarus (1812–67)

The approach to compiling this list was obviously purely personal, as there are no standard procedures in place to facilitate such a task. Pugilists were selected and rated by analysing both their recognized records (with amendments having been made where proven) and the nature of their performances. Regarding the former, as well as a fighter's win/loss ratio, caliber of opposition was necessarily taken into account, and attention additionally paid to the extent of career activity (albeit that protagonists then usually had far fewer contests). In particular, it should be pointed out that editions of *Fistiana; or, The Oracle of the Ring*, the series of "official" record books from the bare-knuckle era, were not accepted unconditionally, there being serious doubts on occasions as to their accuracy, consistency, and comprehensiveness which had to be considered.[6] Moreover, little attention was given to online record compilations and career summaries, as they are, in the main, often rather unreliable for the bare-knuckle period. With regard to performances, emphasis was primarily placed on contemporary source comments and opinions (relating to displayed fighting qualities, including skill, strength, courage, and endurance), especially necessary as obviously no film footage could be viewed. Some consideration was also paid to the general fistic esteem in which a pugilist was held. (The differing circumstances, though, true of the time, such as the evolving style of fighting and practices, as well as an extensive rule change, were of course far more difficult to factor into the equation.)

Four of the choices here have been inducted into the Pioneer Category of the International Boxing Hall of Fame (Daniel Mendoza, 1990; Dutch Sam, 1997; Barney Aaron, 2001; and Young Barney Aaron, 2007). Few ring historians are likely to dispute the first two selections. The accomplished and scientific Mendoza's success in fistic affairs was believed by the radical reformer Francis Place to have led to less abusive treatment being experienced by the Jewish community. He became a prominent public figure, and indeed some families within another minority group, the Gypsies, even used "Mendoza" as a forename (given the Romany tendency to name their children after well-known people). The celebrated Dutch Sam, reported in the *Sporting Magazine* of August 1804 to have "by a peculiar mode, struck his blows upwards," and generally credited today with having introduced the uppercut, was particularly famed as a remarkably hard hitter. At the very least, however, the positioning of the remainder is more subjective. A pugilist who fought in America or Australia has been considered if born in England, but any transitional period combatants competing with the "raw'uns"[7] were not taken into account (and the odd glove contest for protagonists in the bare-knuckle era itself has been ignored). It should be noted that some name variants are occasionally given below but names of fighters are usually shown as they occurred most frequently (especially with regard to fistic activities) in contemporary sources. (A major exception is that of the well-known, American-based Young Barney Aaron,[8] not that often referred to as such in his lifetime, in the main just being called Barney Aaron, but generally termed the former more recently in order not to confuse him with his noted father, the renowned "Star of the East.") Wherever pugilists were better known by a cognomen, their probable or accepted real names are provided in brackets.

Based on his record and performances Young Dutch Sam (Samuel Evans), like Dutch Sam, his believed sire (although Samuel Evans is actually named as his father on his marriage certificate), would definitely have been highly placed. However he does not feature because of strong doubts as to whether, according to rabbinic law (or traditional Jewish law), he met the requirement relating to Jewish status descending through the matrilineal line. Certainly

Pierce Egan (*c.* 1772–1849), considered the foremost fistic chronicler of the bare-knuckle era (despite being somewhat prone to bias), opined some two years after Young Dutch Sam's death, having first known him as a newsboy, that he was not Jewish since his mother had not been a Jewess.

Another to whom the same situation apparently applied was the unfortunate Harry Lazarus (1838–65), a third generation, it appears, of the fighting Lazarus family. However, although he inherited his father Izzy's ability, and despite receiving some minor recognition as lightweight champion of America (notwithstanding being more usually considered a featherweight), he seems to have had too limited a bare-knuckle career (as confirmed by Izzy under cross-examination at the trial of Harry's murderer[9]) to justify being selected in any case. Likewise the circumstances of his mother not being Jewish are obviously also true of Harry's somewhat lesser-known younger brother Johnny. Moreover his actual career with the "raw'uns" appears to have been even less active, with some contests which should be on Izzy's record occasionally attributed to him, whilst his assuming the right to the American lightweight title the year before he apparently had in fact fought in the prize-ring not surprisingly aroused some objections.

Conversely, though, there is no question from the point of view of the matrilineal line requirement (or with regard to the level of fistic activity) of the eligibility of undoubted lightweight champion of America, Young Barney Aaron. Although it has been implied at times that whilst his father was Jewish, his mother, being Irish, was not, various genealogical sources show that she was definitely a Jewess, and in fact she was actually born in England. (Of course, in general, it is not always possible to prove categorically a fighter's Jewish status, or even his English nationality, and so where it has been accepted as such, it should be noted that in some cases the benefit of the doubt may have been given.)

The unbeaten Isaac Bitton (1779–1839) also did not warrant an assessment since, quite apart from a very slight possibility that a seemingly good result on an already sparse record could have been erroneously credited to him, his birthplace was actually Holland. Ironically Samuel Elias, despite being known as Dutch Sam, appears to have been born in London (in what was later, and of course still is today, referred to as the "East End," an area famed for producing Jewish fighters, both bare-knuckle and gloved). His cognomen could well have arisen from his parents' nationality given, amongst others, Egan's belief that they were Dutch, although possibly this might also have indicated German origin.

Some combatants, although it could be argued that they were pugilistically well esteemed, were disregarded because, often allied to a relatively sparse record at the very least, there must be significant or complete reservations as to whether they achieved a sufficiently acceptable win/loss ratio. (This is even making allowances for the fact that, despite sizeable weight disparities for a considerable period being hardly unusual, fighters were generally more competitively matched than today since, by and large, their abilities had to be good enough to attract patrons to back them in a genuine "winner takes all" scenario.) Israel Belasco (1798–1866), for instance, younger brother of the more renowned scientific pugilist (and infamous brothel-keeper) Aby, is excluded for this reason (an enhanced summary of his battles given on a rare 1827 handbill for sparring exhibitions being very suspect).

The same is true (and indeed more applicably) of both Himan and Harry Gid(g)eon (although there is some evidence to suggest that they could actually have been the same person despite separate entries for each in *Fistiana*), and additionally of an earlier Lazarus, whose forename is uncertain and would appear to have been Izzy's uncle. With regard to Elisha Crabbe or Crab(b), believed by fellow pugilist Thomas Fewtrell to have been "entitled to much praise, both for skill and bottom," there is the added possibility that he might have been Dutch. Regarding Iky Pig (*fl.*1805–6), who could have been Isaac Pick, although he was later well thought of on account of his having contended with future champion Tom Cribb, he was actually poorly considered by contemporary newspapers. The manner of his defeat against Cribb was generally deemed unsatisfactory and his apparent lack of courage was further emphasized the next year in a since often unrecorded contest against Isaac Wood, an opponent described as distinctly inferior. (In fact, the following decade, the *Morning Chronicle* even reported that a fighter had "deliberately walked away in the Iky Pig style.")

The merits of the likes of Little Puss (Henry Abrahams, d.1820), stated in the *Weekly Dispatch* at his death to have been undefeated in "numerous battles," and perhaps even Gadzee (Godfrey Benjamin, d.1826), certainly considered by Egan a "real good man in his day," could not be evaluated due to their records being either nonexistent or too sketchy, and to their having received insufficient coverage in contemporary newspapers. Likewise, the apparent merits of Joshua Hart, previously overlooked in discussions on Jewish pugilists, but a rare example of Jewish fistic ability in the immediate aftermath of the introduction of the sport's first organized rules, who declared in 1744 in the *Daily Advertiser* that he was unbeaten, having "defeated the famous Mr. Chetham, and several other Bruisers." Nor could the clever lightweight Sol(ly) Reuben(s) be properly assessed, as his record prior to being transported to Australia appears incomplete, given that it does not reflect the assertion in 1829 by *Bell's Life in London* (then beginning to become recognized as the accepted authority on fistic matters) that he had "frequently distinguished himself in the P.R." It is likely, too, that he fought after having been deported; certainly he was scheduled to do so on at least one occasion and *Bell's Life in Sydney and Sporting Reviewer* of August 25, 1849 wrote at his death that he had "left a *hiatus*" in the sport which would not be easily filled. Another transported convict who should also be mentioned here is Aby Davis (1800[10]–64), a combatant in what may be considered the early prize-ring in Australia, and at the time highly thought of there as a scientific pugilist, but whose record in England at least would seem to be a matter of doubt.

A further English-born Jew (and not, as occasionally asserted, an American) who was also well regarded in fistic circles in Australia was Jack Thompson (1844?[11]–90), whose family name was originally Solomon. However sometimes referred to as an amateur, he only appears to have engaged in one regular, albeit well-known, bare-knuckle affair in Australia (and then not until 1877). Moreover, he seems not to have participated in any contests when in England, nor is there apparently any evidence to support occasional twentieth-century claims of his fighting with the "raw'uns" in America prior to going to Australia. (The only indication of fistic activity for Thompson there appears to have been the reference in a *New York Clipper* pen picture, dated January 29, 1881, to his having sparred in "about 1865" with the infamous Matt "Rocky" Moore, a business partner of Harry Lazarus's murderer.) Indeed Thompson's brother, Barney, categorically stated that he had not taken part in any such fights in America, with the aforementioned Australian encounter against (former police detective and royal bodyguard) John Mitchell Christie being his sole appearance in the bare-knuckle arena.

It is therefore clear that, although there appears to have been no lack of English-born Jewish participants in the bare-knuckle period, merely a handful can definitely be classed as being of the first rank. Today only the names of Daniel Mendoza, and perhaps Dutch Sam, are familiar beyond the community of boxing historians. Nevertheless it is certainly not unreasonable to suggest that, generally, appearances in the prize-ring of Jewish combatants improved, at least to some extent, the negative way in which Jews were viewed. With the exception of Iky Pig and perhaps one or two others, their ongoing (albeit to a varying degree) participation in a sport associated with notions of manliness and Britishness would have helped dispel a general perception of Jews as foreign and cowardly, and made them seem more acceptable to the belligerent English lower orders. In fact, it could be said that the involvement of Jews in pugilistic matters demonstrated that the Jewish poor were adopting the English working-class habits and tastes (thus incurring the disapproval of both the Jewish elite and the reform-minded English middle classes), and this embracing of such practices would surely have facilitated their easier assimilation. However, while lower-class Jews becoming a presence in the sport (both as protagonists and spectators) made them more like their English counterparts, paradoxically their involvement appears to have been an expression of Jewish assertiveness.

NOTES

1 Although there were earlier newspaper mentions of bare-knuckle contests in England, it was not until the 1720s that the first regular such encounters, usually termed "trials of manhood," occurred. Nevertheless "trials of skill" involving weapons still remained more numerous. (Contrary to some beliefs, protagonists did not fight with weapons and fists in the same contest, and in fact it was rare to find a combatant able to contend competitively with both, it being considered "much beneath a Swordsman" to box.) The bare-knuckle era subsequently survived various vicissitudes and endured for nearly 150 years. It was followed by a transitional period, with the acceptance for professional purposes of the Marquess of Queensberry Rules (for gloved combat) gradually taking hold. However, traditional bare-knuckle encounters definitely did not disappear overnight, and it was certainly not unusual for a pugilist then to compete with knuckles (albeit generally only being tested in one or two such affairs), as well as gloves, at some time during his career. It should be noted that in other countries the bare-knuckle sport's time frame and circumstances differed from those of England. In America and Australia this was particularly true with regard to when and how it actually became well established. (In both countries the former did not occur until the nineteenth century, although in the American South a much more brutal, no-holds-barred style of fighting had gained popularity in the previous century.)

2 Besides being a prominent minority group in the ring, Jewish pugilists enjoyed the active encouragement of their co-religionists, who not only provided the money to back them but were also a conspicuous physical presence at their fights. Certainly mentions in contemporary accounts, for instance, of a strong following from Duke's Place (described by the eminent historian of Anglo-Jewry, Todd M. Endelman, as "the center of the Jewish settlement within the City of London," and a term used to "refer to the Jewish community in general") indicate large Jewish support at a significant number of their contests. In fact, it is Endelman's belief that such "matches became rallying points for ethnic assertiveness."

3 According to the fighter's memoirs, Daniel Mendoza was born in 1764 (and historians have also given 1763). However, the published Bevis Marks Records of the Spanish and Portuguese Synagogue show that he was circumcised in 1765, making that year for his birth a lot more probable. There do not seem to be any actual birth records covering the years in question (as confirmed by the Synagogue's Hon. Archivist, Miriam Rodrigues-Pereira).

4 It is generally accepted that Dutch Sam's real name was Samuel Elias, although an opinion did exist that it was Elias Samuel, and occasionally references were made in contemporary newspapers to his surname being Samuels.

5 The year 1836 was usually stated in contemporary sources for Young Barney Aaron's birth. However, the entry for him in the 1900 United States Federal Census gives 1833, and this is in accordance with the contention of Shirley Atkins, Aaron descendant and researcher, that actually Young Barney was almost certainly, in fact, Abraham Aaron, one of Barney Aaron's sons, whom she maintains was born in that year.

6 It has not been possible to view editions for all the years that *Fistiana* was produced (and indeed there are conflicting opinions as to the year when the final edition appeared). However, it seems as though the record book was always published at the office of *Bell's Life in London and Sporting Chronicle* (the newspaper which was for many years the premier source of sporting news in England, and the recognized authority on the prize-ring), with its editor given as the author. Unfortunately, *Fistiana* did not always live up to the high standards of *Bell's Life*, appearing at times to have been compiled in a rather slap-dash fashion and containing entries that were not consistent with the actual fight reports in the newspaper itself.

7 "Raw'uns" was a phrase particularly favored by newspapers, especially around the second half of the nineteenth century, when referring to bare fists (another being "nature's weapons").

8 Young Barney Aaron was a notable figure in nineteenth-century American sporting circles. Lightweight champion during his fighting career and a decidedly rare example of a Jewish pugilist in the American ring at a time when another ethnic group, the Irish, were dominating, he continued to be involved in the sport, in various capacities, following his retirement. Whilst it was usual for bare-knuckle combatants to remain active as seconds, and often as boxing instructors, somewhat more uncommonly Aaron's services were also sought in a variety of other roles, such as those of referee, fight trainer, master of ceremonies, and umpire, and additionally he was involved in the organization of some fistic events. He was also associated with wrestling and pedestrianism (as a trainer of pedestrians he seems to have been almost as well regarded as in pugilistic matters).

9 In January 1865, Harry Lazarus was fatally stabbed by one Bernard Friery, a partner in the New York drinking establishment next door to that of his victim. Friery was tried the following month, and Harry's father, Izzy, was amongst those who testified. The trial, which generated great interest, particularly among the sporting fraternity, concluded with Friery being found guilty of murder in the first degree. Following a respite pending appeals, he was eventually hanged in August of the next year.

10 Although it has been suggested that he was born in 1801, various New South Wales convict records for the twice-transported Aby Davis give a birth year of 1800.

11 Whilst 1843 has been given as the birth year of Jack Thompson, one of his brothers, Barney, in a letter published in *The Referee* in August 1918 correcting diverse information regarding his late sibling, asserted 1844.

SELECT BIBLIOGRAPHY

Books

The American Fistiana, Showing the Progress of Pugilism in the United States, from 1816 to 1873, New York: Robert M. DeWitt, [1873?].

Cohen, Shaye J. D., *The Beginnings of Jewishness: Boundaries, Varieties, Uncertainties*, Berkeley, CA: University of California Press, 1999.

[Dowling, Francis], *Fistiana; or, The Oracle of the Ring*, London: Office of *Bell's Life in London*, 1868.

[Dowling, Francis], *Fistiana; or, The Oracle of the Ring*, London: William Clement, Jun., Office of *Bell's Life in London*, 1866.

[Dowling, Vincent], *Fistiana; or, The Oracle of the Ring*, London: William Clement, Jun., Office of *Bell's Life in London*, 1852.

[Dowling, Vincent], *Fistiana; or, The Oracle of the Ring*, London: William Clement, Jun., Office of *Bell's Life in London*, 1841.

[Egan, Pierce], *Boxiana; or, Sketches of Ancient and Modern Pugilism*, vol. II, London: G. Smeeton, 1812.

Egan, Pierce, *Boxiana; or, Sketches of Modern Pugilism*, vol. II, London: Sherwood, Neely, and Jones, 1818.

Every Gentleman's Manual: A Lecture on the Art of Self-defence, London: Sherwood and Bowyer, 1845.

New Series of Boxiana: Being the Only Original and Complete Lives of the Boxers, vol. II, London: George Virtue, 1829.

Endelman, Todd M., *The Jews of Britain, 1656–2000*, Berkeley, CA: University of California Press, 2002.

The Jews of Georgian England, 1714–1830: Tradition and Change in a Liberal Society, Philadelphia, PA: Jewish Publication Society of America, 1979.

Fewtrell, Thomas, *Boxing Reviewed; or, The Science of Manual Defence*, London: Scatcherd and Whitacker, 1790.

Gee, Tony, *Up to Scratch: Bareknuckle Fighting and Heroes of the Prize-ring*, Harpenden, England: Queen Anne Press, 1998.

Levi, John S., *These Are the Names: Jewish Lives in Australia, 1788–1850*, Carlton, Australia: Miegunyah Press, 2006.

Miles, Henry Downes, *Pugilistica: Being One Hundred and Forty-four Years of the History of British Boxing*, vols. I & II, London: Weldon & Co., [1880].

Young England, *The Yorkshire Fancy-ana, for 1845, Comprising a Faithful Record of the Ring and the Turf*, Leeds: Milner and Stephenson, [1845?].

Newspapers And Periodicals

ENGLAND

Annual Register
Bell's Life in London and Sporting Chronicle
Daily Advertiser
Dorset County Chronicle

Morning Chronicle
Morning Post
Sporting Magazine, The
Star Daily Evening Advertiser
Weekly Dispatch
World, The

AMERICA

National Police Gazette
New York Clipper
New York Herald
New-York (Daily) Tribune

AUSTRALIA

Australasian, The
Bell's Life in Sydney and Sporting Reviewer
Referee, The
Sydney Monitor

Articles

Ford, Anne, "Shaws and Welchs," *Romany Routes*, vol.12 (December 2014).
Gee, Tony, "Mendoza, Daniel (1765?–1836)," *Oxford Dictionary of National Biography*, edited by H. C. G. Matthew and Brian Harrison (2004).
MacDougall, Gwen, "The Fighting Belascos," *Shemot*, vol. 11 (March 2003).

Other Sources

Handbill for Israel Belasco sparring exhibitions, Whitby, England, May 1827 (Pierre Spake Collection).
N.B. Extensive use was also made of the following records – birth, circumcision, census, convict, marriage, death and burial.

13

RANDY ROBERTS

Joe Louis: "You Should Have Seen Him Then"

In February 1964, journalist Robert Lipsyte traveled to Miami to cover what his editor at the *New York Times* had concluded was an inconsequential heavyweight title fight between the seemingly indestructible champion Sonny Liston and the loud-mouthed challenger Cassius Clay. Only later would he realize that this was a transitional political and cultural moment – about three months since the assassination of President John Kennedy, nearly four months after the assassination of South Vietnam's President Ngo Dinh Diem, and during the worst times of the civil rights struggle, when a violent white reaction in Birmingham, Alabama, caused many to question Martin Luther King's nonviolent tactics. Culturally, a new age was showcased on *The Ed Sullivan Show* on February 12, 1964, when four mop-topped musicians sang "I Want to Hold Your Hand" to wildly ecstatic and screaming young girls.

Lipsyte had gone to Miami to cover a boxing match, but he discovered something more. In the last weeks of February, the city had become the center of an evolving America. The Beatles were there, as was Malcolm X, former minister and spokesman for the Nation of Islam, suspended from the sect the previous November for making controversial remarks about the Kennedy assassination, who had attached himself to Clay's camp. Not asking too many questions about what the controversial Malcolm was talking about with the challenger, Lipsyte rightly judged that Clay was the story. Larry Merchant, Jerry Izenberg, and other younger sportswriters agreed that Cassius represented a new America – a brash, confident, and outrageous America full of entertaining possibilities.

A few days before the title match, Joe Louis, the forty-nine-year-old former heavyweight king and friend of Sonny Liston, appeared in Clay's camp. Promoters had paid him to show up for media events, talk to reporters, and generally lend his considerable prestige to the fight. The contrasts between Clay and Louis were stark – Clay was young, opinionated, and controversial; Louis was old, quiet, and bland. Clay seemed to dance on air like a pugilistic Astaire; Louis plodded dead-legged and heavy-footed. For Lipsyte, Louis was "a black Dwight D. Eisenhower," a relic from his father's generation. Yet such older sportswriters as Jimmy Cannon, Red Smith, Arthur Daley, and Barney Nagler moved from Clay to Louis like a pack of paparazzi deserting a D-lister for a superstar.

Lipsyte was mystified. Later he asked Nagler why he and the others had wanted to talk to Joe. "How can you hang around that mumbling old has-been, when here's this young beautiful hope of the future?" he inquired. Clay was alive and interesting. Nagler looked at Lipsyte almost sadly, because he knew that he could never explain. "You should have seen him then," was the best he could offer.

You should have seen him then. Back then. What was it like back then? Back then blacks, or Negroes, as they were politely called, were all but invisible. Unless they rioted or committed a particularly heinous crime, they were hardly mentioned in the mainstream (white) press. Back then a solid wall of Southern senators and congressmen prevented all legislation meant to improve the lot of African Americans from reaching the floor. Back then baseball's major leagues were lily white, except for a few Native American players, and just before Louis's time, boxers of his race could not fight for the heavyweight title.

Back then were the darkest days of the twentieth century, the years of the Great Depression and the Second World War. Ernest J. Gaines wrote about that time in his novel *The Autobiography of Miss Jane Pittman* (1971): "When times get really hard, really tough, He always send you somebody. In the Depression it was tough on everybody, but twice as hard on the colored, and He sent us Joe. Joe Louis was to lift the colored people's heart." Joe Louis emerged out of those hard times, and not only did he lift the hearts – if only temporarily – of black Americans, he altered the way white Americans thought about race.

On meeting novelist and activist Richard Wright, prominent University of Chicago sociologist Robert E. Park reportedly asked, "How the hell did you happen?" How did Wright escape Jim Crow Mississippi and develop a literary voice that spoke to the very soul of the great American dilemma? The same question could have been posed to Joe Louis, born Joe Louis Barrow in an Alabama sharecropper's shack on May 13, 1914. Asked toward the end of his career if he could have imagined his rise from red-clay poverty to fame and wealth, he shook his head, adding, "I couldn't dream that big."

Dreams were in short supply for most Alabamans during Louis's childhood, and particularly for poor people of Joe's color. His father, Munroe "Mun" Barrow, escaped the grinding poverty and debilitating responsibility of his large family by drifting away from reality and landing in the Searcy Hospital for the Colored Insane. Pat Brooks, who married Joe's mother, Lillie Reese Barrow, escaped the all but immutable plagues of black Alabama – the scourge of the boll weevil, the humiliation of Jim Crow, and the reign of the Ku Klux Klan – by moving his family out of the South. He was one of the more than 1.5 million blacks who between 1914 and 1940 left the rural South for the urban North. Brooks established a base in Detroit, and then in 1926 brought his family to the city of Henry Ford, where the dream of a $5 workday had taken shape. For most African Americans it was just a dream, but there were lower-paying jobs in the Ford, Dodge, or other automotive plants (at least until 1929–30, when the onset of the Great Depression dealt a crippling blow to dreams).

Teachers and administrators judged Joe Louis a "slow" student and eventually assigned him to the Bronson Trade School. But after his stepfather lost his job at Ford, Joe dropped out of Bronson and took what menial work he could find. He swept factory floors, delivered ice and coal, and accepted about any odd job that required a strong back and arms.

Hard times made for hard men, and many of the hardest tried their hand in the prize ring. It was a virtually unregulated world, populated by hungry boxers, predatory managers, exploitive promoters, and a wide assortment of gamblers, mobsters, hustlers, and bottom-feeding trolls looking for a quick buck or a long-term meal ticket. The chances for a boxer hitting it big in the fight game were number-racket small, and most ended their time in the sport broke and broken. It was a sort of male prostitution, an activity for the very desperate.

In 1932 and 1933, Louis began to learn to box. He mastered the basic techniques, engaged in amateur matches, and enjoyed the feeling of success. In 1934, he won the Amateur Athletic Union (AAU) and the national Golden Glove light-heavyweight titles. There were small under-the-table cash payments in amateur boxing, but the amounts were negligible. Louis knew that steady and significant money was only to be won in the professional ranks, so in the summer of 1934 he turned professional. His managers were John Roxborough and Julian Black, influential figures in Detroit's and Chicago's numbers rackets. Although both were involved in a variety of shady deals, they were also prominent figures in the African American communities of their cities, and Roxborough especially had a great fondness for Louis.[1]

They employed Jack Blackburn, an outstanding former boxer and experienced trainer, to teach Louis the nuances of the sport. Blackburn fought with his own demons; he was a mean drunk, with a violent temper, who had served time for killing a man. But he was a great trainer. At first, he was unenthusiastic with Louis, not because of Joe's ability but on account of his color. "I won't have no truck with a colored boy," he told Roxborough. "Colored boys ain't got much chance fighting nowadays – unless they just happen to be a world-beater." But times being what they were and money hard to come by, Roxborough convinced Blackburn to train Louis, and the trainer soon realized that Joe was a world-beater.

Blackburn's initial hesitation was well grounded. He had boxed professionally during the era of Jack Johnson, the controversial first black heavyweight champion. Blackburn knew that Johnson's independent behavior had so outraged white Americans that it muddied the waters for black heavyweights for a generation. "You know, boy," the trainer told Louis, "the heavyweight division for a Negro is hardly likely. The white man ain't too keen on it. You have got to be something to go anywhere. If you really ain't gonna be another Jack Johnson, you got some hope. White man hasn't forgot that fool nigger with his white women, acting like he owned the world."

To counter the lingering legacy of Jack Johnson, Roxborough and Black sculpted a set of rules for Louis that clearly rejected the behavior and lifestyle of the first black champion. Johnson had broken racial taboos by consorting with and marrying white women; Louis was forbidden from even having his photograph taken alone with a white female. Johnson had talked loud, boasted constantly, and enjoyed a flamboyant night life; Louis was told never to humiliate an opponent, gloat over a victory, or visit a nightclub alone. He was coached to express little, say even less, and allow his fists to give meaning to his existence. His managers made sure that he was matched against quality fighters and that all his bouts were on the level, and they insisted that he live and fight cleanly. Although Louis's "deadpan" expression mystified white reporters, it could never be confused with Jack Johnson's "golden smile." Everything Louis did, every image he projected, carried the same message: "I am not Jack Johnson." No verbal boasts, no flashy smiles, no public sexual exploits – just machine-like fighting and Bible-reading innocence.

Even with his consciously shaped anti-Johnson image, Louis experienced some trouble advancing into the upper echelons of prizefighting. Between July 1934 and May 1935, he fought primarily in the Midwest, demonstrating in a series of sensational knockouts his superior punching power and ability to finish opponents. But his managers had difficulty arranging a major fight in New York, the Mecca of boxing. In a telephone conversation, Madison Square Garden matchmaker Jimmy Johnston explained the facts of life to Roxborough, whom he assumed was white. "Well, you understand he's a nigger," Johnston said, "and he can't win every time he goes in the ring." Not putting too fine a point on it, Johnston implied that when ordered Louis would have to throw a few fights. Roxborough responded that he too was black and then hung up. Johnston was unconcerned, telling a white associate, "We don't need the nigger."

Fortunately for Louis, Johnston had a rival, Michael Strauss "Uncle Mike" Jacobs, a ticket speculator and general promoter who had made his way into boxing during the 1920s. The sport interested him hardly at all, but money did. A sharp businessman who understood the art of promotion, he had learned how to market a prizefight from George "Tex" Rickard, the master who had spun gold from the career of Jack Dempsey. Jacobs saw in Joe Louis his Jack Dempsey, a fighter of rare explosive ability who could fill outdoor ballparks. And, incidentally, he understood that the promoter who controlled Louis's career would become the most significant force in the fight business. In the end, Johnston's racism gave Jacobs the opening he needed to wrestle control of boxing away from the Madison Square Garden Corporation.

All Louis had to do was take care of business in the ring. Jacobs, as well as Roxborough and Black, would take care of the rest. Joe's debut on the New York stage occurred in Yankee Stadium on June 25, 1935, in front of more than 64,000 people. His opponent was former heavyweight champion Primo Carnera, whose physical size was in direct inverse proportion to his fighting ability.[2] Although he was one of the largest title holders in the history of the sport, many of his victories were probably fixed fights, and he possessed neither boxing ability nor punching power. But long before the opening bell clanged, Jacobs had worked with sportswriters to clarify the issues at stake in the contest, for in boxing the narratives woven around the fight were more important than the match itself.

Two narratives, one domestic and the other international, dominated the public discourse about contest. The domestic narrative underscored Louis's socially benign nature. If Jack Johnson was the "bad nigger," the "angry beast" who threatened to disturb America's racial status quo, Joe Louis was the "good Negro," the "good colored boy" who read the Bible, lived clean, and "knew his place." In hundreds of newspaper articles, sportswriters portrayed Louis as an animal in the ring – dubbing him "the dark destroyer," "the tawny tiger," "the ebony elephant," "the chocolate cobra," and "the brown bomber," among scores of other nicknames – while adding that he was as harmless as a puppy outside of the ropes. They suggested that during his spare time he liked nothing more violent than eating ice cream, taking naps, and pond-fishing. One story suggested that Louis would never have fit in with the bumblebee pace of the Ford assembly line. It concluded, "It is doubtful if this husky colored lad, who was born to be a singing cotton picker, could ever have wholly adapted himself to being part of a silent, smooth-running factory machine."

The international narrative focused on Italian imperial designs on Ethiopia (Abyssinia). By June 1935, a border dispute between Italian Somaliland and Ethiopia had led to several violent clashes and threatened to escalate into a war. The incidents were part of Fascist leader Benito Mussolini's plan to build his new Roman Empire at the expense of Haile Selassie's Ethiopia nation and to avenge Italy's humiliating defeat at the hands of Emperor Menelik II in 1895, when the Italian army tried to invade Ethiopia through Eritrea in response to Menelik's renunciation of a 1889 treaty between Italy and Ethiopia. Selassie's call for intervention from the international community to halt Italian aggression fell on deaf ears. The events in Africa provided the backdrop for the Louis–Carnera match. Especially on the East Coast, African Americans followed the worsening crisis in the black press. Since the 1920s when Marcus Garvey's United Negro Improvement Association celebrated racial pride, lectured about Africa's rich heritage, and implored blacks to return to their ancestral homeland, Africa – and especially Ethiopia, one of the last independent black African nations – had occupied a central place in racial thinking.

Sportswriters transformed Louis and Carnera into symbols for the smoldering conflict in Africa, surrogates in an elaborate morality play. Although neither boxer was even remotely political, their fight was portrayed as "Little Abyssinia and big Italy." Political cartoons portrayed Italy as a gigantic Carnera moving toward a small, black Louis labeled Abyssinia. The result of the international narrative was that Louis became a viable symbol of anti-colonialism in Africa and racism in the United States. Even before his first major match, Joe Louis had transcended the ring, becoming an iconic emblem of the African American struggle on a global stage.

The contest was not much of a fight. Louis's skill and power overwhelmed Carnera, who fought bravely but was horribly beaten. In the sixth round the referee stopped the fight. Although the mainstream press portrayed Louis's victory as the triumph of a jungle animal – Grantland Rice noted that he stalked his prey like a "black panther," and Davis J. Walsh wrote that "something sly and sinister, and perhaps not quite human came out of the African jungle" – black Americans, as well as the African American press, celebrated Louis's win. "HARLEM GOES 'MAD WITH JOY'," headlined the *Pittsburgh Courier*. And the celebrations were not restricted to New York. The sheer excitement of the festivities in Harlem and in other "Negro sections," the crush of the crowds, the explosion of energy, the volume of people and noise, frightened many white authorities, reminding them of the riots after the 1910 Jack Johnson–Jim Jeffries fight. But Louis's spokesmen quickly calmed such fears. "We will see to it that Louis never does anything that will in any way bring about public criticism," Jack Blackburn asserted. "There will be no public statements belittling opponents, no gloating over victims, no act of any kind that can be offensive." A reporter quoted the trainer as promising, "We will not let Louis follow in the footsteps of Jack Johnson. He will be an example and a help to the colored race."

In his first New York fight, Louis reached an unprecedented status in black America. Equal part avenging angel, delivering Moses, and resurrected John Henry, he seemed to communicate directly with an aching need of his people during the hard times of the mid-1930s. The speed with which Louis captured the imaginations of black Americans of all political proclivities demonstrated his power as a symbol. Three months after demolishing Carnera, he faced Max Baer, another former champion, in Yankee Stadium.[3] The official count for the attendance was more than 84,000, but unofficially it probably reached 95,000. And, of course, many millions more listened to the live radio broadcast of the match.

On the night of September 24, 1935, aspiring novelist Richard Wright was one of the millions who heard the radio broadcast. Sitting in a tavern on Chicago's South Side, surrounded by other black patrons, he listened nervously, knowing that the prizefight was so much more than just an athletic contest. For him and millions of other African Americans, Louis carried their dreams of equality and advancement into the ring; he epitomized their desires for respect and pride.

And once again, he delivered, knocking out Baer in the fourth round. The victory once more set off passionate celebrations. In Chicago, Wright left the saloon and wandered the streets, watching as the euphoria spread like a river spilling over its banks. Witnessing the scene, he wrote, "Negroes poured out of beer taverns, pool rooms, barber shops, rooming houses and dingy flats and flooded the streets." They chanted "LOUIS! LOUIS! LOUIS!," throwing their hats in the air and walking through dingy slums like they were in a magical kingdom. "They shook the hands of strangers. They clapped one another on the back. It was like a revival," he continued. "Really, there was a religious feeling in the air. Well, it wasn't exactly a religious feeling, but it was *something*, and you could feel it. It was a feeling of unity, of oneness."

Whites surely must have felt, Wright speculated, "that *something* had ripped loose, exploded." With the joy came bitter memories – of slights, insults, abuses, punishments, and injustices they had suffered at the hands of whites. Some of the celebrants stopped street cars, a few smashed a few windows. "Thought Joe was scared, didn't you? Scared because Max talked loud and made boasts. We ain't scared either. We'll fight too when the time comes. We'll win too." Wright was sure he knew what was happening in

Chicago – and across America – in the hours after the fight. "A something had popped out of a dark hole, something with a hydra-like head, and it was darting forth its tongue." It was a sincere expression of dreams too long suppressed.

Joe Louis united black Americans. "[E]very Negro must feel that his fate is inexorably bound" to the success or failure of Louis, wrote an editorialist for the *New York Amsterdam News*. "This apparently holds true from the highest to the lowest Negro in America." His appeal rested on undeniable superiority of performance. One fact should not be lost: his reputation was won by pummeling white boxers. As one editorialist cogently suggested, "[W]hat he is doing as a fighter will do more to show up the fallacy of 'inherent inferiority' of Negroes than could be done by all the anthropologists in the nation – so far as the ears and eyes of the white masses are concerned. One flash of his mighty brown arm is a better argument than a book – to a great majority of men. His personality is more impressive than a thousand sermons, for he will be felt where no sermon would ever be heard."

Although the NAACP and the Communist Party were supporting black advancement in the courts and the streets, their failures were often greater than their successes, and even their achievements were never clear cut and occasionally ambiguous. Louis's knockouts were stunningly absolute, devoid of nuance or equivocation. Hence Joe's victories were all the more meaningful.

Capturing the meaning of the Louis–Baer match, Richard Wright observed, "Four centuries of oppression, of frustrated hopes, of black bitterness, felt even in the bones of the bewildered young, were rising to the surface. Yes, unconsciously they had imputed to the brawny image of Joe Louis all the balked dreams of revenge, all the secretly visualized moments of retaliation, AND HE HAD WON! Good Gawd Almighty! Yes, by Jesus, it could be done! Didn't Joe do it? You see, Joe was the consciously-felt symbol. Joe was the concentrated essence of black triumph over white... And what could be sweeter than long-nourished hate vicariously gratified?" Wright recognized Louis's force, understood how millions of blacks interpreted him. "From the symbol of Joe's strength they took strength, and in that moment all fear, all obstacles were wiped out, drowned. They had stepped out of the mire of hesitation and irresolution and were free! Invincible! A merciless victor over a fallen foe! Yes, they had felt all that – for a moment."

Testaments of Louis's importance are legion in African American culture. Minister Martin Luther King, Jr., jazz musician Miles Davis, poet Maya Angelou, singer Lena Horne, and actor Ossie Davis all left eloquent accounts of listening to broadcasts of Louis's matches. In addition, no athlete, and probably no person since Jesus Christ, inspired more recorded songs. At least forty-three records featuring the exploits of Louis were released in the 1930s and 1940s. From "He's in the Ring (Doin' the Same Old Thing)" to "Joe Louis Is the Man," the songs celebrate Louis's race as much as his feats, taking pride in his modesty, strength, courage, and success.

Victories, of course, were the essential ingredients for the Louis cultural phenomenon. Unbeatable fighters are not supposed to be beaten, and at Yankee Stadium on June 19, 1936, the unimaginable happened to Louis when he was knocked out by yet another former champion, Max Schmeling of Germany. Almost no one outside of Schmeling's camp thought the German had a chance, which made the outcome all the more shocking. Listening to the contest between sets in Cincinnati's Moonlite Gardens, where she was performing with the Noble Sissle's band, Lena Horne grew increasingly agitated as Louis absorbed terrible punishment. "I was near hysteria toward the end of the fight when he was being so badly beaten and some of the men in the band were crying." Joe was the one black man who stood up to whites, beat them in fair contests, and, for Horne, he "carried so many of our hopes, maybe even dreams of vengeance. But this night he was just another Negro getting beaten by a white man." As tears marred her performance, her mother became outraged. "Why you don't even know the man." "I don't care, I don't care," Horne yelled. "He belongs to all of us."

Some fighters never overcome a defeat like the one Schmeling inflicted on Louis. But after a few confidence-building matches, Joe was again tracking toward a title fight. Through an odd assortment of backroom deals that bypassed Schmeling, the kind of negotiations that have contributed to the sport's unsavory reputation, Louis got his chance to fight James J. Braddock for the championship on June 22, 1937, in Chicago's Comiskey Park. It was Braddock's first and last title defense, and it marked the first time that a black boxer contended for the title since Jack Johnson lost it in 1915. In the eighth round Joe landed a devastating overhand right on Braddock's chin. As Louis recalled, "I laid it solid, with all my body, on the right side of his face, and his face split open. He fell in a face-down dive." Braddock was knocked cold, and his body did not so much as twitch as the referee completed the count.

Although Louis won the title from Braddock, he would not feel like the champion until he defeated Max Schmeling in a rematch. Jacobs scheduled the fight for June 22, 1938, in Yankee Stadium, and from the moment Louis and Schmeling signed the contact, it was recognized as a match that rose above the world of sports and had global significance.

By 1938 the course of Adolf Hitler's Nazi Germany was certain. The Blood Purge, arrests of political opponents, and Nuremberg laws, combined with the reoccupation of the Rhineland, *Anschluss* with Austria, and the

Axis Pact with Italy, stood as stark proof of Hitler's racist ideology and imperialist intentions. And Max Schmeling, though not officially a member of the Nazi Party, was closely aligned with Hitler and leading Reich officials. His 1936 defeat of Louis had elevated him into the pantheon of German heroes, certifying him as the poster child of Nazi strength and manhood. It also atoned for his 1933 loss to Max Baer, whose father was a Jew. Similarly, Louis's success had made him something of an emblem of American strength, openness, and democracy. The match, then, shaped up as a battle between opposing world views – "them" and "us," fascism and democracy, repression and freedom.

America seemed to stop for the fight. At shortly before 10 p.m., the voice of Clem McCarthy began to fall like a blanket across the nation. Activity inside restaurants, movie theaters, baseball parks, and other public places stopped as people leaned into the airwaves. Out on the nation's streets traffic quieted to a whisper as McCarthy's voice drifted through raised windows into the summer night. Woody Guthrie, whose songs were the conscience of Depression America, recalled walking through the narrow alleys and streets of Santa Fe, New Mexico, that evening, listening to the broadcast of the fight. But nowhere were citizens listening more intently than in the black neighborhoods across the country, places where Joe Louis was the embodiment of hope and accomplishment.

Worldwide, nearly 100 million people listened to the fight. The bout was freighted with meaning, but perhaps its greatest significance was for America's black population. For the first time in the history of the United States, a black man carried the hopes of his countrymen and the promise of his nation. Future comedian and civil rights activist Dick Gregory recalled listening to the fight with his family in St. Louis. Almost seventy years later he could still recall the voices of the announcers: "There was a difference in announcers' voices. That night it sounded like they loved him. Sounded like he wasn't a nigger to them. Joe had become an American."

The fight was violent and brief. Louis stunned Schmeling with a punch to the kidneys, and then finished him off. The official time was two minutes and four seconds of the first round, one of the shortest heavyweight championship fights in history. A number of spectators had not reached their seats before the bout ended; others had become distracted and missed the action. It was that fast. In his dressing room after the fight a reporter asked Louis how he felt. "Now I feels like the champ," he answered. And so he was – America's champ.

Joe Louis had transformed black into red, white, and blue. Probably never before in American history had a black man received so much praise in the mainstream press. In a moment of democratic peril, with Japan on the move in China and Germany talking about annexing the Sudetenland, Joe Louis had with his fists made a bold, direct statement about the vitality of democracy. He had done what American, English, and French politicians had failed to do – achieve a victory, even a symbolic one, against Hitler. A cartoon in the *Chicago Daily News* made the essential point: It showed a plane named the Brown Bomber dropping a bomb next to Adolf Hitler. No caption was needed.

The Second World War underscored Louis's symbolic role. Still champion when Japan bombed Pearl Harbor, Louis immediately displayed his patriotism in a series of highly symbolic acts. On January 9, 1942, he defended his title against Buddy Baer and donated his entire purse to the Navy Relief Fund; then, on March 27, 1942, he risked his title again, this time against Abe Simon, and donated his share of the match to the Army Relief Fund. At a time when some black Americans questioned the commitment of the US government to equality, Louis eloquently demonstrated his commitment to America.

On January 12, 1942, Louis took a further step and enlisted in the US Army. His role in the military was largely a symbolic one. He toured bases in America and overseas, engaged in almost 100 exhibition matches, appeared in two military-related films, and generally did what the leaders in the Office of War Information (OWI) asked. In the government's and the mass media's search for an authentic black icon, one who was heroic but did not really threaten the racial status quo, Joe Louis became the gold standard. As heavyweight champion he already carried considerable street credentials, but even more important, nothing in his past lowered his public image. He was the nation's original brown-eyed handsome man – soft-spoken, modest, and generous; a mother-loving, Bible-reading, and heavy-punching hero. The fact that he knocked Hitler's superman silly in one round – sending Schmeling to a hospital and forcing him to limp out of the United States – added to his aura.[4]

Louis emerged from the Second World War still champion, but he was moving into the twilight of his career and was strapped for money. The final act of his life had overtones of tragedy. Defeated in the ring in a comeback against Rocky Marciano, hounded by the Internal Revenue Service for back taxes, married and divorced several times, and experiencing bouts of drug addiction and paranoia, he nevertheless lived a dignified public life. He appeared as a contestant on Groucho Marx's *You Bet Your Life*; he was the subject of a biopic in 1953 called *The Joe Louis Story*; he became a greeter at Caesar's Palace in Las Vegas, a not ignoble fate that has befallen other noted athletes. He remained the Brown Bomber, the fighter who thrilled millions of Americans, black and white, and meant so much to Richard

Wright and other African Americans. Assessing Louis's importance to his own struggle against the color line, Jackie Robinson said, "I'm sure if it wasn't for Joe Louis, the color line in baseball would not have been broken for another ten years."

"You should have seen him then," Nagler told Lipsyte. Then was a different time. And America was a different place. But Joe Louis played his part in changing it for the better, just as Jackie Robinson would in the 1940s and Martin Luther King Jr. would in the 1950s. And, of course, just as Cassius Clay would, as Muhammad Ali, in the 1960s and after.

NOTES

1 Such black numbers men as Alex Pompex, Gus Greenlee, and Abe Manley had a strong presence in Negro league baseball at this time. And Casper Holstein, a major numbers man in Harlem, was one of the major financial backers of the Harlem Renaissance. Far from being low-rent gangsters, they played important roles in black communities.

2 Primo Carnera was the subject of Budd Schulberg's famous 1947 boxing novel, *The Harder They Fall*, which was made into a 1956 film starring Humphrey Bogart.

3 Max Baer also had an acting career, starring in the 1933 film *The Prizefighter and the Lady*, with Myrna Loy and appearing in over twenty other films. His brother, Buddy, was also a boxer and an actor, knocked by US Marshall Matt Dillon in an early episode of *Gunsmoke*. His son, Max Baer, Jr., was also an actor, most famous for playing Jethro on the *Beverly Hillbillies*.

4 Louis also retained his image as a race man. According to Truman Gibson, civilian aide to the secretary of war, who became Louis's friend and lawyer, Louis was the first person Jackie Robinson contacted when the latter got into trouble in 1944 for refusing to go to the back of the Army camp bus at Camp Hood, Texas. Louis and welterweight boxing champ Sugar Ray Robinson got into a row with a white military policeman who wanted them to use the "colored only" bus while at Camp Siebart in Alabama. Louis received nearly as many complaints from black soldiers about their treatment as Gibson did, and Louis tried, using his friendship with Gibson, to improve conditions in the camps.

14

WIL HAYGOOD

Sugar Ray Robinson's Furious Beauty

Prizefighters are not renowned for grace and elegance. It goes against the job description. The craft requires brutishness, muscle, and any measure of guile and sometimes chicanery. Facial structures will be knocked askew. Fans will gasp at screaming newspaper headlines. There can be glory – which is why men, often born impoverished, climb into the ring – but there will also be pain and often grave disappointment. Yet, sometimes, the boxing gods give us a figure who seems to defy the limitations of the sport, a figure who is a bewildering combination – artistic and vicious – that seems to make the prizefighter immortal. It is the rare prizefighter who comes across as beautiful and at the same time possesses a devil-like ferociousness that cannot bend the beauty. Sugar Ray Robinson, a six-time world champion across various fight divisions, was just such a figure.

He was as comfortable at Boston soirées hosted by rich socialites as he was inside the ring. He was a one-time tap dancer. He slid up to Lena Horne in his Harlem nightclub wearing a herringbone suit, and it made her smile. In Paris, a city he loved and that loved him back, beautiful French women slipped him notes. He could count poet Langston Hughes, trumpeter Miles Davis, and bandleader Count Basie amongst his close friends. Sugar Ray Robinson seemed made for the world of art and artists, but the paycheck was needed, and he earned his cash with gloved fists. He defeated the likes of some of the most dangerous fighters in the history of boxing, men who swung with the force of hammer blows, men who were mighty prideful they were the sons of immigrants, men like Jake LaMotta, Bobo Olson, and Carmen Basilio. And there were the black fighters, men like Henry Armstrong, Tommy Bell, and Tiger Jones, black men born on the wicked and not totally free side of the tracks, just like Sugar Ray, and he whipped them too. He beat them all and afterward appeared – the marcelled hair, the tailored suit – like a well-dressed man ready for an evening stroll. He was movie star handsome and knew it. The radio announcers, the newspapermen, the magazine writers – not to mention the millions of fans – would tell stories about his dazzling life for years to come. And they would always wonder: How does a fighter split his life in two, between blood and beauty?

Children come to be shaped by their upbringing and surroundings. Sugar Ray Robinson – his birth name was Walker Smith Jr. – was born in 1921 in rural Georgia and raised in his early teen years in Detroit. The family suffered the pangs of poverty in both locales. Detroit was particularly wicked, a place where ethnic strife seemed constant. There were Klan rallies and racial murders, not unlike what his parents would have remembered of their southern heritage. In 1932 Robinson's mother, Leila, decided to take her eleven-year-old son and two daughters to New York City. In doing so, she cracked a whole new world open for her only son.

This is what the New York City of the early 1930s was like for the boy who would become Sugar Ray Robinson: Jumpy music flowed from the cabarets; Negroes were dancing in Broadway shows; writers were producing poetry and short stories that told of Negro artistic genius; Negro painters were drawing portraits in their studios. On the streets Negro women in fur posed beside fancy cars as renowned photographer James VanderZee snapped away. And yes, there were plenty reminders of the Great Depression still in evidence, but there was high art and cultural expression on display every day. Negro writers, it seemed, were everywhere: Langston Hughes, Countee Cullen, Claude McKay, Ann Petry, and Arna Bontemps were keeping memories of the Harlem Renaissance – a period of exuberant black artistic expression – quite alive. They were given a name: "the New Negroes." As Arna Bontemps would recall, "In Harlem we were seen in a beautiful light. We were heralds of a dawning day. We were the first born of the dark renaissance."

These were amongst the first images of artistic expression that fastened onto the mind of Sugar Ray Robinson. And he loved it so much that he decreed that he'd become a dancer. And for all those who doubted him, there he was some afternoons, down on Broadway, dancing in circles while gawkers dropped coins at his feet. The symphony of life, of life's literal music, had snared him. His eye saw beauty. But the pure athlete in him caught the attention of someone else.

George Gainford was a has-been fighter who by the early 1930s had turned to training young boys at the Salem Crescent Athletic Club in Harlem. The club was actually a youth boxing team, supported and backed by the Salem Methodist Episcopal Church. That a church was in the business of promoting the talents of youthful boxers – they trained in the basement of the church – represented one of the more peculiar undertakings in Harlem. But the parishioners were bedeviled by juvenile crime in the community, and there existed a collective feeling they had to do something. So they allowed Gainford to form a boxing team, something to lure the boys inside and keep them off the streets. (It was commonly believed at this time that boys required considerably more intense socialization than girls and that sports were a good, wholesome, emotional and psychical outlet for boys, a variation of the principle of CCC, or Civilian Conservation Corps, of giving young adult males fresh air and physical labor so that they might become virtuous rather than sociopathic.) It was on this team that Walker Smith became Sugar Ray Robinson, given the name in upstate New York one evening during a mix-up over another fighter's absence. It was on this team that Gainford sat stunned as the young and gangly Robinson began knocking out opponents with a lightning left hook. It was on this team – fighting up and down the Eastern seaboard in AAU tournaments – that Robinson went on to fight under the klieg lights at Madison Square Garden, becoming, throughout 1938 and 1939, a Manhattan and Golden Gloves sensation. It was on this team that Robinson – who possessed dancing ring footwork – insisted on having a Victrola record player because he wanted to listen to beautiful music – Jelly Roll Morton, Duke Ellington, Fats Waller – while skipping rope. It was on this team that something seemed to click in the mind of the young Sugar Ray Robinson: that beauty itself was also something worth fighting for.

He was a tall and lean welterweight who had the coiled body of a swimmer. When Sugar Ray Robinson turned pro in 1940, he had a peerless amateur record. But fighters came and went (especially at this time when the fight game was still a major attraction for ethnic and immigrant boys seeking a get-out-of-the-tenements-free card.) Many considered it wise to keep predictions measured no matter how sterling an amateur record happened to be. But Sugar Ray Robinson won every professional fight he fought from 1940 to the end of 1942. A total of forty clashes. The New York reporters had to take notice. Nat Fleischer's respected *The Ring* magazine started marking Robinson's career with cover photos and articles. Yes, there were some going-nowhere journeymen in the bunch Sugar Ray had defeated, but there were also some ranked brawlers, among them Fritzie Zivic, Sammy Angott, and Jake LaMotta. The public, of course, adores a winner, and the undefeated Sugar Ray Robinson was soon being toasted about Manhattan. He was a magnet for movie stars and Cotton Club dancers. The gangsters saw something in him that they did not see in Joe Louis: a style that was continental, a kind of music, a kind of beauty even. And as Sugar Ray Robinson certainly knew, the 1940s was a good time to be beautiful in Manhattan.

In the Manhattan that glittered, you might catch a glimpse of Ava Gardner at Toots Shor's nightclub, or Dean Martin at the El Morocco, or

Billy Eckstine at the Copa. Vivien Leigh might be dining at the Stork Club. There were certainly racial boundaries for Negroes, but not necessarily for Negro stars, and by the end of 1946, when he had defeated Tommy Bell in a fifteen-rounder in New York City for the welterweight championship of the world, Sugar Ray Robinson was a star and found himself hanging out with newspaper columnist Walter Winchell, a star magnet. Sugar Ray had married the beautiful Edna Mae Holly, a one-time showgirl. He had a valet and a tailor. He took music lessons. He was named to best-dressed lists in Harlem. He seemed a man fighting against the rough-hewn image of the boxer. He opened a nightclub, called Sugar Ray's, and the beautiful people came: airline stewardesses, showgirls, Hollywood stars. (It had to be a relief to have a place to distance himself against suffering any possible slights in the white-owned nightclubs.) He purchased a car, and it was hard to miss it as it sliced along the Hudson River and down 125th Street. It was a Cadillac, a convertible, and it was pink. No one had ever seen an auto like it.

And still Sugar Ray Robinson fought, and he fought like a champion, and he won like a champion. He became middleweight champion in 1951, having crossed over from welterweight. His ring style was controlled yet furious, his fists flew like birds. Opponents seldom saw the knockout punch coming. He moved his feet like Balanchine. Sometimes, in the ring, he smiled, and his victims loathed the habit. His left hook was delivered like a shotgun blast.

There was a colossal war, from 1942 to 1951, between Sugar Ray Robinson and Jake LaMotta. They fought six times. They were brutal affairs that attracted the beautiful people. In 1942 they fought in New York City. In 1943 they fought twice, both times in Detroit, the immigrant crowd howling in support of LaMotta, the Negroes for Sugar Ray, back in the city where he once lived. In 1945 they fought twice, in New York City and Chicago. Their final clash was on Valentine's Day, 1951, in Chicago. The punches were quick and lethal. LaMotta bled heavily. Women in attendance cried. It was the only one of their fights nationally televised. The *Indianapolis News* – not exactly a fan of the sweet science – would offer: "When Jake LaMotta was permitted to go into the thirteenth round unsound of mind, unsound of body, wobbling and with a mentality that didn't know whether it was 10 o'clock or the Fourth of July, the sport showed its true colors. It is a throwback to the Cromagnon man." The LaMotta whipping was so bad it was quickly referred to as the St. Valentine's Day Massacre, presided over by Sugar Ray, the Esquire man. Sugar Ray won five of their six meetings.

It's obvious that Americans – the world even – loves movies. Stories of romance and nuanced dramas tend to garner a wide appeal. As for sports movies, they more often than not draw a niche crowd. But when an auteur makes a sports movie, people tend to pay attention. So it was in 1980 when *Raging Bull*, directed by Martin Scorsese and starring Robert DeNiro, Joe Pesci, and Cathy Moriarty, was released into the American cineplexes. Scorsese's hypnotic directing – in black and white no less – was highly praised, as was the acting. Given that LaMotta and Robinson had fought those six battles, one might have thought Scorsese would have given ample screen time to the two combatants and their encounters. He did not. Their clashes took up only five or so minutes in the film. One left the movie rather confused when it came to the LaMotta–Robinson fights. If Robinson won five of the six encounters, why did it feel, from the movie, that LaMotta won some kind of victory? For one thing, a former fighter by the name of Johnny Barnes played Robinson. Barnes, an unknown, was simply an unaccomplished actor. Even if in Scorsese's mind the Robinson role was a small one, a gifted actor could have bought depth to the portrayal. Instead, LaMotta-DeNiro dominated the scenes between Robinson and LaMotta. On screen, it was all LaMotta achieving a kind of celluloid victory. The estimable film writer and critic David Thomson thought as much. He would write that "to miss Sugar and fall on LaMotta suggests something very different on Scorsese's mind, and something tricky to spell out." Put another way, Hollywood has long been more enamored of the white prizefighter than the black prizefighter. Sugar Ray Robinson simply won't get his cinematic due until a smart and savvy filmmaker senses the epochal story surrounding his grand life.

One of the very few black prizefighters who did receive screen treatment was heavyweight champion Joe Louis. Hollywood premiered *The Joe Louis Story* in 1953. The budget was small, the casting uninspired, and the movie flopped. The filmmakers, strangely enough, completely ignored the real-life Sugar Ray Robinson–Joe Louis dynamic, which would have made for interesting cinema.

When the young Sugar Ray reached Detroit with his family in 1921, they were as nervous as any family from the rural South suddenly thrust into an urban environment might be. But young Robinson – then still known as Walker Smith – would grow and begin to hang out at the Brewster Recreation Center. It was at Brewster where he first caught a glimpse of the rising and much talked about Joe Louis. When he turned professional years later, Robinson would keep company with Louis – his hero – on the social scenes of Chicago and Manhattan. Their bond deepened when Uncle Sam came calling.

In 1942 Robinson and Louis found themselves in the Army. Their boxing celebrity got them the cushy assignment of conducting fitness exhibitions from Massachusetts to Alabama. Joe was a sturdy presence; Sugar Ray, six years younger and a Harlem hepcat, was looser, more quick with his tongue against slights than Louis. It was in Gadsden, Alabama, where trouble brewed.

Robinson and Louis had been waiting on a Negroes-only bus to take them from the Army base into town. Louis grew impatient waiting on the bus and went over to a whites-only area and stepped into a phone booth to call a taxi. A white military policeman shot him a cutting look, then when Louis emerged from the phone booth, the MP raised his billy club in Louis's direction and scolded him about using the whites-only phone booth. Sugar Ray, idling nearby, fuming, suddenly attacked the MP. There was a spasm of wrestling motion; Robinson avoided using his fists. Still, it was otherworldly to see a black man attack a white MP. Calm returned, but Louis and Robinson both were summoned before Army brass. The Army did not want a national scandal and did not press charges against Robinson or Louis.

But this hardly ended the dramatic turns of Sugar Ray Robinson's Army service.

Before war's end Robinson and Louis found themselves at Fort Hamilton, in Brooklyn. They were waiting to be shipped overseas. Such a prospect made Robinson quite uneasy. He feared being killed in an overseas battle; he had yet to get a shot at a championship belt. It was March 29, 1944, when Robinson abandoned a card game on the Army base and vanished like a puff of smoke. He went AWOL. Six days later Robinson was discovered in a Staten Island hospital, his head wrapped in bandages. He claimed amnesia, told Army brass he truly had no idea how he got there. He seemed delirious. Some imagined Robinson – a star in the Negro world of celebrity – would surely be either harshly disciplined or face a court martial. It was, yet again, a tricky tightrope for Army brass. First Lady Eleanor Roosevelt was keen to mistreatment of the Negro soldier. Army officials wanted to show a cohesive home front. In their hands they now had the fate of one of the rising Negro figures in world boxing. When they allowed Sugar Ray Robinson to leave the Army with an honorable discharge, it surely was an example of Army benevolence at its best.

The hepcats, the numbers runners, the jazz musicians, even many who lived on the shadowy edges of society, all seemed to adore Sugar Ray Robinson. Robinson was respectful of the fighters who came before him, especially the Negro fighters who had fallen on hard times. They could get a free meal at his restaurant. But he also realized he was cutting a different path from them. For all of Joe Louis's courage, he could seem socially timid. He would not challenge the promoters who took advantage of him. There was no such timidity on Sugar Ray's part. He took boxing commissioners to court over unfair treatment. He demanded larger portions of gate receipts and railed against the International Boxing Club, which ruled boxing in the 1950s by buying Joe Louis's heavyweight title, was linked to criminal elements and fixed fights, controlled boxing on television for a decade, and was investigated by the United States Congress. Sugar Ray forged his own freedom with stubborn defiance. He also remained a true dreamer in life.

In 1939 *The New Yorker* writer James Thurber wrote a charming short story about a man named Walter Mitty. Mitty, who comes off as a tender sort, daydreams about being a surgeon, about standing before a firing squad. He dreams about many things outside his present life. There is a buoyancy to the story, a harmless spirit, a kind of call to arms of the everyday heartbeat. Perhaps that is why the story "The Secret Life of Walter Mitty" would become so iconic. In time there would even be stage and film adaptations. As to Sugar Ray Robinson's big dream, he wanted to cavort and play with the big cats of the jazz world, with the likes of Lionel Hampton and Count Basie. How would a champion boxer make such a dream come true? Would he give up the ring, still at the height of his powers?

Maybe it wasn't the wisest choice to make, stepping away from the bigtime fight game at the height of one's career. But there stood Sugar Ray Robinson, at the end of 1952, abandoning the sport. He cobbled together a revue, dancers, and musicians. He was going to travel with Count Basie. The echoes of the Harlem Renaissance had deeply touched him. It was an odd decision, but in its own way it was kind of beautiful too.

First, the beautiful part: He got Ralph Cooper, who had appeared in Negro films, to be his manager. He and Cooper had a high time talking about Negro beauty. Then Sugar Ray asked his buddy Miles Davis to recommend some musicians, and Miles did, and there were jam sessions that lasted deep into the night. Sugar Ray Robinson was about to unleash his Walter Mitty dream. And just like that – after a Manhattan opening attended by stars and celebrities – he was out on the nightclub circuit. The popular TV hosts Kate Smith and Ed Sullivan had him on their shows. He flew west and played Los Angeles and Las Vegas. He played Pittsburgh and Chicago. In Chicago he appeared on stage with one of his idols, Louis Armstrong. Fans would spot him and those musical celebrities kicking back in all-night diners, cackling and having fun. Who could ever had told him that he'd have this opportunity in life – out on the road with some of the greatest musicians in the world? Why, he even got an engagement and found himself tap dancing on stage at Harlem's famed Apollo Theatre.

But for all the joy Sugar Ray Robinson must have gotten from being on the road as an entertainer, he could not escape the reviews. They were, for the most part, dreadful. He decided to cross the Atlantic. In Paris, they loved him more in the ring than on a nightclub stage. The reviews were unkind.

When he was forced to return to the ring, many in the fight world believed his best days were behind him. On January 19, 1955, Tiger Jones beat him in a ten-round slugfest in Chicago. And then the critics began writing an epilogue to the great career of Sugar Ray Robinson. But champions often have something in reserve that mystifies the critics. Eleven months later, also in Chicago, thirty-four-year-old Sugar Ray Robinson stood across from champion Bobo Olson in the ring. Robinson was a 4–1 underdog. In the second round Robinson unloaded a right-left combination that buckled Olson, that saw the crowd jump to its feet, that saw referee Frank Sikora stop it. Champions find a way to rise, and Sugar Ray Robinson had regained the world middleweight title.

But then, the beautiful magic began to fade. There were a few great battles ahead: He beat Carmen Basilio in March of 1958, following a defeat by Basilio six months earlier. He lost a title fight to Gene Fullmer, in 1961, but continued to fight. He turned forty and was still lacing up the gloves. Those who loved him cried.

Sugar Ray Robinson certainly wasn't the first prizefighter to imagine Hollywood coveted his services. In 1967 he found himself living on West Adams Boulevard in Los Angeles. He was going to try his hand at acting. He had befriended so many entertainers – Sammy Davis Jr., Frank Sinatra, Richard Burton, Liz Taylor – and of course they would remember him. But the truth of it is that Robinson, so loose and jazzy in the ring, was stiff and unpersuasive in front of the camera. Sinatra gave him a tiny role in *The Detective,* and there were other roles, just as tiny, in more forgettable films. He had a minor run guest starring on episodic television – *Lost in Space, Mission Impossible, Car 54, Where Are You?* Soon the casting directors stopped calling. It wasn't that all of his bloody fame had vanished; it was simply that fighters must find other callings to salve their wounded ego in light of the aging process.

All during his youth Sugar Ray had fought against the claws of poverty. In retirement he founded the Sugar Ray Youth Foundation. Impoverished kids had a chance to engage in after-school activities. They could take classes on etiquette and modeling, ballet. The sight of so many children doing things that made them happy made the not-so-old prizefighter and his wife, Millie, quite happy.

Like others, he fought too long. His final bout was in 1965. He died in Los Angeles in 1989.

He had swirled through segregation, gangster New York, fifteen-round ring battles, and shady promoters. It was a legendary record: 173 wins, nineteen losses, and six draws. Picture him running – no, gliding – through the woods around Greenwood Lake, New York, where he often trained, where he'd vanish beautifully into the wind.

15

LEWIS A. ERENBERG

Echoes from the Jungle: Muhammad Ali in the Early 1970s

On October 30, 1974, ex-champion Muhammad Ali battled current champion George Foreman in Kinshasa, Zaire, to regain the crown stripped from him in 1967. Like many of Ali's early 1970s fights, this match transcended sport. The $10 million purse was the biggest ever, plus this was Africa's first heavyweight title bout, and the grandest spectacle in boxing history. The "Rumble in the Jungle" represented the fusion of sport and politics in global media spectacles during the 1960s and 1970s that resonated worldwide. As the freedom movement and the Vietnam War transformed sport from escapist playground into an arena where divisive social issues battled for supremacy, black boxers like Ali and Foreman became political and cultural symbols of rebellion against the establishment versus patriotic nationalism and gradual racial progress, all broadcast worldwide via satellite.

The African setting transformed the bout into an international spectacle, which promoter Don King called "a symbolic black happening" where the world would learn "that there is more to Africa than beads, bones, and beating drums." The 1970s witnessed truly global spectacles, represented by international casts of promoters, broadcast of bouts worldwide, and participation by Third World countries in a boxing world no longer ruled by Madison Square Garden. Ali stressed the Rumble's international drama, calling it "a holy war. I'm the freedom fighter and Foreman will be fighting for the establishment." Claiming to represent "all the African people who are fighting for their independence and freedom," Ali painted Foreman "as a Belgian, he is the oppressor of black nations." He linked anti-colonialism to the plight of American "black people who are wine heads and dope addicts." A "politician for Allah," Ali called the match a crusade against Foreman, Christianity, and a racist white America.[1]

The fight projected onto the world stage the clash of 1960s cultural and political values, and would determine that turbulent era's victor. To Ali's supporters, the ex-champ sought vindication against a boxing and political establishment that had unjustly taken his title and cast him into exile.

Now, seven years later, he faced his last chance to regain his title against an invincible Foreman, who represented the establishment versus the waning power of the aging dissident. As the underdog for the first time since his title match with Sonny Liston in 1964, could Ali buck the odds and reclaim his crown? Could he beat the ascendant Silent Majority? The return to Africa also resonated deeply. Just as Ali fans believed white America stole his title, the return to Zaire avenged the enslavement that had exiled blacks from Africa. That the roots of black America lay in civilized Africa rather than savage America served to criticize American oppression and slavery. Meanwhile, Foreman had thanked President Lyndon Johnson's Job Corps for rescuing him from poverty and promising him the American Dream. Fans also remained divided over Vietnam. Ali saw the war as a worldwide war on people of color. Silent on Vietnam, Foreman's waving of the flag at the 1968 Olympics seemed a patriotic response to the black-fist gesture by Tommie Smith and John Carlos, and made him a national hero. Both Ali and Foreman were 1960s symbols, fighting in the 1970s over the validity of the American narrative of freedom and progress. Ali represented 1960s athletes rebelling against racism; Foreman symbolized the establishment and the virtues of an exceptionalist American society. The Rumble highlighted contrasting symbols of blackness and competing national narratives, and revealed lingering 1960s tensions played out in a global sport spectacle during the early 1970s.[2]

While filled with powerful symbolism, the "Rumble in the Jungle" was not the only Ali fight during the early 1970s with significant political and cultural overtones, especially as the war continued and the country remained racially divided. Because of his membership in the Nation of Islam and his refusal to accept the draft, in 1967 he was convicted of draft evasion by an all-white jury and faced a five-year jail sentence and a $10,000 fine. Because state licensing commissions refused him a license, and the WBA stripped him of his title, he was exiled from boxing and became a pariah to much of white America. Yet, foregoing career and wealth to put his body on the line against the government raised his stature to unheard-of heights as a Race Man. Despite his separatist beliefs, his principled defiance made him a hero to the civil rights movement, which faced similar persecution by white officials. Ali became a symbol of courage and conscience around which the freedom and anti-war movements coalesced. As Martin Luther King declared, "He is giving up fame. He is giving up millions of dollars in order to stand up for what his conscience tells him is right. No matter what you think of Muhammad Ali's religion, you have to admire his courage." Similarly, young anti-war whites and blacks found a hero who articulated their opposition to Vietnam War and the draft. That his opposition to the war was rooted in his Islamic beliefs and his charge that white oppression at home was linked to a war on people of color abroad only elevated his as an anti-colonial champion in Third World countries.[3]

In this atmosphere, Ali's return to the ring assumed the quality of a Second Coming, filled with strong religious and political overtones. As the war dragged on, the defiant hero still had to fight his boxing opponents and political foes in matches apocalyptic in nature. His return on October 26, 1970, against Jerry Quarry after three and a half years in exile was greeted as the resurrection of a black folk hero who defied an oppressive government and American racism on behalf of all blacks. Even before the Supreme Court ruled in his favor, Atlanta blacks mobilized their formidable power to break the ban and sanction the Quarry match. As Ali declared, "This is goin' to be the biggest night in ring history, every eye in the world's gonna be on me to see if the government beat me." The bout became a battle between a White Hope and a symbol of Black Pride and was seen as a major civil rights victory. *Jet* described Ali's tune-up exhibition at Morehouse University in religious terms, occurring in Georgia, where the KKK president lived, Lester Maddox was governor, where Martin Luther King was buried, and "Ali is resurrected." Equated with King and Christ, Ali was now a monumental hero whose every fight carried political, racial, and religious import for his many black and white fans.[4]

The majority black crowd celebrated Ali's second coming and "their" victory over arch-segregationist Maddox. The night before, sports writer Bert Sugar recalled, fans at Atlanta's Hyatt-Regency Hotel, "who'd been waiting for his resurrection, looked up cheering" as Ali ascended to the heights in the glass elevator. These were "idolators." Signaling the importance of Ali's return to the black community, the black elite attended in droves, many of whom threw up Black Power salutes led by Jesse Jackson. Among the politicians were the Southern Christian Leadership Conference's Ralph Abernathy, Operation Breadbasket's Jesse Jackson, Georgia state representative Julian Bond, Alderman Q. V. Williamson, Vice Mayor Maynard Jackson, Jewish Mayor Sam Massell, Rodman Rockefeller, Adam Clayton Powell, the Urban League's Whitney Young, Atlanta congressional candidate Andrew Young, and former Student Non-violent Coordinating Committee chairman John Lewis. Many entertainers attended, as did sports stars, a slew of boxing greats, and elaborately dressed hustlers and their ladies who turned the event into a black happening.[5]

Black fans shared in Ali's resurrection and his victory over racism. As *Jet*'s Ronald Kisner noted, Ali "pranced to the center of the ring and simultaneously looked Jerry Quarry, the United States Army, other American cities, and Georgia Governor Lester Maddox squarely in their faces." Maddox, "a historic impediment to Black liberation movements in the South," tried but failed to cancel the match, but called for "A Day of Mourning," summoned Georgians to boycott the fight, and urged "patriotic" groups to express their disgust. "I don't see how this fight, with a man who disgraced his country's uniform by refusing to be drafted," he declared on the evening news, "could be held in this city – or in any other city in this country." As a sign of his crushing defeat, Maddox was the sole prominent local official not in attendance.[6]

Fans saw "a man who may possibly be the greatest fighter [to] don a pair of gloves" slice up Quarry for a bloody third round TKO. Ali defied Father Time and appeared as good as ever. "But," Kisner concluded, "viewers were also witness to an important victory for Atlanta and US blacks." The black community's struggles and Ali's were intertwined. As Ali declared, they were there to celebrate "one nigger the white man didn't get." In recognition of his symbolic importance, after the bout Mrs. Coretta King and Ralph Abernathy gave Ali the Dr. Martin Luther King Memorial Award "for his contributions to human dignity." Mrs. King proclaimed him "a champion of justice and peace and unity," while Abernathy called Ali "a living example of soul power, the March on Washington in two fists."[7]

The battle of a John Henry-like Ali versus boxing's white establishment became clearer six weeks later. Ali's bout with Argentina's Oscar Bonavena at Madison Square Garden was made possible only after the NAACP Legal Defense Fund successfully sued the New York State Athletic Commission, charging that it had violated Ali's Fourteenth Amendment rights on political grounds despite licensing over ninety convicted felons. Veterans groups protested the fight's being held on December 7, but the battle over the right to a boxing license was over. Despite this legal victory, Bonavena proved troublesome, hitting Ali endlessly and forcing him into the fifteenth round, where he managed a dramatic knockout. Many blacks saw a persecuted black hero versus a brutish White Hope, supported, said *Jet*, by bigots, white sportswriters, and promoters. Ali's dramatic victory, notes historian Michael Ezra, "further endeared him to the public, because it embodied the same kind of resolve, endurance, and determination that had fueled him throughout his exile." Furthermore, the bout's metaphoric relationship between the Bonavena bout and Ali's battles outside the ring was obvious. "Against an indefatigable foe, he had called upon his deepest reserves to pull out a dramatic victory."[8]

As with Quarry, however, there were ominous portents that exile had diminished his skills, slowed his legs and weakened his punches. With his legs weakened, he less easily danced out of trouble, and was hit more than before the exile. Ali's doctor, Ferdie Pacheco, noted he "absorbed more punishment against Bonavena than he had in any previous fight," and needed five months to recover. Instead, with prison still a possibility, Ali jumped at the chance to fight Joe Frazier for the title. Now Ali was not just a standard-bearer against an oppressive government, he fought to survive the ravages that the government and Father Time had imposed upon him. In this he embodied another 1970s theme: the fight to survive disaster, which he demonstrated against Bonavena and in more dire circumstances against Frazier.[9]

The "Fight of the Century" between "the People's Champion" and the undefeated champion Joe Frazier on March 8, 1971, a match embroiled in the national conflict over the war and black power, pitted opposite styles of blackness against each other. The fight, noted sports writer Robert Lipsyte, fit into a "live unrehearsed allegory here that transcends a simple punch-up." Two undefeated champions fought for the right to be the true champion. Plus, as the Supreme Court was to decide Ali's draft case momentarily, the match pitted a draft dodger/anti-war hero against a supporter of doing one's duty. According to author Budd Schulberg, the lingering resentments over race and the war transformed Frazier into a white man's hero. Many whites wanted Ali beaten for his loud mouth, his opposition to the war, his religion, and his vocal challenge to white supremacy. Many young whites and blacks, however, saw him as the first free black champion up against "the house nigger of the white chauvinist pigs." For black sports commentator Bryant Gumbel, Ali symbolized 1960s racial and political rebelliousness versus a more complacent black man. If Ali lost, "it was as if everything I believed in was wrong." To young anti-establishment blacks, "he was a heroic figure, plain and simple." Ali "was the very symbol of black pride, parading black feelings about black heritage, speaking out against racial injustice." Frazier, however, "was more like your parents were. He just kind of went along. He did his job." No fan of the old order, "he didn't fight it either." Vietnam was the litmus test. Ali "was dead set against the war"; Frazier remained quiet, though he "was supported by those who backed the war." Fighting their hero, Frazier "became a symbol of the oppressors." Public opinion also favored Ali as it turned against the war, though he still faced massive opposition by white southerners and working-class ethnics who saw Ali as "the symbol of national dissent" and Frazier as a the working-class guy to button Ali's lip.[10]

Despite a valiant effort only four months since his return, Ali lost a narrow fifteen-round decision when he suffered a brutal knockdown after being mauled by a relentless Frazier. Ali fans, however, took heart that he survived being knocked down. Fans were clearly divided over who won, influenced much by the war. Ali-haters were elated. Arthur Kronenberg told *The Ring*,

"I saw the Muslim get a beating just short of a KO." Kronenberg's hatred lay in his Vietnam experience. "[I served but] came back alive with a fungus which is driving me nuts, and this guy Clay gets $2,500,000 … I despise Clay for what he is." Many fans, like Franklin Crandall, believed Ali won. Crandall supported Ali's draft battle, stating, "[I wish I] had his money and strong arguments to stay out of the Army myself. I am due to go in soon and I am not a CO. Merely a draftee who has no desire to fight in Viet Nam."[11]

Many fans were devastated. Gumbel "felt as though everything I had stood for had been beaten down" by the hard hats and the silent majority. In Ali's loss, the promise of the 1960s turned sour. The devastation occurred worldwide, especially among Muslims. Libyan President Qaddafi declared a day of mourning. Ali claimed he heard about similar sentiments in Kuwait, Saudi Arabia, Indonesia, Pakistan Malaysia, Egypt, South Korea, Thailand, and Burma. In Great Britain a Black Nationalist declared, "Tonight the black world weeps that their king has passed away." Whites, he lamented, "had willed that the king should die. But it took the might of the most powerful, most designing judicial system in the world to bring the king down." Frazier, he reasoned, "was the unreckoning tool of that design." This sentiment emboldened Ali and his fans to believe that it was not Frazier's left hooks and unstoppable determination that had defeated Ali, rather his forced exile. Returning too soon, he just needed more time to regain his old form.[12]

As a result, Ali survived to fight on as a 1960s symbol, though against a significant headwind, helped by the Supreme Court decision on June 28, 1971, which overturned his conviction and enabled him to pursue the title without worries of jail. On March 31, 1973, however, he suffered a broken jaw and lost a decision to unheralded Ken Norton, an ex-Marine patriotic symbol in navy bastion San Diego, California. Most observers assumed Ali was through. However, he stayed alive, winning tough decisions against Frazier and Norton and worked his way back as the only logical opponent for the formidable new heavyweight champion George Foreman.[13]

"The Rumble in the Jungle" on October 30, 1974, became the grandest of Ali spectacles, freighted with accumulated political and cultural metaphors, as he sought to reclaim the crown that had eluded him for the last three years. Black promoter and ex-convict Don King transformed the Ali–Foreman fight into a poster for Black Power worldwide in the first ever heavyweight title match in Africa. In the 1970s, new players like King and Zaire's President Mobutu Sese Seko, took advantage of the de-centralization and globalization of boxing. Where race had always redounded to the credit of whites, since the 1960s blackness became a positive characteristic that King tapped in the black-dominated heavyweight boxing world. Derided as an unscrupulous hustler, King believed it "a mediocre word when applied to my talents ... I am a solitary black man up against the weapons of the white power structure, a bow and arrow against an atom bomb." The first black man to wield real behind-the-scenes power, King proved that a black entrepreneur could negotiate complex deals with heads of state. In an era of global black consciousness, King persuaded a reluctant Foreman that black promoters would "show all blacks around the world that we can succeed like no one has ever believed we could. I am black and this is my promotion. No white man gonna rip you off." King also persuaded Herbert Muhammad, Ali's manager and the son of the Honorable Elijah Muhammad, the head of the Nation of Islam, to remember Elijah's message: "You have to help the black man ... And it's being put together by me. A black man."[14]

With the help of Mobutu and Ali, King constructed an African setting for one of the century's great symbolic international spectacles. In King's hands, the bout became black America's return to Africa when many blacks sought roots in their history and in their African past. "I yearn for my home-land with great intensity," he announced. "I am going home and taking my brothers with me." President Mobutu desired a global spectacle to pro-mote Zaire, the former Belgian Congo, as an example of black liberation from European colonialism. Eager to showcase its independence and mod-ernity, Zaire sought prestige as the first African country to stage a "Fight of the Century" with the richest prize in boxing history. Like several other developing nations during the 1970s, Zaire underwrote a sports spectacle to display its mineral wealth, showcase Mobutu as an enlightened leader, strengthen his hold on his vast nation, and attract foreign investment. He put up the $10 million purse, and spent another $15 million to refurbish the stadium, build a modern airport and access roads, and link telephones to the satellite station. He also erected billboards proclaiming the regime's mod-ernity, that Africans and African Americans had a common enemy in white supremacy, and that Black Power was realized in Zaire. There was even a three-day music festival before the fight to highlight the African Diaspora's musical and cultural riches.[15]

Eager to reclaim his title, Ali claimed a mandate from people of color worldwide as "the People's Champion." Foreman, like every champion since 1967, operated in his shadow, and King insisted that Foreman would have to beat Ali to legitimate himself, which fueled his anger and irritated the Zarois. When the fight was postponed five weeks after Foreman was cut in training, Ali traveled the countryside, befriending everyone while George stewed in seclusion. Like Liston he was capable only of brutally destroying an opponent. Ali dubbed him "the Mummy." The wait heightened their cultural and political differences too. Foreman's waving the American flag at the 1968 Olympics and his belief in America because of his Job Corps experience made him seem a black man of an earlier age, and to some, another White Hope. By contrast, Ali assumed the mantle of global Black Nationalism anti-colonialism, painting Foreman as the white oppressor. This theme emerged at the Boxing Writers Banquet when playful scuffling turned nasty as Ali denounced Foreman as "white America, Christianity, the Flag, the White Man, Pork chops." Adding an anti-colonial element, he noted the fight was "in the Congo. In Lumumba territory. When Foreman see my Mau Mau boys he going to be afraid to show up for the fight ... Africans like me better than George." In fact, until his arrival, most Africans assumed Foreman was white. His German shepherd, a symbol of brutal colonial oppression, further tarnished his image. Most Zarois and all of Africa rooted for Ali; George was "the goof who'd waved the American flag." Comfortable as a Pan-African hero, Ali declared his love for the black-run country. "In America we've been led to believe that we can't do without the white man, and all we know about Africa is jungles," but "we in America are the savages."[16]

Despite being a 3/1 underdog, Ali received cards and letters from all over Africa identifying with his quest for redemption. As he entered the ring, the crowd went wild, chanting "Ali, Bomaye" (Ali, Kill Him), while Foreman received sparse applause. When he removed his robe, however, his huge muscles dwarfed Ali's and awed onlookers. Dread settled over audiences everywhere. After three and a half years in exile and losses to Frazier and Norton, Ali seemed old at thirty-two, up against such a formidable twenty-five-year-old lion who had destroyed both Frazier and Norton and was 40–0, with thirty-seven knockouts. "Foreman might be the heaviest puncher in the heavyweight division," observed the *New York Times*' Dave Anderson, "Sooner or later the champion will land one of his sledge-hammer punches, and for the first time in his career, Muhammad Ali will be counted out. This could happen in the first round." Faced with such a monster, could Ali survive with his life?[17]

The fight itself surprised everyone, and added to the Ali legend. As expected, Ali came out dancing and jabbing. Rushing to ring center he threw two right-hand leads, followed by a straight left and right. Foreman, however, responded fiercely, cutting off the ring, and forcing Ali to the ropes, where to everyone's horror, Ali leaned back on the ropes and let Foreman pound away, blocking shots and leaning back on the ropes. Like a black trickster, Ali led Foreman to destruction like the cartoon wolf "is tricked into some extravagantly ghastly trap laid by a sly mouse." Foreman threw bombs, Ali blocked. George remained unconcerned. "I knew he was going down, just as every opponent of mine had." His corner implored Ali to stay off the ropes, but to no avail. Foreman pressed, hitting Ali constantly, while periodically Ali left his defensive shell to stagger his opponent and puff up his face. Aided by Ali's goading, Foreman's power ebbed after the fifth round, but he kept single-mindedly pounding away like "the mummies of Ali's beloved horror films." In the eighth, a spent champion pinned Ali on the ropes and threw punches in slow motion. Suddenly, Ali lunged forward, throwing lefts and rights that knocked Foreman out. As it became clear that Ali had survived certain destruction, the crowd erupted.[18]

While Foreman was devastated, Ali and his entourage were triumphant. Against all odds Ali dramatically reclaimed his title. Cast into exile he came back to prove he was "the greatest." The way he won only added to the legend. In a morality play rooted in black folklore, the weaker hero outwitted a much more powerful foe. "A bee battered a lion," noted the *New York Times*' Dave Anderson, with brains, just as Ali had predicted. Wit and style beat, as *Time* described Foreman "a robot with gloves." Ali called him "a mechanical man" who failed to improvise. As Ali declared, "Don't ever match no bull against a master boxer. The bull is stronger but the matador is smarter."[19]

David's victory over Goliath also vindicated fans, who also had opposed government injustice. Reticent Foreman represented the flag-waving white "silent majority" eager to stifle Ali, but like government officials, he failed. *Ebony* hit this political note at Ali's Louisville homecoming, where he was honored by the big shots who had shied from him in the past, "when he was considered a traitor and a bum" for "changing his name" and challenging the draft. The crowd greeted him as a folk hero "for whom black people have gained profound respect – for refusing to knuckle under." It was also apt to triumph in Africa, where whites enslaved, oppressed, and exiled blacks, as America exiled Ali. The exile had returned. At Washington, DC's Capitol Theater, nearly all 17,000 black fans rooted for Ali because, noted a doctor, "he was black man enough to stand on his own two feet and suffer the consequences." His victory was thus a victory for all blacks.[20]

The international spectacle also publicized the 1960s narrative linking domestic racism and white imperialism. Ali proclaimed he won for Islam and black colonists struggling for liberation, and praised Zaire's modern civilization as a counter to white supremacy by introducing a black Zairian pilot to the Louisville crowd. "You white folks still think Africans live in trees. Well, this man here ain't no tom-tom beater, he's a highly skilled pilot who can fly a jumbo jet as good as any white man!" Trumpeting African civilization, Ali expressed the Third World view that America represented racial oppression at home and abroad, while he represented the black masses worldwide.[21]

Many black intellectuals and artists hailed Ali's victory as a triumph for a fading 1960s radicalism. Poet Quincy Troupe declared, "The joy felt by his victory was felt throughout the world," but he was surprised that so many young whites agreed. In depressing 1974, beset by recession, waning civil rights energy, the oil crisis, anti-busing riots, and the Symbionese Liberation Army's kidnapping of heiress Patty Hearst and shootout with the police in Los Angeles, which resulted in six dead SLA members, Ali's win, like Nixon's resignation, was "a spiritual victory" for all. Like Ali, white and black protestors were "silenced by murder and jail sentences, or shouted down as "irresponsible and radical – 'un-American.'" Troupe believed the victory vindicated dissenters, proving that conservative forces were bankrupt and the new spiritual forces would challenge and survive political adversity. Retaking the title, Ali "represented the millions upon millions of people who, also in the face of odds ... had said, 'No.'" In a battle between two black heavyweights, one black image triumphed. For young whites and many blacks, Ali was a folk hero who symbolized the cultural explosion of the 1960s and black vernacular culture with his verbal agility, poetry, and bragging. Playwright Clay Goss noted that blacks "recognize in Ali our own struggle for dignity, beauty and survival in a hostile America. He has been a mirror image of our own collective struggle for freedom and dignity in this racist-to-the bone, hypocritical country." Despite his flaws, Ali's victory over a flag-waving, silent Foreman vindicated black and white 1960s political and cultural dissent.[22]

While the victory confirmed Ali's place in boxing history and marked a triumphant exile's return, the bout dramatized the conflicting domestic and international forces in a global sporting spectacle. Under worldwide scrutiny, Ali challenged Cold War assumptions, embodied by Foreman, that America was an exceptional beacon of freedom regardless of race. Rather, this global event highlighted a 1960s counternarrative. While previous black artists and intellectuals had linked domestic racism to international imperialism, Ali brought these themes to global center stage. Anti-colonialism was a major current of the 1970s, and Ali was a hero of liberation abroad and de-colonization at home. This egalitarian attack on racial hierarchies continued the 1960s' thrust into the 1970s. Yet growing international egalitarianism merged with the triumph of market relations. Significantly, Zaire was a triumph for Don King, who became the first major black promoter in a white-run industry. The fight boosted his prestige among black heavyweights enthralled by his talk of black pride and giant purses. New black players entered boxing's business side, but as unbridled capitalists. Similarly, the bout helped legitimate Mobutu's dictatorship, which reaped the profits but oppressed the people. Despite the triumph of market forces, however, the fight's African setting encouraged blacks to identify with roots that lay outside American cultural ideals. Imperialism was dying, and in 1974 cultural de-colonization vied with market values for predominance.[23]

Although Ali remained champion through the late 1970s, his role as an oppositional hero waned after 1974. With the war over and President Nixon in disgrace, President Ford invited him to the White House as part of his reconciliation policy. Ali continued to fight abroad, but these international bouts featured more subdued rhetoric. "The Thrilla in Manila," his third match against Joe Frazier in 1975, for example, displayed less talk of war and black power, and more about personal pride and animosity. Plus, the general public was agog at Ali's personal life, mired in sexual scandal and eventual divorce, as it was revealed in Manila that Ali introduced nineteen-year-old model Veronica Porche as his wife while Khalilah remained at home. In an era of militant feminism, his reputation was somewhat tarnished when the public learned that the ascetic Muslim had had a string of "foxes" all along. His actions were part of the shift toward personal indulgence in the "Me Decade." While Ali continued to represent Islamic causes at home and abroad, the shift away from the Nation of Islam's racial separatism toward orthodox Islam after Elijah Muhammad's death softened Ali's anti-white rhetoric. Inside the ring, he fought all the top contenders, but his fights were less about politics and more about survival. In each succeeding fight, he stayed on the ropes more and took more punishment, surviving, as in the Jimmy Young and third Ken Norton matches with the help of favorable judging. By the time he lost and then regained the crown against the inexperienced Leon Spinks, the fire had gone out of the oppositional hero just as 1960s rebelliousness gave way to the demands of the market of the late 1970s.

NOTES

1 King quoted in "George Foreman vs Muhammad Ali," *Sportsworld*, September 1974, p. 11. For the international promotion see "The Cash," *Sportsworld*, September 1974, p. 10. Ali quoted in Dave Anderson, "Chant of the Holy War: Ali, Bomaye," *New York Times*, 28 October 1974, in Ali Vertical Files, Schomburg Center for Research in Black Culture, New York.

2 The theme of exile was suggested by Gerald Early, "Some Preposterous Propositions from the Heroic Life of Muhammad Ali: A Reading of 'The Greatest: My Own Story,'" in *Muhammad Ali, The People's Champ*, ed. Elliott Gorn (Urbana, IL: University of Illinois Press, 1995), 83–84. For Ali as a 1960s symbol, see Mike Marqusee, *Redemption Song: Muhammad Ali and the Spirit of the Sixties* (London: Verso, 1999), and Budd Schulberg, *Loser and Still Champion: Muhammad Ali* (Garden City, NY: Doubleday, 1972). For Ali and the athletic revolt of the 1960s, see Amy Bass, *Not the Triumph but the*

Struggle: The 1968 Olympics and the Making of the Black Athlete (Minneapolis, MN: University of Minnesota Press, 2002); Harry Edwards, *The Revolt of the Black Athlete* (New York: Free Press, 1969); Douglas Hartmann, *Race, Culture and the Revolt of the Black Athlete, the 1968 Olympic Protests and Their Aftermath* (Chicago, IL: University of Chicago Press, 2003); and Othello Harris, "Muhammad Ali and the Revolt of the Black Athlete," in *Muhammad Ali*, ed. Gorn, 54–69.

3 Michael Ezra, *Muhammad Ali, The Making of an Icon* (Philadelphia, PA: Temple University Press, 2009), 120–134; King quoted, 124.

4 Ali quoted in Mark Kram, *Ghosts of Manila: The Fateful Blood Feud Between Muhammad Ali and Joe Frazier* (New York: HarperCollins, 2001), 102; for more on the Quarry bout, see 99–104. "Ali Does It: Stages 8-Round Bout in Atlanta," *Jet*, 17 September 1970, p. 56.

5 Sugar quoted in Thomas Hauser, *Muhammad Ali: His Life and Times* (New York: Simon and Schuster), 1991, 210. The entire list is in "Mrs. Ali Misses Who's Who Celebrity Guests," *Jet*, 12 November 1970, p. 14. For the Nixon administration's persecution of black militants as equated with Ali's jail sentence as part of it, see John H. Britton, "Black Militants Showdown in Struggle to Avoid Prison," *Jet*, 16 January 1969, pp. 14–20.

6 For the victory over Quarry and Maddox, see Ronald E. Kisner, "Ali Quells Quarry on Maddox 'Day of Mourning' Before Capacity Crowd," *Jet*, 12 November 1970, pp. 51–56.

7 Kisner, "Ali Quells Quarry on Maddox 'Day of Mourning' Before Capacity Crowd." Abernathy quoted in "Purse for Bout above Estimate," *New York Times*, 28 October 1970, p. 37, as in Ezra, *Muhammad Ali*, 150. For Ali quote, see "The Black Scholar Interviews Muhammad Ali," June 1970, reprinted in *The Muhammad Ali Reader*, ed. Gerald Early (Hopewell, NJ: Ecco Press, 1998), 89. For Mrs. King quote, see Robert Lipsyte, "'I Don't Have to Be What You Want Me to Be,' Says Muhammad Ali," *New York Times Magazine*, 7 March 1971, reprinted in *The Muhammad Ali Reader*, 97.

8 "U. S. Judge Helps Flatten New York Boxing Body," *Jet*, 1 October 1970, p. 50. For racial overtones see Cordell S. Thompson, "Ali's Purse Put at $600,000; Looks to Frazier," *Jet*, 24 December 1970, pp. 52–54. Ezra, *Muhammad Ali*, 150–51.

9 Pacheco quoted in Hauser, *Muhammad Ali*, 216. For Ali's declining skills, see Thompson, "Ali's Purse Put at $600,000," *Jet*. For the 1970s theme of the survival, see William Graebner, "America's Poseidon Adventure, A Nation in Existential Despair," in *America in the Seventies*, Beth Bailey and David Farber, eds (Lawrence: University Press of Kansas), 157–80.

10 Lipsyte, "I Don't Have to Be," in Early, *The Muhammad Ali Reader*, 98–99. For "house nigger," see Schulberg, *Loser and Still Champion*, 106–07, 128. Gumbel quoted in Hauser, *Muhammad Ali*, 223–24.

11 For the first Ali–Frazier match, see Kram, *Ghosts of Manila*, 141–47. "And this One, Too," Letter to Editor, *The Ring*, July 1971, p. 32; Franklin Crandall, "How About This?" ibid., p. 32.

12 Gumbel quoted in Hauser, *Muhammad Ali*, 224–25. Ali's remembrance of the reaction by Qaddafi and the Islamic world is in Muhammad Ali with Richard Durham, *The Greatest* (New York: Ballantine Books, 1975), 249–51. For Black Nationalist quotes, see Ambalavaner Sivanandan, "On the Passing of the King,"

April 1971, reprinted in *A Different Hunger: Writings on the Black Resistance* (London: Pluto Press, 1982), 69. For an example of his resentment of this rhetoric, see Joe Frazier, "Cassius Who?" *Ebony*, May 1972, pp. 68–76.

13 For the Supreme Court decision, see Suzanne Freedman, *Clay* v. *United States, Muhammad Ali Objects to War* (Springfield, NJ: Enslow Publishers, 1997), 65–78.

14 For the widening of equality in the United States and around the globe, see Thomas Borstelmann, *The Seventies* (Princeton, NJ: Princeton University Press, 2012). For blackness as a resource to be claimed, see Eric Porter, "Affirming and Disaffirming Race," in Bailey and Farber, *America in the Seventies*, 54–55. King quoted in Ali, *The Greatest*, 452, and "The Amazing Saga of the New King of Boxing," *Sepia*, October 1975, pp. 26–33.

15 King in Leonard Gardner, "Stopover in Caracas," *Esquire*, October 1974, p. 310; Jack Newfield, *The Life and Crimes of Don King: The Shame of Boxing in America* (London, Virgin: 1966; reprint, ed., Sag Harbor, NY: Harbor Electronic Publishers, 2003), 70, 78–80.

16 For "Mummy," see Hauser, *Muhammad Ali*, 266. For Foreman as of an earlier era and a white hope, see Wells Twombly, "Champ," *New York Times Magazine*, 24 March 1974, n.p., George Foreman vertical file, Schomburg Center; Tim Tyler, "George Foreman: The Great White Hope," *Sport*, July 1973, pp. 79–80; 84–85. For Ali's quotes about Foreman, see Gardner, "Stopover in Caracas," p. 306; Ali, *The Greatest*, 489, 491. For goof, see George Foreman and Joe Engel, *By George, The Autobiography of George Foreman* (New York: Villard Books, 1995), 107–108. Ali on savages, Hauser, *Muhammad Ali*, 265.

17 Dave Anderson, *New York Times*, 27 October 1974, as in Hauser, *Muhammad Ali*, 260. Odds in Dave Anderson "Foreman 3-1 over Ali in Zaire Tonight," *New York Times*, 29 October 1974, p. 45. Ferdie Pacheco, *Fight Doctor* (New York, 1976), 128.

18 "Sly mouse" and "mummies" are in George Plimpton, "Breaking a Date for the Dance," *Sports Illustrated*, 11 November 1974, pp. 23–26; Foreman, *By George*, 110.

19 For "bee," see Dave Anderson, "Ali Regains Title, Flooring Foreman," *New York Times*, 30 October 1974, p. 93; for "robot," see "Violent Coronation in Kinshasa," *Time*, p. 100; for "matador," see "Muhammad on the Mountain Top," 11 November 1974, p. 85.

20 Charles Sanders, "Muhammad Ali Challenges Black Men," *Ebony*, January 1975, pp. 121–26.

21 Sanders, "Muhammad Ali Challenges," p.133; Olu Akaraogun, "The Meaning of Muhammad Ali for the Black World," *Indigo*, January 1975, pp. 60–64.

22 Quincy Troupe, "The Spiritual Victory of Muhammad Ali," *Black World*, January 1975, pp. 34–40; Clay Goss, "Ali as Creative Black Man," ibid., pp. 30–33.

23 For anti-colonialism and market values, see Borstelmann, *The Seventies*.

16

MICHAEL EZRA

The Unusable Champions: Sonny Liston (1962–1964) and Larry Holmes (1978–1985)

This chapter explores why Sonny Liston and Larry Holmes, two of the best-fighting heavyweight champions, have failed to make enduring impressions on popular culture commensurate with their peers. Hollywood has shown no interest in either man, and there are no books about Holmes, save his autobiography. The HBO documentary on Liston was as murky as the few other biographical inquiries into his life, combining hearsay, speculation, and rumor without shedding light on the important questions about his private life, mysterious death, exceedingly controversial fights with Muhammad Ali, and involvement with organized crime. Few traces of cultural evidence exist to suggest that many people care to make meaning of either man's story, even as boxing fans rate them all-time greats.

Rankings have always been important to the culture of boxing, not so much the official ones that determine who gets title shots, but the historical ones that fans have long used to compare fighters of different eras. Their significance emerges most powerfully through lists of the ten greatest heavyweight champions of all time. Fight fans have always been better prepared to produce such lists than to identify the division's current top ten. Although fictional and subjective and unknowable, it is a common discussion that is important to boxing fans. A short explanation of your particular choices can serve as your calling card.

These all-time heavyweight rankings reflect the values of the individuals and societies that produce them; they assess more than just boxing talent. Muhammad Ali and Joe Louis, in that order, are usually at the top. The enduring idolatry of Ali and Louis as historical figures has inspired an investment in their professional abilities that once did not exist, and their primacy is ensured as much by perceptions of their societal impact as their ring dominance. The 1970 motion picture *The Super Fight* had Rocky Marciano knocking out the prime Ali. Esteemed *The Ring* magazine founder Nat Fleischer never had Louis higher than sixth in his rankings. The Ali and Louis mythologies, for the time being, guarantee their status as leading men.

Few top-ten lists exclude Jack Johnson, Marciano, Jack Dempsey, George Foreman, Joe Frazier, Liston, or Holmes, but the latter pair has garnered the least media attention if the measures are things like biographies, motion pictures, ad campaigns, and documentaries. There are fewer attempts to make retrospective meaning of the lives of Holmes and Liston than any of the others. Lesser heavyweights, including Mike Tyson and Floyd Patterson, have also outshined Holmes and Liston as objects of sustained, if sporadic, media attention. Why have the stories of Holmes and Liston remained relatively resistant to reconsideration?

During their championship years Holmes and Liston often had an oppositional lean, not always by choice, and sometimes as dictated from the very highest levels of society. Presidential insult tarnished each man's crowning moment. John F. Kennedy urged Patterson to deny Liston a title shot, even though Sonny had been waiting for years as the world's best heavyweight. Gerry Cooney's dressing room had a phone line installed for Ronald Reagan to call if he were to beat Holmes in their match. Holmes had no such setup, despite three years as champion and the win over Cooney being his twelfth title defense and eleventh by knockout. Two months earlier, Reagan had waived the military requirement so that Louis could be buried in Arlington National Cemetery. After Ali beat Foreman to regain the belt, Gerald Ford invited him to the White House. Decades later, George W. Bush awarded Ali the Presidential Medal of Freedom. During the Second World War, Franklin D. Roosevelt told champion Louis, "Joe, we need muscles like yours to beat Germany." Such stories highlight the low regard for Liston and Holmes, especially in comparison to Ali and Louis.

Liston was not destined for cultural obscurity. Highly scrutinized in his prime, he was cast as a mysterious and intimidating figure, thought to be one of the best fighters who ever lived, but also the worst man that black America could possibly offer for the job of heavyweight champion. There was limited public sympathy for him despite his cruelly impoverished upbringing. As his career wound down, however, Liston recovered from the shame of the Ali fights and his resulting banishment from US rings, recapturing a degree of renown with a series of wins and by using his loathsome persona ironically for comedic intent (for example, in a television commercial with Andy Warhol). Had he not died prematurely and on such unseemly terms, Liston might have enjoyed the opportunity for benign reincarnation like Tyson. Since his death, though, we have gotten little closer to deconstructing the meaning of Liston's life.

Whether Liston craved mainstream respect is a point of contention, but his attempts to get it usually floundered. Merely to be allowed to fight for the title, Liston had to go through all sorts of shenanigans involving relocations, rehabilitations, and priests, none of which were convincing. Without all these procedures that signified redemption and clean living, Liston couldn't get state athletic commissions to license him, nor convince champion Floyd Patterson (whose angelic public persona was the product of his own redemption story, well-marketed as *Victory over Myself*) to give him a title shot. His devastating knockout record played into his brutish persona, and it took a fall from grace as radical as the Ali fights to shatter his aura of invincibility and make Liston usable as the man you saw sitting next to Warhol on the airplane.

It has long been clear that Larry Holmes will never capture the public imagination. Stalwart fan indifference marked his long and impressive title reign, even though Holmes was strongly suited to his time period as a Reagan-era capitalist whose earnings in boxing became the basis for a more diversified financial portfolio. Holmes always said that it was all about the money, and as an "up by the bootstraps" black man from meager origins who never left his hometown of Easton, Pennsylvania, was a good enough symbolic representative of his championship years, though Cooney's whiteness was to most Americans more emblematic than anything Holmes could ever muster. Even at the peak of his career, when he wanted desperately to be one, Holmes was no celebrity. In his biggest bouts, it was his opponents Ali and Cooney who were responsible for the blockbuster gates. And though the heavyweight champion is usually boxing's most bankable star, it was during the Holmes era that fighters from the lighter weights became the sport's richest draws. Since his retirement, boxing fans have warmed to Holmes as an all-time great, but there has been hardly any popular cultural interest in reexamining his meaning.

Holmes wanted mass regard even though he bobbled some of his best chances to cultivate it. The Ali and Cooney fights notwithstanding, in which he fought well on the sport's biggest stage, Holmes could not emerge from the shadows of the past, tainted as Ali's former sparring partner. Holmes may have hastened his journey to cultural obscurity with his gracelessness following a controversial loss to Michael Spinks, which prevented Holmes from breaking Marciano's undefeated record streak. "Rocky Marciano couldn't carry my jockstrap," was one of the few things that Holmes could have said – even if it were true – that for many would turn him from the sympathetic figure of a great champion, who suffered a controversial decision loss that denied him a hallowed record, into a boor.

Can we blame someone for missing a moment in history when his professional excellence would tap into the political or cultural zeitgeist and become the basis for iconic status? Liston contended for the title as an ex-con when African American respectability was a key undercurrent to civil rights assertiveness, and champion Patterson was more than enough role model for the nation's youth. Holmes faced white hope Cooney only months after Reagan won a landslide victory in a racially polarizing campaign in which millions of white Democrats shifted their votes. Both Holmes and Liston won their biggest fights easily and impressively, but the national climate perhaps resisted heroic exploitation. This would not be a first. In perhaps the biggest boxing match in history, and despite an extraordinary performance, Joe Frazier somehow came out diminished as a result of his 1971 victory over Muhammad Ali, written off by the likes of Bryant Gumbel as a white man's champion.

Liston and Holmes had the misfortune of bracketing Ali's championship years, and Ali's legacy overshadowed both men's careers; they were dwarfed by the magnitude of his celebrity. And few fighters, including Foreman, came out more heroic as a result of their tussles with Ali. Our failure to understand Ali increases the difficulty of making meaning of Liston and Holmes. The public clearly has no idea who Ali was, as evidenced by its widespread belief in a sanctified rendition of the man that doesn't even come close to the real deal. Despite the formidable, decades-long literary and media interest surrounding Ali, there is still no biography of him that comes close to hitting the target, and probably never will be. The betting odds of Ali's bouts with Liston and Holmes show just how mistaken people can be. Although humiliated by Ali in their first bout, Liston was still favored in the rematch, a fight he seems to have thrown. And although smart money knew that Ali would lose badly to Holmes, it was the ex-champ who was favored in their match.

Unlike some of their peers who are regarded as top-ten material, including Frazier, Marciano, and Foreman, there is no questioning the quality of Liston's or Holmes's accomplishments. Until the Ali debacles, many thought Liston to be the greatest heavyweight who ever lived. He was the best in his division for at least three years prior to getting a title shot, and his decisive victories over contenders Mike DeJohn, Cleveland Williams, Nino Valdes, Zora Folley, and Eddie Machen – all of whom champion Patterson refused to face – should be seen as nothing less than title defenses. The prime Ali defended the crown against Patterson, Williams, and Folley years after Liston had wrecked them. Holmes racked up a championship streak surpassing in quality even that of Joe Louis. Throughout his long reign he withstood challenges time and again from younger, hungry, talented fighters like "Terrible" Tim Witherspoon, James "Bonecrusher" Smith, Carl "The Truth" Williams, Renaldo "Mister" Snipes, and Cooney, all of whom would beat the average Bum of the Month.

Their accomplishments while at their peaks notwithstanding, something truly notable about both Liston and Holmes is that they remained dangerous opponents for a long time after their primes, which is when the all-time greats redefine the scope of their genius. Henry Clark and Ray Mercer would learn this the hard way. Liston's post-title reign of terror was especially brutal. Fifteen wins in sixteen fights, all but one by knockout, against solid opposition. Holmes's only losses in his fifteen-plus post-championship years were in title fights, and during that period he beat twenty-one fighters with winning records, making many of them look amateurish.

It was not a foregone conclusion, therefore, that neither Holmes nor Liston would catch on long term. It's not that either man lacked completely in charm or personality or charisma, and even if that were the case you'd somehow have to explain the enduring interest in the flinty Marciano, who could be quite disagreeable. Both Liston and Holmes have in-ring résumés that surpass those of most of their peers. Both men's stories were enough in touch with the times to be turned potentially into heroic meaning, either mainstream or oppositional. That they bookended Ali is not the explanation, because Foreman emerged from Ali's specter to become a mass-media icon. And it's not that each man was ruined by any single particular failure to give people what they wanted at opportune moments. It was not Liston's response, "I ain't got no dog-proof ass," when asked why he didn't participate, like Floyd Patterson had, in civil rights marches. It was not Holmes's dismissiveness toward Marciano's legend. Neither of those faux pas was as bad, for example, as Jack Dempsey's wearing patent-leather shoes in a photo depicting him doing supposed war service. Nor were they as scandalous to as many people as what Jack Johnson did on a daily basis. Mike Tyson is a convicted rapist who went on to have a one-man show on Broadway and HBO, and an animated television show in his name. So why have Liston and Holmes been so resistant to reconsideration, much less heroic iconography or hagiography?

There are many differences between their stories, of course, but one common aspect of Liston's and Holmes's failures to become folk heroes was their conscious resistance to the clear public expectations that called upon African American heavyweight champions of any significance to embody a tangible vision of what it meant to be black that either challenged or reinforced the public's racial consciousness. Liston and Holmes steadfastly refused to impress upon the public a sense of their racial politics during a long period of history when the only way most people understood how to make meaning of an African American heavyweight champion was through the lens of race. Holmes and Liston neither defied nor satisfied these cultural expectations. You never really knew whether or not Holmes and Liston cared about being loved or hated by the public, white or black. At times they were accommodating, at others they were oppositional. They neither materially resisted nor symbolically endorsed the American racial order and could neither be called race men nor sellouts. Their inability to be categorized, symbolically or otherwise, as either integrationists or racial militants rendered them less usable than their peers. Operating in today's climate, however, Liston or Holmes might have avoided this fate, like Tyson has.

Being a race man is a chancy play in today's sports world, as Colin Kaepernick's case proves. The safest way to go for an African American athlete that wants to achieve iconic status, whether in boxing or any other sport, is to refuse serious engagement with black identity. Think Michael Jordan, Tiger Woods, and LeBron James. Race as a political consideration has rarely, if ever, been even a minor or implicit subplot in their celebrity narratives. Floyd Mayweather publicly references his black identity from time to time, but only as a bargaining chip for personal enrichment and almost always in ridiculous fashion, like in the buildup to his bout with Conor McGregor or when he compared his stance on drug testing to the work of Malcolm X and Martin Luther King, Jr. Liston, therefore, might have been marketable today, now that an African American heavyweight champion no longer has to consciously and publicly grapple with his meaning for being black on this earth if he is to reach the heights of commercial relevance. But in his day the lack of consideration was inexcusable, and the legacy of this has impeded his status. Holmes, too, would have been better off now, without having to define himself beyond craftsmanship and consistency, which were always his greatest strengths, but back then those things didn't speak loudly enough to elevate an African American heavyweight champion to hero status.

17

MARK SCOTT

Emile Griffith: An Underrated Champion

On a summer's day in 1973, in Monaco, a thirty-five-year-old man, balding and with a squat build, was the opponent for Carlos Monzon, the glamorous world middleweight champion. Monzon was considered by many to be the best "pound-for-pound" fighter in the world at that time and was rivalled only by Sugar Ray Robinson for the claim of the greatest middleweight boxer of all time. Yet his opponent in Monaco, half a foot shorter, was not tiring as the fight progressed and was not taking the usual beating that Monzon meted out to his opponents. In the exchanges, Emile Griffith, the challenger, was landing the cleaner blows and even staggering the great Monzon, time and again. Who was this aging fighter who refused to follow the script and appeared on the verge of dethroning the supposedly unbeatable middleweight champion?

Emile Griffith was one of the greatest fighters of all time, a five-time champion at welterweight and middleweight, whose accomplishments were nearly eclipsed by what happened during twenty seconds of a televised bout in 1962. That night, in New York, world welterweight champion Benny "The Kid" Paret and the challenger Griffith were fighting fairly evenly when midway through the twelfth round the announcer Don Dunphy said, "This is probably the tamest round of the entire fight." Twenty seconds later, Paret was knocked out on the canvas, never to regain consciousness. During those twenty seconds, Griffith threw a barrage of punches after hurting Paret with a right cross. That barrage of punches, the kind that boxers are routinely trained to use in order to end a bout, would haunt Griffith for the rest of his life. And yet between his first Paret fight and the Monzon fight in Monaco, Griffith fought in twenty-two world title fights and defeated such great boxers as Luis Rodriguez, Dick Tiger, Nino Benvenuti, Bennie Briscoe, and numerous others. Emile Griffith holds the record for boxing the most title-fight rounds, 339.

One boxing writer[1] rated Griffith the best fighter of the 1960s, based on his overall record and particularly the world-class opponents he faced at welterweight and middleweight. Griffith, however, is rarely placed near the top of any lists of all-time greats of either division.

When Emile Griffith came to the United States in the 1950s as a teenager, he would have seemed the least likely of that era's immigrant boxers to become the best fighter of the next decade. He was working in a boutique, arranging flowers, when a local ex-boxer noted his powerful physique and invited him to a local boxing gym. Griffith proved to be a natural fighter and won the Golden Gloves, and then turned pro.

Many of the greatest boxers of all time were consummate artists, such as Sugar Ray Robinson and Muhammad Ali. Such fighters made for good matches against street toughs of the Jake LaMotta or Sonny Liston type. Griffith fit the artist mold much more than the stone-cold killer image of a Liston or Carlos Monzon, both of whose legacies were tarnished by violence outside of the ring. Griffith was a clever boxer and, before the Benny Paret tragedy, threw knockout blows with either hand. In the first Paret fight, which took place on April 1, 1961, Griffith knocked his opponent cold with one perfect left hook, as graceful as the arc of a dolphin over the ocean waves.

The circumstances surrounding the third Griffith–Paret fight, and Paret's death as a result of the bout, were the subjects of a feature-length documentary, *Ring of Fire*. Paret had made insulting remarks about Griffith's sexual preferences and then took a beating in the ring that was seemingly the cause of his death. However, Paret had taken a horrible beating in his previous fight against Gene Fullmer, a full-fledged middleweight who had twice defeated Sugar Ray Robinson, considered by many boxing experts the greatest boxer who ever lived.

Griffith, it should be noted, did not hit Paret when he was down, during a break, or in any way commit a violation of the rules of boxing. In the heat of battle with a world title at stake, he did what a boxer is trained to do. Paret got caught in the ropes and thus did not fall as he would have done in ring center. But during the twenty seconds between when Don Dunphy declared that the twelfth was "probably the tamest round of the entire fight," and when the referee stopped the bout, Griffith had no way of knowing that Paret was at death's doorstep.

The aftermath of the Paret fight nearly caused the banning of boxing in America. Photos of Paret were grim, and the press had a feeding frenzy showing them over and over. Griffith fell into a depression and only emerged gradually.

Griffith's legendary trainer Gil Clancy was interviewed for the 2005 documentary *Ring of Fire*. Clancy had told Griffith during all three Paret fights that he needed to be more aggressive, and that if he hurt Paret he should keep punching until the referee intervened or Paret fell. This was sound advice given that Griffith had lost a disputed decision in the second Paret fight on September 30, 1961.

A year after Paret's death the featherweight champion Davey Moore died from brain injuries after losing his title to Sugar Ramos on national television. Boxing fell into the doldrums; and public pressure to abolish the sport may have grown insurmountable if not for the arrival upon the scene of Muhammad Ali, then known as Cassius Clay.

Griffith persevered, however. In his next few fights he fought tentatively, but he did keep winning. He always carried himself with class and dignity. According to Jose Torres in *Ring of Fire*, the boxing community thought that Griffith was gay. Griffith was quoted in *Sports Illustrated* as saying that he "like[d] both men and women," but preferred women. He was married in 1971 to a female dancer, Mercedes Donastorg. They had no children, but Griffith adopted Donastorg's daughter. Griffith never seemed to make a spectacle of his personal life, and in any case his ring career was a huge credit to any group he may have represented.

In 1963 Griffith successfully defended his welterweight championship several times. He lost by a knockout to the hard-hitting Ruben "Hurricane" Carter. Carter would later spend two decades in prison on a murder conviction that was eventually overturned. Other than the Paret tragedy, Griffith is perhaps best known for this loss, because of the media attention paid to the life of Hurricane Carter. Griffith's loss is the opening scene of the movie, *The Hurricane*, in which Denzel Washington played the title character.

Griffith came back from the loss, and in fact was named as *The Ring*'s Fighter of the Year in 1964. There was not an ounce of quitter in Emile Griffith. He kept fighting and beating the best boxers of his era. In 1966 Griffith fought and beat fellow Hall-of-Famer Dick Tiger to win the world middleweight championship. A year later he lost the title in a very close bout against Hall-of-Famer Nino Benvenuti in *The Ring*'s Fight of the Year. Griffith won their rematch and then lost their third bout, again in a very close fight. The third Benvenuti bout marked the end of Griffith's time as a world champion.

Griffith kept fighting at a world-class level. After the Paret fight, Griffith lost his instinct for finishing off an opponent, and scored very few knockouts. At 5' 7", he became a rarity in that he was a master ring technician who would consistently outbox taller opponents. If there had been a well-established junior middleweight division in Griffith's time, he probably would have dominated that division.

In 1973, at the age of thirty-five, he gave Carlos Monzon the fight of his life in a bout that many thought Griffith won. Carlos Monzon dominated middleweight boxing in the 1970s, in a way more so than Muhammad Ali dominated the heavyweights, or Roberto Duran dominated the lightweight division. Both Ali and Duran lost during that period, while Monzon never did. Monzon had "matinee idol" looks and was in fact a movie star, appearing in such films as the 1977 Spaghetti Western *El Macho*. His bouts were held in such glamorous locales as Paris, Buenos Aires, and Monaco. When Monzon fought Griffith in 1973, Monzon was in his prime at age thirty. Celebrities such as former Miss America Phyllis George, various rock stars, and Hollywood stars could always be found in the front rows of Monzon's fights. His star power among boxers was eclipsed only by that of Muhammad Ali. Monzon had twice battered Nino Benvenuti into defeat. Benvenuti had been named the best boxer of the 1960s Olympiad, selected over the light-heavyweight tournament winner Muhammad Ali, then known as Cassius Clay. Monzon had the height, reach, and power to destroy the contenders he faced. He was also a master of defense who rarely took a solid punch. Against the older Griffith in their 1973 fight in Monaco, however, Monzon looked confused at times and was hurt on several occasions during the latter rounds. Film of the fight shows that Monzon, a head taller, never dominated Griffith as he routinely did with his other opponents. The second Monzon–Griffith fight in 1973 was extremely close and hard to score. Griffith slipped most of Monzon's punches, but had difficulty getting inside his long arms. Griffith staggered Monzon in round eight, and Monzon's head was snapped back with regularity. Griffith had a great sense of distance, which enabled him to out jab Monzon throughout the fight. From the film footage, most of the rounds are too close to score. In the rounds that Griffith wins, he rocks Monzon with power shots. The rounds that Monzon wins are close and he wins because of his jab and his reach. Griffith clearly wins five rounds, while Monzon clearly wins three of the first four rounds when Griffith can't get inside. The rest of the rounds are too close to call with any certitude. Monzon was given a close decision. After the bout, Griffith's trainer, Gil Clancy, discussed filing a protest over the decision, but nothing came of it. Griffith fought on for a few more years, losing several close decisions in world title fights. An outstanding boxer, Griffith never had the instinct for knocking his opponent out after the Paret tragedy.

In 1976 Emile Griffith was a last-minute replacement for Sugar Ray Seales, the only American to win a gold medal in boxing during the 1972 Olympic Games, in a world title fight against Eckhardt Dagge, on Dagge's home turf in Germany. The bout was for the world light-middleweight championship. Griffith, nearly forty years old at the time, lost a close split decision in a fight where many thought Dagge had received a "home country" gift decision.

For most of Griffith's career, the light middleweight division was not broadly recognized. If it had been, Griffith probably would have had a long and prosperous reign, as 154 pounds was his best fighting weight. Throughout his career, he had trouble making the welterweight limit of 147 pounds and often had difficulty with the taller middleweights at 160 pounds. He could have been rated as the all-time greatest light-middleweight if the division had been widely recognized one or two decades before it became a money-making division, as it is today.

In his later years Griffith trained boxers. His Caribbean voice can be heard in the corners of fighters such as Juan Laporte in his bout against the great Julio Caesar Chavez, a fight that Laporte came very close to winning in a junior-lightweight bout. Another tragedy befell Griffith when he was assaulted one night in New York by a gang when Griffith had been drinking and could not properly defend himself. He suffered some degree of brain damage from this incident.

A 2005 documentary, *Ring of Fire,* about Griffith's tragic bout with Paret featured a poignant meeting between Griffith and Paret's grown son. In Griffith's final years the author of this chapter met Griffith at the International Boxing Hall of Fame in Canastota, New York. He had recovered, though not entirely, from his brain injuries and could converse well enough for a former world class fighter in his seventies, who had endured more rounds of championship boxing than any fighter in history. Like a veteran warrior who has seen death in combat, Griffith didn't want to talk about his twenty years of ring wars, much less brag about his long and dominant boxing career. He was like the happy Warrior in the William Wordsworth poem, "in confidence of Heaven's applause," content to be among boxing fans who accepted him for the champion he was.

Emile Griffith died of kidney failure on July 23, 2013, a man of peaceful nature who made his way in a violent world.

Bouts Described Above

Emile Griffith vs Carlos Monzon, June 2, 1973, Stade Louis II, Monte Carlo, Monaco.

Emile Griffith vs Benny Kid Paret, March 24, 1962, Madison Square Garden, New York, NY.

NOTE

1 Bivins, Ryan. "10 Reasons Why Emile Griffith Is One of the Best to Ever Lace Gloves," *Bad Left Hook,* July 24, 2013. www.badlefthook.com/2013/7/24/4552 260/10-reasons-why-emile-griffith-is-one-of-the-best-to-ever-lace-gloves

18

ADAM CHILL

Pierce Egan, Boxing, and British Nationalism

Pierce Egan was the most important chronicler of boxing in its early nineteenth-century golden age. Much of what we know about famous boxers of that era – fighters such as Jem Belcher, Tom Cribb, Tom Molineaux, Jack Langan, and Tom Spring – can be traced to Egan's original work. Moreover, beyond his role as boxing's most widely read reporter, Egan was a tireless and bombastic promoter of the sport. The claim that boxing was indicative of British national greatness was a recurring theme in his writing. Despite such nationalist bluster, however, he was sympathetic to the many Irish boxers who participated in the sport – so much so that his biographer argued that he was "exceptionally partial to Irish boxers."[1] While this is certainly an exaggeration, Egan nevertheless suggested throughout his work that Irish boxers could and did demonstrate the heroism that he claimed buoyed the British nation. In this way, his writing on boxing constructed an idea of Britishness that included Irish men.

The fact that Egan was himself Irish seems to have been the chief basis for his critics' claim that he was unfairly sympathetic to Irish boxers. He descended from a prominent Anglican family from County Cork in Ireland – his grandfather was the Vicar of Templeodane, and his uncle John "Bully" Egan was a prominent barrister and chairman (or lord) of the Manor of Kilmainham. The same uncle was also a member of the Irish House of Commons and a fierce opponent of the Union of Great Britain and Ireland that passed in 1800.[2] Pierce was likely born in Ireland in 1774. His father, for reasons that are unclear, moved his family to London and took work as a laborer when Pierce was very young. At the age of twelve or thirteen, the boy became a printer's apprentice. From there he gradually moved into writing, serving as a parliamentary reporter as a young man.[3]

Egan's development as a writer coincided with the rise of boxing, which was becoming increasingly popular in the first decade of the nineteenth century. Being a parliamentary reporter, he may have heard William Windham – a disciple of Edmund Burke and one of the most respected orators of his time – defend "manly, athletic exercises" such as boxing against the attacks of moral reformers. In a speech in the House of Commons in April 1800, Windham claimed that the "sports of a people went a great way to form their national character."[4]

Around the time of Windham's speech, Egan went to work for Joseph and George Smeeton, prominent printers and engravers of materials related to sport. During this period he also gained a minor reputation as a "racy reporter," writing about the scandals and pastimes of aristocrats, including boxing.[5] While spectatorship at boxing matches had been an almost exclusively aristocratic preserve in the late eighteenth century, just a few decades later boxing matches attracted a much broader audience and many more Britons than before were interested in reading about the sport. In 1810 and 1811, British boxer Tom Cribb fought African American immigrant (and ex-slave) Tom Molineaux in two of the most celebrated bouts of the early nineteenth century. The popularity of these fights raised the profile of the sport; some weekly newspapers began to devote a page to boxing news, and the biggest fights drew more than 10,000 spectators. In order to take advantage of this new market, George Smeeton turned to Egan, who was already well acquainted with the sport, to write a history of boxing. The work Egan produced was called *Boxiana*.

The publication of *Boxiana* brought Egan immediate notoriety. Although he had written it anonymously, readers quickly discovered his identity, and the success of this work cemented Egan's reputation as the premier reporter of boxing. Indeed, he ultimately published five volumes over a seventeen-year period, between 1812 and 1829. His evocative style, reproducing the slang of the boxing community, made the books immensely popular. They sold thousands of copies and became an "indispensable part of a sporting gentleman's library."[6] *Boxiana* was also popular because Egan laced it with heavy doses of British nationalism, arguing that British strength derived from the courage and fortitude naturally possessed by its men. Effeminacy, which he equated with political radicalism and continental Europeans, threatened to erode this natural manliness. In the introduction to his third volume, for example, Egan argued that boxing "teaches men to admire true courage" and "to despise a coward." The success of the sport in Britain, he claimed, "makes a man feel proud that he belongs to such a nation."[7] In the fifth and final volume, he argued that boxing was "truly NATIONAL, and ... completely interwoven with the ... prosperity of the British Nation."[8]

Even as Egan and other lesser-known journalists rhapsodized about the national importance of boxing, Irish pugilists played a crucial role in the sport, often as foils for English boxers. As early as 1742, London fighter John Francis published a challenge to Irish boxer Patrick Henley, noting that

Francis was not "ashamed to mount the stage when my manhood is called into question by an Irish Braggadocia."[9] In July 1800, as the Act of Union worked its way through the British Parliament, Irish boxer Andrew Gamble fought a match against English soldier Noah Jones. The *Whitehall Evening Post* noted that the match would "ascertain whether England or Ireland be the most capable of supplying, at this time, the best pugilist!"[10] After defeating Jones, Gamble fought English champion Jem Belcher. *The Times* reported that Irish sedan-chair drivers "call it the *Union-battle*."[11] Nervous British authorities reportedly made some military preparations in the event of an insurrection.[12] By 1824, when Dublin-born Jack Langan fought the Bristol boxer Tom Spring for the championship, the characterization of a match as a battle between England and Ireland was a familiar theme. The newspaper *Bell's Life in London* claimed that the match would "decide to whom the enviable distinction of 'Champion of England,' and of 'Ireland,' was to belong."[13]

One would expect that this large Irish presence in boxing and the nationalist overtones of their matches with English boxers would lead Pierce Egan – with his penchant for enthusing about the British nation – to dismiss or be hostile to Irish boxers. The two islands had long had a troubled relationship, one that was recently punctuated by the bloody 1798 rebellion and the subsequent Act of Union, which was meant to put a permanent end to Irish rebelliousness. Egan, however, argued that Irish boxers exhibited the qualities of British men. He claimed, for example, that eighteenth-century Irish boxer Peter Corcoran possessed "bottom [stamina and courage] which could not be excelled." Similarly, he described Michael Ryan, who twice fought for the championship in the 1780s, as "manly" and noted that his "courage kept pace with his science." The match between Andrew Gamble and Noah Jones in the summer of 1800 was "contested with the most determined resolution and heroic firmness."[14] He even claimed (erroneously) that Irish boxer Dan Donnelly was knighted by the Prince Regent in 1819.

Egan's most clear association of the manly British values of boxing with an Irish fighter came in his description of Jack Langan's life. Egan's short biography, written on the occasion of Langan's championship match with Englishman Tom Spring, highlighted Langan's manly heroism. Early in the account, Egan described an incident that occurred when Langan served with the merchant marine in Portugal in which Egan claimed that two stiletto-wielding Portuguese attacked Langan. According to Egan, Langan's "courage ... did not desert him for an instant, although he was attacked in such an assassin-like manner" and he ultimately "made the cowards run before him."[15] The contrast between cowardly, knife-wielding continental Europeans and sturdy, courageous British men was an image frequently used during and after the Napoleonic wars. Later, Egan described Langan's journey to South America in 1817 to aid rebel forces in their fight against Spain. Once there, Langan and his comrades found themselves trapped with no food and so, to prevent starvation, he and two others snuck into a village to procure a pig. The noise made by the captured pig aroused the residents of the neighborhood, who came out to confront the thieves. Langan's two companions fled but, as Egan put it, "*Running away* from the scene of action was so contrary to the feelings of our hero" that he did not follow. Instead he hid in a thicket while his pursuers thrust bayonets into the brush. One of these blows plunged into Langan's thigh. At this point, Egan asked his readers to "[j]udge of the feelings of Langan." His "*game* was put to the test. To *cry* out would have cost him his life." Of course, the courageous Langan managed to keep quiet and eventually hobbled back to join the rest of the crew.[16] In this description, as in the rest of the account, Langan demonstrated the core values of Britishness so prized by Egan.

Not all journalists agreed that Irish boxers were exemplars of Britishness. Although he made similar arguments to Egan's about the importance of boxing to the British nation, John Badcock, one of Egan's main writing rivals in the 1810s and 1820s, frequently ridiculed Irish pugilists. After recounting Tom Belcher's victory over Irish boxer Jack O'Donnell in the first volume of his boxing compendium, Badcock sarcastically remarked that O'Donnell was "christened by his countrymen, as usual, 'Irish hero.' " When describing O'Donnell's fall from grace in a cheating scandal, he triumphantly noted: "so much for *heroism*, and the *respectable* eulogy of Jack's veracious countrymen." Badcock also ridiculed Irish national aspirations, writing that Irish boxer Dan Dogherty chose to face Tom Belcher "*on national grounds* – or rather we might say *provincial*, for Ireland is but a component part of the Empire, let her warm-headed sons say what they will." Badcock mocked Egan's claim that Donnelly was knighted as well. He hoped that, if the knighthood had in fact occurred, "no improper person shall be admitted to the honour of knighthood" in the future.[17]

Badcock's sarcastic dismissal of Irish boxers puts Egan's celebration of them in sharp relief. Early boxing journalism was a font of British nationalism and many British nationalists, especially in the wake of the French-inspired 1798 rebellion, characterized the Irish as, at best, ignorant yokels and, at worst, treacherous enemies within. Egan, however, believed not only that the Irish could be loyal subjects but that Irish men, as much as English men, represented the qualities that made Britain great. Some scholars have noticed Egan's ardent British nationalism while others have highlighted his sympathies for Irish boxers. The dismal history of the union between Ireland and Britain makes these two positions seem antithetical, but Egan's work reminds us that, in the early nineteenth century at least, a union of equals could still be imagined.

NOTES

1 J.C. Reid, *Bucks and Bruisers: Pierce Egan and Regency England* (London: Routledge & Kegan Paul, 1971), 4.

2 Charles Phillips, esq., *Recollections of Curran and Some of his Contemporaries* (London: T. Hookham, Jun., 1818), 95.

3 The account of Egan's ancestry and early life comes from Reid, *Bucks and Bruisers*, 2–6.

4 *Sporting Magazine* 26, no. 1 (April 1800), 35.

5 Dennis Brailsford, "Egan, Pierce (1772–1849)," in *Oxford Dictionary of National Biography*, ed. H. C. G. Matthew and Brian Harrison (Oxford: Oxford University Press, 2004), accessed February 26, 2014, www.oxforddnb.com/view/article/8577.

6 Reid, *Bucks and Bruisers*, 2.

7 Pierce Egan, *Boxiana; or, Sketches of Ancient and Modern Pugilism: from the days of the renowned Broughton and Slack to the heroes of the present milling era*, vol. 3 (London: Sherwood, Neely, and Jones, 1821), 4.

8 Pierce Egan, *Boxiana; or Sketches of Ancient and Modern Pugilism*, vol. 5 (London: George Virtue, 1829), iv.

9 Challenge from John Francis printed in an advertisement for George Taylor's Theater, May 4, 1742. Reprinted in *Sporting Magazine,* 1, no. 2 (November 1792), 79.

10 *Whitehall Evening Post*, July 3, 1800.

11 *Times*, December 27, 1800.

12 *Morning Post and Gazetteer*, December 23, 1800.

13 *Bell's Life in London*, January 11, 1824.

14 [Pierce Egan], *Boxiana; or Sketches of Ancient and Modern Pugilism, by one of the Fancy*, vol. 1 (London: G. Smeeton, 1812), 84, 225, 241.

15 Pierce Egan, *Boxiana; or Sketches of Ancient and Modern Pugilism*, vol. 4 (London: George Virtue, 1828), 337.

16 Egan does not mention whether Langan's assailant noticed any blood on his bayonet. *Weekly Dispatch*, January 11, 1824.

17 [John Badcock], *The Fancy, or, True Sportsman's Guide: Being Authentic Memoirs of the Lives, Actions, Prowess, and Battles of the Leading Pugilists, from the Days of Figg and Broughton to the Championship of Ward*, vol. 1 (London: J. McGowan and Son, 1826), 74, 300, 325–26.

19

ADEYINKA MAKINDE

Jose Torres: The Boxer as Writer

Figures from the field of literature have long strived to make sense of the boxer's world, by penetrating his mind, reflecting his feelings and interpreting his environment. But if seminal works such as William Hazlitt's 1822 essay "The Fight" and Norman Mailer's 1975 book *The Fight*, are laudatory explorations by the writer-enthusiast aimed at achieving these ends, they both have the common shortcoming of having not emanated from the pen of a pugilist.

What, then, to give for a boxer who could lucidly and compellingly articulate the proceeds of the examination of his own psychological inclinations within the perimeters of the ring as well as outside of it?

What also to give for such a figure acting as a non-combatant observer whose experiences in the challenging environment of boxing could be utilized to give an insider's perspective of the action of boxing and the outside forces that shape a fighter?

Jose Luis Torres, a Puerto Rican-born light heavyweight champion of the world, was such a man. Indeed, he was much more.

Often referred to as "boxing's renaissance man," Torres not only wrote books and newspaper articles, he once served as the boxing commissioner for the state of New York. He was a social activist who, though remaining proud of his Puerto Rican heritage, was imbued with a humanistic outlook that influenced his decision to befriend and serve as an advisor to arguably the last American presidential candidate to embrace the politics of idealism: Robert F. Kennedy.

He was a raconteur par excellence, often sought out by producers as a talking head on matters concerning boxing. He lectured before hundreds, sometimes thousands. He even proved that he could sing and hold a tune before a nationwide television audience on *The Ed Sullivan Show*.[1]

This was not the trajectory expected to be taken by a boxer who typically, as the story goes, did not complete his high school education. Observing him closely for *Sport* magazine in 1965, soon after he had dethroned Willie

Pestrano to become the first Latino world champion among the light heavies, Leonard Schecter described Torres's English as "poor and slurred," adding that he "is difficult to understand."[2]

But Torres was, as Schecter acknowledged, a bright spark. Those who knew him instinctively sensed his intellectual curiosity. And those who would speak to him as a coming-through-the ranks contender, then as a champion and as a retired fighter, were struck by his warm-heartedness, his enthusiasm for life, as well as the authority and the conviction with which he conveyed his words when speaking about the things in which he believed.

He was born on May 3, 1936, in Playa Ponce. It was an atypically large Puerto Rican family of seven, with Jose the second-born son, known from childhood to the hereafter by his nickname, "Chegui."

He discovered boxing while serving in the army, the decision to enlist in 1954 having been one that he admitted was based on a desire to "look important and sophisticated." The way Torres told it, he settled for boxing in the army's special services unit because his first choices, track and field, basketball, and baseball, had finished their seasons.[3]

That he had enjoyed engaging in childhood fisticuffs was the deciding factor in recommending himself to the sport. Commencing his amateur career as a welterweight, his first victories were knockouts, which appeared to him to have been rooted primarily in an instinctual ability at delivering concussive blows. But it was in competing with a formidably powerful and skilful opponent in Panama that Torres learned a lifelong-held truth that the difference between winning and losing is "in the brain and not in the fist."[4]

After the bout, which Torres recalled as being for the "Caribbean Championship," the army sent him first to Fort Dix in New York and then to Fort Mead in Maryland. It was in Maryland that he met Pat Nappi, a Syracruse-based trainer who coached Olympic-aspirant fighters. Nappy saw much potential in Torres and began devoting a lot of his time and effort on his development.

Torres's confidence was bolstered when he beat a Pan-American champion in only his ninth bout. His underlying self-belief and developing understanding of the fighter's need to blend the twin requirements of mental agility and physical prowess was consolidated when he beat an opponent named Ed Crook in the All Army Championship.

This bout was pivotal because Torres, for the first time, consciously assessed the strengths and weaknesses of an opponent in order to map out a strategy for victory. The maxim of boxing being '10 percent physical and 90 percent mental' is a truism to which he readily subscribed, because Crook had won the tournament for the past four consecutive years.

After winning army championship and inter-service tournaments, Torres entered the Olympic trials and ended up representing the United States in the light-middleweight division at the 1956 Melbourne Games, where he won the silver medal after losing to the veteran Hungarian campaigner, Lazlo Papp.

Torres was discharged from the army and made his way to New York at the invitation of Cus D'Amato, the trainer of world heavyweight champion, Floyd Patterson. Torres recalled that sometime in 1957, a neighbor came to his home waving a newspaper that proclaimed: "Cus D'Amato interested in becoming Chegui Torres's manager." One week later, accompanied by his father, he flew to New York and became a member of D'Amato's boxing stable.[5]

D'Amato was a complex man composed of equal parts compassion and irascibility. But whatever his eccentricities, he was profoundly a boxing man well versed in its history and in its traditions.

To students such as Torres, he disseminated a training regimen that stripped down the art of punching to each type of punch being represented by a number, which would then be ordered in combinations designed to be applied to the vulnerable points of the opponent's anatomy.

He was not merely a motivator, he was a fight teacher.

While Pat Nappi had been the crux of his amateur career, D'Amato would be the fount of knowledge for Torres in the professional ranks. It was while training with D'Amato that Torres became identified with a particular mode of fighting: the "peek-a-boo" style.

This involved a hands-held-high approach, with the gloves situated around the boxer's face to form a protective guard. The modus operandi of the style is to begin with defense. From the standard posture of a near vertical torso and bent knees, the idea is to create possibilities and exploit them by bobbing and weaving and blindsiding an opponent. Fighting off from a jab, the fighter stalks his opponent using footwork in the conventional sense of dragging one foot behind the other, but when primed to attack, he may adopt an unorthodox two-footed approach to create the angles from which punches may be delivered.

But even in offense, D'Amato's style consciously strove to maintain an effective defense: for every type of punch the fighter throws, there is an accompanying head movement, thus preserving the primary principle undergirding scientific boxing: to hit and not be hit.[6]

It was a style that Torres felt suited him perfectly because it played to his strengths. The peek-a-boo is particularly effective for fighters in possession of very good hand speed, which Torres certainly had. The strategy of constant head movement and shifting footwork would consistently enable him to launch effective attacks, in particular the explosive left hook that he would unleash from a left-leaning stance toward a target behind his opponent's right elbow. This maneuver would be used to particularly devastating effect when flooring Wayne Thornton and Willie Pastrano in world title bouts.

He completed his amateur career under D'Amato's tutelage. In 1958, he won the national Amateur Athletic Union (AAU) championship and the New York Golden Gloves tourney in the middleweight division. After turning professional, he would develop a following among the New York-based Puerto Rican community and his fights held at the St. Nicholas Arena became sell-outs.

Torres picked himself up after losing to the Cuban fighter Florentino Fernandez and put together a string of victories against the likes of Don Fullmer and the former middleweight champion, Carl "Bobo" Olsen. His naturally stocky physique created increasing difficulty in making the middle-weight limit, and so he moved up to the light heavyweight class.

A new Latin hero was born when Torres won the world's light heavy-weight title in 1965 by a ninth-round knockout of Willie Pestrano. The rau-cous crowd which was dominated by Puerto Ricans, bayed for him and after his victory, carried him out of the ring. He had earlier refused to fight if the Puerto Rican anthem was not played alongside the "Star Spangled Banner" before the fight.

The following day, Torres stood on a fire escape on the corner of Lexington Avenue and 110th Street and, holding his championship belt aloft, announced: "This is for everyone."

It was inevitable that he would make a defense in Puerto Rico, where a crowd of 150,000 people had gathered to meet him after his world title triumph. But fighting before his home crowd did not seem to bring him luck. Although securing a unanimous points victory over Tom McNeely, a journeyman heavyweight, Torres sustained a body attack that many believe irreparably diminished him as an athlete. The hands-held-high style that had served him remarkably well was also one that had the drawback of leaving Torres vulnerable to strikes aimed at the sides of his abdomen.

Torres ended up with an inflamed pancreas and admitted that he had come close to death. It put an end to any ideas that he had had of fighting Muhammad Ali. In December 1966, he lost his title to Nigeria's Dick Tiger, and after failing to regain his title by a close split-decision in the aftermath of which his Puerto Rican supporters rioted at Madison Square Garden, Torres's years as an elite boxer were over.

The truth, as he often put it, was that he had been fast losing interest in the sport.[7] He had already received his calling as a writer and was by the mid-1960s being often referred to as a darling of the "Norman Mailer-George

Plimpton set." The reactions of the traditionally hard-nosed boxing community, however, were not nearly as hostile as that of a previous era when Paul Gallico had huffed about heavyweight champion and George Bernard Shaw confidant Gene Tunney having "hurt his own game with this cultural nonsense."

Earlier in Torres's career, he had become friendly with a number of young journalists, including Pete Hamill, who had helped secure him a regular column at the *New York Post*. He also wrote a Spanish-language column for the New York-based paper *El Dario La Prensa* in which he focused his energies on the affairs of the Latino community.

Whereas Torres had alluded to D'Amato as "the man who created the fighter," he would credit Mailer as being the one who "created my intellectual capacity." He felt that the biggest obstacle that he had to surmount as a writer was to think in English.

This was a barrier he quite clearly overcame when, in 1971, he produced a masterfully crafted biography of Muhammad Ali entitled *Sting Like a Bee*. It is a book still acknowledged as one of the better books on one of the most widely written about figures in American sports history.

What made it, and still makes it, a classic of boxing writing is how Torres's multilayered deconstruction of Ali and his world provided insightful analyses of the psychology of the fighter that could only be garnered from having gone through the experience of being a champion fighter. The contest of wills, the control of fear, and the management in the fighter's head of the distracting politics outside the ring were all given a fresh airing and a new resonance.

The game of boxing, Torres would assert, is predicated on a series of deceptions, and that Ali's ability to dominate his opponents was rooted in his masterful employment of the art of deceiving them. As Torres put it, "Champions and good fighters are champions and good fighters because they can lie better than the others."[8]

The feint employed by boxers seeking an opening against a fellow combatant embodies this at its most basic level. With Ali, Torres wrote, the deceptions related to the willful abrogation of boxing orthodoxies: keeping his hands low, pulling his head back from punches rather than blocking them, aiming punches exclusively to his opponent's head while eschewing the art of punching to the body. These "errors," Torres maintained, were used by Ali "to fool the other guy."[9] He put it thus: "Ali knows when he's doing wrong. He invites you to take advantage of it. But Ali is two steps ahead. He knows what your next two punches are going to be."[10]

Ali's strategy meant that fighters hit him at a far lower rate than he hit them. The outcome, according to Torres, was frustration in the opponent, which inevitably led to a psychologically induced state of tiredness. In other words, Ali was apt at deceiving properly trained adversaries into a mindset that they were fatigued.

Another example of Torres's brand of fighter's insight is clear from his descriptions and analyses of how boxers control fear in the dressing room just prior to fighting. Some boxers embark on a prolonged and somber meditation on the opposition. Others, such as Floyd Patterson, Torres noted, induce a temporary state of slumber; in Patterson's case, not waking up until an official from the boxing commission would enter the dressing room to inform him that it was time to enter the ring. Torres could use the direct analogy of his own dressing room habit in explaining that Ali coped with this segment of the rituals of the sport by actively seeking distractions.

Whereas others would have construed Ali's posing for a drawing by artist LeRoy Neiman prior to a bout with Billy Daniels as an encumbrance and his banter with Howard Cosell before taking on Joe Frazier as a nuisance, Torres judged the presence of Neiman to be a "tremendous relief" to Ali, and Cosell's questioning together with Ali's playfully barbed responses as a necessary measure to keep his mind off the impending battle.[11]

Torres's knowledge of Ali was bolstered by an acquaintance both men had developed over the years. And although he did not get to fight him for real, both men can be seen engaging in an intense sparring session in the film *The Fighters*, which documented the buildup to and the aftermath of the first Ali–Frazier confrontation.

Torres's contacts in the boxing and literary fields were important in bringing the project to fruition. He had been approached with the idea of writing a book on Ali by Burt Randolph Sugar, the editor of *Boxing Illustrated*, six weeks before Ali's "Fight of the Century" with Joe Frazier in 1971. His mentor Norman Mailer, who wrote the book's preface, would serve as an unofficial editor as Torres toiled at his typewriter in Vermont that summer, while Budd Schulberg, author of *The Harder They Fall*, contributed the epilogue. LeRoy Neiman also provided some sketches. Published by Abelard-Schuman, the book sold well, and the reviews were overwhelmingly positive.

Leonard Gardner's review for the *New York Times* described it as "a study of the psychic content that in boxing is the hidden part of the iceberg," and *Publishers Weekly* praised the work as "acrid, penetrating, a book fuming with the ammonia of the prize ring and the psychic steam of champions."

Torres's other biography, *Fire and Fear: The Inside Story of Mike Tyson*, charted the tumultuous rise of a champion who, like Torres, had been tutored by Cus D'Amato. It also predicted Tyson's imminent demise.

Torres was uniquely placed to give insight into Tyson the person and fighter. He had, after all, been "present at the creation," knowing Tyson intimately from the time the twelve-year-old delinquent was placed under the care of D'Amato.

In the book he recounts how in February 1979, D'Amato had gently placed his hand over Tyson's head and predicted that the boy was going to be the heavyweight champion of the world someday "if he maintains interest and desire in the game."[12]

Then, speaking softly and with a trace of the lisp that would become familiar to millions, Tyson, with his eyes fixed to the floor, told Torres: "Someday I wanna be like you ... what you were ... champion of the world."[13]

Tyson would over the coming years stay for periods at Torres's family home up to the time when he became the heavyweight champion.

The book reveals much about D'Amato as the molder and shaper not only of the fighting skills of the boxers under his charge, but also of the development of their outlook to life. Thus, Tyson's tutelage was composed of daytime physical drills and evening character-building sessions. The evening discussions did not include the matters pertaining to boxing technique because, according to Torres, D'Amato believed that the "development of the physical side of a champion was 'incidental' to during both the first and last stages of his career."[14]

D'Amato's rationale about boxing as a blend of metaphysical, psychological, and physical components is consistently given airing. At one point, Torres informs the reader of the inspiration of the book's title. "Boxing," Torres quotes D'Amato as telling the young Tyson, "is a sport of self-control. You must understand fear so that you can manipulate it. Fear is like fire. You can make it work for you: it can warm you in the winter, cook your food when you're hungry, give you light when you are in the dark, and produce energy. Let it get out of control and it can hurt you, even kill you ... fear is a friend of exceptional people."[15]

Some suspected a mercenary motive in his decision to write the book – that Torres had jumped onto a money-making opportunity. But he countered his detractors by insisting that it was an effort he felt compelled to make because of his belief that the course Tyson's career and life was taking was completely antithetical to the values he believed D'Amato had consistently striven to instill in his fighters.[16]

The circus surrounding Tyson and his reckless behavior only served to support the views of those whom Torres felt could only deal with the world of boxing as a disreputable sport that bore the vestiges of "our basic animal instinct."

The biographies on Ali and Tyson are the only books written by Jose Torres. While he produced no similar works on his mentor Cus D'Amato or his stable-mate Floyd Patterson, his books and other writings did provide material on both.

So far as Patterson is concerned, Torres presented a portrait of his shy and enigmatic counterpart in *Sting Like a Bee*. It was a straightforward, honest recounting of Patterson's humiliation by Ali in their first fight, in 1965. It was a one-sided match, with Patterson famously fighting with an injured back. Although many boxing writers wrote about Ali having refrained from scoring a knockout in order to deliberately prolong the bout to spite Patterson for his derogatory comments about Ali's Muslim faith and his refusal to acknowledge his change of name from Cassius Clay, Torres thought differently.

He could see that Patterson was focusing on his defense and consciously absorbing the blows, which he could not evade. And Patterson's comments to Torres that Ali had hit him many times on the chin but that he "didn't feel the damned punches," served as a confirmation of Torres's theory of the knockout: they are more likely to occur when the fighter does not see the blow coming.

Torres consistently acknowledged Patterson to be one of the best fighters he had ever seen. His greatest attribute, Torres wrote, was that of delivering a fast-paced combination of punches, punches that followed each other at such speed that he once saw Patterson start a five-punch combination in which the first blow knocked the opponent out but the momentum created and speed was of such alacrity that the other punches could not be withheld, thus leaving the descending fighter to be hit by the remaining four.[17]

Such was the confidence and fluidity of Patterson as a fighter at the summit of his powers, which Torres places at the time of the series of bouts leading up to and including the one in which Patterson won the title in an eliminator with Archie Moore, that Torres reached an interesting thesis. While he opined no heavyweight champion, including Joe Louis and Rocky Marciano, could beat Muhammad Ali in his 1960s prime, Patterson, he asserted, had "the speed then to destroy Ali's assets."[18]

Torres's abilities as a writer in recreating the battles in which he himself was involved were no less compelling. For instance, in his obituary of his former foe, Dick Tiger, he recounted with great lucidity and humor an incident during their first bout, which encapsulated his waning resolve as a fighter and the superior willpower of an opponent against whom he possessed all the physical advantages of height, reach and, weight.

Torres sees Tiger off balance and throws a combination of punches. He is sure that Tiger will fall to the canvas, and he steps back relaxed and unguarded, only to feel the sensation of being hit. As he struggles to realign his momentarily discombobulated senses, from a distance his refocusing lenses begin to make out the outlines of Tiger's mouthpiece: Tiger was smiling at him.[19]

A number of career moves and achievements underpin Torres's reputation as a trailblazer. Aside from the precedent set in winning the world light heavyweight title, he was the first Latino to have a regular English-language column appearing in the *New York Post*. He was also the first Latino and the first professional fighter to hold the office of chairman of the New York State Athletic Commission (NYSAC).[20]

His appointment came under the auspices of New York State Governor Mario Cuomo in 1984, and he held the position until his resignation in 1988. Torres's intimate connections with the Democrat Party machinery in New York, in the context of which he had undertaken responsibilities at the New York City Council and the office of the president of Manhattan Borough, would have been a major factor in securing the position.[21] He vowed to promote educational opportunities for boxers to enable them at least to be able to "read their contracts."

His concerns about the image of boxing and the standards by which it was run served as a guide to several of Torres's initiatives. One of his first acts on assuming office was to institute compulsory CAT scans for fighters. He was also a driving force behind the creation of the Association of Boxing Commissions, which had the objectives of harmonizing rules and regulations as well as coordinating good practices between the independent boxing commissions of members. The official book *Laws and Rules Regulating Boxing and Wrestling Matches* was revamped.

He was a purposeful administrator, although one who (as was the case with both his predecessors and successors) was unable to stem what is often seen as the malign influence of promoters and sanctioning bodies. His pledge to make sure that the men who control the fighters "are worthy" would come under scrutiny. For instance, he was heavily criticized for sanctioning the WBA heavyweight title bout between Tim Witherspoon and James '"Bonecrusher" Smith in December 1986 when it was reported that both men were managed by Carl King, the son of promoter Don King.[22] A subsequent investigation by New York State's inspector-general, Joseph Spinelli, recommended the resignations of three of Torres's underlings.[23]

The continuing economic attractions of Las Vegas and Atlantic City as staging posts for big money championship bouts meant that Torres had little success in bringing back big-time boxing to New York.

Critics would cite a conflict of interest in his handling of bouts involving Mike Tyson because of his unabashed cheerleading of a Cus D'Amato-affiliated fighter. It was his decision to write the biography on Mike Tyson that in fact prompted his decision to resign the post.[24]

Torres returned to boxing administration when he was elected as the second president of the recently formed World Boxing Organization (WBO) sanctioning body in 1990. Formed by a group of Dominican and Puerto Rican businessmen who broke away from the World Boxing Association (WBA) in 1988, Torres held the position until his resignation in 1995. His appointment was an indication of the level of Torres's prestige within the boxing world as the WBO struggled to achieve credibility in its early years.

Jose Torres died of heart failure on January 19, 2009, at his home in Ponce, where he had relocated after being beset by health issues, the most notable of which was a diabetic condition. There were warm tributes from the world of boxing, politics, and the Puerto Rican community whose interests he had been steadfast in serving.

In Puerto Rico, the authorities declared three days of national mourning and ordered all flags to be flown at half-mast. A speech given in the House of Representatives of the United States Congress eulogized Torres as a "trailblazer for his people and a renaissance man who made a positive impact in boxing, literature and civil rights."[25]

The New York State Senate passed a legislative resolution to pause in its deliberations to mourn the passing of a "distinguished citizen and devoted member of his community." The recounted highlights of his life praised Torres's "commitment to excellence," and noted that "his spirit of humanity, carried over into all fields of enterprise, including charitable and civic endeavors."[26]

From his ready humor and his distinctively earthy laughter to his perpetually inquisitive tone and propensity for candidness, Torres conveyed a richness of character in his interpersonal engagements as well as in his writing.

He loved the sport of boxing and sought to validate this affection by defending the sport from attacks emanating from the wider society, which consistently registers feelings ranging from uneasiness to outright hostility. He rejected the views of those who blamed Muhammad Ali's Parkinson's syndrome on his boxing career just as he rejected the insinuations that linked pugilism to the Alzheimer's disease suffered by Floyd Patterson.[27]

Boxing, for Torres, was always more than a glorified barbaric spectacle in which each combatant bashes his opponent around the head and body with his fists until one reaches a state of physical impotence. His experiences as a fighter whose career had enabled him to achieve a high level of social mobility and his conceptualization of the sport as one that is rooted in the understanding of the primacy of the deployment of the boxer's cerebral resources as the deciding factor that separates the winner from the loser and the champion from the contender made him a consistent advocate in support of the social utility of the sport.

As he wrote in the *New York Times* in 1988, Torres's goal through his writing as well as his administrative capacities, was to persuade society to view the sport "from a more humane point of view, making them understand that, ultimately, boxing is a contest of will and character where triumphs are decided by the power of the mind, not of the flesh."[28]

NOTES

1 *The Ed Sullivan Show* (Apr. 11, 1965) "Toast of the Town," Season 18; Episode Number 18. Broadcast live on a Sunday evening. Jose Torres sang "Un Poco Mas."

2 Schecter, Leonard (Jul. 1965). "Torres! Torres! Torres!" *Sport.*

3 Iamale, David (Jul. 28, 1997). "An Interview with 1997 International Boxing Hall of Fame Inductee: Jose Torres," *The Cyber Boxing Zone Journal.*

4 Evans, Gavin (Aug. 2006). "Dick Tiger," *African Perspective*, BBC World Service radio.

5 Torres, Jose (1989). *Fire and Fear: The Inside Story of Mike Tyson*, 1st edn, Warner Books, p.46. Note: Torres acknowledged that his day-to-day trainer in the professional ranks was Joey Fariello, a disciple of D'Amato's who taught him "mechanically" while D'Amato functioned as a guru, speaking to him often and strengthening his psychological resources. Source: Torres interview with David Iamale.

6 Abramowitz, Adam (Dec. 13 2013). "Q&A: Dr. Scott Weiss on Cus D'Amato Part I," *SaturdayNightBoxing.com.*

7 Makinde, Adeyinka (2005). *Dick Tiger: The Life and Times of a Boxing Immortal*, Tarentum: Word Association, pp. 187–88.

8 Torres, Jose (1990). *Sting Like a Bee: The Muhammad Ali Story*, London: Simon & Schuster, p. 39.

9 Ibid., p. 41.

10 Ibid., p. 41.

11 Ibid., pp. 177–79.

12 Torres, Jose (1989). *Fire and Fear: The Inside Story of Mike Tyson*, 1st edn, New York: Warner Books, p. 37.

13 Ibid., p. 38.

14 Ibid., p. 49.

15 Ibid., p. 50.

16 Torres received a $350,000 advance from Warner Books to write the biography.

17 Torres, Jose (1990). *Sting Like a Bee: The Muhammad Ali Story*, London: Simon & Schuster, p. 43.

18 Ibid., p. 43.

19 Torres, Jose (1972). "The Toughest Ninety Minutes I Ever Had." *Boxing Illustrated*, p. 37.

20 Floyd Patterson would serve as chairman of the New York State Athletic Commission from 1995 to 1998. Wilbur McClure was the head of the Massachusetts Boxing Commission from 1993 to 1998.

21 Torres had worked for Democrat Party politicians Paul O'Dwyer and Andrew Stein when the former was president of New York City Council and the latter served as Manhattan borough president.

22 Carl King was not licensed to manage in New York, and neither Smith nor Witherspoon was licensed to box there. See Brubaker, Bill (Feb. 20 1989) "A Champion at Self-promotion Rises to King of the Heap," *The Washington Post.*

23 Berger, Phil (Jan. 31 1987) "State Seeks Shake Up on Boxing Panel," *The New York Times.* Note: Spinelli, an ex-FBI agent who was the godfather to Torres's son, had spent a considerable amount of time investigating corruption in boxing.

24 Torres's time at the helm of the NYSAC which one journalist described as having been "stormy," came to an end on May 19, 1988, when he tendered his resignation to Governor Mario Cuomo. His departure brought about speculation that he had been asked to step down by Cuomo, something which Torres categorically denied. Although announcing that he did not wish to "go to my grave as a bureaucrat" and stressing his desire to become a writer again, there was an implied admission on his part that he left before accomplishing all that he had wanted. He left three proposals on the table, as he put it: First, the creation of a legal advisory board to aid boxers embroiled in disputes linked to their profession; second, the creation of an oral and written test for prospective managers and trainers; and third, reform of New York law allowing managers to take a third of his charge's purse, along with a 10 percent cut for his trainer. Sources: Associated Press, (May 20 1988). "Sports People: Torres Steps Down," *The New York Times* and Torres, Jose, (Jun. 5 1988). "Views of Sport: Looking at the New York State of Boxing," *The New York Times.*

25 The speech was delivered on February 9, 2009 by Charles Rangel, a Democrat representative from New York. Source: Congressional Record (Monday, February 9, 2009) Volume 155, Number 26.

26 http://open.nysenate.gov/legislation/bill/J207-2009 (accessed on September 18, 2017).

27 Interview with Scott Simon on NPR News' "Weekend Edition," May 13, 2006. Transcript: "Fellow Champ Torres Remembers Floyd Patterson" at www.npr .org/templates/story/story.php?storyId=5402887 (accessed on September 18, 2017). Torres would often tell interviewers that his non-boxer father became debilitated by Parkinson's disease and also revealed that both of his parents suffered from Alzheimer's disease.

28 Torres, Jose, (June 5 1988). "Views of Sport: Looking at the New York State of Boxing," *The New York Times.*

SOURCES

Books

Makinde, Adeyinka (2005). *Dick Tiger: The Life and Times of a Boxing Immortal,* Tarentum: Word Association

Torres, Jose (1989). *Fire and Fear: The Inside Story of Mike Tyson,* 1st edn, New York: Warner Books.

  (1990). *Sting Like a Bee: The Muhammad Ali Story,* London: Simon & Schuster.

Magazines

Boxing Illustrated
Sport

Newspapers

The New York Times
The Washington Post

Web

Iamale, David (Jul. 28, 1997). An Interview with 1997 International Boxing Hall of Fame Inductee: Jose Torres. *The Cyber Boxing Zone Journal,* www .cyberboxingzone.com/news/archives/00005176.htm.
Abramowitz, Adam (Dec. 13, 2013). Q&A: Dr. Scott Weiss on Cus D'Amato Part I. *SaturdayNightBoxing.com,* www.saturdaynightboxing.com/2013/12/q-dr-scott-weiss-on-cus-damato-part-i.html.

Radio

Evans, Gavin (Aug. 2006). "Dick Tiger," *African Perspective,* BBC World Service radio.
Simon, Scott (May 2006). "Fellow Champ Torres Remembers Floyd Patterson," *Weekend Edition,* NPR News.

20

KASIA BODDY

"Well, What Was it Really Like?" George Plimpton, Norman Mailer, and the Heavyweights[1]

During the late 1940s and early 1950s, boxing – with its well-lit, narrowly confined setting and cast of two – was briefly the "darling" of the new medium of television.[2] In 1950, only 9 percent of Americans had TV, but by 1955, television was available in more than half of all homes, and commentators marvelled at the very idea of sports being available "from a sofa!"[3] "The most vibrant memories I bear from my childhood," writes Gerald Early, "are of my uncles crowded around a very small black-and-white television, drinking beer and watching the Gillette Friday-night fights."[4]

Reports of "vibrant memories" of watching TV fights are not uncommon and yet, since the 1950s, a persistent theme in sports writing has been to point out how inauthentic such memories, and experiences, are. "One cannot really imagine the impact of blows on another man's head and body by way of the television screen in its eerily flattened dimensions," insists Joyce Carol Oates.[5] Television "*seems* to get you close enough to see almost everything and taste the flying sweat," argues Carlo Rotella, "but its appeal lies in its cool distance."[6] It is only in the stadium, adds A.J. Liebling, that the spectator can experience a "*feeling* of participation."[7]

These remarks are not untypical of writing about all sorts of sports and stem, I would argue, from the Romanticism inherent in so much of it. Hans Ulrich Gumbrecht, to take an unabashed example, contrasts the at-home "television viewer" with the on-the-spot "beholder" whose recollections are not merely "vibrant" but bodily: "as you hold on to [the key moment in the fight or game] in memory, you feel an impulse running through your own muscles, as if to embody what your hero achieved."[8] Of course Gumbrecht and the others realize the limits of their identification – it is only an "as if," an approximation. Nevertheless, the assumption is clearly that the experience of "sport at one remove" is not only better but *truer* than "at two removes."[9] And it is this experiential truth that most sports writers claim to be able to provide for the reader.

Some, however, also suggest that they can get just a little closer to what it is "really like" – by picking up the bat or putting on the gloves themselves. The "manifesto" of this approach, now known as "participatory sportswriting," is Paul Gallico's 1937 essay "The Feel."[10] Gallico's subject is knowledge and his target not even radio listeners but those spectators who, sitting "in the stands," *think* they understand what's going on. Gallico is quick to disabuse them: "it is impossible to … know anything about the speed of a forehand drive hit by a champion until you have one fired at you," he insists; "nobody knows what real golf is like until he has played a round with a professional." "It is fairly obvious," he concludes, "that a man who has been tapped on the chin with five fingers wrapped up in a leather boxing glove and propelled by the arm of an expert knows more about that particular sensation that one who has not." Gallico's first "experiment" was to be knocked out by the heavyweight champion Jack Dempsey "for the express purpose of learning the sensation."[11] Here it is important to note that Gallico is not suggesting we get the "'feel' of things" by playing some tennis in the park or by sparring in the local gym. "Knowledge," as he defines it, is confined to the charmed circle of initiates who have access to "a champion," "a professional" or "an expert."[12]

"The Feel" was the essay that, twenty years later, inspired George Plimpton to "try [his] hand" at something similar.[13] On the one hand, Plimpton maintained the idea that he, and *Sports Illustrated*, were conducting "research" into "athletic skills at their best" and "the society of athletes" – the kind of "leisurely, longish" research that television and the daily papers couldn't hope to conduct.[14] On the other hand, he admitted that his own response to participatory journalism was less a feeling of initiation into new knowledge than one of simple "envy": "what a lucky guy Gallico was to have experienced all this." Perhaps he too could enjoy some "self-indulgences."[15]

The fact that television had taken over as "the dominant force in spot-news reporting" did not diminish the appetite for print stories about boxing.[16] On the contrary, television served to create an increased market for stories about the fighters who regularly "flash[ed] on the screen," and the 1960s and 1970s have come to be seen as a "kind of golden age in magazine writing."[17] That writing worked hard to distance itself from "spot-news" – the journalistic formula Gay Talese identified as the "'five Ws' – who, what, when, where, why" – and it went about its business neither "succinctly" nor "impersonally."[18] Talese, whose 1962 profile of Joe Louis, "The King as a Middle-Aged Man," is often cited as a founding piece of what became known as the New Journalism, openly admitted that he was "influenced more by the fiction writers I preferred reading" – the Hemingway tradition of John

O'Hara and Irwin Shaw – than by "the practitioners of 'objective' non-fiction."[19] Talese's boxing essays – he wrote extensively on Floyd Patterson in particular – are not, however, strictly "participatory." Rather he presents his subject from multiple points of view: the subject's own viewpoint, the perspectives of those around him, and, hovering "unobtrusively" on the edge, that of the writer himself. That unobstrusiveness paid lip-service at least to the principles of spot-news reporting. As William Howarth said of John McPhee, another sportswriter of the period, Talese believed that in order "to see and hear clearly," he needed to keep "his eyes open and his mouth shut."[20] George Plimpton and Norman Mailer were different.

*

> When people say to themselves "I want to be happy," they could as well be saying "I want to be George Plimpton": one achieves, one is productive, and there's pleasure and ease in all of it.[21]

A "patrician liberal" who claimed "five or six" ancestors on the Mayflower, co-founded *The Paris Review*, and held court at Elaine's restaurant on Manhattan's Upper East Side, George Plimpton was widely admired and envied as "the ultimate Good Fellow," "a playful, debonair, deeply inquisitive man of the world."[22] His journalistic persona, on the other hand, was that of "a "bumbling amateur athlete up against the mighty pros … cast by his ineptness in the role of the virginal victim."[23] "I am very poor on skates," begins *Open Net*, Plimpton's book on his time playing ice hockey with the Boston Bruins; "I tend to skate on my ankle bones."[24] "Being very lean and thin, along the lines of a stick" were hardly the ideal "credentials" for American football, nor boxing nor golf.[25] At six-foot-four Plimpton was (in his own words) "a monstrous manned colossus poised high over the golf ball, a spheroid that is barely discernible 14 stories down on its tee."[26] Each new sport brought forth a new simile – contemplating boxing, he described himself as "a bird of the stiltlike variety" – and a new confession of physical weakness – "I can slide my watch up my arm almost to the elbow. I have a thin, somewhat fragile nose which bleeds easily."[27] The joke ran again and again and, as Graydon Carter noted, Plimpton was not only "in on" it, "he created the joke," assuming, as many commentators noted, a role akin to that of the eponymous hero of James Thurber's 1939 short story "The Secret Life of Walter Mitty."[28] Within ten years of that story's publication, the noun "a Walter Mitty" had entered *Webster's Dictionary*, to refer to a "commonplace unadventurous person who seeks escape from reality through daydreaming." Plimpton's stories often begin by relating commonplace childhood fantasies and humiliations before presenting the "daydreaming kid" with a chance to fulfill the fantasy or redeem the humiliation.[29]

Shadow Box (1977) begins with the story of young Plimpton handing over twenty cents rather than fight some bigger boys, and admitting that "the shame of it lasts to this day." The scenario is the starting point of a hundred comic-book stories but, whereas those usually content themselves with the fantasy of the boy with the "pipestem arms" beating the school bully, Plimpton decides to get into the ring with the heavyweight boxing champion Archie Moore. Boxing, he argues, is "the ultimate confrontation" and the pinnacle of participatory journalism; "I could hardly go on ... without investigating the sport."[30]

Unsurprisingly, most of his essay is devoted to his preparations (the fight itself consists of only three rounds, the last of which is cut short when his coach advances the clock), and the emphasis is very much on comic incongruity. Plimpton prepares for the bout by going to the Racquet Club on Park Avenue to read Pierce Egan's nineteenth-century reflections on the English prize ring, attends the weigh-in dressed in a Brooks Brothers suit, and then heads off for a lunch of "eggs benedict, a steak diane and a chocolate-ice-cream compote"; "the food, arriving in silver serving dishes, helped me forget where I was going to be at five that afternoon."[31] Moore is simply there to play the straight man to Plimpton's buffoon, and all we hear about him is that he was unsure "how to comport himself" in this unusual situation, and that his "comforting face" reminds Plimpton of a "Haitian mammy."[32] Perhaps that's because Plimpton is not trying to capture "the feel" of being Archie Moore so much as that of a writer who "sparred whenever he had the chance" – the feel, that is, of Ernest Hemingway.[33] The fight with Moore offers Plimpton a way of making up with Hemingway, with whom he'd fallen out over a *Paris Review* interview, but, in displaying his insouciance, Plimpton is also able to distinguish himself from the man he had worshiped in his youth. "Sometimes I think [Hemingway] got the priorities mixed up, thinking that it wasn't to provide material for notebooks that I was fighting as much as to undergo a physical test – truly as if what I was after was Archie Moore's championship."[34]

The rest of *Shadow Box* focuses on the boxer who, a few months later, in November 1962, correctly predicted that "Archie Moore ... must fall in four" – Cassius Clay (soon to become Muhammad Ali). Plimpton never got in the ring with Ali – a planned exhibition fight in 1973 "never came off" – and so *Shadow Box* reverts to non-participatory journalism. There is a little more comic incongruity (for example, when he takes the modernist poet Marianne Moore to write a verse with Ali) but mainly Plimpton uses his access to the boxer's entourage to tell the story of Ali's career, culminating in the October 1974 "Rumble in the Jungle," when Ali defeated George Foreman to regain his title. The final seven chapters of the book are

set in Kinshasa, but the fight, and the fighters, occupy only a small proportion of its pages. As Plimpton acknowledges, "a lot of other stuff seems to
creep in."[35] An emphasis on other stuff ("mumbo jumbo" in particular here)
distinguishes the New Journalists from the "true sportswriters," but the New
Journalists are themselves part of the stuff under investigation.[36] Plimpton is
fascinated by figures like Hunter S. Thompson, who never filed his story for
Rolling Stone, and in particular Norman Mailer, whose Hemingwayesque
"competiveness" – that is, lack of insouciance – he discusses at length.
Mailer, in his version, notes Plimpton's "quietly buried competitive passion
(large as Vesuvius, if smokeless)."[37]

*

> ... Ali said afterwards, "It'll be a great experience for you remembering that
> you ran with the Champion just a few days before the fight."[38]

Playboy magazine published Norman Mailer's account of Ali–Foreman in
its May and June 1975 issues, and the following month it appeared as a
book called *The Fight*. Here, too, the emphasis is largely on the traditional
journalistic acts of observing and interpreting, but Mailer was also keen to
distinguish himself from the traditional sportswriter whose stories appeared
"like oats on a conveyor belt."[39] The essay begins by reminding readers that
just as there was an art to Ali's boxing, and even to his training, "there was
an art to watching him train and you acquired it over the years."[40] This is
just the start of a long series of comparisons between fighting and writing
that extend to the insistent employment of similes and metaphors presented
as the equivalent of routine and spectacular punches.[41]

The nearest that Mailer gets to participating, in fact rather than by analogy, is when, a few days before the fight, he joins Ali for an early morning
jog. With another dig at Plimpton, who, he says, "would have to keep on
some kind of close terms with Ali or pay a disproportionate price in humiliation," Mailer presents himself as too short, too old, and too heavy even to
think about competing.[42] A five-foot-eight second-generation Jewish son of a
Brooklyn accountant, Mailer offers himself as a kind of anti-Plimpton. When
Plimpton entered the boxing gym, said Philip Roth, "he entered a world no
less glamorous than his own, the world of the ruling class of America's tran-
scendent popular culture": "the only American world that could possibly
equal his own in the prestige his once had."[43] But, for Mailer, the glamour
always existed at a distance. Never really able to *be* an American, he once
said, he could only aspire to "have a love affair with America," an affair
that might make him feel "*like* an American."[44] Plimpton's account of the
Racquet Club lunch he had before his bout with Moore suggests a confident
debonair man about to supplement an already perfectly pleasant day. But

Mailer's pre-jogging meal disgusts rather than charms. He, too, eats "rich food" ("a thick fish chowder and a pepper steak," accompanied by "ice cream, rum and tonic, vodka and orange juice") but the emphasis here – as it never would be in Plimpton – is on "the forces of digestion" that follow.[45] And this is only the beginning of an assault on the "false legend" of his own "machismo."[46] Mailer's comedy – darker and more serious, as well as more abject, than Plimpton's – culminates in his "cool" response to the sound of a roaring lion: "To be eaten by a lion on the banks of the Congo – who could fail to notice that it was Hemingway's own lion waiting down these years for the flesh of Ernest until an appropriate substitute had at last arrived?"[47]

Plimpton having refused to take part, Mailer has offered himself as the "substitute" Hemingway. But what is Ali's role in this performance? Mailer would later insist on "the similarities between Ernest Hemingway and Muhammad Ali": not only do "they come out of that same American urgency to be the only planet in existence. To be the sun," at the heart of each was a dialectical struggle that was somehow both personal and national.[48] The dialectic of *The Fight* is a bit different. The book plays with various versions of magical thinking, but all are designed to the same end – "the powers of regeneration in an artist."[49] In overcoming the odds to beat Foreman, Ali works magic on Mailer, showing him that regeneration is possible; emphatically unlike Hemingway, whose suicide fourteen years earlier haunts the book.[50] Ali, in other words, is another anti-Hemingway – a "fetish" to keep the novelist's lingering power at bay.[51] The lion may have roared, but he roared from behind bars in the Presidential zoo.

In the late 1990s Plimpton wrote a play based on Hemingway's correspondence with F. Scott Fitzgerald; it had eighteen performances, with Plimpton in the role of Fitzgerald, and Mailer as Hemingway.[52]

*

How would you describe yourself? What do you think you are like, compared with those vividly transforming heroes of yours?
I am like someone who is trying vividly to transform himself out of himself and into his vividly transforming heroes. I am very much like somebody who spends all day writing.[53]

In 2007 Philip Roth published *Exit Ghost*, the ninth, and final, novel in a series narrated by Nathan Zuckerman. Zuckerman is sometimes described as Roth's alter ego, but it is perhaps better to think of him as both an authorial impersonator and a conduit into further impersonators. The regressive chain of selves do not match up but instead offer a variety of what Roth, in another novel, called counterlives.[54] He developed the metaphor further and gave it a boxing spin, in *The Human Stain* (2000). There, Zuckerman's impersonator, and best friend, is a man called Coleman Silk who boxed in his youth and specialized in counterpunching, a technique that Zuckerman believes he also adopted outside of the ring. The novel offers Zuckerman's imaginative recreation of Silk's early experiences and his thoughts about his opponents. At one point, he has Silk observe that "the power and pleasure" were not to be found "blabbing" about oneself but "in the opposite, in being counterconfessional in the same way you were a counterpuncher."[55] Roth has made a career out of counterconfessing, and *Exit Ghost* is, among other things, an elegy to others who adopted a similar strategy, a generation of writers who looked for "power and pleasure" in opposites, and in opposition itself. Near the end of the novel, "Roth suspends the story for an eight-page disquisition" on George Plimpton (1927–2003) and Norman Mailer, who was born in 1923 and who died just a couple of months after its publication in November 2007.[56]

"The Twilight of the Gods," remarks Richard Kliman, Zuckerman's impersonator in *Exit Ghost*, as he observes Mailer, "both knees shot" and walking with two canes, struggle to get up to the pulpit at the Cathedral Church of St. John the Divine, to deliver his eulogy to Plimpton.[57] The Nietzsche allusion is a notch up from Leon Gast's formulation, in his 1997 movie about Ali and his literary admirers, *When We Were Kings*, but the object of nostalgia is the same.[58] Like *Shadow Box* and *The Fight*, Gast's film is less interested in what the black boxers themselves experienced or remembered than in the significance of their confrontation for the white journalists who witnessed it.[59] Reading Plimpton and Mailer, we know what it feels like to daydream, impersonate, and "concoct" counterlives, if not exactly as athletic gods or kings, then as comic pretenders to their crowns.[60] Reading their work, we "get the feel" of what it was like to be a white male writer at a time when Hemingway's influence was still seen as a challenge, when sports magazines offered considerable space for literary experimentation, and when writers were encouraged to make things happen on the page that weren't likely to happen on TV. But to answer the question "what was it really like" to be in a boxing ring, we'd do better to ask Archie Moore and Muhammad Ali.

NOTES

1 George Plimpton, Introduction to "Participations," in *The Best of George Plimpton* (New York: Atlantic Monthly Press, 1990), 3–6 (3).

2 Randy Roberts, "The Wide World of Muhammad Ali: The Politics and Economics of Televised Boxing," in *Muhammad Ali, The People's Champ*, ed. Elliott J. Gorn (Urbana, IL: University of Illinois Press, 1995), 24–53 (28). The first fight to be "telecast" was Lou Nova's defeat of Max Baer in June 1939. Benjamin Rader,

In Its Own Image: How Television Transformed Sports (New York: Free Press, 1984), 41.

3   Quoted in Rader, *In Its Own Image*, 18.
4   Gerald Early, "The Passing of Jazz's Old Guard," in *Tuxedo Junction* (Hopewell, NJ: Ecco Press, 1989), 307.
5   Joyce Carol Oates, *On Boxing*, Expanded Edition (Hopewell, NJ: Ecco Press, 1994), 82.
6   Carlo Rotella, *Cut Time: An Education at the Fights* (Boston, MA: Houghton Mifflin, 2003), 8.
7   A. J. Liebling, "Boxing with the Naked Eye," *The New Yorker*, June 30, 1951, reprinted in *The Sweet Science* (New York: North Point Press, 2004), 17–29 (17; my emphasis).
8   Hans Ulrich Gumbrecht, *In Praise of Athletic Beauty* (Cambridge, MA: Belknap Press, 2006), 144, 221, 8, 19.
9   Stuart Chase, *Men and Machines* (New York: Macmillan, 1929), 259–60. For Chase, spectatorship itself was a bad thing – "passive rather than active participation" – and listening to sports on the radio even worse.
10 Zachary Michael Jack, Introduction to *Participatory Sports Writing: An Anthology 1870–1937* (Jefferson, NC: McFarland & Co, 2009), 3–16 (12).
11 Paul Gallico, "The Feel," in *Farewell to Sport* (1937) (New York: Simon and Schuster, 1988), 287–98 (295, 293, 287–88).
12 Gallico, "The Feel," 298.
13 George Plimpton, *Shadow Box* (1977) (New York: Simon and Schuster, 1989), 62.
14 Plimpton, *Shadow Box*, 207.
15 Plimpton, Introduction to "Participations," 4.
16 Gay Talese, "Origins of a Nonfiction Writer' (1997) in *Frank Sinatra Has a Cold and Other Essays* (London: Penguin, 2011), 166–96 (188).
17 David Halberstam, Introduction to *The Best American Sports Writing of the Century* (Boston, MA: Houghton Mifflin, 1999), xix–xxxiii (xxxi).
18 Talese, "Origins," 187.
19 Talese, "Origins," 188. Tom Wolfe described Talese's essay for *Esquire* as an example of the kind of "stylish" work that could be produced if writers were "allowed" greater freedom and a long-lead time. "The New Journalism," in *The New Journalism* (1973) (London: Picador, 1975), 15–68 (24).
20 William Howarth, Introduction to *The John McPhee Reader* (New York: Vintage Books, 1977), viii.
21 Philip Roth, *Exit Ghost* (London: Jonathan Cape, 2007), 250.
22 P.J. O'Rourke, quoted in *George, Being George*, ed. Nelson W. Aldrich, Jr. (New York: Random House, 2008), 22; David Remnick, "George Plimpton: The Very Good Life," *Washington Post*, Nov 4, 1984, H1,2,4 (H2); Roth, *Exit Ghost*, 245.
23 Roth, *Exit Ghost*, 245–46.
24 George Plimpton, *Open Net* (London: Andre Deutsch, 1985), 13.
25 George Plimpton, *Paper Lion* (1965) (Guilford, CT: Lyons Press, 2006), 10.
26 George Plimpton, *The Bogey Man* (1968) (New York: Simon and Schuster, 1988), 1–2.
27 Plimpton, *Shadow Box*, 19.

28 James Thurber, "The Secret Life of Walter Mitty," *The New Yorker*, March 18, 1939, 19–20; reprinted in *My World and Welcome to It* (New York: Harcourt, Brace and Co.,1942) and filmed in 1947.

29 Plimpton, Introduction to "Participations," 3.

30 Plimpton, *Shadow Box*, 15, 13, 16.

31 Plimpton, *Shadow Box*, 36.

32 Plimpton, *Shadow Box*, 43, 41. Miles Davis supposedly asked Plimpton after the fight whether the blood streaming from his broken nose was "black blood, white blood, or red blood," to which Plimpton replied, "That's blue blood." David Amram, quoted in *George, Being George*, 168.

33 Plimpton, *Shadow Box*, 63.

34 Plimpton, *Shadow Box*, 71, 73.

35 Plimpton, *Shadow Box*, 292.

36 Plimpton, *Shadow Box*, 314.

37 Norman Mailer, *The Fight* (1975) (London: Hart-Davis, MacGibbon, 1976), 75.

38 Mailer, *The Fight*, 196.

39 Norman Mailer, "Ten Thousand Words a Minute," *Esquire*, February 1963, reprinted in *The Presidential Papers* (London: Andre Deutsch,1964), 213–67.

40 Mailer, *The Fight*, 9.

41 I discuss this in more detail in *Boxing: A Cultural History* (London: Reaktion Books, 2008), 251–60.

42 Plimpton told Mailer he "didn't have any equipment to run in." *Shadow Box*, 275.

43 Roth, *Exit Ghost*, 249–50.

44 Norman Mailer, *The Armies of the Night* (1968) (New York: Plume, 1994), 171, 48.

45 Mailer, *The Fight*, 75, 77.

46 Norman Mailer, "Of a Small and Modest Malignancy, Wicked and Brisling with Dots," in *Pieces and Pontifications* (1982) (London: New English Library, 1985), 21.

47 Mailer, *The Fight*, 83.

48 Norman Mailer, "Writers and Boxers: An Interview with Michael Lennon," in *Pieces and Pontifications*, 161.

49 Mailer, *The Fight*, 142.

50 Mailer, *The Fight* 109, 142.

51 He returned to the comparison later: "After Ali got old he still won a couple of great fights," while, in contrast, Hemingway "didn't make the big knockout … in his later books." Mailer, "Writers and Boxers," 161.

52 Plimpton tried to arrange a meeting between Hemingway and Mailer in 1960 but, in the end, Hemingway didn't make the promised phone call. J. Michael Lennon, *Norman Mailer: A Double Life* (New York: Simon and Schuster, 2013), 259–60, 715–18; *George, Being George*, 353–56; *Shadow Box*, 259–64.

53 Philip Roth, "*The Art of Fiction*: No.84," interviewed by Hermione Lee, *The Paris Review*, 93 (Fall 1984): www.theparisreview.org/interviews/2957/the-art-of-fiction-no-84–philip-roth

54 Early on in the series, Roth distinguished between an "impersonation" and a "confession." Philip Roth, *Zuckerman Unbound* (1981) (Harmondsworth: Penguin, 1983), 13. *The Counterlife* is the title of a 1986 novel by Roth.

55 Philip Roth, *The Human Stain* (2000) (London: Vintage, 2001), 100. I discuss the implications of this at greater length in "Roth's Great Books: A Reading of *The Human Stain*," *Cambridge Quarterly*, 39, no.1 (March 2010), 39–60.

56 "The original jacket cover was to have shown Plimpton ... seated at the center of a party, in a restaurant." Claudia Roth Pierpont, *Roth Unbound: A Writer and His Books* (London: Jonathan Cape, 2014), 293. Plimpton is Zuckerman's "antonym of doppelgänger." *Exit Ghost*, 252.

57 Roth, *Exit Ghost* 255. For Mailer's account of the memorial service, see *George, Being George*, 371–72.

58 Roth, *Exit Ghost*, 256.

59 See Gerald Early, "Ali's Rumble," *Sight and Sound*, May 1997, 10–12; Grant Farred, "Feasting on Foreman: *When We Were Kings* as Hagiography," *Camera Obscura* 39 (September 1996), 52–77, and Julio Rodriguez, "Documenting Myth: Racial Representation in Leon Gast's *When We Were Kings*," in *Sports Matters: Recreation, Race and Culture*, eds John Bloom and Michael Nevin Willard (New York: New York University Press, 2002), 209–22.

60 Roth, *Exit Ghost*, 246.

21

SCOTT D. EMMERT

Jack London and the Great White Hopes of Boxing Literature

Boxing exhilarated Jack London. Its drama sharpened his appetite for vivid stories, and its spectacle of violent survival justified his Darwinian convictions. He needed no further motivation to become a boxing journalist and the first American writer to turn the sport into material for adult fiction.[1] Notoriously, London has also been given credit for inventing the phrase "great white hope"[2] to name the desire by white boxing fans for a white champion in the wake of Jack Johnson becoming the first black man to earn and defend the heavyweight title. Like almost all whites in the early twentieth century, London was a racialist who agreed with what Madison Grant called in 1916 "the modern and scientific study of race" that positioned Nordic as superior and Negro as inferior.[3] A black man holding the heavyweight title threatened the assumed superiority of white Americans, and the threat made whites angry.[4] Although in his journalism London admitted that Johnson was a tremendous boxer, in his second boxing novel, *The Abysmal Brute* (1913), he created a larger-than-life white boxer, the great white hope, to comfort his white readers by relieving anxieties that undermined their self-image.

As a journalist London covered many of the era's best-known bouts, including those between Tommy Burns and Jack Johnson in 1908 and James Jeffries and Johnson in 1910. In his reporting, London favored Burns and Jeffries because they were white and Johnson was black. His report for the *New York Herald* – dateline Sydney, Australia, December 27, 1908 – freely expresses his desire to see Tommy Burns defeat Jack Johnson: "I was with Burns all the way. He is a white man, and so am I. Naturally I wanted to see the white man win."[5] Yet London also gives Johnson his due: "Because a white man wishes a white man to win, this should not prevent him from giving absolute credit to the best man who did win, even when that best man was black. All hail to Johnson. His victory was unqualified."[6] Unqualified, but still a bitter pill, and London objects to Johnson's "clown"-like demeanor in the fight, his smiling throughout with "teeth flash[ing] forth like the rise of a harvest moon," and to the apparent insouciance with which he "played with Burns from the gong of the opening round to the finish of the fight."[7] In the end of his Burns–Johnson report, London calls for James Jeffries, a long-retired, white, ex-heavyweight champion, "to emerge from his alfalfa farm and remove [the] smile from Johnson's face."[8]

That called-for fight would take place on July 4, 1910, and again Johnson would defeat the white hope. London begins his post-fight article: "Once again has Johnson sent down to defeat the chosen representative of the white race, and this time the greatest of them all."[9] Johnson remains a mystery to London, however: "No one understands him, this man who smiles ... And where now is the champion who will make Johnson extend himself, who will glaze those bright eyes, remove that smile and silence that golden repartee?"[10] Although here London does not call expressly for a *white* champion, as scholar Kasia Boddy writes, his opposition to "Johnson as a clown or a minstrel drew upon the myth of black shiftless gaiety peddled by 'coon songs' ... [and] Sambo cartoons."[11] Heavyweights have always borne the heaviest symbolism, and London clearly could not square his sense of racial superiority with the fact that a black man held the heavyweight title. If Burns and Jeffries could not defeat Johnson, then what white man could?

London would find the answer in fiction by imagining a white champion in *The Absymal Brute*. The novel is a direct response to the Jeffries–Johnson bout. Begun soon after that fight and published first in *Popular Magazine* in September 1911 and then as a separate book in 1913, *The Abysmal Brute* appeared when the nation still recalled Johnson's successful defense of the heavyweight title.[12] Early in the novel, protagonist Pat Glendon is called "the hope of the white race" and "Jeffries" is mentioned two sentences later.[13] Critic Michael Oriard notes that although Glendon never fights a black man, his "real opponent in the story, though he never appears, is Jack Johnson himself, still enjoying his championship before he would be driven from the country for outraging white Americans."[14] *The Abysmal Brute* is the most prominent great white hope fiction in American letters. It is also largely a fantasy of purity – racial, sexual, and national.

Glendon is London's ideal American. He is presented as "pure natural,"[15] as a product of America's bucolic innocence and not of its urban decline. Manager Sam Stubener recognizes Glendon's innate superiority: "He seemed a creature of the wild, more a night-roaming figure from some old fairy story or folk tale than a twentieth-century youth."[16] Eventually, Glendon is attracted to Maud Sangster, and she to him. The attraction, however, is more conceptual than sexual. Pat Glendon and Maud Sangster are London's essential male and female, impermeable gender categories. Soon after their meeting, Glendon thinks, "Here was a woman, a WOMAN,"[17] and the capitalization underscores London's fundamentalism. Pat and Maud are America's Adam and Eve,[18] though they never sin. Their honeymoon in a "vast virgin forest"[19] is prelapsarian bliss. Neither character can possibly fall from natural grace.

Saint and redeemer in one supreme, male, white body, Glendon seeks to restore boxing's competitive code after he learns that Stubener has been colluding with other managers to fix fights. Before his last match, Glendon makes a grandiloquent speech exposing boxing as "crooked," a "graft" "run on business principles."[20] He then knocks out his opponent to thwart the prearranged dive and "retire[s] from the ring forever."[21] While London depicts no black challenger, he is nonetheless careful to maintain racial hierarchy. Significantly, Glendon knocks out "Pete Sosso, a Portuguese fighter from Butchertown,"[22] in the fourth round, but he battles into the fourteenth round with "the Flying Dutchman … a young Swede who possessed an unwonted willingness to fight and who was blessed with phenomenal endurance."[23] Clearly, the best skin in this game is Nordic.

In its mythic themes, *The Abysmal Brute* is a seminal American sports novel,[24] the forerunner to sports stories in which winners are ultimately incorruptible and so are the readers who embrace them. However, *The Abysmal Brute* did not invent the great white hope narrative. In 1812 Pierce Egan recounts the second heavyweight bout between Tom Molineaux, a black American boxer, and Tom Crib, a white Englishman, in 1811 – a fight in which Englishmen of all social ranks invested great symbolic capital, though it went largely unnoticed in America.[25] Included in *Boxiana*, Egan's account of Molineaux, whom he repeatedly calls "the *Moor*" (italics in original), views the black boxer as more American than African American, as a national upstart opposing a great English hero in Crib. Historian Elliot J. Gorn explains that the English saw "national honor" as the stakes in the two matches between a black American and *their* champion. With his two victories over the upstart American, Crib affirmed his nation's sense of superiority.[26]

English pride and the vitality of its upper classes are similarly reinforced in George Bernard Shaw's *Cashel Byron's Profession* (1886), another precursor to London's white hope novel. Byron, a white heavyweight, is the fictional embodiment of Shaw's fascination with the dominance of a boxer who, alone against a single opponent in the ring, emerges as "supremely vigorous and powerful, moral and courageous – in short, as a superman."[27] Through his title character, Shaw explores the elasticity of British social class, for Byron fights his way into the upper classes even though, as it turns out, he was first born to this prominence. Although boxing is illegal and considered "low," Byron proves that he belongs among gentlemen, in part by defeating Paradise, a "new man from the black country."[28] Paradise possesses the visage of "an ourang-outang."[29] He is further set apart from the white Byron when spectators insist that the black boxer "ain't … the gentleman."[30] During an exhibition before an African king, Byron and Paradise end up in a brawl in which Paradise displays a "sly grin" – a description that prefigures Jack London's offense at Jack Johnson's smile.

The king is so impressed by Byron that he offers "to provide him with three handsome wives if he would come out to Africa."[31] By refusing miscegenation, Byron helps prove his love for Lydia Cashew, an intellectual seemingly above his class. Later Byron defeats Paradise to become "champion of the world and a gentleman as well. The two things have never happened before and never will again."[32] After Byron retires from boxing, Paradise becomes the heavyweight champion, successfully defending the title twice before descending into alcoholism and poverty. In this way, the white Byron becomes to the black Paradise both a physical and moral superior.

After *The Abysmal Brute* came other white hope stories, such as *The Mucker* (1914), a serialized novel by Edgar Rice Burroughs. In chapter 17, protagonist Billy Byrne spars with "Battling Dago Pete" to become the next white hope: Byrne "fought, crouching, much as Jeffries used to fight, and in his size and strength was much that reminded [fight promoter] Cassidy of the fallen idol that in his heart of hearts he still worshiped." In the end, Byrne contracts to fight the black champion, and though the match is not depicted, Burroughs leaves no doubt who would win. Other authors were less indirect. In the *The White Hope* (1913) by W.R.H. Trowbridge, white boxer Jack Delane knocks out black title-holder Sam Crowfoot to gain the middleweight championship. The crowd cheers "their 'white hope' wildly,"[33] and Trowbridge makes clear that the better race and man has won: "Crowfoot's colour was against him and his reputation as a bruiser and foul-fighter made his defeat appear just and well merited."[34]

Such overt white hope fiction was soon subject to historical and cultural change, however. Significantly, black boxers were marginalized in the late teens and the 1920s and posed less threat to white heavyweights. In the years between Jack Johnson's loss of the heavyweight title to white boxer Jess Willard in 1915 and the rise of Joe Louis in the 1930s, white heavyweight champions consistently refused to fight black challengers; as a result, white readers had less psychic need for white hope fiction. Indeed, in this period black boxers are almost erased from white popular culture. This elision can be seen in the preeminent boxing magazine *The Ring*, which featured white fighters on its covers almost exclusively from its inception in 1922 until 1940. On the rare occasions that black boxers do appear in *The Ring*'s cover art, they do so with a number of white boxers in face shots only. In March 1940, Louis is finally shown alone and in full fighting posture.[35] The first pulp magazine exclusively devoted to boxing fiction, *Fight Stories*, similarly championed white boxers. From initial publication in June 1928 until April 1932, only white fighters are depicted on its monthly covers. *Fight Stories* then ceased publication for four years, and the cover of its second edition in 1936 depicts Louis with white boxer James J. Braddock.[36] The stories inside these covers also sidelined African American characters. An extensive survey by John Dinan finds that "[t]he majority of sports fiction in the pulp magazines was white, male, and professional."[37]

Nevertheless, bigoted characterizations of black athletes were still, as Dinan puts it, part of the "common racism of the day."[38] The many examples include an Arthur Conan Doyle story from 1926, "The Adventure of the Three Gables," in which Sherlock Holmes and Dr. Watson sneer at a "savage" black boxer.[39] And racist dialect abounded. *Knockout Magazine*, for instance, published "Gloves for a Ghost" (1937) which features in a white boxer's retinue the character Sambo Mullins, "who speaks in Stepin-Fetchitese."[40]

The African American press responded to this racism. Scholar Chris Vials notes that African American artists "exalted the ring" in the 1930s and championed Armstrong and Louis in print and song.[41] The hero-worship of black boxers by African Americans takes an original turn in Victor R. Daly's "Private Walker Goes Patrolling" (1930), in which a black American soldier and a German battle hand-to-hand in a fashion more sweet science than frantic combat. Toward the end of the story, Sergeant Bill Dade and a German soldier exchange "uppercut[s]" and "lefthook[s]." Daly describes the action like a boxing scribe eager to involve his readers in an unseen fight: "So there they stood in the quiet, peaceful valley, in the gathering dusk, toe to toe, the Bavarian butcher and the stevedore from Memphis, trading punches, blow for blow."[42] After Private Jerry Walker coldcocks the German with his sidearm, Daly comments wryly, "Jerry had stopped the fight."[43] The friendship between black soldiers in this story, which not incidentally reverses the white hope narrative, results from Dade's prowess as pugilist and Walker's resolve as referee.

Among the white literati in the 1930s, furthermore, the white hope plot became decidedly unfashionable. Vials examines the emerging trend of "stories of white ethnic boxers"[44] by Depression-era writers, including Clifford Odets, Dashiell Hammett, and Nelson Algren. These writers depicted boxers of, for example, Irish and Jewish heritage to suggest their masculine credentials for counting as Americans. These white writers also contested a simplistic white–black racial divide to attempt an "antiracist class unity."[45] Boxing fiction became, then, less about the social divides of race, a great white hope, and more about the longed-for unity of a polychromic nation in dire economic straits, a great working-class faith. This desire for racial unity can be seen in Sherwood Anderson's distaste for the racism he witnessed before a fight between Joe Louis and Jorge Brescia in 1936. Anderson reports a drunken man's boast that the "smoke's a sucker for a right" and a newspaper account emphasizing the "Nordic blood in [Brescia's] veins."[46] Sitting in the uppermost seats among a mostly black crowd, Anderson roots for Louis to beat Brescia so "our Joe, the Brown Bomber" can again fight Max Schmeling.[47] Here the great hope is "our Joe," the American boxer who "had got us all, white men and Negro men" in the desire to see the "German Nazi" defeated.[48]

Before and especially after the Second World War, serious boxing literature does not develop in the direction of the white hope fantasy of *The Abysmal Brute*, but instead takes its cue from London's first boxing novel, *The Game* (1905), in which a fighter is killed in the ring. In the 1930s and after, literary writers overwhelmingly took a similar naturalistic view of the sport, creating white boxers whose fates are sealed. Nelson Algren in *Never Come Morning* (1942), Budd Schulberg in *The Harder They Fall* (1947), Irving Schulman in *The Square Trap* (1953), W.C. Heinz in *The Professional* (1958), and Leonard Gardner in *Fat City* (1969) all take defeat as a boxer's lot in life. Moreover, like much post-Second World War fiction in America, these naturalistic boxing novels – stories of loss and misplaced optimism – challenge readers to consider whether the United States lives up to its ideals now that the nation is a global superpower and putative moral leader.

Schulberg's *The Harder They Fall*, for example, dramatizes corruption in sports to question America's professed dedication to truth and fairness. Narrator Eddie Lewis, a press agent for mobster Nick Latka, writes puff pieces for fighter Toro Molina, whom Latka sets up in a series of fixed bouts. Molina, an Argentine peasant and gentle giant, eventually kills a man in the ring and later suffers a punishing defeat at the hands of a more experienced and legitimate boxer. Latka and his mob make money while Molina will have to go on taking a beating because he is dependent on crooked promoters. Eddie, telling himself that he needs to be as wealthy as possible before he can settle down to serious writing, cannot act to save Molina or redeem himself. *The Harder They Fall* ranks with Bernard Malamud's *The Natural* (1952) as an indictment of an American consumer culture that worships only money and turns athletes into products to be sold and discarded.

Heinz's *The Professional* offers a more subtle critique of a winning-is-all American society. Though its title is singular, the novel portrays three professionals: boxer Eddie Brown, manager Doc Carroll, and sportswriter (and narrator) Frank Hughes. Each character takes his profession seriously, seeking success through complete dedication to craft. Confident of his natural ability, Eddie nonetheless trains hard, for boxing is his livelihood. Though Eddie is his best hope for a champion, Doc nonetheless cares about the art of boxing more than about winning and money. For a single magazine story, Frank spends a month at training camp as Eddie prepares for the middleweight championship; and though Frank admires Eddie and Doc, he protects his journalist's objectivity and keeps a careful distance from his subjects. In his own way, each character is presented as an anachronism in an era in which TV broadcasts of fights have led fans to relish flash over substance. In the end, Eddie loses because he tries to finish the fight too early instead of patiently out-lasting the champ: "It was all over in one minute and forty-eight seconds."[49] All Eddie and Doc have, finally, are the years and effort they put in to prepare for this one fight. The reader is led to admire them both, and in that way the novel emphasizes that loving a "winner" is too easy. As Frank says, "The shame is that we all lose, Doc, including that champion who right now is being slapped on the back and told again that he's a great champion. For a second there Eddie made him an honest man, but now he'll believe this because the honest winners are so few. Everybody in this place lost tonight, Doc, but they don't know it."[50] Ultimately, *The Professional* dramatizes that hard work and right action stand little chance in a culture that cares too much for meretricious success and too little for out-of-view self-sacrifice.

Boxing fiction since the Second World War also offers a curious omission: Although in these years many of boxing's greatest athletes have been African Americans, as Gerald Early has noted, "no major black writer" has published a novel about an African American boxer.[51] To be sure, Ralph Ellison dramatizes a travesty of boxing in "Battle Royal," first published as a short story and later as the first chapter of *Invisible Man* (1952), to expose the power dynamics of race and gender by depicting the common practice of blindfolding black boys and having them fight en masse for the amusement of white men. In the twentieth century, certain other African American novelists attempted portrayals of black boxers. For example, in the late 1920s, Walter White began and abandoned a novel about a black heavyweight.[52] In the mid-1930s Richard Wright was, without success, submitting to publishers the novel *Tarbaby's Dawn*, the story of a teenager who migrates to Chicago with the intention of becoming a boxer.[53]

And in the 1940s, before embarking on a career in historical fiction, Frank Yerby tried unsuccessfully to publish a novel with a black boxer as protagonist.[54] Publishers, it appears, were not interested in novels about African American boxers, so dominated had the genre become by white authors and characters.

Portrayals of boxers in contemporary novels continue to come from white writers who find boxing amenable to their themes. Robert Lipsyte, for example, creates a black boxer in the young adult novel *The Contender* (1967) to emphasize the virtues of exertion and dedication. Pete Hamill's *Flesh and Blood* (1977), reminiscent of the white ethnic boxing novels of the 1930s, depicts the pugilistic fall but existential rise of Bobby Fallon, a working-class New Yorker on the make. Joyce Carol Oates in *You Must Remember This* (1987) embroils an ex-boxer in an affair with his teenaged niece to connect sexual passion with violence and thereby suggest the threat to identity posed by both. To be sure, tremendous nonfiction about African American boxers, including essays by Early and Oates,[55] abounds. However, a novel on boxing by a leading African American writer may never materialize – perhaps, in part, due to the sport's decreased popularity. Still, the potential for such a novel is rich. Early likens "race in America" to the doubloon nailed to the mast in *Moby-Dick*. Race is the symbol "hammered in our consciousness," and in it we may read how we understand the world.[56] Gazing into this symbol, Paul Beatty in the brilliant basketball novel *The White Boy Shuffle* (1996) satirizes the nation's racial perceptions, illuminating blindspots and viewpoints alike. Beatty's novel eschews the earnest patterns of sports fiction established by pioneers such as Jack London. In long fiction, boxing still awaits such an unrestrained treatment.

As does boxing in contemporary film. Today's movies about boxing, from *Rocky* (1976) to *Southpaw* (2015), are often beholden to Jack London's interest in the progress of white characters, though their racial preference is more subtly conveyed. In fiction, as Oriard astutely observes, the pastoral idealism of *The Abysmal Brute* moved readily into much subsequent fiction about baseball, a supposedly rural sport bearing little of boxing's urban tensions.[57] Baseball novels such as W.P. Kinsella's *Shoeless Joe* (1982) often devise a largely white, bucolic ideal. On film, similar daydreams of great white hopes live on in movies such as *Rocky* and *Cinderella Man* (2005), and even in the basketball-focused *Hoosiers* (1986).[58] Today, Jack London's racialism may shock readers[59] – but if in America racial allegiance is now more covertly expressed, that in itself allows us neither to condemn London nor to congratulate ourselves.

NOTES

1 Oriard, Michael. *Dreaming of Heroes: American Sports Fiction, 1868–1980.* Chicago, IL: Nelson-Hall, 1982, 9.

2 George Kimball and John Schulian give full credit to London for being "the originator of the term" (Kimball, George and John Schulian, eds. *At the Fights: American Writers on Boxing.* New York: Library of America, 2011, 1). Kasia Boddy allows only that "the phrase seems to have been coined by London" (Boddy, Kasia. *Boxing: A Cultural History.* London: Reaktion Books, 2008).

3 Grant, Madison. *The Passing of the Great Race; or The Racial Basis of European History.* 1916. Fourth rev. ed. New York: Scribner's, 1936, 12.

4 After Johnson defeated James Jeffries in 1910, white violence against blacks erupted in a nationwide series of race riots and lynchings.

5 London, Jack. "Burns–Johnson Fight." *Jack London Reports: War Correspondence, Sports Articles, and Miscellaneous Writings.* Eds. King Hendricks and Irving Shepard. Garden City, NY: Doubleday, 1970, 258–59.

6 Ibid., 259.

7 Ibid., 263.

8 Ibid., 264.

9 London, Jack. "Jeffries–Johnson Fight." *Jack London Reports: War Correspondence, Sports Articles, and Miscellaneous Writings.* Eds. King Hendricks and Irving Shepard. Garden City, NY: Doubleday, 1970, 293.

10 Ibid., 301.

11 Boddy, *Boxing,* 182.

12 Oriard, Michael, *Dreaming of Heroes,* Introduction, viii.

13 London, Jack. *The Abysmal Brute.* 1913. Lincoln, NE: University of Nebraska Press, 2000, 5.

14 Oriard, *Dreaming of Heroes,* Introduction, ix.

15 London, *The Abysmal Brute,* 15.

16 Ibid., 22.

17 Ibid., 80.

18 Oriard, *Dreaming of Heroes,* Introduction, xii.

19 London, *The Abysmal Brute,* 133.

20 Ibid., 153.

21 Ibid., 169.

22 Ibid., 47.

23 Ibid., 56.

24 Oriard, *Dreaming of Heroes,* Introduction, xiii.

25 Gorn, Elliott J. *The Manly Art: Bare-Knuckle Prize Fighting in America.* Ithaca, NY: Cornell University Press, 1986, 34.

26 Ibid., 20.

27 Peters, Sally. *Bernard Shaw: The Ascent of the Superman.* New Haven, CT: Yale University Press, 1996, 86.

28 Shaw, George Bernard. *Cashel Byron's Profession.* 1886. Carbondale and Edwardsville, IL: Southern Illinois University Press, 1968, 125.

29 Ibid., 159.

30 Ibid., 160.

31 Ibid., 164.

32 Ibid., 194.

33 Trowbridge, W. R. H. *The White Hope*. Leipzig: Bernhard Tauchnitz, 1913, 291.

34 Ibid., 293.

35 Stephenson-Payne, Phil, comp. "Fight Stories." *Gallactic Central*. Jan. 12, 2014. Jan. 13, 2014. <www.philsp.com/mags/fight_stories.html>

36 "*The Ring* Magazine Covers." *Boxtree Encyclopedia*. Nov. 30, 2007. Jan. 13, 2014. <http://boxrec.com/media/index.php/The_Ring_Magazine_Covers:_1940>.

37 Dinan, *Sports in the Pulp Magazines*. Jefferson, NC: McFarland, 1998, 42.

38 Ibid., 91.

39 Doyle, Arthur Conan. *The Complete Sherlock Holmes*. Vol. 2. Garden City, NY: Doubleday and Company, 1930. 1023.

40 Dinan, *Sports in the Pulp Magazines*, 91.

41 Vials, *Realism for the Masses: Aesthetics, Popular Front Pluralism, and US Culture, 1935–1947*. Jackson, MS: University Press of Mississippi, 2009, 5.

42 Daly, Victor R. "Private Walker Goes Patrolling." *The Crisis*. Jun. 1930: 201.

43 Ibid., 213.

44 Vials, *Realism for the Masses*, 4.

45 Ibid., 8.

46 Anderson, Sherwood. "Brown Bomber." *At the Fights: American Writers on Boxing*. Eds. George Kimball and John Schulian. New York: Library of America, 2011, 45.

47 Ibid., 49.

48 Ibid.

49 Heinz, W. C. *The Professional*. 1958. Cambridge, MA: Da Capo Press, 2001, 321.

50 Ibid., 330.

51 Early, Gerald. "The Grace of Slaughter: Joyce Carol Oates's *On Boxing*." *Tuxedo Junction: Essays on American Culture*. New York: Ecco Press, 1989, 168.

52 Suggs, Jon-Christian. "'Blackjack': Walter White and Modernism in an Unknown Boxing Novel." *Michigan Quarterly Review* 38.4 (Fall 1999): 514–40.

53 Ward, Jerry W., and Robert J. Butler, eds. *The Richard Wright Encyclopedia*. Westport, CT: Greenwood Press, 2008, 369.

54 Hill, James L. "Frank Yerby." *The Concise Oxford Companion to African American Literature*. Eds William L. Andrews, Frances Smith Foster, and Trudier Harris. Oxford: Oxford University Press, 2001, 452.

55 Read Early's *Tuxedo Junction* and *The Culture of Bruising*, and Oates's *On Boxing*.

56 Early, "The Grace of Slaughter," 168.

57 Oriard, *Dreaming of Heroes*, Introduction, xiii.

58 See Ron Briley's analysis. Briley, Ron. "Basketball's Great White Hope and Ronald Reagan's America: *Hoosiers* (1986)." *Film and History: An Interdisciplinary Journal of Film and Television Studies* 35:1 (2005): 12–19.

59 London's racial ideas underwent significant changes. See Reesman, Jane Campbell. *Jack London's Racial Lives: A Critical Biography*. Athens, GA: University of Georgia Press, 2009.

BIBLIOGRAPHY

Anderson, Sherwood. "Brown Bomber." *At the Fights: American Writers on Boxing.* Eds. George Kimball and John Schulian. New York: Library of America, 2011, 45–51.

Beatty, Paul. *The White Boy Shuffle.* 1996. New York: Picador, 2001.

Boddy, Kasia. *Boxing: A Cultural History.* London: Reaktion Books, 2008.

Briley, Ron. "Basketball's Great White Hope and Ronald Reagan's America: *Hoosiers* (1986)." *Film and History: An Interdisciplinary Journal of Film and Television Studies* 35:1 (2005): 12–19.

Burroughs, Edgar Rice. *The Mucker.* 1914. New York: Ballantine, 1966.

Daly, Victor R. "Private Walker Goes Patrolling." *The Crisis.* Jun. 1930: 199–201, 213.

Dinan, John. *Sports in the Pulp Magazines.* Jefferson, NC: McFarland, 1998.

Doyle, Arthur Conan. *The Complete Sherlock Holmes.* Vol. 2. Garden City, NY: Doubleday and Company, 1930. 1023–33.

Early, Gerald. *The Culture of Bruising: Essays on Prizefighting, Literature, and Modern American Culture.* Hopewell, NJ: Ecco Press, 1994.

"The Grace of Slaughter: Joyce Carol Oates's *On Boxing.*" *Tuxedo Junction: Essays on American Culture.* New York: Ecco Press, 1989, 160–70.

Egan, Pierce. "Egan's *Boxiana.*" *The Unlevel Playing Field: A Documentary History of the African American Experience in Sport.* David K. Wiggins and Partick B. Miller. Urbana and Chicago, IL: University of Illinois Press, 2003, 11–13.

Gorn, Elliott J. *The Manly Art: Bare-Knuckle Prize Fighting in America.* Ithaca, NY: Cornell University Press, 1986.

Grant, Madison. *The Passing of the Great Race; or The Racial Basis of European History.* 1916. Fourth rev. ed. New York: Scribner's, 1936.

Heinz, W. C. *The Professional.* 1958. Cambridge, MA: Da Capo Press, 2001.

Hamill, Pete. *Flesh and Blood.* New York: Random House, 1977.

Hill, James L. "Frank Yerby." *The Concise Oxford Companion to African American Literature.* Eds. William L. Andrews, Frances Smith Foster, and Trudier Harris. Oxford: Oxford University Press, 2001, 451–53.

Kimball, George and John Schulian, eds. *At the Fights: American Writers on Boxing.* New York: Library of America, 2011.

Lipsyte, Robert. *The Contender.* 1967. New York: HarperCollins, 1992.

London, Jack. *The Abysmal Brute.* 1913. Lincoln, NE: University of Nebraska Press, 2000.

"Burns–Johnson Fight." *Jack London Reports: War Correspondence, Sports Articles, and Miscellaneous Writings.* Eds. King Hendricks and Irving Shepard. Garden City, NY: Doubleday, 1970, 258–64.

"Jeffries–Johnson Fight." *Jack London Reports: War Correspondence, Sports Articles, and Miscellaneous Writings.* Eds. King Hendricks and Irving Shepard. Garden City, NY: Doubleday, 1970, 293–301.

Oates, Joyce Carol. *On Boxing.* 1987. New York: Harper Perennial, 2006.

You Must Remember This. New York: Dutton, 1987.

Oriard, Michael. *Dreaming of Heroes: American Sports Fiction, 1868–1980.* Chicago, IL: Nelson-Hall, 1982.

"Introduction." *The Abysmal Brute.* Lincoln, NE: University of Nebraska Press, 2000. v–xiv.

Peters, Sally. *Bernard Shaw: The Ascent of the Superman*. New Haven, CT: Yale University Press, 1996.

Reesman, Jane Campbell. *Jack London's Racial Lives: A Critical Biography*. Athens, GA: University of Georgia Press, 2009.

"*The Ring* Magazine Covers." *Boxrec Encyclopedia*. Nov. 30, 2007. Jan. 13, 2014. <http://boxrec.com/media/index.php/The_Ring_Magazine_Covers:_1940>.

Schulberg, Budd. *The Harder They Fall*. 1947. Chicago, IL: Elephant Paperbacks, 1996.

Shaw, George Bernard. *Cashel Byron's Profession*. 1886. Carbondale and Edwardsville, IL: Southern Illinois University Press, 1968.

Stephensen-Payne, Phil, comp. "Fight Stories." *Gallactic Central*. Jan. 12, 2014. Jan. 13, 2014. <www.philsp.com/mags/fight_stories.html>.

Suggs, Jon-Christian. "'Blackjack': Walter White and Modernism in an Unknown Boxing Novel." *Michigan Quarterly Review* 38.4 (Fall 1999): 514–40.

Trowbridge, W.R.H. *The White Hope*. Leipzig: Bernhard Tauchnitz, 1913.

Vials, Chris. *Realism for the Masses: Aesthetics, Popular Front Pluralism, and US Culture, 1935–1947*. Jackson, MS: University Press of Mississippi, 2009.

Ward, Jerry W., and Robert J. Butler, eds. *The Richard Wright Encyclopedia*. Westport, CT: Greenwood Press, 2008.

Wiggins, David K., and Patrick B. Miller. *The Unlevel Playing Field: A Documentary History of the African American Experience in Sport*. Urbana and Chicago, IL: University of Illinois Press, 2003.

22

LEGER GRINDON

Body and Soul of the Screen Boxer

The boxer stands alongside the cowboy, the gangster, and the detective as a figure that has shaped America's idea of manhood. Beyond the sport itself, the boxer's significance has been vividly developed in motion pictures. The pugilist became popular in Hollywood cinema with the coming of sound and appeared in over 100 feature films between 1930 and 1960, including such hits as *The Champ* (1931), *Kid Galahad* (1937), *Gentleman Jim* (1942), and *Somebody Up There Likes Me* (1956). During the decade 1975–85, the screen boxer experienced a comeback in numerous films, including the enormous commercial success of the *Rocky* series (1976–2018) and the critically esteemed *Raging Bull* (1980). More recently, *Million Dollar Baby* (2004), *Cinderella Man* (2005), and *The Fighter* (2010) testify to the boxer's continuing presence.

The screen boxer embodies the physical: a strong man striving for power in a metropolis dominated by money, position, and cunning. His body becomes a commodity that is consumed in his struggle for dominance. As a result, the boxer dramatizes oppression. Like the gangster, the boxer is tragic; he personifies a division between the body and the spirit, and because time dictates the deterioration of the flesh, he is destined for a fall. His story generally follows a rise and fall pattern in which he reaches a pinnacle of physical prowess, becomes champion, and then declines with the aging of his body. The reason for and purpose of suffering arise as central questions. The boxer's agony sparks a search for values beyond the body, raising questions about American materialism. Thus, the boxing film genre addresses the limitations of the physical and a quest for a worthy alternative.

At the foundation of boxing films is a series of dramatic conflicts that represent widespread social concerns. Though not every conflict is evident in every film, these related conflicts give boxing films unity and flexibility over time. Six key conflicts distinguish boxing films. They are (1) the conflict between body and soul or material versus spiritual values; (2) the critique of the success ethic expressed in the conflict between individual competition fostered by market forces versus human cooperation and self-sacrifice; (3) a conflict between the opportunity success offers the boxer for integration into mainstream society versus loyalty to the marginalized community from which he arose; (4) a masculinity crisis arising from the gender conflict between the manly ethos of the ring and a woman's influence traditionally associated with romance. And finally a problem for male emotion arises from two related conflicts: (5) anger at injustice clashes with powerlessness to eliminate oppression; and (6) a stoic discipline in the face of life's cruelty conflicts with sensitivity toward others. These conflicts pose problems, vital to the experience of the audience, that receive a variety of treatments throughout the genre's history. For example, *Fat City* (1972), with its critique of masculinity, poses many of the same gender conflicts found in *Hard Times* (1975), which valorizes masculinity. The dramatic conflicts central to the genre allow for a range of resolutions and attitudes, a flexibility that ensures the evolution of the form.

The boxer embodies the physical ideal of old-fashioned, self-reliant masculinity: a strong man of action who finds himself disarmed by guile, finance, technology, changing times – in short, the forces shaping the modern city. Like the gangster, he strives to rise from the crowd and grasp the success warranted by his physical power. Unlike the gangster, whose work is done in private, and whose mode is conspiratorial, the boxer is a public figure, whose body is fully exposed to be applauded or sometimes reviled. However, he is seldom idealized. Rather his rage, simplicity, or a misguided consciousness highlights his common nature. Competition in the ring may allow the boxer to understand himself as a man, or else he is doomed to suffer a grim fate, trapped by the limitations of his body.

The male protagonist is often a dual figure – the boxer and the manager. Though most boxing films foreground the prizefighter, some films, such as *Kid Galahad*, highlight the manager. In many films, such as *Iron Man* (1931), *Hard Times*, and *Million Dollar Baby*, the boxer and the manager receive comparable treatment. The division between these figures emphasizes the body–mind split and expresses key conflicts. The manager is the technician and strategist, a rationalist; he is frequently compromised because he represents business, a rival to the family. The boxer embodies the natural and intuitive individualist who resists social rules, whereas the manager represents institutional wisdom and community values. Figures circling near the protagonist further develop this character. For example, the trainer usually assumes that role as the caretaker of the body, though he may, like Ben (Canada Lee) in *Body and Soul* or Poe (Strother Martin) in *Hard Times*, also minister to the soul. Others, like Mickey (Burgess Meredith) in *Rocky,* combine the roles of manager/trainer along with the values of the mind and the heart.

The antagonist in the boxing film mirrors the protagonist in comprising a dual figure: the gangster-promoter and the hero's chief rival in the ring. For example, in *Champion* (1949), Harris, the gangster-promoter, replaces the manager, leading to Midge Kelly's (Kirk Douglas) fall, while his counterpart is Johnny Dunne, Kelly's ring opponent. The gangster-promoter, an evil transformation of the manager, is associated with the corruption of money and the moral compromises necessary to prosper in business. In the economic analogue underlying the genre, the boxer represents physical labor; the manager, technical expertise; and the promoter, capital. Sometimes the manager betrays his loyalty to the boxer by serving the gangster-promoter, as in *Body and Soul* and *The Set-Up* (1949). As a gambler, the promoter is a shadow investor who uses capital to make money from the physical toil of others. For him, value lies not in labor and craft, emblematic of the work ethic, but in wealth itself. The promoter also violates the code of fair competition, for as a gangster he uses force outside the boundaries of the ring and employs others to execute his violence. A personification of the soul's degradation, the promoter is solely interested in financial gain. Like market forces, he is impervious to human feeling.

The hero's ring opponent physically portrays the moral assault undertaken by the gangster-promoter. Whereas the gangster-promoter signifies exterior social forces pressuring the boxer, the ring opponent often becomes a phantom or psychological antagonist representing a weakness inside the boxer. For example, in *Right Cross* (1950), Heldon (Eddie Lou Simms), the inconsequential opponent of champion Johnny Monterez (Richardo Montalban), recognizes that Monterez drops his left hand as he throws a right punch. The champ's weakness allows Heldon to score an upset. More to the point, the flaw in Johnny's defense represents a character flaw, his exaggerated feeling of being victimized by prejudice. This motif invites, and frequently receives, a racial treatment, with African Americans assuming a symbolic function as the black phantom that personifies psychic turmoil. For example, in *Golden Boy* (1939), Joe Bonaparte (William Holden) kills Chocolate Drop in the ring and as a result comes to terms with the violence in himself. Ray Robinson embodies LaMotta's troubled psyche, inflicting defeat and retribution upon Jake (Robert De Niro) in *Raging Bull*. Gerald Early has noted there is "a very simple and very old idea here, namely, that the black male is metaphorically the white man's unconscious personified."[1] So the antagonist in the boxing film takes on the body/soul division, splitting into exterior social forces portrayed by the gangster-promoter and interior psychic turmoil embodied by the ring opponent.

The opposition between body and soul and the critique of the success ethic shape the romance as the boxer's affections move from the neighborhood sweetheart to the vamp. Whether the librarian of "Dynamite Hands," the painter of *Body and Soul*, or the manager's convent educated younger sister in *Kid Galahad*, the sweetheart is associated with the uplift of the spirit under the rubric of family, religion, or culture. On the other hand, the vamp, like Grace (Marilyn Maxwell) in *Champion*, offers the pleasures of the flesh; she preys upon the hero's body just as she drains away his money.

Romance also poses the gender conflict. How can a man retain his masculinity and achieve a fruitful union with a woman? The heroine of the boxing film does not simply represent romantic fulfillment, but challenges the exclusive male world of the ring. Marriage, domesticity and family mean giving up the diversions of fighting and the male coterie of the gym. In order to cultivate his soul, the boxer must take on attributes associated with the feminine; otherwise he will perish with his body. *The Champ* (1931) portrays the fighter as an overgrown boy, and similar childlike qualities mark Kid Mason (Lew Ayres) in *Iron Man* (1931; remade in 1951 with Jeff Chandler), Joe Bonaparte, and Kid Galahad. Like the schoolteacher in the Western, the heroine of the boxing film acts in opposition to a male ethos that the hero must overcome in order to mature.

Within the ring two questions are posed. Can the boxer master his body? And can the boxer embrace his soul? The first is resolved when the protagonist gains the championship. At this point the fighter achieves an idealized command over his physical self. The culmination of the boxing film, however, comes with the climactic bout in which the boxer must come to terms with the aging of his body and can only overcome this physical decline through an understanding of his spirit. Typically this moment comes with the realization that the boxer must not throw the fight after all, as in *Body and Soul*. The existence and nature of a spiritual alternative to physical being thus becomes a vital concern for these films.

The ring is the site of sanctioned violence and becomes the key setting for exploring the consequences of anger and the meaning of suffering – that is, can the aggression characterizing the boxer be understood and redirected? In the climactic bout the boxer endures a severe beating in the ring, and even if he emerges victorious, as in *Golden Boy*, the boxer retires after the fight. How is the boxer's suffering to be understood? As a proof of self-worth (*Rocky* [1976], for example)? As punishment (*Champion*)? As a source of purification in preparation for renewal (*Body and Soul*)? Or perhaps the boxer's ordeal is rendered meaningless, as one could argue is the case in *Fat City*. The climactic bout explores the boxer's inner self and asks whether violence bred by anger will destroy or liberate the spirit. The bouts present a struggle in which the boxer must finally learn from loss, that is, learn from the decline of his physical prowess or be trapped within the decaying body. The theme of resurrection commonly attributed to *Raging Bull* seems upon reflection to be endemic to the boxing genre as a whole.

Champion boxers have themselves found their way onto the screen, from Max Baer in *The Prizefighter and the Lady* (1933), to Joe Louis in *The Spirit of Youth* (1937), Muhammad Ali in *The Greatest* (1977), and perhaps most notably Ken Norton in *Mandingo* (1975). But maybe their greatest contribution to the screen boxer is in an advisory role, such as when Jake LaMotta helped to train Robert De Niro for *Raging Bull* (1980) and contributed to the design of the boxing sequences in the film.

Noir Classic

Body and Soul is the seminal work in the post-war noir cycle of boxing films, complemented by three other influential movies, *The Killers* (1946), *Champion*, and *The Set-Up*. In this cycle the boxing world is a competitive marketplace where money talks, duplicity reigns, and human values are degraded. The struggle for success in the ring has transformed the talented young man into a corrupt cynic marked by anxiety and regret. He asks himself if it is too late to escape from the materialist jungle and recover the values he once held.

In the years after the Second World War, new influences, social and cinematic, refined the boxing film. These influences included criminal investigations into the corruption of prizefighting; Ernest Hemingway's stories about boxers; and the film noir style. The intersection of these influences produced the most celebrated boxing films of the studio era.

In December 1946, District Attorney Frank S. Hogan of New York began a crusade to clean up professional boxing, which received widespread press attention. The investigations and press reports revealed a nationwide racket controlling professional prizefighting. The publicity sparked the boxing film's popularity and reanimated its link to the rise of the social problem film after the Second World War. Ethnic and racial prejudice also became conspicuous in boxing films. The influence of Joe Louis, who remained heavyweight champion until 1949, grew increasingly evident. *Body and Soul* featured the African American Ben Chaplin (Canada Lee) in a prominent role as the exploited champ defeated by Charlie Davis for the title. As a result, the noir cycle saw the gangster-promoter and the set-up become dominant elements in the genre.

Meanwhile, the style and values of film noir reinvigorated the conventions of the boxing tale of the 1930s. By 1946 the noir movement already had hit films like *The Maltese Falcon* (1941) and *Double Indemnity* (1944), and its practices were incorporated into other urban crime films. The noir style featured darkness as its signature element; its shadowy black and white photography expressed the loss of ideals, moral ambivalence, and the corruption at the foundation of a nightmarish world. An example of the noir touch opens *Body and Soul* when the silhouette of the swaying body bag awakens Charlie Davis (John Garfield) from his anxious sleep. Flashbacks create a complex temporal scheme in the noir style whereby the past controls the present and confines the protagonist. This self-conscious style employed unstable compositions, startling editing shifts, and voice-over narration emphasizing a tormented psychology attracted to doom. Lust is often privileged over romance, as in the vamp Alice's predatory sexuality in *Body and Soul*, and violence takes on a brutal edge in beatings in and out of the ring. The serious fight takes place outside of public view, after the lights go out and with odds stacked against the lonely boxer. Between 1946 and 1949, screen boxing became a racket. Hoods populating the corrupt underworld controlled the boxer. Battered and dispirited, or equal to the mobster in his ruthlessness, the fighter teetered on the verge of breakdown. The guilt-ridden, nightmare realism of film noir portrayed the conflicts of the screen boxer in a fresh and compelling fashion.

Body and Soul opened in New York City in November 1947 and was an immediate hit. The film earned enthusiastic reviews and three Academy Award nominations: Best Actor for John Garfield, Best Original Screenplay for Abraham Polonsky, and Francis Lyon and Robert Parrish won the award for best editing. *Body and Soul* set the trend for the post–Second World War noir cycle and became the key boxing film for the Hollywood studio era.

Ernest Hemingway's story "Fifty Grand" (1927) provided a model upon which to frame the tale of the rising fighter and invest the fiction with a noir mood. Like "Fifty Grand," the film uses a fix as the crisis that organizes the plot. The film pivots around a noir flashback beginning in training camp just before the big fight, reviews the course of the boxer's career for the bulk of the film, and ends with the title bout anticipated in the opening. The two episodes in "Fifty Grand," the training camp where the fix is set and the bout where the plan goes awry, serve as bookends for *Body and Soul*. The insomnia motif is also borrowed from the short story. In Hemingway's story, Jack Brennan can't sleep in training camp, soured at his declining skills and then compromised by his willingness to take the dive. On screen, Charlie Davis opens the film waking from a troubled sleep and wanders the city at night. Eventually his nap before the bout cues the flashback. The closing bout also offers a reversal on the fix, but it lacks the complexity of Jack Brennan's victory in defeat. Most important, Hemingway's hard-boiled fiction incorporates the noir mood. The plot develops the internal crisis facing the boxer, and the conflict between body and soul becomes a choice between money and integrity.

In the noir tradition the film sets a dark tone, but only gradually reveals the source of the boxer's anxiety. The night before his title defense, Charlie abruptly departs from his training camp for the city where, at his boyhood home, he seeks out his mother and encounters his former fiancée, Peg Born (Lilli Palmer). An unexplained estrangement drives the boxer away, and he leaves to find consolation with Alice (Hazel Brooks), a nightclub singer. The next day, as Charlie tapes his hands in the dressing room before the fight, Roberts (Lloyd Goff), the promoter, visits to remind the boxer of their agreement. The bets are placed for Charlie to lose. After Roberts departs, the champ lies down, and a flashback shows an innocent young Davis applauded for his amateur boxing talents. From here the typical rise and fall pattern of the boxing genre's master story ensues. However, the opening sequence emphasizes feelings of guilt, loss, and melancholy. This plot foregrounds Charlie's fall and in the noir manner intensifies the psychological. The boxer has already sold out; the flashback explains why. In the 1930s, screen boxers, such as Kid Galahad, Joe Bonaparte, and Danny Kenny, were frequently threatened by gangsters or compromised by their managers, but the protagonist boxer had never taken a dive. His attraction to the gangster was motivated by impulse or indiscretion, but he resisted dirty deals. In most cases, the villainous gangster was allied to the hero's ring rivals. From the beginning of the film, Charlie is morally compromised and, like Hemingway's Jack Brennan, the consequences haunt the story. The screen boxers who defined the post–Second World War pugilist are fallen souls whose awareness of their sins invests them with the doomed self-consciousness typical of film noir.

Roberts, the gangster-promoter, has been transformed from a criminal into a businessman. Addressed only by his last name, restrained in speech, polite in manner, he emphasizes calculation rather than violence. In his finely tailored suits, Roberts appears to be the chairman of the board rather than a street thug. Roberts's visit to Charlie's dressing room sets the tone, as he confirms the fix with veiled threats while forcefully twisting Charlie's hand. Taking cues from the revelations of District Attorney Hogan's grand jury investigation, *Body and Soul* displays an institutional understanding of how gangster-promoters control boxers by programming the principal urban arenas and demanding a dominant financial interest in boxers before they can compete in premier matches. The upstanding athlete has little choice but to strike an alliance with criminals. Otherwise, his career would be permanently blocked. So the criticism falls on the competitive system rather than simply the immoral behavior of individuals. Boxing has become equated with business, and Charlie represents the upwardly mobile man on the make ready to sacrifice human values for financial success. *Body and Soul* intensified the social criticism in the boxing film to produce one of the most politicized films in classical Hollywood.

Forces fighting for the human spirit contest the subservience to money. In *Body and Soul* these forces are chiefly portrayed through romance, the art motif, and compassion for the oppressed. Peg Born is the boxer's sweetheart. An art student, she sketches Charlie and recites poetry. She gives the fighter her self-portrait and the picture comes to haunt Davis long after their estrangement. One night during a party in Charlie's apartment, the portrait is accidentally revealed, staring out at the veteran champion. The surprise motivates the boxer to seek out his former fiancée and woo her with the news that his next fight will be his last. The romance amplified by the art motif functions as an expression of spirit in the conflict between body and soul. Together the mother and the beloved condemn ill-gotten wealth because it threatens the values of family, education, and art. In choosing to turn from the fix and win the closing bout, Charlie loses his payoff. He must reject the money to claim the beloved, reunite with his mother, and affirm his spirit.

Furthermore, compassion for the oppressed stirs Charlie's conscience and rekindles his spirit. The first image of the film, the shadow of a body bag swaying in the night over an empty boxing ring, provokes Charlie's nightmare cry: "Ben." The outburst establishes the former champion's haunting influence as Charlie's trainer after Ben retires. Though the African American boxer only slowly emerges as the gangster's victim during the flashback, such suggestive images and persistent foreshadowing magnify his presence. In a climatic confrontation with Roberts, Ben vents his righteous fury on the gangster, but consumed by his frenzy, Ben collapses, dead. Ben's death brings the flashback to its climax and sets the stage for Charlie's defiance of the racketeer. Ben serves as the focal point of oppression and provokes Charlie's tormented conscience.

The closing bout in *Body and Soul* is among the most innovative in the boxing film genre (others include *Kid Galahad*, *Somebody Up There Likes Me*, and *Raging Bull*). The veteran Davis faces his final test in his championship defense against Jack Marlowe. The set-up engineered by Roberts promises Charlie $60,000 if he allows Marlowe to win by decision. Roberts agrees to spare Davis the knockout; Charlie can box the distance without going down. The quality of the boxing sequence was widely celebrated. James Wong Howe's creative cinematography brings the audience forcefully into the ring.

The noir variation on the classic design of a boxing sequence uses a cluster of visual devices to portray Charlie Davis's entrapment. Close shots and tight framing of the boxers, the spectators, and even the bell at ringside convey a menacing confinement. The lighting is dark and a harsh contrast between shadows and glaring illumination contributes to the threatening atmosphere. In the closing three rounds, a strobe-like popping from ringside flash bulbs imparts a pulsating intensity. The editing is fast, with the average shot length down to 3.23 seconds. Unbalanced compositions, especially during the frenzied closing rounds, frequently frame the fighters off center. The shots within the ring are well integrated with the ringside perspectives, while the movement of the hand-held camera conveys the tension, vulnerability and dynamism of the struggle. The uneven lighting and the mobile shots contribute to a newsreel-like imagery, investing the fight with the mix of realism and expressionism distinctive to noir.

The closing three rounds intensify the bout. This climax frequently has the camera within the ring versus the orthodox ringside perspective. Charlie begins the bout as a prisoner to Roberts, but Roberts and Marlowe betray the deal by trying for the knockout. With the double-cross, Charlie's spirit revives, and he fights to win, thereby regaining his soul.

The variety of shots of the boxers in action, as well as the mastery of tempo, movement, and continuity, make this sequence a landmark. Here the expertise that won Lyon and Parrish an Oscar for editing is on display.

The postfight departure brings the opposition between the spiritual and the material to its resolution. As Charlie walks from the ring, cross-cutting begins between the boxer and Peg making her way through the crowd to join him. Just outside the ring Davis is congratulated by the boxing commissioner, the representative of fair play. Opposite stands Alice, the vamp, whom Charlie snubs. The two figures underline the counterpoint between righteousness and hedonism. At the exit from the arena, Roberts waits. Instead of looking up at the fixer as Charlie did at his entry, now they face each other eye to eye. "Get yourself a new boy; I retire," Charlie declares. "What are you gonna do," he continues, "kill me? Everybody dies." At this moment Peg rushes to the champ's side. "Are you all right?" "I never felt better in my life," says Charlie. The film ends. Charlie resolves the spiritual and material opposition embodied by Peg and Roberts by placing his arm around the beloved and walking away from the ring.

Comeback: *Rocky* (1976) and the Revival of the Screen Boxer in the 1970s

From *Hard Times* and *Mandingo* in 1975 through *Raging Bull* and *Any Which Way You Can* in 1980, the boxing film experienced an astonishing resurgence. The 1970s movies include stage hits (*The Great White Hope*,

1970), literary adaptations (*Fat City*, 1972), "blaxploitation" films (*Hammer*, 1972), parodies (*Movie, Movie*, 1978), remakes (*The Champ*, 1979), romantic comedies (*The Main Event*, 1979), and biographies (*The Greatest*, 1977; *Raging Bull*, 1980). *Rocky*'s enormous success stood at the center of the cycle. The Sylvester Stallone film spawned an ongoing seven film series; each of the first four ranked among the top three box office hits in the year of its release. The decade generated the most important cycle of boxing films since the close of the studio era. The causes can be summarized around two phenomena: the film industry revival that came to be known as the "New Hollywood" and the comeback of heavyweight champion Muhammad Ali.

The "New Hollywood" arose in the wake of the near collapse of the old studio system. The motion picture business began the 1970s in crisis and roared back to prosperity at the decade's close, the revised industry dubbed "New Hollywood." The industry recession of 1969–71 was the most severe slump in Hollywood since the Great Depression. Among the many failures were two boxing films directed by Hollywood stalwarts Martin Ritt and John Huston – *The Great White Hope*, a lavish production based upon the Pulitzer Prize-winning Broadway play, which nonetheless lost over $7 million, and *Fat City*, a critically acclaimed literary adaptation that died at the box office. As a result of the crisis in Hollywood, management changed in the film industry, and new filmmakers got unprecedented opportunities.

An upswing in the industry was apparent in 1972 with the enormous success of *The Godfather*. For the remainder of the decade business continued to improve. By 1980 Hollywood was once again prosperous. Benchmark works for the Hollywood comeback were *Jaws* (1975), *Star Wars* (1977), and *Halloween* (1979). Steven Spielberg and George Lucas assumed the leadership of the industry. The boxing film played a role in the turnaround. Walter Hill's *Hard Times* was a mythic valorization of the boxer (Charles Bronson) combining a nostalgic setting in the 1930s with tough action. Its physical ideal of masculinity reasserted old-fashioned individualism. Furthermore, the relaxed ratings code in the "New Hollywood" allowed for a more intense portrayal of ring violence. By the close of the decade, three leading male action stars, Charles Bronson, Sylvester Stallone, and Clint Eastwood, had portrayed the boxer in hit films. Two boxing films, *Rocky* and *Every Which Way But Loose* (1978), registered blockbuster profits.

Rocky became the most popular boxing film in screen history. Produced on a modest budget of $1 million, the brainchild of Sylvester Stallone earned over $100 million in its initial run. *Rocky* won three Academy Awards for 1976, including "Best Picture" and "Best Director." Near the close of the century, *Rocky* was voted among the "100 greatest American movies" in a poll conducted by the American Film Institute.

The screen boxer from the 1970s responded to the challenge to manliness after the military defeat in Vietnam; to the challenge to masculinity posed by the women's movement; to the economic threat to the middle class as the US economy stagnated; and to the pressure felt by the white ethnic working class from other subordinate groups, particularly African Americans. Whereas during the Depression and after the Second World War the boxer expressed a liberal ethos critical of dominant values and sympathetic to minority groups, the cycle of films from the 1970s shifted this political sensibility. In many respects the contrast between Joe Louis and Muhammad Ali suggests the change. Louis was associated with racial justice; he gained almost universal admiration, especially during and after the Second World War. Ali was a more complex celebrity, who excited hostility and devotion while embodying the tumultuous changes of his time. Their personalities and their public personas were also polar opposites: Louis, during his heyday as champion, was quiet, serious, humble, and patriotic; whereas Ali was brash, a braggart, a comedian, and a dissident.

The comeback of Muhammad Ali was the highlight of boxing in the 1970s. During Ali's first reign as heavyweight champion, he excited controversy by embracing the militant politics of the Black Muslims. In 1967 Ali was stripped of his crown for refusing to be drafted; his trial resulted in a fine of $10,000 and a five-year prison sentence. During his legal appeals, Ali became a symbol for social change, denouncing racism and the Vietnam War. In October 1970, Ali's boxing license was reinstated and a title fight was scheduled against the champion Joe Frazier. The social conflicts dividing America became associated with the fight. Though an African American, Frazier was positioned by Ali and the press as a representative of tradition, the white man's champ. Ali spoke for the counterculture, a black separatist and a war resister who proclaimed his opposition to prevailing values. On March 8, 1971, Ali lost a fifteen-round decision to Joe Frazier in one of the most socially resonant championship bouts in boxing history. Later that year the US Supreme Court ruled unanimously to overturn Ali's conviction. By the time of Ali's 1974 bout with George Foreman, in which he regained the title, he was a popular favorite. The public was disenchanted with the Vietnam War, and the Muslims now seemed tame compared with the militancy of such groups as the Black Panthers. Ali was invited by President Gerald Ford to the White House and was named *Sports Illustrated*'s "Sportsman of the Year." Just as Joe Louis influenced the boxing films of his era, Muhammad Ali became a catalyst for the comeback of the screen boxer in the 1970s. His personification of black pride influenced the blaxploitation films. Stallone acknowledged that *Rocky* was inspired by an actual fight, the March 24, 1975 heavyweight championship bout between Muhammad Ali and Chuck Wepner, an unheralded "white hope" selected by Ali. Stallone saw the crowd reaction when the underdog Wepner knocked Ali down late in the fight and believed that this was the path to the emotions of his audience. The cinema had to produce the greatest "white hope" for Ali to face, Rocky Balboa, who fought champion Apollo Creed, a surrogate Ali, in *Rocky*. As Sylvester Stallone explained, "Apollo Creed was a thinly disguised impersonation of Ali. If Ali didn't exist, I don't think people would have bought the premise of *Rocky*."[2]

In the films of the 1970s, boxing is typically associated with the values of a racial, ethnic, or class community. A veteran fighter finds his identity at stake in a decisive ring battle with an outsider, and he must make a comeback to assert his self-worth. *Rocky*'s commercial success prompted the pathos of *The Champ* (1979) and the seven *Rocky* sequels. In opposition to the sentiment found in *Rocky* and *The Champ*, there arose an opposing group of boxing comedies that mocked the ring sport and its primitive masculinity. *The Main Event* was the most conspicuous of these productions, whereas the "Dynamite Hands" segment of *Movie, Movie* supplied a well-observed parody. Whereas *Rocky* and *The Champ* express a conservative ethos, the boxing comedies display a more liberal sensibility. Clint Eastwood combined pathos and humor in *Every Which Way but Loose*. These contrasting attitudes also contributed to the complexity of Martin Scorsese's *Raging Bull*. This biography film of middleweight champion Jake LaMotta mixes genre conventions and the aesthetics of the art cinema and is, for many, the stellar achievement of the Hollywood boxing film.

The boxing film of the 1970s arose from the classic fight film, but it developed distinctive traits. Though the plot featured the elements of the standard rise and fall story, a "comeback" variation, which followed the fighter's revival of his career, was conspicuous in films such as *Fat City*, *Rocky*, *The Champ* (1979), and *The Main Event*. The genre, like the boxer himself, sought to compete once again. The motif recalled Muhammad Ali, who regained the heavyweight championship twice in the 1970s. The comeback also had social implications. Rivalry with competing racial and ethnic groups replaces the villainous gangster promoter who represented harsh forces of the market in the 1930s and 1940s. Rocky Balboa's beleaguered Italian American loses his gym locker to an African American, finds a black woman from television peppering him with questions, and is threatened with humiliation by Apollo Creed. Resisting outsider threats to the native community replaces the problem of assimilation. Rather than exhibiting the progressive ethos of the Popular Front era, the 1970s boxer displayed a backward look. There was often a longing for values that prevailed before the movements for racial justice and the Vietnam War. As a result, the boxing films of the 1970s exhibited a nostalgic, old-fashioned, even retrograde quality.

Rocky uses racial antagonism to mask fears of class division, contrasting the challenger's mental simplicity with the champ's wit. In the champion's first appearance on television, Apollo is elegantly dressed with a beautiful woman at his side. Articulate and self-confident, he urges viewers to give up sports and get an education. Creed embodies what Rocky lacks. Typical of the genre, the black opponent personifies anxieties inherent in the boxer himself. Class differences associated with education are presented in the division between African American and Italian American. *Rocky* expresses the distress of common people who can no longer secure a livelihood based on physical labor in the absence of professional skills. The film projects this legitimate fear onto African Americans – a population equally, if not more, vulnerable to these conditions – and this displacement reveals what Vincent Canby describes as "latent racism that may not be all that latent."[3]

Anxiety over changing gender roles and the women's movement is conspicuous in the 1970s boxing film. The economic threat posed by the Depression and the scars of the Second World War had prompted the boxer's torment during the classic era and female characters often embodied these fears. However, during the 1970s cycle women themselves were the problem. The opposition between the neighborhood sweetheart and the scheming vamp no longer portrayed women along a moral divide. Women, such as the TV newswoman in *Rocky*, appeared to be out of place. Or sympathetic companions, such as Lucy (Jill Ireland) in *Hard Times*, became too demanding even though their requests were modest. Seducers, like Lynn (Sondra Locke) in *Every Which Way but Loose*, were puzzling to the point of mystery. No longer did the boxer attract a forceful, dynamic companion, such as Peg in *Body and Soul*. Instead, *Rocky* features the timid Adrian (Talia Shire), or *Every Which Way but Loose* the compliant Echo (Beverly D'Angelo). The boxer frequently retreats toward self-sufficiency or anchors himself in the male world rather than pursuing romance.

The 1970s boxer continues to be the working-class laborer, but with a more primal, unreflective character. There are no more wise guys like Charlie Davis in *Body and Soul*. Instead an intensified innocence, reminiscent of Frank Capra's Mr. Smith or Joe Pendleton from *Here Comes Mr. Jordan* (1941), becomes the model. The psychic struggle that Robert Wise uses to deepen character in *The Set-Up* and *Somebody Up There Likes Me* is exchanged for an emphasis on the body. Charles Bronson, Sylvester Stallone and Clint Eastwood give the boxer's physical presence new stature. Training often features body building rather than sparring. Instead of recognizing the ephemeral nature of the body and turning to spiritual values, the boxer allies himself with horses, cats or orangutans. The motif associates the boxer with the strength, loyalty and grace of animals. In casting aside sophistication, the boxer is more than a brute. He aspires to an almost Franciscan sense of innocence apart from a calculating intelligence or a complex psyche. The trend emerges into a retrograde longing for childhood, a time before confusing adult problems arise. The body versus soul conflict fades, as the physical becomes an avenue to an elevating simplicity.

Ali's comeback influenced the boxing film revival of the 1970s, but it wasn't consonant with it. On the whole, these films tried to stare down the disillusionment arising from the social turmoil of the 1960s, and fight back social change. The result was an unusual mixture of pathos and humor; a concern for innocence and the body, and a puzzling look at the cultural divide between men and women.

Raging Bull serves as a counterpoint to *Rocky*, and many consider it the greatest boxing film because of its intensity and complexity. Instead of a lovable hero, the biography film of middleweight champion Jake LaMotta (Robert De Niro) portrays a despicable anti-hero. Our shifting allegiance to the protagonist guides the audience response through a dynamic of attraction and repulsion. In its nine distinct boxing sequences, the director Martin Scorsese creates an unrivalled intensity in our bonding with LaMotta in the ring. The flashback plot engenders a pose of reflection both in the characters and about the Italian American culture portrayed. The realistic elements vividly ground the milieu of the 1940s and 1950s while allowing a critical evaluation of the historical period. The naturalistic performances convey immediacy to characters whose persuasive power disarms any sense of artistry. The traditional conflicts of the boxing genre are portrayed with freshness and remarkable force.

Perhaps the most noteworthy trend in the boxing film since the comeback cycle of the 1970s is the rise of the woman boxer in hit films such as *On the Ropes* (1999), *Girlfight* (2000), and *Million Dollar Baby* (2004). Here the female boxer storms into the ring to prove that even the outer limits of masculinity are within her reach. Even *The Fighter* (2010) gave the boxer's mother an Academy Award-winning role as the manager. The new attention to gender brings a fresh perspective to ring stories, but gender conflict has always been central to the boxing film. While bringing a new perspective to male–female relations these films also exhibit a creative understanding of the conventions of the boxing film genre.

Some of the most notable recent boxing films include *Southpaw* (2015), starring Jake Gyllenhaal as a fighter beset by personal tragedy; *Hands of*

Stone (2016), a biopic of famous Panamaian boxer Roberto Duran, who quit in his championship rematch against Sugar Ray Leonard; and *Creed* (2015), another installment in the Rocky series featuring the illegitimate son of Rocky's famous black opponent, Apollo Creed, seeking out an aged, cancer-stricken Rocky to be his trainer. These films have their merits and flaws. They do not thematically break any new ground in the boxing film genre, relying very much on the formula of the boxer's relationship with his trainer. *Creed* might almost be interpreted as the Rocky series taking a redemptive turn to expiate its racist beginnings by having Rocky teach Creed's son. It is surprising that *Hands of Stone* was not a Spanish-language film (Duran spoke almost no English, as he refused to learn the language) and marketed as such. That might explain why it failed at the box office. What is more striking is that two of the three films (*Creed* and *Southpaw*) were directed by African Americans: Ryan Coogler and Antoine Fuqua. The fact that Coogler was not nominated for an Oscar for his directing (its only nomination was Stallone for Best Supporting Actor) was one of the reasons that African Americans in Hollywood launched the #OscarsSoWhite protest of 2015.

For a more comprehensive study of the boxing film, including a detailed analysis of *Raging Bull* and the women boxing films, see *Knockout: The Boxer and Boxing in American Cinema* by Leger Grindon.

NOTES

1 Early, Gerald. "'I Only Like It Better When the Pain Comes': More Notes Toward a Cultural Definition of Prizefighting," in *Reading the Fights*. New York: Henry Holt, 1988, 50.
2 Hauser, Thomas. *Muhammad Ali: His Life and Times*. New York: Simon and Schuster, 1991, 301.
3 Canby, Vincent. "'Rocky,' Pure 30s Make Believe," *New York Times* (November 22, 1976), 19.

SELECT BIBLIOGRAPHY

Canby, Vincent. "'Rocky,' Pure 30s Make Believe," *New York Times* (November 22, 1976), 19.
Early, Gerald. "'I Only Like It Better When the Pain Comes': More Notes Toward a Cultural Definition of Prizefighting," in *Reading the Fights*. New York: Henry Holt, 1988, 36–60.
Grindon, Leger. *Knockout: The Boxer and Boxing in American Cinema*. Jackson, MS: University Press of Mississipi, 2011.
Hauser, Thomas. *Muhammad Ali: His Life and Times*. New York: Simon and Schuster, 1991.

23

REBECCA WANZO

Black Slaver: Jack Johnson and the Mann Act

On June 25, 1910, Congress passed the White Slave Traffic Act, also known as the Mann Act:

> That for any person who shall knowingly transport or cause to be transported, or aid or assist in obtaining transportation for, or in transporting, in interstate or foreign commerce, or in any Territory, or in the District of Columbia, any woman or girl for the purpose of prostitution or debauchery, or for any other immoral purpose, or with the intent and purpose to induce, entice, or compel such woman or girl to become a prostitute or to give herself up to debauchery, or to engage in any other immoral practice; who shall knowingly procure or obtain, or cause to be procured or obtained, or aid or assist in procuring or obtaining any ticket or tickets, or any form of transportation or evidence of the right thereto, to be used by any woman or girl in interstate or foreign commerce, or in any Territory or the District Columbia, in going to any place for the purpose of prostitution or debauchery, or for any other immoral purpose, or with the intent or purpose on the part of such person to induce, entice, or compel her to give herself to the practice of prostitution, or to give herself up to debauchery, or any other immoral practice, whereby any such woman or girl shall be transported in interstate or foreign commerce, or in any Territory or the District of Columbia, shall be deemed guilty of a felony, and upon conviction thereof shall be punished by a fine not exceeding five thousand dollars, or by imprisonment of not more than five years, or by both such fine and imprisonment, in the discretion of the court.[1]

The name of the act was a bit of a misnomer because nothing in the language of the law states that only nonwhite women could be trafficked without penalty. But white slavery was one of the "moral panics" preoccupying progressive reformers in the early twentieth century.[2] In the report supporting the bill, the concern was over women "who, if given a fair chance, would in all human probability, have been good wives and mothers and useful citizens."[3] Although the legislation was ostensibly about the commercial traffic in prostitution, the inclusion of "immoral purpose" and "debauchery" made it possible to prosecute people who were not engaged in commerce. Unsurprisingly, "debauchery" could be interpreted quite broadly in the early twentieth century, and the breadth of the law allowed the state to use the Mann Act to target those who were considered undesirable US citizens.

The Act was the product of anxieties about a rapidly changing new century. More women were moving into the workforce and the city. In the first decade of the twentieth century, more than eight million immigrants arrived, and concerns about the sexual morality of women immigrants in particular would make them a target of the state.[4] Urbanization brought increased anxieties about red-light districts that the police often seemed to accept as part of the landscape.[5] And African Americans continued to pose, as W.E.B. Du Bois famously phrased it, a "problem" for many white Americans unwilling to accept their continued demands for rights and encroachment on traditionally white spaces.[6]

All of these changes threatened the preservation of homogenous white spaces and narratives of white female purity. The circulating discourses about the Mann Act reveal wide-ranging attempts to contain suspect citizens and exclude outsiders, as well as a schizophrenic relationship to the "victims" the act was supposed to protect. On the one hand, narratives about white slavery would focus on the need to protect white female innocence. On the other hand, these narratives suggested that women were morally weak and easily led astray. Concerned and titillated citizens could read "thrilling stories of actual experiences of girls who were lured from innocence into lives of degradation" in *From Dance Hall to White Slavery: The World's Greatest Tragedy* (1912) and in other pamphlets and books.[7] In 1913, thousands of people went to see *Traffic in Souls*, a salacious story of a Swedish woman kidnapped by a pimp.[8] Sometimes the victims were incarcerated for aiding in their own "debauchery" or placed behind bars in the process of prosecuting the accused.[9]

Enforcement of the Mann Act focused "new" immigrant European women and native-born white women. "New" European immigrant women were often viewed as not quite white and bringing a deviant sexuality to the country, and some women were deported on white-slavery grounds. The prosecutorial targets of the Mann Act were thus quite varied – not only men and women who were procuring and trafficking prostitutes were the objects of state action, but anyone whose deviance from model US citizenship could invite surveillance and persecution from the state. The Mann Act was one of the means by which the FBI expanded its power.[10] J. Edgar Hoover would use the Mann Act to pursue people he believed could be dangerous dissidents (and as is now well known, he found many people dangerous). In the 1940s, Charlie Chaplin would be charged with violating the

Mann Act; however, evidence suggests that the Bureau was more concerned that he had Communist sympathies.[11]

But in the early years of the Mann Act enforcement, the noncommercial cases focused on regulating sexual morality and protecting whiteness. And who threatened notions of white purity – and supremacy – more than Jack Johnson in the early twentieth century? When Jack Johnson definitively beat white heavyweight champion Tommy Burns in 1908 in Australia, it was, as Gail Bederman writes, "unthinkable – a black man has been crowned the most powerful man in the world!"[12] In his mastery over white men in the ring and ability to possess what was still often thought of as property – white wives – he would represent to many whites the world they feared after the fourteenth amendment granted slaves freedom.

It is not a coincidence that the decade that birthed the Mann Act would also result in the resurgence of the Ku Klux Klan.[13] People consuming white slavery narratives would also see D.W. Griffith's successful film *Birth of a Nation* (1915), an adaptation of Thomas Dixon's 1905 novel *The Clansman*, as a romantic rendering of the birth of the KKK. A key scene in the film depicts a freed black slave chasing a white woman who jumps to her death to escape him. (In the novel, she is raped and both she and her mother jump to her death because of the shame of it.) Her death propels the romantic hero and Klan into taking back the South from the animalistic and uncivilized freed slaves. The narrative of the "black male rapist" had widespread support, just as the story of white slavery did. Although the Mann Act would pass through Congress quickly, Congress was not interested in seeking protection for the black men who were increasingly the target of lynching since the 1890s. In the first decade of the twentieth century alone, 858 African Americans were lynched in the United States, in contrast to 104 whites.[14] Supporters of vigilante justice argued that unchecked black criminality – particularly sexual violence – produced white retaliation. But as Ida B. Wells would demonstrate in her crusade against lynching, prosperity could be a strong impetus for white mob violence.[15] Ironically, it was the White Slavery Act that propelled blacks to push for federal anti-lynching legislation as the act set a precedent for the federalizing of a state crime.

And Jack Johnson was arguably the most high-profile, successful African American in the early twentieth century. This success would make him a powerful target for whites seeking to preserve power. While married, Johnson had a number of extramarital relationships. Evidence suggests that one of these affairs was with eighteen-year-old Lucille Cameron, who he met in his Chicago club, Café de Champion. He hired her, allegedly as a "stenographer" and "companion to his wife."[16] After his first wife committed suicide, in the nightclub, he continued to have a relationship with Lucille, and a reporter called her mother and asked if she knew that her daughter was "under the influence of Jack Johnson."[17] When Cameron's mother could not convince her daughter to leave, she hired a lawyer and went to the police and accused Jackson of kidnapping her daughter. Because she was eighteen – and the police didn't believe the kidnapping charge – she went to the newspapers to get public sympathy for her claim.

Johnson received a massive amount of negative and sensational news coverage for his behavior. Even many African Americans would condemn him. The local black newspaper, *The Chicago Defender*, would remain on his side, but papers like *The Philadelphia Tribune* would run stories with disapproving headlines: "Jack Johnson Dangerously Ill, Victim of White Fever."[18] Both blacks and whites would take issue with Johnson's preference for white women. Such a claim from black leaders had a great deal of strategic value when African American leaders were trying to convince whites that African American men posed no threat to white womanhood. Johnson's dedicated pursuit of white women also suggested that he saw African American women as inferior romantic and sexual partners, an idea that certainly would be rejected by African Americans who had a full dose of racial pride and supported racial uplift.

In 1912, Johnson would be charged for trafficking Cameron. But Lucille Cameron posed some problems for the prosecution. She would not turn on Johnson. She had been a prostitute before she met him, so he did not coerce her into prostitution. As in a number of other Mann Act cases, the victim was incarcerated in pursuit of the accused. Her mother would bring charges of disorderly conduct against her daughter to keep her from Johnson.

Without Cameron's cooperation, the case fell apart, but the FBI continued to pursue Johnson. They received a tip that led them to Belle Schreiber, a prostitute who had seen Johnson several times over a number of years. Bitter that Johnson had not continued a relationship with her, Schreiber testified that he took her over state lines. On November 7, 1912, he would be charged with transporting Schreiber from Pittsburgh to Chicago, in 1910.

While on bail Johnson married Lucille Cameron, whom he had at first been accused of trafficking, and that caused even more public outrage. When *United States* v. *John Arthur Johnson* began on May 5, 1913, the jury would be told that he violated the Mann Act by transporting Schreiber for immoral purposes and by giving her money to set herself up as a madam. The federal prosecutor argued that, as a professional boxer, he threatened Schreiber with his fists.

The jury took less than two hours to convict. In a telling statement, prosecutor Harry Parkin did not say that the verdict was evidence of the evils of prostitution. Instead, he argued that the case was a forerunner "in laws to be passed in the United States that we may live to see – laws forbidding miscegenation." Parkin stated that Johnson was the "foremost example of the evil in permitting the marriage of whites and blacks."[19] In response to the verdict, Johnson fled before sentencing and lived in exile until he surrendered himself in 1920. He served his one-year sentence and was released in July 1921.

Jack Johnson knew that the government targeted him under the Mann Act because of his racial transgressions as an African American man. As he said to a group of black businessmen:

> First I want to say that nothing is ever said of the white man who waylays the little colored girl when she goes to market. Nobody has anything to say about that. But when the Negro does something that is not nearly so serious there is a great hue and cry ... But I do want to say that I am not a slave and that I have the right to choose who my mate shall be without the dictation of any man.[20]

Although not a slave, Johnson was, as many African Americans found for decades after emancipation, still subject to the prescriptions of what black people should be able to do in the early twentieth century. His case demonstrated the law's reach when it wished to contain African American success. Public vilification, exile, and incarceration were the cost of his transgressions. But the state that failed to recognize his persecution when he was alive would care about him after death. In a rare act of bipartisanship during President Barack Obama's administration, the United States Senate and House of Representatives would vote to pardon Johnson posthumously, in 2009.[21] But it would not be the first African American president who got it done. Ironically, Donald Trump would pardon him in 2018.[22]

NOTES

1 US 61st Congress, 2nd Session, H.R. 12315, White Slave Traffic Act. Washington Government Printing Office, 1910.

2 Erich Goode and Nachman Ben-Yehuda, *Moral Panics: The Social Construction of Deviance, 2nd Edition.* (Oxford: Blackwell, 2007), 5.

3 61st Congress, 11.

4 Deirdre Moloney, *National Insecurities: Immigrants and US Deportation Policy Since 1882* (Chapel Hill, NC: University of North Carolina Press, 2012).

5 David J. Langum, *Crossing Over the Line: Legislating Morality and the Mann Act* (Chicago: University of Chicago Press, 1994), 21.

6 William Edward Burghardt Du Bois, *The Souls of Black Folk Essays and Sketches, 7th edition* (Chicago, IL: A.C. McClurg & Co, 1907), 2.

7 H.W. Lytle and John Dillon, *From Dance Hall To White Slavery: The World's Greatest Tragedy* (Chicago, IL: Charles C. Thompson Co, 1912).

8 *Traffic in Souls*, directed by George Loane Tucker (1913; Fort Lee, NJ: Independent Moving Pictures Company of America).

9 Moloney, 52.

10 Kenneth O'Reilly, "A New Deal for the FBI: The Roosevelt Administration, Crime Control," *Journal of American History* 69 (1982): 640.

11 Langum, 176; 193.

12 Gail Bederman, *Manliness and Civilization: A Cultural History of Gender and Race in the United States, 1880–1917* (Chicago. IL: University of Chicago Press, 1996), 2.

13 Nancy L. Maclean. *Behind the Mask of Chivalry: The Making of the Second Klu Klux Klan* (Oxford: Oxford University Press, 1995).

14 Unknown Author, "Lynching, Whites & Negroes, 1882–1968," Tuskegee University Archives Online Repository. http://192.203.127.197/archive/bitstream/handle/123456789/511/Lyching%201882%201968.pdf?sequence=1.

15 *Southern Horrors and Other Writings: The Anti-Lynching Campaign of Ida. B. Wells*, edited with an introduction by Jacqueline Jones Royster (Boston, MA: Bedford Books), 1997, 29.

16 Geoffrey C. Ward. *Unforgivable Blackness: The Rise and Fall of Jack Johnson* (New York: Alfred A. Knopf, 2004), 287.

17 Ward, 299.

18 Ward, 307.

19 Ward, 344.

20 Ward, 310.

21 CBS News, "Congress Achieves Jack Johnson Pardon," July 30, 2009, www.cbsnews.com/news/congress-approves-jack-johnson-pardon/.

22 Jacob Bogage, "Boxer Jack Johnson is Posthumously Pardoned by President Trump." *Washington Post*, 2018 May 2018.

24

Yesternow: Jack Johnson, Documentary Film, and the Politics of Jazz

Heavyweight champion Jack Johnson attracted controversy during his ring career, but even the act of remembering him has been contentious. Johnson's story has been told in two substantial nonfiction films: Bill Cayton and Jim Jacobs's feature *Jack Johnson* (1970) and Ken Burns's television documentary *Unforgiveable Blackness: The Rise and Fall of Jack Johnson* (2004).[1] These visual retellings largely agree on facts and themes while employing the music of prominent jazz trumpeters for their soundtracks. But the films come from different places in the culture, and their composers, Miles Davis and Wynton Marsalis, are two of the most well-known and argued-about figures in jazz, whose soundtracks reveal differing attitudes toward race and the meaning of the past.

Johnson himself was well aware of his own significance as both an athlete and racial symbol. "I am astounded when I realize," Johnson recalled, "that there are few men in any period of the world's history, who have led a more varied or intense existence than I." That life ranged from a childhood of poverty in Galveston, Texas, to a string of prizefights that spanned the globe, to prison and a tenuous life as an aging celebrity in changing times before his death in 1946. In the early years of the twentieth century, no black American was more famous. After he won the World Colored Heavyweight Championship in 1903, Johnson refused to fight black opponents, instead pursuing a title bout with the white heavyweight champion, a move that proved controversial to the black community – sensing abandonment – and inflammatory to whites. When Johnson defeated champion Tommy Burns for the heavyweight title in Sydney, Australia, in 1908, the white press demanded a "Great White Hope" that would put the threat of Johnson and his pretensions to equality to rest. Johnson responded by defeating a string of white challengers before what was billed as "The Fight of the Century," a bout with former champion James J. Jeffries in Reno, Nevada, on July 4, 1910, that is unquestionably one of the greatest sporting events of the twentieth century.

After months of unprecedented buildup, Johnson's victory over Jeffries in the fifteenth round before 20,000 shocked spectators prompted anti-black violence throughout the country, resulting in the deaths of at least twenty people, and the film of the fight quickly became the most intensely debated, censored, denounced, and most significantly, viewed film in the medium's history until D.W. Griffith's feature *Birth of a Nation* in 1915. Johnson stoked the controversy by openly dating white women (his three wives were all white) and cultivating a glamorous lifestyle complete with flamboyant tailored clothes, flashy automobiles, and cosmopolitan travel. In 1912, federal authorities arrested Johnson for violation of the Mann Act, passed by Congress in 1910 to combat prostitution ("transporting women across state lines for immoral purposes"). Johnson had an adulterous but consensual relationship with a former prostitute, Lucille Cameron, but the interracial nature of the couple left an opening to end the boxer's flaunting of American social propriety. Convicted in 1913, Johnson fled to Canada and thence to Europe. In 1915, he lost the heavyweight title to Jess Willard in a twenty-two-round bout in Havana, Cuba. Eventually settling in Mexico, Johnson struggled to make a decent living. He surrendered to US authorities in 1920 and served his one-year prison term at Leavenworth.

Johnson, a passable bassist and practiced raconteur, toured with Fletcher Henderson's jazz band, made humorous spoken-word recordings recalling his exploits for Ajax Records in 1924, took occasional film roles, published an autobiography, *Jack Johnson: In the Ring and Out*, in 1927, and continued to box with less success as he aged. He finally stopped fighting at age sixty in 1938, but made a final ring appearance in a benefit for US War Bonds in 1945. He died the following year in a high-speed highway crash in North Carolina after being refused service at a segregated restaurant.[2]

This was the man remembered in the two later documentaries, a man whose talents and transgressions angered whites and embarrassed many blacks. By his senior years in the 1930s, boxing fans had a new Negro champion, but Joe Louis's carefully managed public image intentionally contrasted with Johnson's.[3] The ubiquity of Johnson's image in photography and film – an irritant to his enemies when he was the champion – proved a boon to later filmmakers. Common to both *Jack Johnson*s are still photographs and, crucially, footage from the early cinema, itself born only a decade or so prior to Johnson's rise. "Actuality" films were documentary in the pure sense decades before Kenneth Macpherson coined the term. They showed the wider world to curious nickelodeon viewers and theatergoers. Boxing films remind us that the thirst for footage of real events did not end with the ascent of fictional storytellers such as Edwin S. Porter and Griffith. Indeed, the attraction of viewing two men slugging it out in the ring was a constant source of moral concern in a culture already spooked by film's privileging of the visual and its transgression of class lines.[4] Film of Jack Johnson made his blackness the central and unavoidable element in the story for viewers on both sides of the color line. At the moment of Johnson's 1908 triumph over Burns in Australia, authorities shut down the cameras the moment the referee stopped the fight. Johnson's later victory over Jeffries led to a congressional ban on the transport of boxing films across state lines.

Johnson's racial intervention into the white domain of the boxing ring also disrupted visual spaces defined by a clear color line. Johnson exhibited films of his own bouts and those of others at theatrical appearances during his travels around the world. His championship fight contracts always included terms for film rights and distribution. By the time of the epic Johnson–Jeffries fight in Reno, boxing films were receiving international distribution, and moving images of Johnson in action helped make him an international icon of resistance among nonwhite peoples.[5]

Decades later, advertising man and boxing enthusiast Bill Cayton began licensing, collecting, and preserving prints of early fight pictures – including precious footage of the Johnson bouts – for the early television series *Greatest Fights of the Century*. Eventually teaming with his partner Jim Jacobs, he later created a series of feature documentaries under his The Big Fights, Inc., umbrella.[6] Cayton pitched the soundtrack for *Jack Johnson* to Miles Davis, a boxing fan who occasionally stepped into the ring for training sessions and counted several important fighters as friends. Davis readily agreed and spent hours at Cayton's offices watching old footage.[7] Perhaps hoping to capitalize on the success of Howard Sackler's 1967 play *The Great White Hope* (itself filmed by Martin Ritt and released in 1970), *Jack Johnson* would be made by boxing insiders and boxing lovers.

Working with his Columbia Records producer Teo Macero (musical director for the film), *Jack Johnson* sent Davis even deeper into the jazz-rock vein of experimentation he had begun a couple of years earlier. Davis later said he had made music with "that boxer's movement in mind, that shuffling movement boxers use … "[8] Playing at a physical peak, in part due to well-documented boxing workouts (he had been photographed in the gym for *Rolling Stone*), Davis's solos on the tracks recorded for the film put to rest doubts about his ability to reach and sustain high notes. Davis's music during the period was determined more by extensive experimentation and jamming in the studio than by preconceived composition in the traditional sense. For the rousing "Right Off" (sometimes known as "Theme from Jack Johnson"), guitarist John McLaughlin, bassist Michael Henderson, and drummer Billy Cobham started a loping, bluesy jam before Davis entered with a high-note solo cued in the film by voice actor Brock Peters declaring Johnson's love of getting into the ring, "waiting for the sound of the bell."[9] The strutting rhythm of "Yesternow" is matched to footage of Johnson training for a title bout. Macero also provided material from an earlier Davis album, *In a Silent Way*, for train sequences.[10]

Davis interpreted Jack Johnson both as a personal inspiration and a cultural pioneer who would have fit right in with his own times. In a liner note to the soundtrack album the trumpeter assesses Johnson's contemporary meaning. "The rise of Jack Johnson to world heavyweight supremacy in 1908 was a signal for white envy to erupt," the note begins. "Can you get to that?" Davis notes that Johnson's "flamboyance was more than obvious," referring to Johnson's preference for white women and for expensive clothes and automobiles. Davis's own consumption – of fast cars and of sundry vices – found a historical analogue in Johnson. He called the boxer "a living-color nightmare for the anti-Johnson Americans who couldn't get ready" for the champion's transgressive attitude and racial pride, perhaps thinking as well of his own run-ins with law enforcement, including a publicized arrest outside Birdland in 1959.[11] Davis titled the album *A Tribute to Jack Johnson*, signaling admiration for both the boxer's fighting prowess and his definition of black masculinity.[12]

Davis's attitude toward the subject accords with the unusual approach taken by Cayton and Jacobs's ninety-minute film, in which actor Brock Peters gives fictional voice to Johnson, providing commentary from the boxer's point of view both in the ring ("Show me $35,000 worth, Mr. Tommy. You sure bounce easy") and out ("They always talk about me. Let 'em. I'll give my answer in the ring"). This violation of *verite* complicated the film's documentary status years before this kind of obvious intervention laid to rest the myth of objectivity in the genre. Peters had already played the role of an unjustly persecuted black man in Robert Mulligan's feature *To Kill a Mockingbird* (1962), and his rendering of Johnson's in-ring taunts and expressions of pride leave a strong impression, even if they are not based on original documents.[13] Peters intoned opening and closing lines for the film that Davis also mixed into the end of his soundtrack album: "I'm Jack Johnson, heavyweight champion of the world. I'm black. They never let me forget it. I'm black all right. I'll never let *them* forget it." In the era of Muhammad Ali, Black Power, James Brown's "Say It Loud – I'm Black and I'm Proud," and Blaxploitation heroes like *Superfly*'s Priest and *Shaft*'s title character, the project's construction of Johnson as black folk hero seemed right on time.

Jack Johnson does not seem to have secured a wide release, premiering in Detroit in July 1970 but not in New York until November 1971 at the

Whitney Museum of American Art in a limited run.[14] It has never been available on home video even though it was nominated for an Academy Award in 1971 for Best Documentary Feature. Davis's soundtrack album disappeared quickly, Columbia having put little marketing resources into it and disappointing the artist, who thought the music would connect with rock and rhythm and blues fans. Cayton and Jacobs eventually become boxing managers – they were Mike Tyson's first management team – and Cayton went on to sell his vast library of boxing films to Disney/ESPN in the 1990s.

While *Jack Johnson* had been the work of boxing aficionados, the next major documentary on the champion would be made by academics and celebrities. Ken Burns's Florentine Films produced the 220-minute *Unforgiveable Blackness*, broadcast in 2004 on PBS. Burns took a decidedly more sober approach to Johnson's story in film, with a soundtrack provided by perhaps the most important jazz musician to emerge since 1980, Wynton Marsalis, label mate of Davis's on Columbia early in his career. At roughly the same age Davis had been when he recorded *A Tribute to Jack Johnson*, Marsalis – himself a boxing fan who grew up in the age of Ali – took a different approach that reflects his interest in the jazz tradition. His music creates something like what legendary (and unrecorded) New Orleans trumpeter Buddy Bolden might have done had he provided the soundtrack to Johnson's silent boxing films. Unlike Davis, Marsalis worked directly with a rough cut of the film "the old-fashioned way, with a metronome and a stopwatch."[15] Doug Wamble's guitar and banjo stylings emphasize the blues feel to the music, and the Marsalis score's emphasis on Reginald Veal's old-timey walking bass lines remind us that Johnson himself played the instrument. Marsalis emphasizes ensemble playing rooted in early hot jazz over his own soloing. To fill out the nearly four-hour film, the soundtrack uses material from other Marsalis recordings and a few other artists. The Marsalis soundtrack comes across as a corrective to Davis's work.[16]

While Davis's liner notes on Johnson had punctuated his soundtrack release, Marsalis surprisingly did not provide commentary on his own, odd given that he had been a voluble on-camera and important off-camera presence in the creation of Burns's ten-part *Jazz* documentary from 2001. His only additional contributions to the DVD release are a short video of stills from recording sessions accompanying a medley of soundtrack tunes and an interview for the brief "Making of" featurette. Moreover, the music itself is far lower in the mix in *Unforgiveable Blackness* than Davis's had been in *Jack Johnson*, privileging Keith David's Emmy-winning voiceover narration and the informative quotes gleaned by Burns's research team. Nothing distracts from Samuel L. Jackson's renderings of Johnson's words, taken from the fighter's writings and interviews.

Burns uses his patented approach of alternating period photographs and footage under narration with contemporary intellectuals, in this case essayists Stanley Crouch and Gerald Early, boxing writer Bert Sugar, Johnson biographer Randy Roberts, and actor James Earl Jones – who had played Johnson in *The Great White Hope* – most prominently. While Sugar looks like a refugee from the world of The Big Fights with his anachronistic fedora and cigar, the commentary ranges from the memorably salty (especially Crouch), to the interpretively bold (Jones) to the merely factual. By the time of *Unforgiveable Blackness*, Burns and his key writer, Geoffrey Ward, had already created "event" programming for PBS with such popular titles as *The Civil War* (1990), *Baseball* (1994), and *Jazz* (2001), all of them in one way or another concerned with race in America. Each had drawn some criticism on interpretive grounds and choices of emphasis, although the facts Burns presented were rarely in dispute.[17] Burns's style had also crystallized into a recognizable and influential "effect": slow pans over still photographs – with some striking but dissociated ones to illustrate the narration. But in *Unforgiveable Blackness*, Burns uses more dramatic zooms and montage editing to convey the action of the fights. At times he sacrifices resolution in order to capture Johnson in ring close-ups that show him smiling and bantering. It is perhaps Burns's most focused and dynamic filmmaking.

Burns had become revered for his rare determination to tell a story in-depth (*Baseball* ran to eleven episodes) and occasionally mocked for earnest excesses. But Burns's commitment is clear in his note to Marsalis's soundtrack album. "In the end," he writes, "this is a story about freedom, and one black man's insistence that he be able to live a life nothing short of that of a free man," an interpretation endorsed by his composer. "Ken Burns is dealing with a certain truth in the United States," Marsalis offers.[18] To that end, the film concentrates on Johnson's sex life and its ramifications for his career as well as the problem of the color line throughout American society. While *Jack Johnson* revels in footage of Johnson racing automobiles with Barney Oldfield, the much longer *Unforgiveable Blackness* dispenses with the episode entirely, apparently deeming it extraneous to the documentary's agenda. If *Jack Johnson* had been a project of insider passion for the boxer as flamboyant outlaw, *Unforgiveable Blackness* was a triumph of research and the mobilization of resources in the service of racial liberalism.[19]

What spices consideration of these jazz-inflected ruminations on Jack Johnson are the disparate poles in the music represented by Davis and Marsalis in the intervening decades. In the curious world of jazz politics, the elder Davis is often considered an artist who restlessly worked his way through various styles that influenced the course of the music's development.

For the younger traditionalist Marsalis, Davis's later innovations – including the jazz-rock of *Jack Johnson* – represented at best an artistic dead end and at worst a craven sellout. Marsalis and his intellectual mentor and sleeve-note writer, Stanley Crouch, made this point repeatedly in interviews and articles published in the years before and after Davis's 1991 death.[20] Indeed, over time Marsalis became known as much for his role as critic and educator as for his actual music. His muted presence in *Unforgiveable Blackness* may be due to a certain discomfort with Johnson himself. Johnson's flouting of middle-class values, disturbing to black elites in his own day, runs counter to Marsalis's own agenda of promoting jazz as an uplifting alternative to lowest common denominator entertainment – including rap, rock, and pop.[21]

Although both musicians had been born into middle-class black professional families (Davis's Garveyite father was an East St. Louis dental surgeon, Marsalis's a New Orleans university teacher and musician), Davis cultivated an anti-bourgeois street image amplified by his co-writer, Quincy Troupe, in his 1989 autobiography. Burnishing his pop credentials and dressing in what Crouch called "the expensive bad taste of rock 'n' roll," in the 1980s, Davis explored material by Michael Jackson and Cyndi Lauper with bands that leaned toward rhythm and blues.[22] Davis had left the Juilliard School for the college of bebop at his first chance in 1944; Juilliard graduate Marsalis became the first recording artist to win Grammy awards in both the jazz and classical categories in 1982, giving him a high-cultural credibility that jazz musicians had struggled to achieve for decades. In a curious kind of patricide via homage, Marsalis led 1980s bands that looked and sounded like no one so much as the Miles Davis groups of the early to mid-1960s. The controversy's pivotal moment occurred in 1986, the near midpoint between the two *Jack Johnson*s. When Marsalis took the stage uninvited (and perhaps at Columbia's bidding) at a Davis gig at the Vancouver Jazz Festival, Davis cut the band and ordered the upstart away. Davis left Columbia after thirty years shortly thereafter.[23]

Of course, when it comes to Jack Johnson, neither Miles Davis's nor Wynton Marsalis's work can ever be definitive. Davis's willingness to forgo the myth of history – the accurate representation of the past – is of a piece with the way he conducted his entire career. He had to be persuaded to revisit his own classic material from the 1950s and 1960s even when he sensed the end of his life in 1991. Jack Johnson's relevance to the current moment is not only undisguised in Davis's *Tribute*; it is celebrated as the reason for remembering Johnson at all.[24] Marsalis's faith in the idea that the past can be known and that there are object lessons to be learned from it run in quite another direction. His is the kind of faith that builds and sustains institutions of public culture and education such as Jazz at Lincoln Center and PBS and that led to original music for *Unforgiveable Blackness* that sounds like it emanates from Johnson's time, though of course it is as much a musical fiction as is Davis's jazz-rock. That Jack Johnson could provoke these two trumpet titans to such disparate approaches to telling his story in music is testament to his ongoing cultural power. Both Davis and Marsalis responded to Johnson as a subject with music that expressed their deepest instincts as musicians and, crucially, as fellow black men in America acutely aware of how contemporary *that* history continues to be. Davis gave it a name: "Yesternow."

NOTES

1 Directing credits for *Jack Johnson* are unclear. Cayton and Jacobs were partners and collaborators. The soundtrack album and a contemporary review in the *New York Times* lists Cayton as director and Jacobs as producer, while prints of the film and the Internet Movie Database say the opposite.

2 Biographical and related sources include Theresa Runstedtler, *Jack Johnson, Rebel Sojourner: Boxing in the Shadow of the Global Color Line* (Berkeley, CA: University of California Press, 2013); Randy Roberts, *Papa Jack: Jack Johnson and the Era of White Hopes* (New York: Free Press, 1985); Jack Johnson, *Jack Johnson, In the Ring and Out* (various reprints); and Tim Brooks, *Lost Sounds: Black and the Birth of the Recording Industry 1890–1919* (Urbana, IL: University of Illinois Press, 2004). The most recent detailed study of Johnson's bouts is Adam J. Pollack, *In the Ring with Jack Johnson, Part 1: The Rise* and *Part II: The Reign* (New York: Win by KO, 2013, 2015).

3 See Lewis A. Erenberg, *The Greatest Fight of Our Generation: Louis vs. Schmeling* (New York: Oxford University Press, 2007).

4 Lary May, *Screening Out the Past: The Birth of Mass Culture and the Motion Picture Industry* (Chicago, IL: University of Chicago Press, 1980), 35.

5 On Johnson and boxing films, especially that of the Jeffries fight, see Runstedtler, *Jack Johnson, Rebel Sojourner*, 68–100. Runstedtler calls Johnson "the world's first black movie star," 69.

6 Cayton and Jim Jacobs are both members of the International Boxing Hall of Fame. See Cayton's online biographical entry at www.ibhof.com/pages/about/inductees/nonparticipant/cayton.html

7 John Szwed, *So What: The Life of Miles Davis* (New York: Simon and Schuster, 2002), 307. Davis apparently slept with a photo of Johnson next to his bed during this period.

8 Miles Davis with Quincy Troupe, *Miles: The Autobiography* (New York: Simon and Schuster, 1989), 315.

9 Listeners may trace the development of the music in Miles Davis, *The Complete Jack Johnson Sessions*, a five-CD box set published by Columbia/Legacy in 2003.

10 This was "Shhh/Peaceful," a tune whose original title had been "Morning Fast Train From Memphis To New York."

11 The Birdland incident involved Davis escorting a white woman to the curb in front of the club. See Benjamin Cawthra, *Blue Notes in Black and White: Photography and Jazz* (Chicago, IL: University of Chicago Press, 2011), 125–28.

12 For more on Davis, boxing, and black masculinity, see Gerald Early's "Miles Davis in the Ring: The Boxer as Black Male Hero" in *Miles Davis: The Complete Illustrated History* (Minneapolis, MN: Voyageur Press, 2012), 188–91.

13 Peters's career is a significant indicator of the black renaissance in film of the late 1950s to the early 1970s. In a way, his *Mockingbird* role was a setup for audiences. He had starred as Crown, the sexual predator in Otto Preminger's 1959 film version of *Porgy and Bess*, joining a cast that included Sidney Poitier, Dorothy Dandridge, and Sammy Davis Jr., among others. In 1972, just after his work on *Jack Johnson*, he starred in Ossie Davis's *Black Girl*, a film challenging the prevailing "blaxploitation" tropes of the day.

14 Weiler, A.H., review of *Jack Johnson*. *New York Times* (November 5, 1971).

15 Marsalis interview, "The Making of *Unforgiveable Blackness*," *Unforgiveable Blackness: The Rise and Fall of Jack Johnson*, directed by Ken Burns. PBS Home Video, 2004.

16 Gerald Early had called for precisely this in an essay on Miles Davis published three years earlier. Early, "The Art of the Muscle: Miles Davis as American Knight and American Knave," in Early, ed., *Miles Davis and American Culture* (St. Louis, MO: Missouri Historical Society Press, 2001), 12.

17 In particular, academic historians scrutinized *The Civil War*, debating its interpretative choices in academic journals and in Robert Brent Toplin's edited volume *Ken Burns's The Civil War: Historians Respond* (New York: Oxford University Press, 1997). *Jazz* disappointed some of the music's fans and cultural historians such as George Lipsitz, who contributed his critique "Songs of the Unsung: The Darby Hicks History of Jazz," to Robert G. O'Meally, et al., eds, *Uptown Conversation: The New Jazz Studies* (New York: Columbia University Press, 2004), 9–26.

18 Ken Burns, notes to Wynton Marsalis, *Unforgiveable Blackness: The Rise and Fall of Jack Johnson* (Blue Note, 2004), n.p. Wynton Marsalis interview, "The Making of *Unforgiveable Blackness*."

19 Florentine Films had important allies on the project. General Motors had been Burns's corporate sponsor since 1987. Six members of Wynton Marsalis Enterprises are also credited.

20 A sample: "Miles Davis is now no more than a winged death's head floating on the hot air of insipid writers and gullible listeners ..." Stanley Crouch, "Miles in the Sky: The 60s," *The Village Voice*, August 1986, jazz supplement. Reprinted in Gary Carner, *The Miles Davis Companion: Four Decades of Commentary* (New York: Schirmer, 1996), 98–102.

21 For Marsalis as jazz critic and public intellectual, see Eric Porter, *What Is This Thing Called Jazz? African American Musicians as Artists, Critics, and Activists* (Berkeley, CA: University of California Press, 2002), 287–334.

22 Stanley Crouch, "Play the Right Thing," *The New Republic* (February 12, 1990). Reprinted in Carner, *The Miles Davis Companion*, 22.

23 For an examination of the "New Jazz Renaissance" of the 1980s and the Marsalis–Davis controversy, see John Gennari, *Blowin' Hot and Cool: Jazz and Its Critics* (Chicago, IL: University of Chicago Press, 2006), 339–72.

24 An extensive discussion on the topic of objectivity in historical writing may be found in Peter Novick, *That Noble Dream: The "Objectivity Question" and the American Historical Profession* (Cambridge: Cambridge University Press, 1988).

FILMS

Jack Johnson, directed by Jim Jacobs. The Big Fights, Inc., 1970.
Unforgiveable Blackness: The Rise and Fall of Jack Johnson, directed by Ken Burns. PBS Home Video, 2004.

MUSIC

Davis, Miles. *A Tribute to Jack Johnson*. Columbia/Legacy 93599, 2005.
  The Complete Jack Johnson Sessions. Columbia/Legacy 86359, 2003.
Unforgiveable Blackness: The Rise and Fall of Jack Johnson. Original soundtrack recording by Wynton Marsalis. Blue Note Records 64194, 2004.

25

ROSALIND EARLY

Opera in the Ring

No one would expect much overlap between the crowd sitting ringside at the MGM Grand in Las Vegas and the one watching the Ring Cycle at the Metropolitan Opera in Lincoln Center. But in 1936, when Jack Johnson, the first black heavyweight champion in the United States, appeared in Verdi's *Aida* (in a nonspeaking role) he mused, "it's the same crowd and the same lights." While lights and crowds are part of almost any live entertainment, Johnson was right to notice a parallel – boxing and opera are both exaggerated spectacles; one of violence, the other of melodrama and music.

Boxing legends like Johnson, Muhammad Ali, Joe Louis, and Floyd Mayweather Jr. epitomize this melodrama, fighting bouts that captivate the country and sometimes the world. Louis and Ali are both already the subjects of operas: *Shadowboxer*[1] is about Joe Louis; and *Approaching Ali*, based on the memoir *The Tao of Muhammad Ali*,[2] is about a writer's friendship with the champ.

Different entirely is Emile Griffith, the subject of *Champion*, a recently commissioned boxing opera.[3] Noticeably less famous – even those who don't follow boxing have heard of Ali and possibly Louis – Griffith is most widely known for killing someone in the ring and, long after he retired, revealing that he was bisexual.

How Griffith's life became an opera is a story that begins in 2008, when Opera Theatre of Saint Louis, a nonprofit, English-language opera company that has staged more than twenty-five world-premiere operas, and Jazz St. Louis, a nonprofit jazz club and education program, commissioned world-renowned jazz trumpeter and composer Terrence Blanchard to compose an opera.

Though he's scored more than fifty films and won five Grammy Awards, Blanchard seemed an unlikely choice, having never before written an opera. But Blanchard grew up listening to the genre. His father, Joseph Oliver, had sung baritone with a group called The Harlem Harmony Kings and played opera at home. "As soon as it came on, you'd hear doors closing," Blanchard recalled with a laugh.

Blanchard got his own start touring with jazz vibraphonist Lionel Hampton and later became the trumpeter and music director for Art Blakey's Jazz Messengers. In the late 1980s, Blanchard scored Spike Lee's *Do the Right Thing* and has scored every Spike Lee film ever since, as well as other movies.

When Opera Theatre and Jazz St. Louis approached Blanchard, they told him that he could pick his opera's subject. Years ago, Blanchard had taken up boxing and become friends with former heavyweight champion Michael Bentt, who had told him about Emile Griffith.

Timothy O'Leary, then general director for Opera Theatre, remembers his response when Blanchard announced his opera's subject. "We all said, 'That's wonderful! Who is Emile Griffith?'"

When former welterweight champion Emile Griffith died on July 23, 2013, most of his obituaries began by recounting another death. This one from March 24, 1962, when Griffith fought for the welterweight championship of the world against Benny "Kid" Paret before 7,600 fans at Madison Square Garden. Griffith pummeled Paret into a coma on ABC's *Saturday Night Fights*, a live broadcast. Ten days later, Paret died. Although fighters had been beaten to death in the ring before, this was a firestorm because it was nationally televised. The furor against boxing further intensified when defending featherweight champion Davey Moore died just three days after his March 21, 1963, nationally televised bout against Sugar Ramos.

Griffith was spat on in the street and afraid to answer his own door. ABC stopped broadcasting boxing, and the governor of New York, Nelson Rockefeller, created a commission to investigate the sport. (Not the first time boxing was investigated by a governmental body.) Public denunciation of boxing – in the form of newspaper editorials and television commentary – was so fierce that the sport itself appeared to be on life support.

At the weigh-in the morning of the fight, Paret had teased Griffith and called him a *maricon*, Spanish for faggot. There had always been whispers about Griffith's sexuality. Griffith had a high voice and wore tight pants and frilly shirts. His apartment in Weehawken had wall-to-wall red carpeting, French provincial couches, and a pink princess telephone. Before becoming a boxer, he had wanted to design hats, and Griffith was known to visit gay clubs.

It seemed that Paret's insult drove Griffith to the merciless beating. (Griffith denied that anger was behind the incident. Paret also teased Griffith at the weigh-in for their previous bout on September 30, 1961, and Griffith had lost that match.)

Killing Paret haunted Griffith for the rest of his life and shaped him as a boxer. "I was never the same fighter after that," he said in a 2005 documentary. "After that fight, I did enough to win. I would use my jab all the time. I never wanted to hurt the other guy."

"Emile's story is powerful because he was constantly looking for redemption, for forgiveness," says Blanchard. "Here's a person who was a reluctant fighter to begin with but had natural talent and rose to the highest level of achievement in his sport, but he was saddled with the experience of taking another man's life."

Blanchard contacted Pulitzer Prize-winning playwright Michael Cristofer (writer of 1977's *The Shadow Box*, which is not about boxing) to write the libretto. The two had worked together before: Cristofer is also a director and Blanchard scored his films *Gia* (1998) and *Original Sin* (2001).

"I've always been very taken with the whole world of Italian opera," says Cristofer, who listened to it as a kid with his grandfather. But Cristofer had never written a libretto before. "I approached it pretty much as if I were doing a play, and as if I was doing a long poem," he says.

Blanchard composed the music, drawing on the blues, spirituals, Afro-Caribbean beats, hard bop, and classical to create a hybrid sound that wasn't a jazz opera like Duke Ellington's musical-esque *Queenie Pie* or Anthony Davis's atonal *X: The Life and Times of Malcolm X*. Instead, the music drew from Blanchard's work in film and occasionally "threatened to slide into background music" according to *St. Louis Post-Dispatch* reviewer Sarah Bryan Miller. But it also worked, as film scores do, to enhance dramatic tension and action. "It's perfectly suited to its dramatic purpose," Miller wrote. "There are only a few moments that sag in the course of it."

Blanchard called *Champion* an opera *in jazz*. It's also an opera *in boxing*. "The excitement and thrill of the competitive nature of fighters is what inspired the music," Blanchard said. "And also the very solitary nature of being a fighter played a big role, because fighters live a very lonely life."

In 2005, filmmakers Dan Klores and Ron Berger made a documentary about Griffith, *Ring of Fire: The Emile Griffith Story*. In it, they set up a meeting between Paret's son, Benny Jr., and Griffith, who was already suffering from *dementia pugilistica* – dementia brought on by boxing.

Griffith, wearing sweatpants and a leather jacket, strides through the Central Park. When he sees Paret, he haltingly asks, "Are you The Kid's son?" Paret nods, and Griffith starts to cry. "I didn't go in there to hurt no one," he says. "But things happen."

"That scene was so powerful when I saw it," says Cristofer. "Suddenly I had the idea that this whole opera would happen on the day when Emile was going to meet Benny Paret's son."

The opera, which is basically true to the narrative of Emile's life, opens with Old Emile (sung by bass Arthur Woodley) getting dressed in his Long Island apartment. His caretaker and adopted son Luis (sung by tenor Brian Arreola) checks on him regularly. While he's getting ready, Old Emile's life comes back to him in a series of flashbacks divided into ten rounds. Emile walks through his old life and even speaks to his younger self.

In round one, "The Kid from St. Thomas," Young Emile (sung by bass-baritone Aubrey Allicock) arrives in Manhattan from the US Virgin Islands, where he grew up. He finds his mother Emelda (sung by mezzo-soprano Denyce Graves), who initially mistakes him for another of her seven children. (Emelda is portrayed as a loose and venal woman, who had seven kids by seven different men. She actually had five children with her husband who abandoned the family to work in the United States. Emelda left her children with relatives to work in San Juan to support the family. While there, she had two more children by another man.)

Emelda takes Emile to ask milliner Howie Albert (sung by baritone Robert Orth) for a job making hats, but when Howie sees Emile's physique, he convinces Emile to become a boxer instead. Howie becomes manager and trainer (in real life Gil Clancy was Griffith's trainer) to the reluctant but talented welterweight.

After a string of victories, the fateful fight comes and the first act ends with Griffith killing Paret in the ring. In a *Sports Illustrated* article from April 2, 1962, about Griffith's life after killing Paret, Gilbert Rogin writes, "The despised Paret is mourned by Griffith, child of misfortune, a naïf perhaps burdened now with more manhood than he can endure."

The question of manhood is central in the opera. Most characters refer to Young Emile as boy, kid, honey, or baby. His mother even calls him monkey. Then Emile heads "down the street that's got no name, / Through that door that's got no sign, / Past them people with no faces / To that room that's got no light, / Only shadows in the dark. / Only shadows in the night." There he finds Kathy Hagan (sung by mezzo-soprano Meredith Arwady) and her gay bar, Hagan's Hole. Kathy is the only character to call Young Emile a man, referring to everyone around him in the bar – comically oversized drag queens included – as boy. Only in this shadowy nowhere is Emile's masculinity recognized.

"What Makes a Man a Man?," the opera's central aria, takes up the issue again. Young Emile sings it during the untitled round four in the locker room right before his fateful bout with Benny Paret (sung by tenor Victor

Ryan Robertson). Emile is trying to explain to Howie that he's bisexual, and that's why Bennie's taunts bothered him.

"No, Emile. It ain't true." Howie sings. "Not in this world. / Not in this man's world / Will it ever be true. / No fighter in this fight world / Is ever gonna be / Less than a man." To which Emile responds, "But listen to me, Howie. / I am a man."

Through euphemism, Howie tries to explain that real men aren't bisexual and then leaves Young Emile by himself. "What makes this man a man?" Emile wonders aloud. "Is it the life he's lived? / The yesterdays? Or what he dreams / For the tomorrow-days? / Inside? Outside? / There is a heart, I know, somewhere inside, / You hear it beat, / You hear it sing / It cries and talks to you / And tells you what you feel / Is what you feel."[4]

These questions about manhood also lead Emile to questions about belonging, which are threaded throughout the opera. Old Emile's dementia exhibits itself as confusion about where his clothes go. The opening lines, for instance, are "This is my shoe. / My shoe goes where? / Where does it go? Hey, man. / It goes where it belongs." Young Emile's confusion about whether he belonged in boxing rings or gay clubs (or if he could possibly belong in both) now manifests itself in everything he does.

The second act unfolds briskly. Emile continues to win bouts, impetuously marries a beautiful young woman, Sadie (sung by soprano Chabrelle Williams) – in real life he did marry Mercedes "Sadie" Donastorg after a whirlwind two-month courtship; the marriage quickly fell apart – and then hits the skids. The decline of his career is told in a montage of losses. Howie retires Emile when he notices the signs of dementia setting in.

As he's leaving a gay bar one night, Young Emile is attacked by a group of homophobes and nearly beaten to death, hastening the onset of his dementia. In round ten, "The End of the Day," Old Emile goes to the park to see Benny Paret Jr., and is finally able to forgive himself for what he did in the ring decades before.

Champion became one of the most talked about and reviewed operas of the season when it premiered in June 2013. Having a famous composer helped, but also NBA basketball player Jason Collins and boxer Orlando Cruz had both come out of the closet a few months beforehand, starting a national conversation about sexuality and sports.

Reviews of *Champion* were largely positive. Ray Mark Rinaldi's rave in the *Denver Post* was also one of the most insightful critiques. "Remarkably impure as opera and as jazz, really, but unrelentingly true to itself, over-the-top when it needs to be and unapologetic, just like Verdi," he wrote. "The piece bridges a divide between the European forms we still love and the American spirit that always seduces us. *Champion* makes its stands, politically and artistically. It is black-and-white and black and white, moving forward in a world defined by gray hair and old customs. It has a giant ego and it is an important work."

The *Chicago Tribune* called it a "*rara aves*: a new work of quality *and* staying power, one that deserves to be taken up by other opera producers far and wide." And since its premiere in 2013, the opera has been performed around the country including at the SFJazz Center in San Francisco, the Washington National Opera in Washington, DC, and the John F. Kennedy Center for the Performing Arts in New York City.

The *St. Louis Post-Dispatch* wrote that it was the "single most important world premiere in the 38-year history of Opera Theatre of Saint Louis." And in early 2014, the International Opera Awards announced that *Champion* was a finalist for best world premiere of 2013.

Dallas Morning News critic Scott Cantrell was one of the few who didn't like the production at all, calling it a "bewildering shuffle of episodes ... Blanchard's inexperience with vocal writing is evident in stilted word-setting."

But even Cantrell appreciated director James Robinson's production and Allen Moyer's sets. (Vivien Schweitzer of *The New York Times* even called them "a treat.") Robinson used video projections on either side of the stage to enhance the set, showing, for instance, the view out of Emile's Long Island apartment. He also used video during fight sequences to give the audience the feeling that they were seeing the fight both live and on television.

Most reviewers commented on – and many complained about – the expletive-laden libretto.

"I knew I was writing about characters who lived and spoke a certain way," Cristofer says. "I also knew that the story had to be told in a really strong way, and that we couldn't be polite about this stuff."

George Loomis of the *Financial Times* gave the production only three stars out of five, writing that "Blanchard never exerts the firm artistic leadership demanded of an opera composer and seems constrained by Cristofer's problematic libretto, [which] flits from subject to subject, so that the opera sometimes seems like a revue."

The opera did cover a large portion of Griffith's life. There were even flashbacks within the flashbacks to Emile's boyhood. This meant there were a lot of scenes and rapid transitions in time and place. It didn't leave much room for Griffith to be portrayed as much more than a tragic figure, trapped by his own talent in a career he didn't want.

But boxing, though the cause of Griffith's infamy, was always his means of redemption, too.

On January 31, 1972, when he entered the ring at the Anaheim Convention Center, Griffith was thirty-four years old – a fighter in his twilight. That night, his opponent was the undefeated Armando Muniz, the West Coast's great new hope, who was fighting in front of a hometown crowd. In addition to winning sixteen professional bouts over the last two years, Muniz was also studying to get his master's in educational administration.

From the start, Griffith dominated the match, showing Muniz it was possible to be outgunned by someone nine years your senior. By the eighth round, Muniz was pouring blood. A large purple mouse under his left eye had split. Instead of going for the knockout, Griffith lowered his blows and refused to hit Muniz in the face anymore. Those nearest to the ring could hear Griffith encouraging his opponent.

"Don't give up," Griffith exhorted. "Keep punching."

Muniz did. And he lost. Griffith was declared the winner and the crowd that had been mocking him in the press as both a pansy and a murderer let out a roar and crowned a new hero, their gentleman boxer.

"As long as I can move these two hands," Griffith told *Sports Illustrated* in 1962, "I'll make them like me." And that night in Anaheim, he did.

NOTES

1 *Shadowboxer* premiered in 2010 at the Maryland Opera Studio. Composed by Frank Proto with a libretto by John Chenault, the opera is actually similar to *Champion*. Both are told in a biopic style and blend opera with other genres of music. *Shadowboxer* received mixed reviews though they seemed to be more favorable than not.

2 *Approaching Ali* debuted at the Washington, DC, Kennedy Center in June 2013. The author of *The Tao of Muhammad Ali*, Davis Miller, wrote the hour-long opera together with more experienced librettist Mark Campbell, while D.J. Sparr composed the music. Reviews were generally favorable.

3 Boxing and opera have crossed paths other times, including in the 1943 Broadway musical *Carmen Jones*, an adaptation of Bizet's *Carmen* that featured African American characters. In it, the matador who seduces Carmen in the original is now a champion boxer. Also *Cavalleria rusticana* plays during the opening of *Raging Bull*, Martin Scorsese's film about middleweight champion Jack LaMotta.

4 The name of the aria is clearly a nod to French-Armenian musician Charles Aznavour's 1972 song "Comme ils dissent," which he translated to "What Makes a Man a Man." In it, a drag performer talks about his lonely life with his mother and unrequited love.

26

COLLEEN AYCOCK

The Voice of Boxing: A Brief History of American Broadcasting Ringside

Boxing broadcasts began as round-by-round descriptions written and posted by newspapermen. With the advent of radio, the broadcaster was a sole figure behind the microphone calling the rounds in real time. But when sponsors began using the boxing ring to market their products, additional announcers were placed ringside to supply color and commercial commentary. As television became popular, film celebrities took their seats at the broadcast table to add color commentary. During the last two decades ring broadcasters have come predominantly from the ranks of boxing, as former professional boxers, trainers, and cornermen. Only recently have color commentators been women, who have yet to take a permanent seat behind the symbolic mike.

Boxing is full of descriptive terms and larger-than-life appellations. A century ago the announcer's first electronic aid, the Magnavox microphone, was called the Super Vox. Newspaper writers, competing to broadcast fight results to the public, replaced their yell-leader megaphones with this super voice that could send their announcements into the air for all to hear. On July 2, 1921, outside the San Francisco offices of William Randolph Hearst's newspaper *The Examiner*, a sportswriter tested the mike and began reading the round-by-round results of a title fight 3,000 miles away on the East Coast between World Heavyweight Champion Jack Dempsey and World Light Heavyweight and European Heavyweight Champion Georges Carpentier. The newsman's voice could be heard over three city blocks by a crowd estimated to have grown to 10,000. It was like something out of an H.G. Wells novel.[1]

Before the heyday of sports radio broadcasts, fans eager to hear immediate fight results had to visit a newspaper office or railroad station to await the postings. As soon as the telegraph operator could decipher the results of the three-minute rounds, encrypted in Morse code, he would either announce those results from his notes or hand them to an assistant to post on a board, much like the leaderboard seen in tournament golf.

Men, women, and children were drawn to the nearest telegraph station for the fight news like later generations were drawn to movie theaters for their leisure entertainment.

As gate attendance approached six digits in the 1920s for Tex Rickard's million-dollar fight promotions, the likes of which had not been seen since the days of the Roman Coliseum, amplifying the announcer's voice became a ring necessity. Aided by the new Magnavox, ring announcer Joe Humphries could actually be heard introducing Jack Dempsey and Georges Carpentier to the 90,000 fans sitting on yellow pine benches at Boyles Thirty Acres in Jersey City, on a sweltering afternoon in 1921. Simultaneously, fans at home, limited to seven broadcast areas in the East, listened in real time to the action of the first world title fight transmitted over the radio. Sitting ringside next to newspaper reporter Nat Fleischer was Major J. Andrew White, editor of *Wireless Age*. White dictated the rounds by telephone to J.O. Smith, working in a hut under the stands to announce the fight's progress through radio connections to his rather limited listening audience.

Out of such humble beginnings came two of the early pioneers of boxing broadcasting in the 1920s: Sam Taub and Graham McNamee. Taub began his broadcast career as a sports journalist at the *New York Morning Telegraph* working under Bat Masterson (the famous lawman before turning referee before turning journalist). Taub was one of the early blow-by-blow boxing broadcasters for the National Broadcasting Company (NBC) founded in 1927 by the Radio Corporation of America (RCA). Taub called over 7,000 contests during his long career, announcing such fights as the second Lou Nova–Max Baer heavyweight bout in 1941 and the Tony Zale–Rocky Graziano middleweight bout in 1947. In 1978 the Boxing Writers Association of America designated an award in his honor: the Sam Taub Award for Excellence in Broadcast Journalism. The list of award recipients is a Who's Who of broadcasters who worked the boxing rings.

Graham McNamee became the most recognized voice of boxing in the 1920s and 1930s as a result of his association with the Gillette Company and Madison Square Garden. After a failed audition as a singer for a New York radio station, McNamee was hired in 1923 to help newspaper sportswriters (the first broadcasters) liven up their radio play-by-play reporting of baseball games. While not entirely knowledgeable about baseball, he made up for it by adding enthusiastic detail; hence he became one of the first broadcast color commentators. That same year he transitioned to the boxing ring as the announcer for the world middleweight title fight at the Polo Grounds, between Harry Greb and Johnny Wilson. In two short years, with his deep melodic voice, he was considered *the* celebrity boxing announcer. In 1927, he broadcast the heavyweight bout in Chicago between Gene Tunney and

Jack Dempsey. In 1935, he called the famous upset at Madison Square Garden when James Braddock beat Max Baer for the heavyweight title. For each, fight listeners waited in anticipation for McNamee's opening lines directed at both men and women: "Good evening ladies and gentlemen of the radio audience. This is Graham McNamee speaking."

Before the Baer–Braddock fight, McNamee famously introduced the Gillette Razor Company to the fight world. Now, added to and sandwiched between frenetic reporting, he had to give a nod to a sponsor. Here is a brief transcript of his opening broadcast: "This is Graham McNamee speaking, direct from the ringside of the Madison Square Garden Bowl in Long Island, New York, with a blow-by-blow description of the fifteen-round fight. This contest is the outstanding pugilistic contest of the year. For eight weeks, the Gillette Safety Razor company has been completing arrangements to broadcast from coast to coast over a nation-wide hookup." No time was wasted. Every second was filled with telegraphic, run-on commentary, difficult to read in transcript but easily processed by the radio listeners. Prior to Baer and Braddock entering the ring, McNamee introduced Ward Bond who would add commercial commentary to the fast-paced broadcast. This is what the radio audience heard from Bond in sixty seconds:

> Thank you Graham. I know you listeners are plenty anxious to catch Al Frazen's voice who is substituting for Joe Humphries tonight. You of course heard the news about Joe. I know you're anxious to hear that gong, sending these two great heavyweights into action. While we are waiting for the boys to come into the ring, we want to tell you about the big new Gillette contest in which the Gillette Safety Razor Company is awarding thousands of dollars-worth of prizes just for naming Max Baer's dog, that wiry little fellow that Max recently adopted. Folks you should see this dog of Max's. He's the most loveable little fox terrier you ever saw, white, wiry hair with spots of brown, and a snappy wide awake look that says, "Boy I'm ready for fun." And what a pal he's been to Max. Day after day dominating Max's training camp, he's been right up to the ringside and bark as the champ snagged a sparring partner with that famous right. But be one of the last to get one over on Max, and the snappy little he-dog will bark and growl as if to say, "You can't do that while I'm around." You all would all love this little fella if you could see him, and we know you're going to get a lot of fun suggesting a name for this dog. Be the first to submit winning names for this dog. Gillete is awarding over $17,000 dollars in prizes: a grand prize of $1,000 in cash, 120 new 1935 RCA victor magic ring radios, complete with antennas valued at $125.50 each.

Gillette had planned its extended media promotion on the fact that every Gillette executive, along with the betting public, expected Baer to win. The company's management failed to understand a fundamental principle of boxing – that it's anyone's game. After the upset, the name of Baer's dog fell in importance to the advertiser. (A winning name was eventually selected: the Livermore Gay Blade.)

In those early days of radio broadcasting, Gillette and Graham McNamee were names synonymous with boxing. Recognized years after his death for his achievement in the entertainment industry, Graham McNamee was among the initial honorees for a brass star on Hollywood's Walk of Fame.

When the enormous gates of the late 1920s peaked, promoter Tex Rickard blamed the situation on the radio, saying that fans had elected to stay home to enjoy the fights in the comfort of an easy chair. The same argument would be used when a newer technology, the television, emerged. However, the new media and its new, star-quality boxers, supported by sponsors, only fanned the popularity of the sport.

Don Dunphy was perhaps the best-known ringside announcer of the middle decades, a voice still remembered today by a generation of Baby Boomers. His broadcast career began in 1934 during the Great Depression, when he earned $7 a week as a radio announcer, a hearty first paycheck when the penny daily cost two cents, beer was a nickel a glass, and a winning prize for a local boxing match was $5. Like most young working men then, he carried his earnings home to his mother.

By 1936 corporate money was freed up for marketing. Following Gillette's foray into sport promotions, the Ford Motor Company sponsored the 1936 World Series on radio. The Atlantic Refining Company attached its name to sport by sponsoring college football for the first time. Don Dunphy was asked to do the color and commercial commentary for the Cornell games in upstate New York. At the time, his broadcast idol was Stan Lomax, the distinctive voice of a daily sports show for Mutual Broadcasting System in New York.[2] Prior to the Second World War, a time considered the golden age of radio, Mutual Broadcasting, specializing in news, sport reporting, and radio dramas, was the largest of the four American national networks (with NBC, CBS, and ABC) that would add television to their broadcast media.

In 1941, Mutual Broadcasting selected the Gillette Company as exclusive sponsor for the fight promotions at Madison Square Garden. This partnership would be the inception for the *Cavalcade of Sports*, a series that would not get fully under way until 1944. Dunphy was invited to be the new radio broadcast announcer for Gillette and Madison Square Garden. His first fight was a title fight pitting the great heavyweight title holder Joe Louis against Billy Conn, a fighter who had never been knocked out before June 18, 1941. Conn had given up his light heavyweight title to challenge Louis for his heavyweight title. The exciting fight proved no tongue twister for the adroit twenty-eight-year-old announcer. Through the first twelve rounds Conn was leading on points, about to upset the champion. Then in the thirteenth round Louis put an end to his own misery with a barrage of uppercuts that put Conn down, ending the fight. Dunphy's coverage of that fight would catapult him into broadcast fame. He would go on to be the play-by-play radio announcer, the voice of boxing for Gillette for over 2,000 fights during the next two decades, transitioning from radio to television. Dunphy was at the announcer's mike for the Garden's first televised broadcast, and he remained at the mike through Muhammad Ali's last career fight in 1981, Dunphy's last broadcast.

At the end of his career, Don Dunphy summarized the art of broadcasting by saying that if you can do the job and have confidence in yourself, the rest is easy. Seasoned practitioners, however, know that nothing is easy about blow-by-blow broadcasting. The first requirement is to have the voice and physical ability to do it. The mental acuity required for the tongue-tripping, rapid-fire, staccato style necessary to announce fifteen or twenty rounds of boxing late in the evening is physically exhausting. Actually, Dunphy thought that blow-by-blow radio announcing was easier than announcing for television because the radio announcer didn't have to think; he just had to describe the action as fast as it occurred. He believed that a good television announcer shouldn't be a radio announcer. The television audience can see the right jabs and the left hooks. The job of the television announcer is to tell the audience what it cannot see because the viewer isn't sitting at ringside. Dunphy instructed, "I might point out that [Sugar Ray] Leonard's jab, which was short of the mark in the early rounds, is now finding its mark."[3]

The transition from radio to television came in 1939 when NBC produced the first live boxing event on television, the first Lou Nova–Max Baer fight at Yankee Stadium. The evolution of the new media, however, would be interrupted by the Second World War. And when the Great War was finally over, returning soldiers, and Americans in general, were ready to be entertained. Post-war prosperity and the novelty of television in the late 1940s gave momentum to set production and commercial sponsorships. Television followed radio in that broadcasters signed with sponsors. Bob Hope, for example, a radio broadcaster for *The Pepsodent Show* became host for the *Chevy Show* when he transitioned into television. The leading television shows of the early 1950s were identified by title with commercial sponsors, such as *Texaco Star Theater*, *Philco TV Playhouse*, and the *Colgate Comedy Hour*. Unlike American television, British television was reluctant to adopt commercially sponsored programming.

Boxing transitioned from radio to television in America with the Gillette Company. In an arrangement with Mike Jacobs at Madison Square Garden, NBC launched Friday Night Fights in 1944 in a series called *Gillette*

Cavalcade of Sports. The first fight featured featherweight champion Willie Pep and former champion Chalky Wright. Like radio, boxing was made for television programming. Boxing was not a seasonal sport; its popularity was already established, and the one-on-one action could be seen more easily than other sports on the tiny, black and white screens. Other major networks were not serious contenders for the boxing audience, choosing instead to cover news or the blue-chip sports. NBC's *Cavalcade of Sports* fight announcer Jimmy Powers remained with NBC from 1949 to 1960 and brought a unique perspective to broadcasting. He believed in the picture telling the story and detested wordy broadcasters. He once went an entire three-minute round of boxing without uttering a single word.[4] NBC would remain the leader of boxing entertainment until it dropped the show in 1960. ABC replaced NBC as producer of the show for the next three years. When *Cavalcade of Sports* left the air, it had been the longest continuously running series in television history, producing 600 nights of boxing.[5] (Unrelated to NBC, a similarly named program, *Cavalcade of Sport*, aired in the United Kingdom in the mid-1950s.)

By the late 1950s, boxing had become one of network television's most valued programming assets until news broke of underworld racketeers Blinky Palermo and Frankie Carbo working to fix fights with Frank Norris, who served as president of the International Boxing Club of New York (IBC) from 1949 to 1958, headquartered at Madison Square Garden. US Senate investigations followed, and by the end of the 1950s, the networks' zeal for boxing programs had waned. Then came the 1960s.

All aspects of sport in America were affected by the seismic shift in social attitudes that came with the 1960s. Helping to integrate college sports, the Civil Rights Act of 1964 outlawed discrimination based upon race, color, religion, sex, or national origin. The Title IX educational amendment in 1972 barred discrimination under any educational program on the basis of sex. Inside the ring, boxing had been mixing the races for decades, but for broadcasters and others outside the ring, the sport reflected the status quo of the white male professional. Title IX would change that.

Joe Bostic, a popular radio host for New York's *Gospel Train*, was offered the job of the late Johnny Addie as ring announcer for Madison Square Garden in 1972. Bostic had been a current radio announcer and a former sports announcer for the Negro leagues in the 1940s, but his debut as the first black ring announcer on a regular basis at the most prestigious boxing venue in New York didn't occur until 1972. And while *Friday Night Fights* had been considered family entertainment for the previous two decades, it wasn't until 1972 that reporter Lee Arthur became the first woman allowed in the press section with her male peers at Madison Square Garden. (It would take forty-plus years before a woman would be handed a microphone at a major televised boxing event. Laila Ali, former boxer and daughter of Muhammad Ali, became a ring corner analyst for only a few shows when NBC returned to the continuous fight programming in 2015 with *Premier Boxing Champions*.)

ABC entered the sports market programming boom in 1953 with a series called *Game of the Week* hosted by a man with a homespun style, former ball player Dizzy Dean. ABC would stay happily married to baseball and football during the Norris boxing mayhem until it picked up a most unusual color commentator in 1961, Howard Cosell. Cosell would eventually move to boxing and cement ABC to the sport. As premier announcer for the network, Cosell would at first rankle then amuse his television audience. Born Howard Cohen, Cosell brought his unique voice and personality to broadcasting. Announcers in the past were wary of stepping into the hotbed of social issues. Cosell on the other hand, was fearless about such topics. No one could predict what would come out of his mouth, and his justification for whatever he said became his catch phrase: "I'm just telling it like it is." Viewers were drawn to the suspense. Representing the tone of the 1960s, Cosell was to broadcasting what Muhammad Ali, born Cassius Clay, was to boxing: brash, arrogant, highly intelligent, and very, very clever. Cosell enjoyed banter, particularly when interviewing Ali. As a trained lawyer before venturing into broadcasting, Cosell was personally anguished by the New York Boxing Commission's decision to revoke Ali's boxing license on the basis that Ali refused to be drafted into the military for religious reasons during the war in Vietnam. The broadcaster and the boxer became iconic figures forever linked.

Cosell became the richest sports broadcaster of his era. As his celebrity grew, he became less of a maverick and more of a prima donna, pushing his way into press conferences and making demands on his network.[6] Where previous boxing announcers had played a secondary role to the boxer, Cosell enjoyed the spotlight. His distinctive voice differed from the rapid-fire, tell-it-like-it-is style of sports journalism. His gutsy arrogance and nasally, evenly accented, lethargic quality was frequently mimicked by comedians. It seemed that everyone who knew him had a Cosell story to tell.

Journalist Robert Lipsyte recalls in his memoir that when Cosell was asked to name someone for whom he could pass the torch, or in this case, the broadcaster's mike, "He cleared his throat and glared, and coldly said he didn't think there was anyone in broadcasting who could cover the range of topics he had covered with similar intelligence or morality."[7]

Before the 1960s, the television announcer was usually the only person speaking from ringside. But by 1970, ABC began airing NFL games on

Monday Night Football, using the controversial color commentator Howard Cosell alongside a celebrity announcer, former Dallas Cowboys football quarterback, Don Meredith. The publicity benefit was enormous and other networks followed the trend by adding celebrities to the broadcast mix.

With the advent of celebrity commentary during sport broadcasts, the play-by-play announcer's job at ringside became increasingly complicated, which explains why throughout his career Don Dunphy preferred to do his job alone. Often the announcer would have two or more people speaking over themselves. The untrained commentators could be wordy or long-winded. The announcer frequently had to cut off these showmen mid-sentence to be able to follow the action in the ring. For the Ali–Frazier fight in 1971, Dunphy was given Burt Lancaster and Archie Moore as co-commentators. Wisely, he would only allow them to speak between rounds.

Every career broadcaster has had a difficult moment during a live presentation. Dunphy's came when he was announcing the Joe Frazier–George Foreman fight in Kingston, Jamaica in 1973. As mentioned, Dunphy preferred working the mike alone; but Don King was the promoter of the fight, and he had "assigned" musical actress Pearl Bailey as co-announcer, who was a huge fan of George Foreman. Once the fight began, she proceeded to cheer her man, a cardinal violation of unbiased reporting. In addition to interrupting Dunphy's commentary with her loud enthusiasm, she obscured his vision with her large presence by frequently jumping out of her chair. When Foreman floored Frazier, she was so excited that she struck Dunphy on the back and sent his papers flying to the floor in disarray.[8] Broadcasters can sympathize with Dunphy's plight.

By the 1980s, the networks had standardized three talking heads at ringside, usually a broadcaster, a color commentator, and a former professional boxer. These positions were highly competitive, with many announcers shifting from one network to another, and with virtually everyone-but-his-mother vying for a chance at the mike. Since the inception of radio, broadcasters came to the profession from the field of communications. During the 1980s many of the jobs were given to men who had never been sportscasters. Even network executives, such as Alex Wallau, who came from ABC management, became an announcer before returning to a position in management. Before the decade was out, most of the talking heads for the three networks were drawn from the sport of boxing.

NBC had Dr. Ferdie Pacheco (Ali's former physician), Dick Enberg (an honorary doctorate degree recipient), and Sugar Ray Leonard (Fighter of the Year in 1979, Fight of the Year with Tommy Hearns in 1981, and Upset of the Year with Marvin Hagler in 1987).

CBS had Gil Clancy (former trainer of boxers such as Emile Griffith, Muhammad Ali, Joe Frazier, George Foreman, Gerry Cooney, and Oscar De La Hoya), Angelo Dundee (trainer and ring cornerman for Carmen Basillio, Willie Pastrano, George Foreman, Sugar Ray Leonard, and Muhammad Ali), and Tim Ryan (Ryan called fights for both NBC and CBS, involving Muhammad Ali, Joe Frazier, Floyd Patterson, Oscar Bonavena, Bernard Hopkins, Tommy Hearns, Sugar Ray Leonard and Marvin Hagler).

ABC had Howard Cosell, with virtually no one remembering whether anyone co-announced or commented with him – Cosell *was* ABC Boxing.

During the 1980s, the new cable networks filled much of their programming with sports, allowing broadcasters to experience many roles, much like those in the earliest days of sports broadcasting. And two broadcasters, Al Bernstein and Jim Lampley, came into the broadcast business for the cable networks at this time.

Originally, Lampley was host for ABC's *Wide World of Sports*, calling forty boxing matches during the 1980s at a time when his analyst was Alex Wallau. Lampley credits Wallau for teaching him how to recognize many of the subtleties of the fight game. Lampley called the action for HBO on *World Championship Boxing*, and was seen as the quarterback for the team, a compliment coming from his co-announcers Larry Merchant, Ray Leonard, Emmanuel Steward, and George Foreman. Known for his forthright opinions, Lampley has not been afraid to voice his thoughts and is perhaps best remembered for his final comment on the Lennox Lewis–Evander Holyfield decision in 1999, which everyone ringside thought went to Lewis. When Michael Buffer announced the fight a draw, Lampley roared, "Out of the cesspool of boxing comes the latest unmistakable stench."[9] Lampley was inducted into the International Boxing Hall of Fame (IBHOF) in June 2015.

IBHOF member Al Bernstein is recognized as the voice of boxing, first for ESPN and currently for Showtime. Like many of the Baby Boom Generation, Bernstein's idol at ringside was Don Dunphy. Later when the mentor became an admirer, Dunphy was asked by a magazine interviewer, "Who is your favorite boxing announcer?" His reply was Al Bernstein.[10]

Bernstein is remembered today as a one-man show, although he has partnered with many of the best sports journalists and professional boxers over several network projects, co-announcers Sal Marchiano, Barry Tompkins, Al Michael, and Sam Rosa. Bernstein spent twenty-four years with ESPN, beginning as a commentator for *Top Rank Boxing* in its early days when the global television network was not the giant cable network it is today. In 1980 few people associated the initials with entertainment and sports programming, Bernstein recalls. Many thought it was a network associated with aliens and extra-sensory perception.

For Bernstein, the 1980s were the halcyon days of sports programming, with fighters such as Marvin Hagler and Tommy Hearns, and with the broadcaster wearing many hats, providing commentary, analysis, play-by-play announcing, or conducting interviews. Once, Bernstein announced a fight alone for ESPN in 1986, a 2½-hour *Top Rank* show where he also had to incorporate interviews with the fighters after their bouts in the same programming. Today, he is both the face and voice of boxing for Showtime's *Championship Boxing*, coming full circle by working with director Bob Dunphy, Don's son. And while the voices of boxers and reporters today have become increasingly harsh and less respectful, Bernstein's gentlemanly qualities work to enhance the respectability of the game.

Fittingly, after thirty years in the business, Al Bernstein and Jim Lampley came together to co-announce the most highly anticipated fight in the recent decade, billed as the "Fight of the Century," between Floyd Mayweather and Manny Pacquiao on May 2, 2015, when their respective networks, Showtime and HBO, agreed to co-telecast the fight. The boxing bonanza brought together a mix of broadcast giants. The CBS host for the evening was James Brown, blow-by-blow announcer was Jim Lampley from HBO, color commentator was Al Bernstein from Showtime, and boxing expert was Roy Jones.

The list of boxing sportscasters is a long one, and their broadcasting techniques have been as varied as their personalities. But two things stand out about them all: their appreciation for the sport of boxing and their desire to share that love of the sport with new fans.

In his Hall of Fame acceptance speech in 2012, Al Bernstein gave three important rules for broadcasters: 1) Never be bigger than the event; 2) Don't ever disrespect any athlete, especially a boxer in the sport that is so very difficult to master; and 3) Being fair is more important than being clever.

Ultimately, viewers look to the broadcaster for a good description and fair assessment of what they are seeing. Consequently, the person at the mike has a broad hand in rewarding decorum and fair play, and calling out injustices. In short, words do matter. With every boxer who steps through the ropes, someone comes to a microphone to announce, interview, explain, or comment; man or woman, the sports broadcaster is there to fill the role of the *Super Vox*.

NOTES

1 Colleen Aycock and Mark Scott, *Tex Rickard: Boxing's Greatest Promoter*, 142–43.
2 Don Dunphy, *Don Dunphy at Ringside*, 39.
3 Dunphy, 99.

4   Stephen Bass, "Boxing's TV Picture," *The Ring,* 82.
5   Ron Powers, *SuperTube: The Rise of Television Sports,* 55.
6   Robert Lipsyte, *An Accidental Sportswriter: A Memoir,* 39.
7   Lipsyte, 84.
8   Dunphy, 101.
9   Mark Whicker, "The Voice of Boxing, *The Ring,* 79.
10 Al Bernstein, *30 Years, 30 Undeniable Truths About Boxing, Sports, and TV,* 25–6.

BIBLIOGRAPHY

Aycock, Colleen, and Mark Scott. *Tex Rickard: Boxing's Greatest Promoter,* McFarland: Jefferson, NC. 2012.

Bass, Stephen. "Boxing's TV Picture," *The Ring.* October 1981, 78–84.

Bernstein, Al. *30 Years, 30 Undeniable Truths About Boxing, Sports, and TV.* Diversion: NY. 2012.

Dunphy, Don. *Don Dunphy at Ringside.* Henry Holt: NY. 1988.

Lipsyte, Robert. *An Accidental Sportswriter: A Memoir.* HarperCollins, NY. 2011.

Powers, Ron. *SuperTube: The Rise of Television Sports,* Coward-McCann, NY, 1984.

Mark Whicker, "The Voice of Boxing, *The Ring,* Aug. 2015. 78–81.

27

SHELLEY FISHER FISHKIN

Ralph Wiley's Surprising *Serenity*

"I have always considered serenity to be an admirable state of existence. I have pursued serenity and found it elusive. So I have pursued the company of those I thought possessed it in greatest supply; they understand the futilities of worry and strife. The first person I met who had this serenity was my Uncle Charles, who was once a prizefighter … [W]ith childish logic, I assumed all prizefighters were serene."[1] Thus begins a highly unusual book about boxing and boxers and covering the sport (something Wiley did brilliantly for decades) – a book which is equally about trying to understand why men whose chosen profession regularly subjects them to elemental, extreme physical violence manage to have that elusive quality of serenity in such great supply.

At age ten, Ralph Wiley asked his uncle Charles to teach him how to fight. His uncle replied:

> "Fightin' that's one thing. Boxin's another. You want to know how to box, you say so." His face moved closer to mine. "Boxin's harder to do," he said. He seemed to contract his vulnerable parts, what few of them there might have been, expanded his arms and shoulders and bent forward from the waist. He put up his hands. I could see his eyes between his fists. His feet were slightly scissored apart. He rose on the ball of his right foot and lowered himself onto the heel of his left. At the center of this poised mass, his eyes shone most dangerously of all. This was not my uncle Charles anymore. This was Charlie Boy Taylor, middleweight.
>
> "Were you scared, boy?"
>
> He had broken the trance.
>
> "No sir."
>
> I was an unconvincing liar. Uncle Charles had a good laugh on me before saying, "You got it then, Butch. Boxin's mostly watching the other man. Remember that. What you can see can't hurt you. Now, you shoot your punch like this." He snapped out his right, rolling the hand over with a muscular jerk that was audible in the still air. "Turn your fist. Throw it from behind the

shoulder, with the legs, if you can. Then snap it." He threw four or five punches with each hand, stopping each one within a whisker of my immobile nose. Tell you what else. Cut the grass twice a week. Cut it good and close. Cut it in the morning, when the dew's down." Then he let the subject drop. I had expected him to turn me into a human buzz saw, but tall grass was not the opponent I expected.[2]

In addition to helping his nephew develop muscles while making himself useful, what the former prizefighter was trying to get his puzzled student to learn, beyond the value of discipline and practice, was a concept stunning in its simultaneous simplicity and complexity: "What you can see can't hurt you." The attention the boxer learns to pay to everything he could see – the smallest movement, the most nuanced gesture – is key to any success he wants to have. ("Boxin's mostly watching the other man.") It was also key to his survival.

On the surface, the world of the gritty, brutal boxing ring couldn't be more distant from the world of gaudy nineteenth-century riverboats plying the Mississippi. But the importance of learning how to "see" ("What you can see can't hurt you") was essential to both. Indeed, mortal peril that ensued if you failed to see things you should have seen was as key to the riverboat pilot's survival as it was to the boxer's – which may explain, in part, why Mark Twain's *Life on the Mississippi* was one of Ralph Wiley's favorite books. In both professions, paying meticulous attention to noticing things – learning to see things that non-initiates would miss – was key to staying alive.

Wiley's description of how a master boxing coach tried to teach him about boxing resonates with Twain's description of how a master riverboat pilot tried to teach him about piloting. Here is Dick Sadler, of the New Oakland Boxing Club, who taught Wiley how to "read" his opponent in the ring:

> Sadler had been George [Foreman]'s trainer, and it was he who gave me lessons on the sequence. "There's up and down and there's in and out, and there's what follows what and what counters what," he said. "Every punch that get thrown leave the opening you must see. You must see it, now. But there ain't no real way to explain it. You have to see it for yourself."[3]

And here is Horace Bixby, the celebrated pilot who taught Sam Clemens how to "read" the river:

> You see, this has got to be learned; there isn't any getting around it. A clear starlight night throws such heavy shadows that, if you didn't know the shape of a shore perfectly, you would claw away from every bunch of timber, because you would take the black shadow of it for a solid cape … You can't see a snag in one of those shadows, but you know exactly where it is, and the shape of

the river tells you when you are coming to it … Do you see that long, slanting line on the face of the water? Now, that's a reef. Moreover, it's a bluff reef. There is a solid sand-bar under it that is nearly as straight up and down as the side of a house. There is plenty of water close up to it, but mighty little on top of it. If you were to hit it you would knock the boat's brains out.[4]

The serenity of the boxer and the serenity of the pilot came from a sense of control born of training, knowledge, and sharp observation. "The professional boxer," Wiley writes, "was as competent at his science as a mathematician, as committed to his art as a musician."[5]

The central challenge was knowing enough and being in a position to use the knowledge you had, whether it involved distinguishing a bluff reef from a wind reef on the river or determining whether to feint or jab in the ring:

Men like Sadler and tedious observance by rote showed me that the opening of the boxer's sequence was basic, like the opening moves of a backgammon player. Six-one. Five-three. Four-two … And that was only the first round, the first three minutes. Meanwhile, the boxer who must react instinctively to each offering of the sequence was being subjected to mayhem of the highest order. The better the boxer, the earlier he knows when something is wrong in the procedure. This knowledge is called skill. It's a mixture of speed, acuity, experience, instinct, rough math, and a kind of genius or insanity, take your pick.[6]

The elusive serenity that Wiley finds in boxers stems in part from the confidence they have in their ability to calibrate their own moves by their subtle awareness of what they see their opponent doing. In short, much of it comes from the *craft* they have worked to hone.

The serenity the boxer achieves is not unlike that which the riverboat pilot achieves: each is secure in the fact that he has learned how to notice everything that his survival depends on and to allow that knowledge to shape his performance on the river or in the ring. That quality – knowing that you have trained yourself to notice what counts, and that you have developed your craft to be able to make the most of what you see – is also essential to the writer. It is key to what makes Ralph Wiley's own writing so compelling.

If Dick Sadler was Wiley's boxing teacher, Mark Twain was his writing teacher. In his book *Dark Witness*, Wiley wrote,

Mark Twain is the only man I would call master, and *mean* it … Mark Twain is not the master of the school in which I am enrolled – he built the school, forced its accreditation, made it known and honored worldwide and kept the admissions policies liberal so that even a wretch like me could get a berth.[7]

Wiley, a star pupil in that school, produced, in addition to hundreds of cover stories, columns, reviews, articles, and opinion pieces, four books of his own and four co-authored ones.[8] Many of these focused on sports – but many (even some of those ostensibly about sports) were caustic exposés of racism American-style and of human folly in general. He wrote in many tones and timbres, ranging from staccato play-by-plays to jazz-inflected satirical riffs to raging jeremiads to elegiac meditations – all with nearly perfect pitch. Witness the sober eloquence, for example, with which he describes the scene in Kronk gym in Detroit:

> The gym was packed. These were good-looking fighters. Quick. Whipcord-strong. Willful. Flawed, of course. Most of them were small, with thin arms and legs. Some were the products of the overdosed and undernourished. The best-quality narcotics and the worst-quality produce made it to inner-city Detroit ... But they all seemed to be on their way to being as good as their abilities and physiques would allow ... They were just boys in the end, but they were boys who had uncaring, fully grown demons growling in their stomachs and whispering in the backs of their minds, assuring them that they would have to kick ass in order to survive.[9]

Or watch him, in this jarringly candid passage on boxing and brain damage, help his readers see things they may have ignored or denied about the sport:

> Damage, specifically brain damage, is what boxing is all about. Boxing is assault and battery with deadly weapons called the fists of man ... Boxing is full of brain damage. Ali seemed untouchable. But he has urinated blood after a fight, had his jaw broken, felt his face tighten as it swelled to twice normal size, been knocked on his can, battered his hands beyond repair and suffered several concussions ... Have you ever wondered at the miracle of a cauliflower ear or a nose warped in three directions? Do you know what a smashed Adam's apple feels like? How long it takes for a shattered cheekbone to heal? ... Think this is some kind of game? Ever hear of Frankie Campbell, Jimmy Doyle, Benny Paret, Clevelend Denny, Willie Classen, or Duk Koo Kim?
>
> What would you think if you couldn't get out of bed in the morning because of a traumatized liver? Can you imagine having your jaw broken and not going immediately to the hospital, but instead fighting for ten more rounds? ... Can you imagine thousands of your fellow humans screaming for your blood?[10]

Boxing's victims get the same kind of careful attention in this book as the winners. Wiley's narrative of the sequence of events the night that the Korean fighter Duk Koo Kim was killed by Ray "Boom Boom" Mancini is moving and powerful, with Kim emerging with a pyrrhic victory of sorts through his stunning determination and courage. At this match and others, Wiley saw more and more of "the underside of boxing. It became Pandora's Box – no matter how or where I chose to open it, out jumped more misfortune, more bad luck, more horrors. My job was to record all this."[11] At that point he realized it was time to move on.

Late in the book Wiley writes that he thought he "finally understood the great secret of [Uncle Charles's] serenity. As a child, I thought it had to do with his boxing, with his ability to defend himself from the first act of violence from another man. Maybe it wasn't the boxing, but the *ability* to box that gave Uncle Charles his serenity."[12] This realization leads Wiley to frame a new definition of what serenity is: "the inner peace which comes from doing something well enough to understand it."[13]

For Wiley himself, writing was a source of that "inner peace." Whether he was displaying genial humor or raw outrage, Wiley always showed a passionate commitment to the writer's craft, and gave credit early and often to his writing teacher. Indeed, when Wiley submitted *Dark Witness* to Random House, the subtitle was "In Homage to Mark Twain." Random House balked and stuck him with a different one that he hated: "When Black People Should Be Sacrificed (Again)." (But when he gave his book to friends, he discarded the dust jacket, crossed out Random House's subtitle on the title page, and replaced it with his own.)[14]

Wiley and Twain shared a passion for vernacular voices – black and white ones. Both abhorred using the second cousin of the right word when the right word was just as handy. Both were impatient with people's tolerance for the "lie of silent assertion" – "the silent assertion ... that nothing is going on which fair and intelligent men are aware of and are engaged by their duty to try to stop";[15] and both targeted the lies of silent assertion that undergirded so much of racism in America. Both writers recognized that "against the assault of laughter, nothing can stand."[16] And, truth be told, both writers were fascinated by boxing: In a letter to his wife, Twain described in blow-by-blow detail a match he attended in 1893 at the New York Athletic Club in which Frank Craig, the Harlem "Coffee Cooler," defeated a white opponent, Joe Ellingsworth. "It is absorbingly interesting," Twain wrote.[17]

Serenity: A Boxing Memoir – A Search for the Boxer's Peace of Mind, from Joe Louis to Mike Tyson, was, for Wiley – as so much of his writing was – a labor of love: love for the athletes and the people who guided and sustained them and love for the challenge of capturing clearly and sharply the feats they achieved and endured. It invites the reader to enter a world that is both terrifying and exhilarating. With Ralph Wiley as one's guide, it is a journey well worth taking.

NOTES

1 Ralph Wiley. *Serenity: A Boxing Memoir – A Search for the Boxer's Peace of Mind, from Joe Louis to Mike Tyson*. New York: Henry Holt and Company, 1989, 1.
2 Wiley, *Serenity*, 9.

3 Wiley, *Serenity*, 30.

4 Mark Twain, *Life on the Mississippi*. [1883]. *The Oxford Mark Twain*, edited by Shelley Fisher Fishkin. New York: Oxford University Press, 1996, 103–4, 112.

5 Wiley, *Serenity*, 29.

6 Wiley, *Serenity*, 31.

7 Ralph Wiley, *Dark Witness: When Black People Should be Sacrificed (Again)* (New York: Ballantine, 1996), 33, 35.

8 In addition to *Serenity* and *Dark Witness*, Ralph Wiley wrote *Why Black People Tend to Shout: Cold Facts and Wry Views from a Black Man's World* (New York: Penguin Books, 1991) and *What Black People Should Do Now: Dispatches from Near the Vanguard* (New York: One World/Ballantine Books, 1993). He co-authored (with Spike Lee) *By Any Means Necessary: The Trials and Tribulations of the Making of Malcolm X* (including the screenplay) (New York: Hyperion, 1992) and *Best Seat in the House: A Basketball Memoir* (New York: Crown Publishers, 1997); (with Eric Davis) *Born to Play: The Eric Davis Story – Life Lessons in Overcoming Adversity on and off the Field* (New York: Viking, 1999); and (with Dexter King) *Growing Up King: An Intimate Memoir* (New York: Warner Books, 2001). He wrote twenty-eight cover stories (as well as other stories) for *Sports Illustrated*, over 240 columns for ESPN, and scores of articles and reviews in *Crisis, Dialogue, GQ, National Geographic, Premiere,* the *Oakland Tribune,* and other publications.

9 Wiley, *Serenity*, 153.

10 Wiley, *Serenity*, 227–28.

11 Wiley, *Serenity*, 114.

12 Wiley, *Serenity*, 205.

13 Wiley, *Serenity*, 200.

14 Copy of cloth-bound edition thus corrected (in pink highlighter) in possession of the author. Also a copy of the paperback edition of this book, in which Wiley used a yellow Post-it note to replace the subtitle his publisher foisted on him with the one he originally chose.

15 Mark Twain, "My First Lie and How I Got Out of It." In *The Man that Corrupted Hadleyburg and Other Stories and Essays* [1900]. *The Oxford Mark Twain,* edited by Shelley Fisher Fishkin. New York: Oxford University Press, 1996, 171.

16 Mark Twain, "Chronicle of Young Satan." *The Mysterious Stranger Manuscripts,* New York: Harper & Bros., 1916, 142.

17 Samuel L. Clemens, Letter to Olivia Clemens, January 4, 1894, reprinted in *The Love Letters of Mark Twain,* New York: Harper & Bros., 1949, 287, reprinted at www.twainquotes.com/Boxing.html

28

GERALD EARLY

Muhammad Ali: King of the Inauthentic

The New Island

> By nature, all members of the black nation are Muslims.
> – Elijah Muhammad,
> *Message to the Blackman in America*, 1965[1]

When I wrote in my introduction to *The Muhammad Ali Reader* (1998) that, as a society, we were on the verge of "over esteeming" Muhammad Ali and thus of grossly misunderstanding his significance and deeply diminishing him as a person, I did not see myself as a revisionist but rather a seeker of a new level of nuance, an explorer.[2] Of course, there were some who did see me as a revisionist, or at least saw portions of that introduction as a revisionist text: For instance, conservative writer Jack Cashill in his book *Sucker Punch: The Hard Left Hook that Dazed Ali and Killed King's Dream* (2006) mentioned me favorably as someone who had a certain skepticism of the Ali myth, referring to me as an "Ali iconoclast."[3] When Ali died, I was asked to write an op-ed about him for the *Washington Post*, a difficult task to limit oneself to 700 words about such a gigantic and complex figure in American society. I collapsed my observations to three basic points; the first of which was:

> [Ali] was not a civil rights advocate or activist. The Nation of Islam, which Ali joined in 1964, was, if anything, against the civil rights movement and, as a separatist group, opposed to racial integration. The Nation also thought that whites were unnatural beings, while its millennialist bent made members feel superior to activists.
>
> In fact, the Nation of Islam was criticized by civil rights activists for their lack of participation in the movement. Do not mistake Ali's outspoken denunciation of racial injustice as activism. That was his defense of the orthodoxy of his religion.

This hardly seems a controversial point. In fact, to my mind, it is indisputable and it is one of the major misunderstandings about Ali that occurred after his death, this persistent belief that he was "a civil rights activist," an expression that seems both reductionist and a bit wrong-headedly congratulatory. Ali expressed his dislike of nonviolence as a political tactic and thus his contempt for the civil rights movement even before he became champion and publicly announced that he was a Muslim, "I'm no James Meredith," he told the *New York Post*. He said shortly after: "I'm a fighter. I believe in the eye-for-an-eye business. I'm no cheek turner. The NAACP can say, 'turn the other cheek,' but the NAACP is ignorant."[4] (Ali, of course, by inference, misidentified the NAACP as a pacifist organization.) This was typical NOI rhetoric, *militant* but also *removed* from the arena, as Muslim self-defense oratory at that time was. The attraction of Islam for Ali was its fantastic cosmology, its anti-whiteness as the orthodoxy of a cult. It gave Ali, as Wilfrid Sheed so aptly put it, a "swaggering he-man's religion,"[5] all of whose vehemence was directed inwardly as a form of discipline, conformity, and group authority rather than outward as political activism. All transformation for the NOI was of the convert, not of the world the convert lived in. To the leaders of the civil rights movement the NOI was disingenuous, fake, hypocritical: the Muslims attacked the civil rights movement as being insufficiently real and militant as political activism but when challenged by civil rights leaders to join the fray chose to opt behind the mystical awakening of conversion and the intervention of Allah as their refuge. This, to me, seemed obvious to anyone who was even superficially acquainted with the NOI specifically and a great swath of black American religion more generally. But many did not have even nodding acquaintance with the religion.

A bit later, on the occasion of Ali's funeral, I was interviewed on the *PBS News Hour* and was strenuously challenged by my interrogator when he insisted on calling Ali "a civil rights activist." He said that several people had referred to Ali in this way, to which I responded, "They're wrong."[6] The point is that Ali was a member of a faith community and operated his entire adult life as such and he opposed his government on the basis of being a member of this faith community. One would hardly say that a Shaker or a Mennonite or a Quaker was "a civil rights activist" for refusing induction into the armed services on the basis of religious faith no matter how antiestablishment the action that the faith induces may be.

Some might argue that Ali's was a political religion and the Nation of Islam was surely that, but then again what religious faith does not have political implications of some sort for its adherents, regardless of whether some of the beliefs are openly or obviously political. To say Ali was a civil rights activist is to misunderstand the age that produced him. A faith, any faith, is making demands on how its adherents should live in *this* world, not the next. (Apparently, no one has to be taught how to live *there*, heaven or hell.) Even something as seemingly apolitical as Pentecostalism is political in its insistence of avoiding and condemning the secular. My cousin, George Fernandez, Jr., is a Jehovah's Witness; one of the tenets of that faith is not to rise for the National Anthem or in any way show any deference to the flag. Seeing him do this at a sporting event can be a cause of tension with the other spectators who are present but he is merely following the dictates of his faith. His action is not anti-American (nor now should it be construed as sympathetic with black athletes and other political dissenters as he would not rise for any nation's flag or anthem because his faith demands that he shows no worship for anything except God). His actions could be construed as anti-patriotic or as anti-patriotism itself but it is not an act of resistance that can be rightly understood by calling him "a civil rights activist," in the way people typically use that phrase, a designation he would find bizarre.

African American journalist, Harlem Renaissance novelist, and noted conservative George S. Schuyler wrote a laudatory column immediately following Ali's 1964 defeat of Sonny Liston and his announcement that he was a member of the Nation of Islam. In part, Schuyler wrote: "What was most impressive about young Clay was the manner in which he answered loaded questions about Islam and the so-called Black Muslims. Yes, he said, he was a member and had been for the past five years. Yes, he believed in the teachings of Mr. Muhammad's sect and what he saw of good decorum, proper dress, respect for women and sobriety in the Muslim gatherings which he had attended."[7] Schuyler makes Ali out as a conservative, attracted to the Nation of Islam because of its conservatism and Schuyler was absolutely right. Schuyler clearly saw that so much of the NOI's message was simply a more militant version of a politics of respectability, but on somewhat different terms than the bourgeois version of the same. What must be understood about the 1950s and the 1960s was black people's search for resurrection and restoration as a damaged group of people who needed to make themselves whole and make themselves new. Islam was attractive to many because it promised to do just that and do it better than Christianity ever could. After all, to the Muslim adherent of the 1960s, if Christianity could truly restore black people, why had it not already done so as blacks had been Christians in the United States for over 150 years at least? Islam – not only as Elijah Muhammad preached it with the Nation of Islam, with its practice of gaining converts in prison and redeeming them – but indeed the other branches of Islam that were attracting black people in the United States at this time, all promised to do for black consciousness what Christianity could not and would not do, that is, restore black people and heal them of the psychic damage they had suffered at the hands of whites. The Ahmadiyya Mission, the Sunni Muslims, the Moorish American Temple all attracted blacks, regardless of whether they preached racialist tenets, as the Moorish American Temple did, or whether they preached a multi-racial Islam, as did the Ahmadiyya Mission.[8] Either vision was attractive for many black Americans who found the iconography of Christianity too white and its social practices too segregated and hypocritical.

Black jazz musicians such as pianists Ahmad Jamal, Hasaan Ibn Ali, and McCoy Tyner, saxophonists Yusef Lateef and Sahib Shihab, drummer Art Blakey, and singer Dakota Staton, among others, became Muslims for similar reasons as Ali, not as revolutionaries or as acts of resistance as much as acts of fulfillment and completion, as a way of rediscovering and conserving their virtues and culture as black people. Converting to Islam was a way to make jazz clean, rid it of drugs, alcohol, and its association with American lowlife, to uplift the musicians. (This aspiration was, of course, not always fulfilled, even by the adherents but it is the necessity of the aspiration that counts here.) I cannot number the jazz records made from the 1950s through the mid-1970s that make some reference to Africa or to the east geographically or with some spiritual connotation.[9] Not all of this was Islamic, to be sure, but it was a clear sign of how preoccupied many black musicians were in claiming a certain authenticity in cleaning up the reputation of their profession and their art form and with associating themselves with the east as being regenerative of blackness. Nothing makes this clearer than the 1966 jazz album *Tauhid* by saxophonist Pharoah Sanders who was and is a devout Muslim. This album, whose title is an Islamic theological term about the oneness of God, was popular among a certain set of younger blacks at the time who were seeking not simply political validation but spiritual and psychological repair. The longest track on the album was entitled "Lower Egypt and Upper Egypt." On the Sanders album, *Jewels of Thought*, released in 1969 is a song entitled "Hum Allah – Hum Allah – Hum Allah," which makes clear how much Islam had become part of the zeitgeist of the 1960s for African Americans. Also, consider this: it is said that the Black Panthers began to call the police "pigs" as a result of one of their members reading George Orwell's novel, *Animal Farm*. But by the mid-1960s, younger blacks especially, whether or not they explicitly identified as Muslim, were eschewing pork and denigrating "the pig" as an animal and as a source of food. The pig was emblematic of a past of slavery and degradation. One elevated one's diet and one's consciousness by not eating pork. This was another indication of how much Islam was in the air or how much the air of black America was taking, indirectly, the scent of Islam.

It might also be remembered that at this time a certain number of black Americans became practitioners of Santeria or, what they called in America, the Yoruba faith, as an act of restoration.[10] It was also the period that produced the Seven Principles of the Kawaida,[11] which was invented in the mid-1960s by Maulana Ron Karenga, the leader of US, an organization in southern California that became a rival to the Black Panthers. The Kawaida was a black value system from which the African American holiday of Kwanzaa sprang. Doubtless, much of this fertile tumult of religious and pseudo-religious, ideological, intellectual, and pseudo-intellectual activity arose in part because, as Karenga put it, African Americans suffered from "ideological deficiency,"[12] or certainly felt they did.

We fail to understand the 1960s and what black people were about then, if everything is subsumed under "civil rights activism." A lot of the activism, the seeking, the political impulse of the period, was to correct the mind and the spirit and was meant to create an imagined community that was inherently conservative in nature: black people wanted stable, two-parent families with men in charge, flourishing black businesses, vibrant black schools and an educational system that did not make them feel inferior, a black art that reflected an idealized black reality, and a self-reliant culture that enhanced and supported their view of the world. We fail to understand the 1960s if we fail to see that many blacks who were attracted to Islam were appalled by the liberation that liberalism and the counter-culture wrought that they saw around them increasingly in the white mainstream: the rampant use of illegal drugs, the rise and approval of blatantly recreational sex and pornography, a growing tendency toward acceptance of, or at least less hostility toward, homosexuality, the Satanic and hedonistic expressions in rock music, the rise of women's liberation: all of this for many blacks seeking Islam was an outpouring of white decadence, the moral decay of white society. The Nation of Islam constantly warned against this,[13] as a book like Elijah Muhammad's *The Fall of America* makes abundantly clear. As Elijah Muhammad wrote and his ministers constantly reiterated: "The original man, Allah has declared, is none other than the black man. The black man is the first and last, maker and owner of the universe. From him came all brown, yellow, red, and white people. By using a special method of birth control law the black man was able to produce the white race." This became a central tenet of the Black is Beautiful Movement of the late 1960s, espoused by many younger blacks who were not Muslims. Not only were blacks superior but white people were a genetic mistake. White people were racist, so this thinking went, because they were afraid of being genetically obliterated by the darker races of the world.

Black Americans becoming Muslims were seeking a certain authenticity, racially, politically, and, most importantly, morally. But there was something more to this; as many black Americans were turning to Islam in the 1960s, it was not entirely with the idea of adopting the religion wholly on the terms that it was offered to them by teachers from the east. Certainly, Elijah Muhammad knew the Nation of Islam was different in several important doctrinal ways from orthodox Islam of the Middle East. He had visited Turkey, Ethiopia, the Sudan, Arabia and Pakistan with his sons in 1959 and met "with some of the most influential people of these countries – government people."[14] Malcolm X also went on this trip with Muhammad, which means that he knew that Islam was not a racialist religion in the way that the Nation of Islam presented it long before he left the Nation in 1964. On the topic of whites being naturally and supernaturally evil, Muhammad wrote: "Not only the so-called Negroes are deceived by this race of devils, but even many of the Asiatic Muslims do not know that the white race are devils."[15] Ali himself saw orthodox Islam up-close in the spring of 1964 when he took a tour of Africa to get away from the pressures of the United States where he had just won the title and where he had also just announced he was a member of the Nation of Islam.[16] He visited Ghana, Nigeria, and Egypt, where he met the famed Egyptian president Gamal-Abdel Nasser, who conspicuously called himself both a black man and an African. Nasser, when he spoke at the Asian-African Unity Conference in Bandung in 1955, purposely referred to it as the African-Asian Unity Conference. He was one of the organizers of the 1963 African Summit Conference, helped set the Organization of African Unity, championed Patrice Lumumba and Sekou Toure. It meant something that Ali met with him. Ali spent a month on the continent, two weeks of which were in Egypt. He learned from the visit that he had an enormous following abroad, even if he was deeply unpopular in the United States and he learned the advantage of being a Muslim, how the religion gave a global relevance that few other American boxers, few other American athletes, have ever had. Yes, there were international and Third World dimensions to the championship reigns of Jack Johnson and Joe Louis, but nowhere near the extent of Ali. Yet all of this underscored that as a black American, Ali and other Western blacks needed a different sort of Islam that would make black Americans a part of the so-called black world while still being something distinct, something worthy of being distinct. In this way, what Ali found most useful both politically and psychologically was the Pan-Africanism inherent in the NOI that essentially made Islam new and useable for American blacks.[17] Elijah Muhammad made this clear when he wrote: "Allah will bring about a new Islam. As for the Principles of Belief, they remain the same. There will be no more signs to be watched for the coming of God and the setting up of a new world of Islam. We are seeing this change now and entering into it. The devils oppose this change, and the Orthodox join them in opposing us because of their desire to carry on the old Islam."[18] We will best understand Ali by removing the leftist lens through which we wish to see him as anti-American hero. He is, at best, a very inauthentic leftist. He was not a political radical; he was something that to his own mind was far more impressive, protective, and important: he was a believer in a world of colored believers.

The Draft

> Joining the Muslims was one reason for Clay's decline in popularity, and his views on Vietnam and the draft are others, and I happen to disagree with everything he is saying on these three subjects, and I think the Cassius Clay viewpoint is working against the civil rights movement and the best interests of the nation. I certainly would fight willingly in Vietnam for my country, and have no soft feelings toward the Black Muslims. But what bothers me about Cassius Clay's situation is that he is being made to pay too stiff a penalty for saying and doing what he thinks is right.
> – Heavyweight and Olympic Champion Floyd Patterson,
> "In Defense of Cassius Clay," 1966[19]

Doubtless, in my introduction to the *Muhammad Ali Reader*, my observation that Ali did not sacrifice any more as an athlete when he was suspended from boxing for three and a half years for his stance against the nation's conscription laws and the Vietnam War than those athletes who were drafted during the Second World War and lost significant chunks of their athletic life spans and were, in many cases, in danger on the battlefield to boot was pushback against the leftist version of Ali. Heavyweight champion Joe Louis did not fight competitively from March 28, 1942 to June 18, 1946, over four years, because of Louis's army service during the Second World War. This was a longer layoff than Ali's. We might ask, in Louis's case, what price patriotism? As we ask in Ali's case, what price dissent? (Hall of Fame pitcher Warren Spahn had a layoff from baseball as long as Louis's from competitive boxing during the Second World War. He did not seem to think it hurt his career; rather he thought he might have been aided by it.[20] It is an open question whether the layoff helped or hurt Ali.) In considering Ali's layoff in this context, I simply wanted readers to think about it more in an athletic context in order to reveal something ironical about it politically. What did it mean compared to other young men who lost years in their prime because of military service as he had opposing such service?

But such framing was not meant to suggest that Ali was insincere or, worse, inauthentic as a dissenter, which was precisely the point of a June 4, 2016 piece in the rightwing online journal *Breitbart News* entitled

"Muhammad Ali No Hero, Just Hypocrite, For Dodging Draft,"[21] that compared Ali unfavorably to Boston Red Sox Hall of Fame outfielder Ted Williams, who served as a fighter pilot in both the Second World War and the Korean War, the upshot of which accused Ali of being a draft dodger. (The only other American fighter who was publicly accused of draft dodging was heavyweight champion Jack Dempsey, who avoided conscription during the First World War, accused by his first wife, Maxine Cates, during their bitter divorce in 1919. Dempsey was brought up on charges in federal court of draft evasion in 1920 but was acquitted.[22])

The *Breitbart* article claimed, in essence, that Williams made the greater sacrifice, losing time as an athlete during his prime and risking his life for his country while in combat. But the article misses the point: Ali did not dodge the draft; rather he challenged its legitimacy and was willing to pay the price for the challenge by going to prison if he lost. If he were a true draft dodger, Ali would have tried avoiding both the draft *and* prison by any means he could. Whether his religious grounds for opposing the draft were ethically acceptable or reasonable (he was not claiming to be a conscientious objector in a traditional sense by claiming not to believe in the morality of violence but rather claimed that as a Muslim, he was duty-bound only to the dictates of his religion's call to arms) is not in any way a reflection on whether they were sincere or authentic. In the case of Ali in this instance the Right wants to have it both ways with Islam as a critique of the West: Islam is wrong and it is insincere as a set of religious beliefs with the NOI and someone like Ali; but with Muslim terrorists, the Right underscores that the beliefs are wrong but that they are sincere, if pathological, which makes the Muslims all the more dangerous. But the *Breitbart* article is part of a revisionist interpretation of Ali, to claim he was inauthentic, fake, a fraud, a hypocrite, a shallow man. Ali as symbol and man is thus part of the Culture Wars; the revisionism was not all generated by the Right, by any means, but also by some liberals who became weary and wary of Ali hero-worship in the fighter's declining years and who wanted to challenge the liberal and leftist view of Ali as the grand American dragon-slayer.

It must be remembered that from the very beginning of Ali's boxing career, when he was the flamboyant Cassius Marcellus Clay, there was an undercurrent that he was something fraudulent: the bragging predictions, the poetry spouting, the entire aura of his showmanship was for many not only fake but offensive. He seemed to be nothing more than a gimmick. In the mid-1960s, African playwright, poet, and radical cultural nationalist-turned-Marxist-Leninist Amiri Baraka at first dismissed Clay as something "from the Special Products Division of Madison Avenue."[23] He would amend this view after Clay beat Liston: "Now I think of Clay as merely a terribly stretched out young man with problems one would have hoped would have at least waited for him to reach full manhood. Clay is not a fake, and even his blustering and playground poetry are valid, and demonstrate, as far as I'm concerned, that a new and more complicated generation has moved onto the scene. And in this last sense Clay is definitely my man. However, his choosing Elijah Muhammad over Malcolm X, if indeed such is the case, means that he is still a "'homeboy,' embracing this folksy vector straight out of the hard spiritualism of poor aspiration, i.e., he is right now just angry rather than intellectually (socio-politically) motivated."[24] There is a qualification for Baraka: Clay is an aware black person but insufficiently developed politically if he remains a follower of Elijah Muhammad and does not follow Malcolm X, the patron saint of the new Black Power movement that arose in the wake of his assassination. Clay/Ali remained with the Nation of Islam and did not follow Malcolm from the fold. In fact, while on his 1964 African tour, Ali went out of his way to denigrate Malcolm, who was also in Africa at the time, remarking: "Did you get a look at Malcolm? Dressed in that funny white robe and wearing a beard and walking with that cane that looked like a prophet's stick? Man, he's gone. He's gone so far out, he's out completely." This sounds like he was mimicking the words of the NOI guys who were around him at the time, wanting to make sure that in the American press he was saying nothing that could possibly be construed as loyal or sympathetic to Malcolm. Eldridge Cleaver, the Minister of Information for the Black Panthers, also made note of Ali in the 1960s, writing: "In the context of boxing, he is a genuine revolutionary, the black Fidel Castro of boxing." But he also qualifies this by saying that Ali was "a loudmouthed braggart" and "a Black Muslim racist."[25] Baraka and Cleaver qualify their praise of Ali the radical because he is not a follower of Malcolm X, the preferred black figure of the era for disaffected intellectuals like themselves. There is something about Ali as a member of the Nation of Islam that, if not quite inauthentic politically, seems crude, homespun, even backwards.

Ali was also inauthentic in other ways: old-style boxing heads thought his style of fighting was incorrect, technically flawed, and showy. Ali never threw punches to the body, never slipped punches properly, never knew how to in-fight at all. No traditional trainer would ever teach someone to box the way Ali did. His entire style was inauthentic, a projection of the inauthenticity of the man himself. As A.J. Liebling observed about Ali in his early days, backed by his Louisville syndicate of rich white businessmen, Clay was not a hungry fighter, at least, not in the literal sense. The old school adage is "hungry fighters make the best fighters."[26] Light-heavyweight champion and old school boxing master Archie Moore, who early in Ali's professional career, tried to be his trainer, certainly thought that Ali's recalcitrance, his refusal to accept discipline, his desire always to be treated as someone and something special, would hurt him in the long run. "He was always trying to discipline his superiors, the people who were working with him. To tell you the truth, the boy needed a good spanking, but I wasn't sure who could give it to him."²⁷ Ali refused to accept the claims, the traditions, and the so-called wisdom of his profession. In his anti-authoritarianism, he was a perfect emblem of his age, of the permissive society, as America had come to be known by the 1950s; and the perfect embodiment for the old school of boxing of a talented but ultimately inauthentic fighter. The main predictions for the young Clay/Ali was that he would not last long as he depended entirely on speed, that he did not hit hard enough, and that he could not take a punch. He was as fascinating to watch as someone walking a tight-rope without a net.

To borrow a phrase from literary critic Harold Bloom, Ali suffered from the anxiety of influence on two different fronts: politically, he had to excise Malcolm X from his life once he chose to side with Elijah Muhammad. This only intensified his dogmatic allegiance to the Nation of Islam and to the idea that African American persecution would be solved by divine, super-natural intervention as opposed to Malcolm X's growing belief in leftist, revolutionary politics. Athletically, he had to overcome the presence and the achievement of Joe Louis, not only the most successful heavyweight champion in the history of the sport but a major race hero for the gener-ation of Ali's parents. Ali, in effect, became the anti-Louis: whereas Louis was patriotic and fought in the US armed services during the Second World War, Ali was a dissenter who chose to oppose the Vietnam War and serving in the military; whereas Louis was quiet, largely self-contained, phleg-matic and undemonstrative in victory or defeat, Ali was a braggart, loqua-cious, animated, witty, charming, and at times a hectoring zealot when it came to discussing his religion. Louis was considered by boxing insiders to have been nearly perfect technically as an orthodox boxer with an excel-lent teacher–pupil relationship with his trainer, Jack Blackburn; Ali, on the other hand, reveled in being unorthodox and uncoachable. Ali was a man of obvious contradictions, which underscored for some his genuineness and for others his artificiality: on the one hand, he sided with a form of old-fashioned, storefront, other-worldly black nationalism by following Elijah Muhammad and rejecting Malcolm X, the quintessential figure of modern black political and religious consciousness. On the other hand, Ali seem-ingly rejected tradition with Louis and declared himself a sort of ultimate modern boxer, a self-invented remodeling of Sugar Ray Robinson taken far beyond Robinson himself.

In recent years, the core of revisionist criticism of Ali has particularly centered on the treatment of his arch rival Joe Frazier, whom he beat twice in three fights; much of it about how unfairly and cruelly Ali castigated and belittled Frazier in the pre-fight promotions as an Uncle Tom and a gorilla, and as ignorant.[28] Frazier was always bitter about this, about how, even when he was champion after beating Ali in 1971, he was never given his due because he existed, in the eyes of the press and possibly a good portion of the public, solely as Ali's foil.[29] "Always able to feel the lancing invective with which Ali assaulted him," wrote Mark Kram in *Ghosts of Manila*, "Frazier began to see it as an orchestrated campaign to crush any respect he had in the black community."[30] *Ghosts of Manila: The Fateful Blood Feud Between Muhammad Ali and Joe Frazier* is the ultimate Ali revisionist book, taking Ali down a few pegs for his sexual excesses (while Ali preached abstinence and sex sanctified by marriage), for allowing the Nation of Islam to control his money (much to Ali's financial detriment), for allowing himself to be bullied by the Nation into opposing the draft, almost forcing him to be a martyr, for misusing his own money in ways that were not unusual for a professional athlete but shockingly irresponsible nonetheless, and for denigrating his black opponents, largely for the amusement of his large white audience, despite his proclamations of being a loyal race man. There is nothing that Kram describes that is untrue. But the overall impression is that Ali, like the Nation of Islam, is something of a fake, a bit of a post-modernist confidence game. Nothing underscores this as much as Kram's description of Joe Frazier as being of Gullah ancestry, where Frazier sees himself (and Kram frames him) as a pureblood (Frazier once called Ali "a half breed"), a black from the fields, unassimilated. In short, Frazier represented something that was more racially and culturally authentic than Ali.[31] Kram almost suggests that Joe Frazier became a sort of Caliban to Muhammad Ali's Prospero. From this perspective, Ali virtually colonized Frazier: Ali represented the middle class sensibility that declared his exceptionalism at the expense of the working-class and agrarian blacks that Frazier's background symbolized.

To be sure, Ali politically denigrated his black opponents (who were far more competitive threats to him than the relatively few white fighters he fought) because, first, there were few other options he had to interest the general public in a bout between two black men other than politicizing his fights. Nearly all of Joe Louis's major fights were against whites. The political dynamic of racial and ethnic difference was built into the bouts (something which boxing has always emphasized to get fannies in the seats) and Louis really had to do nothing to stimulate the public's fantasies about what the public imagined was at stake. In the age of the black dominance of the sports, Ali had to resort to something else and in the age of civil rights and Black Power he found a winning formula of three parts or a set of three explanations for what he did: first, cast himself as a race hero fighting the white man's lackey, a feat that reshaped black disunity as the race's own sort of symbolic culture war. Frazier, the homeboy, represented the Old Negro, the throwback, even as Louis did; Ali was the new dispensation. Second, denigrating his opponents also meant that he could celebrate and promote his new racial consciousness and rebirth as a Muslim. Third, trash talking his opponents amplified their significance and intensified their threat as rivals and rivalry underscored Ali's greatness.

To begin with the first point: Ali had, like other champions before him, taken older fighters, retired champions, down on their luck, into his orbit. Louis had been briefly part of Ali's entourage until the two men had a falling out, mostly over a matter of respect. The old lion always thought he could beat Ali had they met in their primes. Ali idolized Ray Robinson but Robinson refused to become his trainer, in part, because he was still, at the time, an active fighter himself, and ultimately the two men fell out over the issue of Ali's military service. Ali fired Ike Williams because the former light-weight champion was caught eating pork.[32] Kid Gavilan, a welterweight champion of the early 1950s, was part of Ali's camp for four years, and the two men got along sufficiently well but in the end Gavilan was dismissed as well. Ali understood the boxing past, boxing history, clearly and compel-lingly, but, on many levels, he had an enduring argument with the past.

Ali identified himself, particularly after the success of the stage and film versions of Howard Sackler's play, *The Great White Hope* (1970 film, 1967 stage debut), with turn-of-the-century heavyweight boxing champion Jack Johnson, as both men challenged and were challenged by federal pros-ecution, one for violation of the 1910 anti-prostitution statue known as the Mann Act and the other for violation of the Selective Service Act. Ali emphasized this comparison to Johnson in his 1975 autobiography, *The Greatest: My Own Story*.[33] One might argue that even this strong identifica-tion with Johnson was meant to be anti-Louis, as Louis came along to win the championship, the first black to even fight for it, twenty-two years after Johnson lost the title to Jess Willard in Cuba in 1915, by presenting him-self as the anti-Johnson: no fooling around with white women (publicly), no smiling at defeated white opponents or taunting white opponents in the ring, no behavior that would in any way reflect poorly on the race. Whether a comparison between Johnson and Ali is intellectually fruitful is an open question, although pushed too far might prove a disservice to both men. However, what is important here is Ali's need to authenticate him-self by defining himself against the great black boxers of the past and how that authentication ultimately is bound up in the contradictions of the politics of respectability, or more specifically the politics of black respectability. Johnson's penchant for white women and his consorting with prostitutes in general made him suspect in many circles of black respectability at the turn of the century. Although he was well liked by songwriter, poet, novelist, and NAACP leader James Weldon Johnson, he was intensely disliked by Booker T. Washington, the most significant black leader of the era. It was felt by many blacks that Johnson jeopardized the race by his actions and his preference for white women was not an act of self-determination but rather an expression of self-hatred. Ali's Black Muslim politics of respectability should have made his feelings about Johnson far more ambivalent than he expressed in his autobiography, no matter how lax Ali himself may have been in practicing some aspects of his faith. But the sheer audacity of Johnson, his enormous capacity to endure both external and self-induced pressure probably reminded Ali of himself and underscored a certain source of heroism that black men should aspire for. In order to understand how Ali saw his black boxing peers, it is important to understand how he authenticated himself with the past, how he saw the black fighters of the past and why he saw them in the way he did.

Addressing the second point: Ali found denigrating his black opponents to be a way to celebrate and defend his new consciousness as a politically aware black man as a result of publicly joining the Nation of Islam in 1964. (He had actually been a fellow traveler since 1961.) This was especially evident in his fights against Ernie Terrell and Floyd Patterson, who both seemed to be fighting as representatives of an old-style, assimilationist or integrationist politics of respectability, largely shaped by New Deal idealism. Being a Muslim athlete made him a new kind of being, a reinvention, a re-imagining, something fresh and different on the scene. In this sense, Ali was an original, even as he copied the trash talking of professional wrestling, some boxers like John L. Sullivan ("I can lick any son of a bitch in the house"), baseball players like Dizzy Dean and Babe Ruth, and the exaggerated claims of modern advertisers and Hollywood trailers, the exaggerations of popular culture. Ali was both P.T. Barnum and the acts that Barnum was trying to sell. In the age of mass culture, what could possibly be authentic beyond what you asserted rhetorically was authentic? For Ali and his generation, authenticity was a belief, not a fact, a manipulation of the truth, not a quest for it. And everyone in the modern world knows authenticity to be a manipulation.

And the third point: as a champion athlete he was a fierce competitor who defined his greatness by his rivalries. How could he truly be great unless he could convince the public he was fighting for more than just money or even fame? Was his rivalry with Frazier really very different or worse than that between Joan Crawford and Bette Davis or between Tesla and Edison or between soul singers Joe Tex and James Brown? Would anyone, outside of professional boxing, remember Joe Frazier now if Ali had not treated him the way he did?

The Last Ali

Ali and I would end up on occasion in planes together, and while I remained in awe of what he was sacrificing by taking on the US government in the name of religious principle, I could never quite figure him out. We'd be talking, and he'd begin fiddling with something in the seat pocket or staring out the window, and I'd be certain he hadn't heard a word. But six months later, when even I'd forgotten what had been discussed, he'd recount our conversation back to me. He was, on the one hand, a child, and, on the other, a shrewd and honorable man.

– Roone Arledge, 2003[34]

There is an awesome blankness about him.
– Wilfrid Sheed, 1975[35]

Now my charms are all o'erthrown,
And what strength I have's mine own,
Which is most faint ...
– Prospero, the final speech in
Shakespeare's *The Tempest*

Elliott Gorn, author of *The Manly Art: Bare-knuckle Prizefighting in America*, organized a conference at Miami University in Ohio entitled "Muhammad Ali and American Culture." The conference took place on April 10 and 11, 1992 and featured Randy Roberts, Michael Eric Dyson, Dave K. Wiggins, Jeffrey Sammons, Michael Oriad, Othello Harris, Thomas Hietala, and myself. We dubbed ourselves professors of pugilism. Journalist Robert Lipsyte, who had covered Ali throughout the 1960s, was the keynote speaker. The proceedings of the conference were published as a book entitled *Muhammad Ali: The People's Champ*, by the University of Illinois Press. There is nothing especially noteworthy about this conference as conferences go except for one fact: Muhammad Ali himself attended, staying for the entire time.

I had heard that Ali had been invited to the conference but dismissed any possibility that he would show up. After all, why should he? I was certain he had more interesting things to do with his time than to sit and listen to a bunch of boring academic papers, even if the papers were about him. Also, Miami University in Ohio seemed a bit off the beaten track, geographically and academically. Maybe he might show up at a conference about him if it were being held at Harvard or Yale, but Miami University did not seem to offer much academic cache, despite the quality of the presenters. But come Ali did.

At the time of the conference, Ali was fifty years old and had not been in a competitive boxing match in over ten years, since the 1981 loss to Trevor Berbick in the Bahamas. He had been diagnosed with Parkinson's Disease and it was being fiercely debated if the punishment he took in the ring had contributed to his now diminished physical condition. He had joined Wallace D. Muhammad's World Community of Al-Islam in 1976, choosing not to stay with the Nation of Islam which was now under the leadership of Louis Farrakhan. Farrakhan maintained most of the racialist and political teachings of Elijah Muhammad. Wallace D. Muhammad, Elijah's son, chose not to and moved closer in the direction of orthodox Islam, with which his father quarreled, telling his followers he was offering a new Islam specific-ally for the black American. Ali dropped the most doctrinaire of the racialist beliefs he espoused in the 1960s and 1970s and never uttered them again. Ali's fame had also diminished since his retirement and the public disclosure of his compromised health. He had not had a significant fight in more than a dozen years. Younger people did not know him. Ali had been eclipsed as a superstar global athlete by Michael Jordan, who, if anything, would become far richer and even more famous than Ali had been. Mike Tyson was the other global superstar athlete, winning the heavyweight championship in 1986 at the age of twenty. In 1992, he was sentenced to six years in prison for rape. It was the biggest story in American sports that year. The other big name in heavyweight boxing at the time of the conference was Ali's old nemesis, George Foreman, who had come back to boxing in 1987 after a ten-year layoff. In 1994, two years after the conference, Foreman, at the age of forty-five, would win the heavyweight title, the oldest heavyweight ever to do so. Muhammad Ali was in a kind of twilight. He did not seem to mind.

Ali was accompanied by long-time friend, photographer Howard Bingham, who was often with the ex-champion during those days. Long gone was the huge entourage of fifty people including cooks, masseurs, go-fors, hangers-on, relatives, and the like. Ali traveled quite whimsically at this time. He was invited to a conference about himself, and so he came. It was that simple. He did not travel as if he did not expect people to recog-nize him. He traveled as if he was very used to people recognizing him and did not desire in any way to be protected from that. Far from thinking that anyone would harm him, he seemed to think that no matter where he went someone would take him in, would be overjoyed to see him. He was not wrong in this assumption.

So, he hung out with the presenters and organizers of the conference for the entire weekend. He listened to all the papers, sometimes even making humorous gestures if someone said something controversial or not so flattering about him, which was, of course, not very often. Jeffrey Sammons was so moved that Ali was there that he broke down and cried when he presented his paper. Ali mounted the stage and consoled him. It was a touching moment. I asked Ali why he had come and why he stayed to listen to all the papers and he said that he felt honored that so many smart people had thought so much about him and had so much to say about his career. He did not speak much, as his speech was very slurred and it frustrated him when people did not understand him as much as it embarrassed people that they could not but wanted to very much. He did magic tricks but would tell anyone who asked how he did it as he said it was against his faith to purposely deceive anyone. (I suppose Ali had always been interested in magic. He appeared on the Ed Sullivan show in 1963, before his first fight with Sonny Liston, and performed a magic trick.)[36] He would come behind people and make a kind of cricket sound near their ear with his hand, making them think an insect was buzzing near them. This amused him very much. He also handed out cards that showed two quotes from the Bible that contradicted each other. I suppose this was his way of promoting Islam. He would sometimes disappear for several moments and Howard Bingham would say he was praying and could not be disturbed. He patiently signed autographs for anyone who wanted one, as long as you spelled the name you wanted him to dedicate the autograph to. The Parkinson's made it difficult for him to write, so it took a real effort for him to do this. One afternoon he must have signed autographs for nearly two hours. I asked him why he bothered to sign all those autographs; he shrugged, remarking that for many people meeting him was one of the most significant things in their lives, and he did not want to disappoint them. He seemed like an aging prince touring his realm with a kind of benign, almost courtly, transcendence.

Strangely, Ali's presence at the conference did not seem to significantly increase the number of attendees. Many people came to get autographs but they did not stay for the conference itself. They were attracted to Ali the celebrity; Ali as an object of study did not interest them. I was actually relieved about that. A big audience was not necessarily the right audience. But even the number of people who sought his autograph was not as large as one might imagine or as large as it would have been a dozen years earlier.

I remember he ate heartily, and with good appetite. He enjoyed the company he was with but there was also the feeling that he could dispense with it completely at any moment, ignore it, withdraw from it, as he wished. He was resigned to himself, which was something of a victory in and of itself. He did not crave completion or affirmation. Perhaps he had gotten his fill of that in life. He did not mind seeing people in his diminished physical state and had little patience or interest in people who felt sorry for him. He told us he was enjoying his life as much as he ever did. The lesson I learned that weekend from Ali was simple: as the rock group Nirvana once sang, when at a social gathering, come as you are.

There was something strangely yet sharply disappointing about meeting him. Perhaps because he had met so many people in his life, had been fawned over by so many, questioned by so many, he seemed now like a combination of a cipher and a rune, a kind of hollowed-out density, a pillow-like opaqueness. There was something about him that seemed empty, drained. It was impossible to talk to him, not simply because of the Parkinson's but because in the end, I thought, we really had nothing to say to him and he had nothing to say to us. It had all been said before, endlessly. We simply were in awe of the spectacle to which he felt nothing but poised indifference, to the spectacle of himself and to our awe. There was something that was rather stunning about all of this. But this I understand more clearly now that I am older than he was when I met him.

On a sunny, warm late Sunday afternoon, he shook hands with all of us, climbed in an SUV with Howard Bingham and drove away down a tree-lined, shadow-speckled street. It was not yet twilight but getting there quickly enough. The whole weekend felt so much like an elegy, like Wordsworth's poem, "Animal Tranquility and Decay": "He is by nature led / To peace so perfect, that the young behold / With envy, what the old man hardly feels."

I also thought of Prospero's words in *The Tempest*, "We are such stuff as dreams are made on, and our little life is rounded with a sleep." As Ali disappeared into the end of the day, I was convinced that he was in the midst of making to all for whom he mattered a long goodbye.

NOTES

1 Elijah Muhammad, *Message to the Blackman in America* (Chicago, IL: Muhammad's Temple No. 2, 1965), p. 70.
2 Gerald Early (ed.), *The Muhammad Ali Reader* (Hopewell, NJ: Ecco Press, 1998), p. vii.
3 Jack Cashill, *Sucker Punch: The Hard Left Hook That Dazed Ali and Killed King's Dream* (Nashville, TN: Nelson Current Books, 2006), p. 30; see also, pp. 125, 182, 214–15, 236.
4 Quoted in Randy Roberts and Johnny Smith, *Blood Brothers: The Fatal Friendship Between Muhammad Ali and Malcolm X* (New York: Basic Books, 2016), p. 106.

5 Wilfrid Sheen, *Muhammad Ali: A Portrait in Words and Photographs* (New York: New American Library, 1975), p. 171.

6 www.pbs.org/newshour/show/the-greatest-was-an-icon-beyond-the-world-of-boxing

7 George Schuyler, "Views and Reviews" in Gerald Early (ed.), *The Muhammad Ali Reader* (Hopewell, NJ: Ecco Press, 1998), p. 41.

8 "Prior to the founding of the NOI, there were at least four African American Islamic movements already established in the United States: (1) Moorish Science Temple (1913), Noble Drew Ali, Newark, New Jersey; (2) Ahmadiyya Movement (1921), Dr. Mufti Muhammad Sadiq, Chicago, Illinois, (3) The Universal Islamic Society (1926), Duse Muhammad Ali, Detroit, Michigan; and (4) the Islamic Propagation Center of America (1928), Shaykh al-haj Daoud Ahmed Faisal, Brooklyn, New York." (From James L. Conyors, Jr., "The Nation of Islam: An Historiography of Pan-Africanist Thought and Intellectualism" in James L. Conyors, Jr. (ed.), *Engines of the Black Power Movement: Essays on the Influence of Civil Rights Actions, Art, and Islam* (Jefferson, NC: McFarland and Company, 2007).

9 A very small sample: "Airegin" (Nigeria spelled backwards) by Sonny Rollins, "All Africa" by Max Roach, "Dahomey" by John Coltrane, "Africa Brass" (album) by John Coltrane, "Prayer to the East" (album) by Yusef Lateef, "East Meets West" (album) by Ahmed Abdul-Malik, "Ancient Aiethopia" by Sun Ra, "Liberia" by John Coltrane, "African Flower" by Duke Ellington, "Eastern Sounds" (album) by Yusef Lateef, "The Griots" by Andrew Hill, "Uhuru Afrika" (album) by Randy Weston, "Afro Blue" by Mongo Santamaria, to name only a few.

10 A rift would develop between those blacks who became practitioners of Santeria and those who sought Islam. For those who became Yoruba, Islam was seen as a foreign, monotheistic imposition on Africans, not an indigenous expression. The Yorubas felt that the black Americans who sought Islam wanted an Arab-cized identity, not an African one, because they were essentially ashamed of being black. From the Muslim perspective, Santeria or Yoruba seemed an atavistic, pagan attempt at recapturing an anti-modern past. Islam was the religion of modernity and civilization. Moreover, the Muslims argued that Islam was, indeed, indigenous to Africa. For more on African Americans and the Yoruba faith, see Tracey E. Hucks, *Yoruba Traditions and African American Religious Nationalism* (Albuquerque, NM: University of New Mexico Press, 2012).

11 The Seven Principles (*nguzo saba*) are *umoja* (unity), *kujichagulia* (self-determination), *ujima* (collective work and responsibility), *ujamaa* (cooperative economics), *nia* (purpose), *kuumba* (creativity), and *imani* (faith).

12 From Samuel T. Livington, "NOI: Divided We Stand," *International Journal of Africana Studies* no. 5 (December 1999), pp. 50–51, quoted in James L. Conyors, Jr., "The Nation of Islam: An Historiography of Pan-Africanist Thought and Intellectualism" in Conyors, *Engines of the Black Power Movement*, p. 164.

13 See Malachi Crawford, "Understanding Elijah Muhammad" in Conyors, *Engines of the Black Power Movement*, pp. 189–90.

14 Muhammad, *Message to the Blackman in America*, p. 59.

15 Ibid., p. 105.

16 "Muhammad Ali as Third World Hero," in Gerald Early, *This is Where I Came In: Black America in the 1960s* (Lincoln, NE: University of Nebraska Press, 2003), pp. 1–35.

17 See Conyors, "The Nation of Islam: An Historiography of Pan-Africanist Thought and Intellectualism," pp. 159–83 and Malachi Crawford, "Understanding Elijah Muhammad," pp. 184–94 in Conyors, *Engines of the Black Power Movement*.

18 Muhammad, *Message to the Blackman in America*, p. 50.

19 Early, *The Muhammad Ali Reader*, p. 70.

20 www.defensemedianetwork.com/stories/warren-spahn-hall-of-famer-was-seasoned-by-world-war-ii/

21 www.breitbart.com/sports/2016/06/04/muhammad-ali-no-hero-just-hypocrite-dodging-draft/

22 Randy Roberts, *Jack Dempsey: The Manassa Mauler* (New York: Grove Press, Inc., 1980), pp. 77–87. Also see Jack Dempsey with Barbara Piattelli Dempsey, *Dempsey*, (New York: Harper and Row, 1977), pp. 126–31; Jack Dempsey as told to Bob Considine and Bill Slocum, *Demspey by the Man Himself* (New York: Simon and Schuster, 1960), pp. 118–25; Roger Kahn, *A Flame of Pure Fire: Jack Dempsey and the Roaring '20s* (New York: Harcourt Brace and Company, 1999), pp. 121–66.

23 LeRoi Jones, *Home: Social Essays* (New York: Morrow, 1966), p. 157.

24 Jones, *Home: Social Essays*, pp. 159–60.

25 Eldridge Cleaver, *Soul on Ice* (New York: McGraw-Hill, 1968), pp. 92, 96.

26 A. J. Liebling, *A Neutral Corner; Boxing Essays* (New York: North Point Press, 1996), p. 165.

27 Thomas Hauser, *Muhammad Ali: His Life and Times* (New York: Simon and Schuster, 1991), p. 34.

28 www.youtube.com/watch?v=0-u_Q3eVYU0

29 www.si.com/boxing/2015/09/24/muhammad-ali-joe-frazier-william-nack-si-vault#

30 Mark Kram, *Ghosts of Manila: The Fateful Blood Feud Between Muhammad Ali and Joe Frazier* (New York: HarperCollins, 2001), 55.

31 Jack Cashill makes this same point in *Sucker Punch*: "Although Ali and his enthusiasts would paint Frazier as the 'great white hope,' it is hard to imagine a more profoundly African experience in America than Frazier's. His family hailed from Gullah country, outside of Beaufort, South Carolina, the one part of the South most spiritually in touch with the African motherland" (p. 10). Cashill in fact criticizes Ali's entire posture as an aggrieved black man, enabled by liberal writers like Joyce Carol Oates, as fake: "In 1942 [the year of Ali's birth in Louisville, Kentucky], wherever one looked in the world, horror reigned – Europe, China, the Middle East, North Africa. Almost everywhere, that is. In assessing Ali's early life, [Joyce Carol] Oates might have posed this sequence of questions: For every 100 children who entered the world in January 1942, how many were born in a modern hospital? How many had two loving parents? How many drove away in their father's car? How many returned to a home with indoor plumbing, running water, and electricity? Indeed, how many could sleep at night without worry of a bomb crashing through their roof?" (p. 7). Cashill's point is that the entire narrative of Ali's grievance as a black man in America

was entirely fake, inauthentic, the product of Ali's father's ranting against the whites in Louisville, the Muslims' supernatural racial politics, and white liberals manufacturing a story of racism to bolster their sense of his heroism and genius. It must be remembered that the police officer Ali went to for help as a boy when his bicycle was stolen, and who steered him to boxing, was white, that Ali's first sponsors as a professional boxer were several white Louisville businessmen who were quite accommodating to him. For Cashill, Ali suffered from the same disease of many privileged blacks in America: a false sense of victimization, a false self-consciousness.

32 http://articles.latimes.com/1991-08-08/sports/sp-386_1_fight-movie

33 Muhammad Ali with Richard Durham, *The Greatest: My Own Story* (Graymalkin Media, 2015, originally published by Random House in 1975), pp. 321–22.

34 Roone Arledge, *Roone: A Memoir* (New York: HarperCollins, 2003), p. 95.

35 Sheen, *Muhammad Ali*, p. 239.

36 Roberts and Smith, *Blood Brothers*, p. 90.

INDEX